How the Nation Was Won

America's Untold Story

1630–1754

by H. Graham Lowry

Executive Intelligence Review • Washington, D.C.

H. Graham Lowry, Patriot teacher

August 31, 1943–July 28, 2003

Cover: View from the Blue Ridge, looking northwest across the Appalachians, toward the Ohio country.

Cover photograph: H. Graham Lowry
Cover design: Virginia Baier

For more information, contact the publisher:

Executive Intelligence Review

P.O. Box 17390

Washington, D.C. 20041-0390

Library of Congress Cataloging in Publication Data
1. United States—History—Colonial period, ca. 1600–1775. 2.
United States—History—Revolution, 1775–1783 3. United States—
History—1783–1789. I. Title.
E188.L865 1987 973.2 86-33326

Amazon Print on Demand Edition © 2018
ISBN: 9781730846557
EIRBK-1988-001-02

How the Nation Was Won

America's Untold Story

1630–1754

by H. Graham Lowry

Executive Intelligence Review • Washington, D.C.

To

Pamela Heitz Lowry

A True American Pathfinder

and my chief scout for the explorations

reported here

Note to the 2018 Edition

Because of the historic importance of this book, we took extra care in preparation of the new ebook and print on demand editions, to improve the resolution and overall quality of the important images presented. This entailed substitution of high resolution, Public Domain original color images for the lower quality black and white versions printed in the early editions. In a few cases original location photographs were replaced with nearly identical Public Domain color photographs taken from similar perspectives.

While graphic improvements will be noticeable in this paperback, the improvements are most visible in the 2018 ebook editions when viewed on devices with color displays--as most portraits and images are now visible in color. Since, the color imagery greatly helps to bring back to life the people and times portrayed by H. Graham Lowry, we recommend that you also buy or borrow an ebook edition and take a second look. Printing such a long historical study as this in color would have been prohibitively expensive to you, therefore in this paperback edition, the imagery, although improved, is still in black and white.

For classroom situations, be aware that this edition has been reformatted and therefore pagination is different from the pagination of the early editions.

Finally, to keep the length of this paperback within bounds, the original extensive Index has been removed. Researchers should search one of the ebook editions. The 2018 ebook editions retain the original index (with original pagination) from the early print editions.

H. Graham Lowry's text has not been altered in any way.

Table of Contents

Maps and Illustrations

Illustrations appear following pages 90, 192, and 378

Foreword

It is now a little over three years since historian Graham Lowry reported to me his discovery of what he then described to me as "the missing link" in the history of the American Revolution. During that meeting, he presented, piece by piece, the proofs that Benjamin Franklin and George Washington were both directly products of a trans-Atlantic conspiracy centered around three leading international figures during the second half of the reign of England's Queen Anne: Gottfried Leibniz in Hanover, Jonathan Swift in London and Dublin, and Cotton Mather in Boston.

Graham ticked off the most crucial pieces of evidence, one after the other. Part way through his report, I became uneasy. I knew already of intellectual connections between Leibniz and Cotton Mather's circles, and Franklin's indebtedness to Leibniz's circles for both Franklin's own scientific work and Franklin's leading role in assembling international political conspiracies for the American cause. The evidence for the role of Swift in this was also conclusive. The problem was, that this by itself did not show how the pre-1763 mobilization of Americans for the Declaration of Independence had been organized directly around the specific ideas of Liebniz, Swift, Mather, Franklin, and so on.

Then, smiling like a cat who had swallowed the canary, Graham presented the case of Alexander Spotswood, that great lieutenant-governor of Virginia appointed by Queen Anne. It was Spotswood, who had brought Virginia out of the intellectual backwater of a mere Tidewater plantation settlement, and transformed it into what became the state of our first Presidents. The work and influence of Spotswood and his projects, made the case a conclusive one. There was no longer a black hole of about fifty years' duration following 1688, in the history of the United States.

Nearly three years of additional work have been needed, to transform that original discovery into a book solidly presenting the case. Since I have been among those privileged to trace the progress of the manuscript over this period, I know how important the additional work in archives has been. Graham's original thesis could have been published as a scholar's paper three years ago; by presenting it publicly first in the form of this book, the thesis is now in the form which makes it unassailable by any honest academic historian, and also in the form needed by patriots across our nation.

Many of us, even those who reject his political philosophy, are obliged to echo George Santayana's famous dictum, that those who fail to study history are obliged to repeat it. As I look toward Washington, D.C., today, I often think that few of those cascading disasters in policy I see daily there could have been tolerated, if even a majority of the members of Congress knew anything of real history. Yet, the benefit of history is not limited to cautioning us against repeating the mistakes of the past. We learn the most valuable lessons from the examples of those great victories snatched from the jaws of defeat. Such is, I think, the outstanding practical importance of this book.

In Britain, the faction rallied around Jonathan Swift and Dublin's Trinity College was defeated. With the death of the heir to the English throne, Leibniz's ally, Hanover Electress Sophie, and the accession of Marlborough ally, George I, the Liberal vandals around the Bank of England and East India Company took charge. Amid the sometimes imagined glories of the later British Empire, for the United Kingdom, Ireland, and much of the world besides, the death of Queen Anne and George I's accession has been a net disaster to all affected nations and peoples generally to the present day.

Yet, had that noble, defeated faction in Britain not made the attempt, as they did, the American Revolution were probably impossible. Similarly, although the Leibniz who might have become the prime minister of England was fired by George I as soon as Electress Sophie had died, there would be no modern science without his efforts, and there would not have existed throughout Europe that network of conspirators who rallied to the American cause from 1763 onward.

Yet, although the wisest policy is too frequently defeated in the nations within which it is deployed, that same policy, continued in other places, becomes the means by which are achieved those victories on whose occurrence depends the very survival and progress of civilization as a whole.

By the onset of the eighteenth century, the American cause was already as hopeless as many might imagine today's prospects for continued existence of the United States as we have known it these two centuries to date. Yet, by aid of the right method of policy-shaping practice, chosen among such as Cotton Mather, Swift, and Leibniz, during 1776–1789 a glorious, global victory was brought from what had been, eighty years earlier, the jaws of crushing defeat.

As the reader may live in his or her imagination through the crises recounted in this book, the reader can not fail to assimilate some part of that method by which our great republic was brought into being. Putting the book down at the end, no patriot would fail to sigh with pleasure, and share with some friend the thought, "You know, after reading this book, I am proud to be an American."

Lyndon H. LaRouche, Jr.

August 18, 1987

Author's Introduction

This is a book about how men move mountains. The description is not simply metaphorical, concerning America's astonishing feat of forging a superpower out of a continental wilderness. It also applies to an extraordinary political fight, waged for nearly a century before the outbreak of the American Revolution: the battle to break beyond the long barrier of the eastern Appalachian Mountain chain, in order to colonize and develop the vast territories to the west.

The vision of developing a continental republic in the New World guided America's colonists as far back as John Winthrop's founding of Massachusetts in 1630. With benefit from the experiences of Captain John Smith, whose similar hopes for such a project in Virginia had failed, Winthrop organized the Massachusetts Bay expedition as a first-stage, space colony might be organized today. He recruited all the skilled persons he could muster, in engineering, toolmaking, construction, and agriculture, to the limits of early seventeenth century technology. His small ships also brought hundreds of dedicated colonists and their families, to undertake a nation-building mission that 'official' opinion of the time considered impossible.

Under self-governing powers of independence, the Massachusetts colony established an in-depth, republican citizenry—and considerable economic power, during its first half-century of existence. Its influence was spread in varying degrees throughout New England, and even into the Mid-Atlantic colonies. As colonial potentials increased for development beyond the mountain barriers, the obstacles became less the mountains themselves, and more the combined political and military opposition of forces in both Britain and France.

The story of how those obstacles were overcome is the subject of this work. A small group of colonial leaders in America, working both openly and behind the scenes, began implementing a strategy in 1710 for an American 'breakout' beyond the Appalachian and Allegheny mountains. What they accomplished was indispensable to American independence. What they inspired was the mission of nation-building, for which Americans would fight a war to ensure its being fulfilled. In the long struggle between the founding of Massachusetts and "the shot heard 'round the world" at Concord Bridge, that sense of moral purpose was repeatedly tested, yet sustained. The bold and hazardous goal of positioning the colonies to develop the West was attained during the French and Indian War, whose veterans provided much of the leadership for the American Revolution. It may seem presumptuous to describe this account as "America's Untold Story." To the author's knowledge, however, the record of the continuous effort to build a continental republic, from the Puritan founders to the Founding Fathers, has never before been presented, as a coherent, ongoing strategic battle. Yet the evidence is there, that the leading figures who brought America to the point it could successfully assert its independence, had worked to establish the necessary preconditions all along.

The evidence is similarly abundant, that a great many Americans—long before the Revolution—thoroughly detested British rule, on precisely the issue of Britain's refusal to permit any real development of the continent. In the colonists' minds, Britain's oppression was underscored by its open collusion with France to destroy colonial attempts to develop the interior. Westward colonization efforts, from New England to the Carolinas, were instant targets for Indian massacres, typically directed by French Jesuit 'missionaries' operating from Canada— or, on the southern flank, from French outposts in Louisiana. American efforts to remove such threats—through appeals to the monarchy for assistance, or by military measures of their own—were repeatedly betrayed by Britain's ruling circles. These political facts of life were known to generations of Americans before the Revolution. Yet according to prevailing historical opinion, the issue of building a nation did not even arise until the 1760s.

Having been 'trained in the trade,' the author knew something of the witting and unwitting combinations which had produced this dismally limited view of our nation's founding. The typically resulting accounts peddle two crucially misleading claims. First, that the Puritan development of New England was some sort of historical quirk, terminated before 1700 by its own irrelevance, without any lasting influence. Second, that the American colonies merely existed during the first half of the eighteenth century, in a static, uneventful mode, with no significant thought or purpose for the future. Then a further claim is generally added, that Americans simply fought the French and Indian War in support of British colonial policy. Only after that war, according to our standard history texts, did the idea of independence emerge, in response to Britain's imperial measures following the 1763 Treaty of Paris.

The final blow is usually thus delivered: the American Revolution was the unpredicted outcome of the colonists' sudden hostility to imperial rule, over such matters as the Stamp Act and the tax on tea. In other words, the founding of the greatest republic in history resulted from nothing more than a spontaneous string of protests, against British infringement upon some petty rights the colonials already 'enjoyed.' There was a time when our citizens were outraged by such efforts to deny the moral purpose of the creation of the United States. Perhaps even to save it now, they must again become so, despite more than a century and a half of deliberate efforts to deprive them of their real history.

It is a simple matter of record that John Winthrop's Massachusetts Bay project was dedicated to establishing a republic in the New World, as a strategic flank against the threatened destruction of Europe, during the first decades of the seventeenth century. The more difficult challenge confronting an historical investigator today, is to find the paths leading from New England's maligned Puritan commonwealth, to the founding of the constitutional republic of the United States. Both before and after our War of Independence, Benjamin Franklin, John Adams, and Samuel Adams all proclaimed the fact of that connection. Their tributes are seldom cited today, and were delivered at the time as though little explanation were necessary. Thus, even with testimony from the Founding Fathers, the historian faces the task of discovering how the battles fought in seventeenth-century Massachusetts led to America's victory at Yorktown in 1781.

There is nothing arbitrary in posing that question. Beyond the evidence provided by Franklin and the two Adamses, who were all sons of Massachusetts, there is the fact that George Washington raised the Continental Army at Cambridge, on the common facing Harvard College— rather than in his native Virginia. Against the usual portrayals of the provincial narrowness dividing the original colonies, Washington's action is itself sufficient reason to ask, what brought a Virginia planter to the former Puritan stronghold, to lead a war for American independence? The question is also raised, what preconditions had already been met in Virginia, such that a war for the right to build a nation, could be declared with reasonable expectations that it could be done? The answer is suggested by the very name given to these fighters for independence: the *Continental* Army.

When Washington took command of his forces, consisting almost entirely of New England militia units, he had worked in collaboration with Benjamin Franklin for nearly a quarter of a century. And for nearly a quarter century before that, Franklin had been in Philadelphia, building a republican movement on the model of Cotton Mather, the last great leader of New England's Puritans. Contrary to all previous accounts, this work documents that Franklin was Cotton Mather's own protégé, and the son of one of Mather's leading republican organizers in Boston. The evidence for an hypothesis of continuity is irrefutable. The proof lies in determining the singularities which account for the fact, that the *idea* of a continental republic, was transformed into a concrete prospect, *before* America's direct challenges to British authority during the 1760s.

Thus, the foundations for America's independence must be proven to have been established through earlier, successful efforts to open the way for developing the West, despite British and French determination to stop it. Throwing aside prevailing historical opinion, in order to take a fresh look at the matter, one can identify a truly remarkable singularity in the pattern of events occurring around the year 1710. New royal governors arrived that year to take command of Virginia and New York, the two most strategically placed colonies for developing settlements beyond the mountains, from the Great Lakes to the Mississippi River. Cotton Mather published his classic manual on organizing a republican citizenry, *Essays to Do Good*. Virginia's Governor Alexander Spotswood immediately announced plans to push beyond the supposedly impassable Blue Ridge Mountains as far as the Mississippi. In New York, preparations were made to secure the Mohawk Valley as far as Lake Ontario, by Governor Robert Hunter, a close personal friend of Jonathan Swift. By the end of that year, Swift had gained entry to the innermost circles of Queen Anne's emerging new government.

The major policy shift in Queen Anne's government had been in the works for several years, and Jonathan Swift—no mere satirist or coffee-house gadfly—played a major role in it. Upon further investigation, it becomes clear that he did so in collaboration with Gottfried Wilhelm von Leibniz, privy councilor to Queen Anne's designated successor, the Electress Sophie of Hanover. In the midst of this international battle, in which Leibniz and his allies sought to break the nations of Europe away from their policies of mutually assured destruction, the nation-building thrust of the American colonies was launched in earnest. It was a great project for other nations to emulate, yet designed to succeed even if they did not—so that mankind might still have a place to pursue its divinely ordained commitment to progress.

The American colonies' true course to independence cannot be charted, without understanding the issues and lessons of the political warfare which shaped the reign of Queen Anne. That story is therefore treated here in some detail—especially since her reign is generally portrayed as a "black hole" in the galaxy of American history texts. Considerable space is also given to another victim of obscurity, Virginia's Governor Alexander Spotswood, whose magnificent accomplishments enraged the opponents of America's continental development at the time. Spotswood's typical treatment at the hands of American historians is a most telling case. They simply bury him anonymously in a potters' field; yet he personally paved the way for America's first colonization beyond the eastern mountains, and documentably created the nation-building faction in Virginia which produced George Washington. Though hundreds of volumes have been written about George Washington, none has explored his political legacy from Spotswood, even though a mere glance at the relevant genealogies establishes a multiple of direct relationships between the Spotswood and Washington families. The fact that it was Alexander Spotswood who appointed Benjamin Franklin postmaster of Philadelphia, should also give one pause, when considering standard historical opinion.

One final point should be stated, concerning the historical method employed in this work. Without the record of New England's republican origins, many of the questions the author confronted would not have been raised. Had he adopted the general axioms purporting to account for the American Revolution, he would never have scrutinized the early eighteenth-century record for evidence of the colonies' nation-building aspirations. Yet even beyond those obstacles, the search is complicated by another problem, which itself reflects a fundamental reality of the period. Following the death of Queen Anne in 1714, the new government of George I began savagely destroying the policy initiatives which had launched America's continental development in 1710. Those who continued the fight—such as Mather, Franklin, Spotswood, and Washington—frequently had to mask their intentions, and operate covertly under the nose of enemy rule. Thus the documentary record of America's challenge to British rule must be examined from another standpoint: that of intelligence warfare, in the mode of resistance against an occupying power. The early career of Benjamin Franklin best exemplifies the case, and for that reason is also given detailed treatment in this work.

H. Graham Lowry

July 4, 1987

Purcellville, Va.

How the Nation Was Won

Was Won

America's Untold Story

1630–1754

1

Giving Thanks for a Nation

Whatever little historical significance Americans today attribute to Thanksgiving is generally bound up with simple images of the Pilgrims of Plymouth Colony, celebrating their successful harvest after enduring near and actual starvation during their first winter in America. In the folklore of today's environmentalists who annually reenact that Thanksgiving at Plymouth, the Pilgrims were a model society, living happily within the 'limits' of nature, in a labor-intensive, feudal stupor.

As a record of the Pilgrims' accomplishment on their own, the folklore reflects a good bit of truth, as ten years after their landing in 1620, the Pilgrims still numbered only 300 people, huddled together and rapidly depleting the natural resources of the land adjoining Cape Cod Bay. But none of this has anything to do with our national tradition of celebrating Thanksgiving. It is time to recall what our Founding Fathers gave thanks for.

The first Thanksgiving Day proclaimed by the United States called upon Americans to thank almighty God for

> his kind care and protection of the People of this country previous to their becoming a Nation; . . . for the peaceful and rational manner in which we have been able to establish constitutions of government for our own safety and happiness, and particularly for the national One now lately instituted.

That first national Thanksgiving—Thursday, November 26, 1789—was proclaimed by President George Washington, fully conscious that he now presided over the realization of America's more than century-and-a-half struggle to become a sovereign republic.

This was not the first day of thanksgiving Washington had declared. As commander-in-chief of the victorious Continental Army, he ordered a cessation of all hostilities with Britain on April 19, 1783 and instructed the army chaplains to hold services to "render thanks to almighty God"—eight years to the day after Massachusetts militiamen delivered the "shot heard 'round the world" launching the American Revolution.

Washington and the Puritans

The thanks George Washington gave for Americans' abilities "to establish constitutions of government for our safety and happiness" is properly directed to the extraordinary efforts launched by the Puritans of seventeenth-century New England, who fought a pitched battle to establish the republican institutions which made possible the founding of the American Republic.

In 1775, then a veteran Virginia militia colonel, Washington rode to Massachusetts to assume command of the Continental Army on Cambridge Common, across from Harvard College. There, almost twenty years before, he had first consulted with Professor John Winthrop, the teacher of John Adams and Sam Adams, and the brilliant physicist and astronomer whom Benjamin Franklin counted as a great friend, and one of America's most invaluable citizens. In his sixties at the outbreak of the Revolution, Winthrop took responsibility for munitions production, inspecting powder mills, advising on the production of sulphur, and trying to stimulate saltpeter production.

Professor Winthrop was also the great-great-grandson of the first John Winthrop in America, the founder and first governor of the independent Massachusetts Bay Colony, birthplace of the American Republic.   During the Revolution, the republican citizenry of Massachusetts, and of the Connecticut colony developed under similar freedoms by Governor John Winthrop's son, contributed sixty percent of the "Continental Line," the regular army for the thirteen colonies that Washington led to victory.

In an 1807 letter to Benjamin Rush, a fellow-signer of the Declaration of Independence, John Adams wrote

> I have always laughed at the affectation of representing American Independence as a novel idea, as a modern discovery, as a late invention. The idea of it as a possible thing, as a probable event, nay, as a necessary and unavoidable measure, in case Great Britain should assume an unconstitutional authority over us, has been familiar to Americans from the first settlement of the country, and was as well understood by Gov. Winthrop . . . as by Gov. Samuel Adams. . . .

Sam Adams, a leader of the Sons of Liberty during the organizing drive for independence and repeatedly governor of Massachusetts during and after the Revolution, horrified the British monarchy at Harvard's commencement ceremonies in 1740, when, as salutatorian for his class, he called for a revival of "the Puritan Commonwealth of our fathers."   He invoked the more than half a century after 1630 that the Massachusetts Bay Colony had maintained the status of a constitutional republic, free from direct governance by the crown.

The New World Republic

From the late fifteenth century onward, with the tightening oligarchical grip on Europe enforced by

Venetian and Dutch banking, plans for establishing a republic in the New World as a strategic flank were plotted among the circles of the Florentine Academy. In the Tudor England of Shakespeare and Marlowe, in a republican culture enriched by such heirs of the Italian Renaissance as Giordano Bruno and Erasmus of Rotterdam, who fled to England from a collapsing European continent, the leadership capability for a bold colonization effort was developed.

John Winthrop, the leader of the Massachusetts Bay Colony, was the grandson of a Suffolk squire who received his lands from Henry VIII and had been a master of the Clothworkers' Company of London, prominent enough to have his portrait painted by Holbein.[1] Winthrop's father Adam, born in 1548, married the sister, and was the long-time friend, of Dr. John Still, from 1576 to 1592 the vice-chancellor of the University of Cambridge and the Master of Trinity College, where much of the Puritan leadership was educated. Adam Winthrop, born in London and trained as a lawyer, also served as auditor of Trinity College from at least 1593 to 1610, when he was sixty-two years old. The diary he kept at his manor in Groton establishes his reputation as a man of learning, to whom friends came to borrow the works of Plato and Petrarch.[2]

John Winthrop, born in 1588, entered Trinity College in 1602, and there began years of often painful religious self-examination, which intensified with England's moral disintegration as a nation under the Stuart kings, James I and Charles I.[3]   The continuing crackdown on even conforming Puritans, by the monarchy and the Anglican hierarchy, may partly explain the very limited account Winthrop leaves of his activities in England after about 1606. The worsening situation was certainly a factor in his decision in 1622 to send his son John, Jr., not to Cambridge for his education, but to Trinity College, Dublin.[4]

The entire strategic situation deteriorated following the outbreak in 1618 of the Thirty Years War, an orgy of oligarchical destruction which would depopulate half of Europe. Time began running out, for the Puritans in England to launch a strategic flank in the New World, when their archenemy William Laud became Bishop of London in 1628. The hour of decision was enforced when Charles I disbanded Parliament in 1629, and placed the country under virtual dictatorship.

A few small advance parties of Puritans were sent over to Massachusetts, mostly to Salem, between 1624 and 1628. Another step toward serious colonization was taken with the dispatch of an expedition to Salem in June 1628 under John Endicott. John Winthrop initially planned to send his son, John, Jr., with Endicott. But with the aid of Puritan merchants in London, delicate maneuverings were under way to seek a charter for the Massachusetts Bay, not as a crown colony, nor as a London-directed trading company, but as an independent commonwealth in New England. Winthrop instead dispatched his son on a fourteen-month mission to Europe, to report on the movements and military engagements of the English and French fleets in the Mediterranean, and to Venice and Constantinople, to investigate current designs of the oligarchically-run Jesuits and the Ottoman Empire. By one account, his diplomatic meetings included officials of the Vatican, and on his way back to England, he met with republican circles in Amsterdam.[5]

In the meantime, the elder Winthrop continued organizing for a large-scale colonization project. His papers include a moving record of the sense of urgency and republican commitment guiding his efforts—his "Reasons to be considered for justifying . . . the plantation in New England."

All other churches of Europe are brought to desolation and our sins for which the Lord begins already to frown upon us, do threaten us fearfully, and who knows but that God hath provided this place to be a refuge for many whom He means to save out of the general calamity, and seeing the Church hath no place left to fly into but the wilderness what better work can there be, than to go before and provide tabernacles, and food for her, against [the time] she cometh thither.

This land grows weary of her inhabitants, so as man who is the most precious of all creatures is here more vile & base than the earth we tread upon, and of less price among us, than a horse or a sheep, masters are forced by authority to entertain servants, parents to maintain their own children, all towns complain of the burden of their poor though we have taken up many unnecessary, yea unlawful trades to maintain them. And we use the authority of the law to hinder the increase of people as urging the execution of the state against cottages and inmates & thus it is come to pass that children, servants & neighbors (especially if they be poor) are counted the greatest burden which if things were right it would be the chiefest earthly blessing.

Against such bestial degradation of humanity, Winthrop hurls the republican call-to-arms for progress:

The whole earth is the Lord's garden & he hath given it to the sons of men, with a general condition, Gen: 1.28. Increase and multiply, replenish the earth and subdue it, which was again renewed to Noah, the end is double, moral and natural, that man might enjoy the fruits of the earth and God might have his due glory from the creature, why then should we stand here striving for places of habitation, (many men spending much labor & cost to recover or keep sometimes an acre or two of land as would procure them many hundred as good or better in another country) and in the mean time suffer a whole Continent, as fruitful and convenient for the use of man, to lie waste without any improvement.

Winthrop's argument for a New England also took direct aim at the Aristotelian plague then rampant in English education.

The fountains of learning and religion are so corrupted (as beside the unsupportable charge of the education) most children (even the best wits and fairest hopes) are perverted, corrupted, and utterly overthrown, by the multitude of evil examples and the licentious government of those seminaries, where men strain at gnats, and swallow camels, use all severity for maintenance   of   caps,   and   other accomplishments but suffer all ruffian-like fashion and disorder in manners to pass uncontrolled.[6]

The Massachusetts Bay Charter

To secure the constitutional freedom required to nurture a republican society, Winthrop and his allies managed a diplomatic coup—with not a little subterfuge and considerable   sums   of   money—which   gave   the

Massachusetts Bay Company a charter, enabling it to govern its own affairs in New England. It was signed by Charles I, just two days after the attempt to arrest Parliamentary leaders who defied the order to dissolve. The language omitted the standard requirement that the governance of the company be based in England. Moreover, the charter empowered the "freemen" of the company to elect their own governor and other officials, and make laws and ordinances for their own benefit and for the government of persons inhabiting their territory. The royal docket item explaining the charter stipulated holding the election of the company's "governor and officers here in England," but no such provision appeared in the charter itself.

Winthrop and other leaders of the company made their intentions clear, in a secret meeting of the company's General Court—to this day still the official name of the Massachusetts legislature—on July 28, 1629. The meeting discussed various "weighty reasons" for the "transfer [of] the government of the plantation to those that shall inhabit there, and not to continue the same in subordination to the company here, as it now is." The company's records note that "by reason of the many great and considerable consequences thereupon depending, it was not now resolved upon." Instead, the members were requested to consider the proposal "privately and seriously" until their next meeting, and in the meantime "to carry this business *secretly*, that the same not be divulged."[7]

In August 1629, John, Jr. returned from his intelligence mission and reported to his father. On August 26, two days before the next scheduled meeting of the General Court, Winthrop and eleven other leaders of the company met at Cambridge and signed an agreement to embark by March 1 of the following year to pass the Seas, (under God's protection,) to inhabit and continue in New England: Provided always, that before the last of September next, the whole Government, together with the patent for the said Plantation, be first, by an order of [the General) Court, legally transferred and established to remain with us and others which shall inhabit upon the said Plantation.[8]

The meeting of the General Court two days later appointed committees to debate "whether or not *the Chief Government* of the Plantation, together with the Patent, should be settled in New England, or here." After discussion the following morning, the General Court voted to establish the government in New England "and accordingly an order to be drawn up."

The significance of the decision, and the open door to sovereignty obtained in the Massachusetts Bay Charter, was not lost on the republicans' enemies already active in New England. Sir Ferdinando Gorges, who, under the authority of the Council of New England, deployed a number of marauding bands to the Bay area during the 1620s, as a blocking move against real colonization, reacted with horror. Gorges charged the Puritans had "surreptitiously" extended their grant of lands and their governing authority.

The Puritan "intruders," he wrote,

exorbitantly bounded their grant from East to West through all that main land from sea to sea. . . . But herewith not yet being content, they obtained, unknown to us, a confirmation of all this from His Majesty, by which means they did not only enlarge their first extents . . . but wholly excluded themselves from the public government of the Council authorized for those affairs, and made themselves a free people.

On October 20, 1629, the General Court unanimously elected John Winthrop governor for one year. However slim the records of his previous activities, there is no doubt of the leadership stature already accorded him by the time of his election. "It is come to that issue," he wrote, "as, in all probability, the welfare of the Plantation depends upon my assistance: for the main pillars of it, being gentlemen of high quality and eminent parts, both for wisdom and Godliness, are determined to sit still if I desert them."[9]

Indeed, the mission was already under way. On April 25, less than two months after Charles I signed the Massachusetts Bay Charter, an expedition of 300 colonists set sail, assigned to establish the infrastructure for the much larger migration to follow. They included engineers to lay out town plans, and carpenters, brick-makers, and sawyers to build warehouses, ships for fishing and shipping, a sawmill, and fortifications. Their cargo included seven cannon as well.

Preparing for dispatch of the next wave of settlers, John Winthrop oversaw logistics as a whole, and raised additional funds to provide transportation for poor families, to maintain ministers, and to build churches, public buildings, and additional fortifications. His son John, Jr. was to stay behind temporarily, to sell Groton Manor and study fortifications. Through Isaac Johnson, the officer in charge of arranging ordnance for the colony, John, Jr. obtained permission to plot the specifications of the fort at the North Seas port of Harwich, and to examine the weapons of the London Military Company.

On June 12, 1630, after a voyage of seventy-six days, four ships with 800 passengers, under command of John

Winthrop, anchored in Salem harbor. Defining the historic significance of the mission in *A Model of Christian Charity*, written on board his flagship *Arbella*, Winthrop declared, "For we must consider that we shall be as a city upon a hill. The eyes of all people are upon us."[10] With more ships already on the way, he was soon to preside over more than 2,000 colonists of the Massachusetts Bay. Winthrop proclaimed the colony's first Thanksgiving on February 22, 1631, upon the arrival of desperately needed supplies after the hard winter of the first year of the new commonwealth.[11]

The Battle for Sovereignty

Though an ocean removed from any immediate actions of the English crown, and armed with the self-governing powers of its charter, Massachusetts Bay was so far only a beachhead for a new republic. Nearly 20,000 colonists would arrive on its shores by 1650, a feat requiring not only extraordinary effort in physical and logistical terms, but a continuing political battle, both to maintain emigration opportunities within England and to defend the freedoms established in New England.

It was not long before the charter came under attack. After a series of efforts, the King's Privy Council in 1634 ordered the charter returned to England. When the demand was presented in Boston, Governor Winthrop politely responded that nothing could be done except by the General Court, which would not convene until September. In the meantime, the population was mobilized against the threat to the charter, and when the General Court met it authorized £600 toward "fortifications and other charges." Winthrop wrote that the measures "were the more hastened" with the news that the Lords Commissioners were sending two Anglican archbishops" and ten others of the council, to regulate all plantations," with power to "make laws, to raise tithes and portions for ministers, to remove and punish governours," and to exercise all judicial powers.

Winthrop and four magistrates of the General Court were given "power to consult, direct and give command for the managing and ordering of any war that may befall us for the space of a year's next ensuing. . . ." Fortifications were stepped up for the defense of the colony at Castle Island in Boston Harbor, Charlestown, and Dorchester, while cannon were provided for Salem, Saugus, and Ipswich, with the priority that "the fort at Castle Island, now begun, shall be fully perfected." Finally, it was ordered that "a beacon be set on Sentry Hill [now Beacon Hill, the site of the Massachusetts State Legislature] at Boston, to give notice to the country of any danger. "[12]

Faced with the threat of armed popular resistance, the crown backed down, but the return of the charter was again demanded in 1638, coupled with the threat that King Charles would otherwise "reassume into his hands the whole plantation." Winthrop replied to the Lords Commissioners, insisting that Massachusetts had loyally abided by the terms of the rights the King's charter granted it. Not so subtly, he hinted at the alternative if they were violated—as John Adams later warned, "in case Great Britain should assume an unconstitutional authority over us." Winthrop's reply concluded:

> Lastly, if our patent be taken from us, (whereby we suppose we may claim interest in his Majesty's favour and protection,) the common people here will conceive that his Majesty hath cast them off, and that hereby they are freed from their allegiance and subjection, and thereupon will be ready to confederate themselves under a new government, for their necessary safety and subsistence."[13]

Winthrop had also moved to expand his forces. He began efforts to establish the United Colonies of New England, or the New England Confederation, which would unite Massachusetts, Plymouth, and the Connecticut River settlements around Hartford, for collaboration on development of the region and for its common defense. Winthrop reports in his journal that "some of the Connecticut magistrates being here, there was a day of meeting appointed to agree upon some articles of Confederation," but, for the moment, the Connecticut towns refused.[14]   When established in 1643, the New England Confederation elected John Winthrop as president, and its Articles of Confederation served as the first step toward realizing a new nation under constitutional rule. Benjamin Franklin would later cite them during the American Revolution, in explaining the Articles of Confederation of the United States to the French government.

Winthrop's "city upon a hill" was beginning to radiate outward. In the still harsh wilderness of New England, a whole society was being established for the first time on the basis of natural law. Despite inevitable challenges—and often malicious disruptions—from both without and within, Massachusetts was determined to build the foundations for a republic in the New World. In doing so, its Puritan leaders defined a constitutional basis for man's freedom to perfect his divine nature.

In his speech, "On Christian Liberty," in 1645, John Winthrop presented one of the strongest affirmations of that freedom ever presented by an American political leader:

> There is a twofold liberty, natural (and I mean as our nature is now corrupt) and civil or federal. The first is common to man with beasts and other creatures . . . it is a liberty to

evil as well as to good . . . and cannot endure
the least restraint of the most just authority.
The exercise and maintaining of this liberty
makes men grow more evil, and in time to be
worse than brute beasts. This is that great
enemy of truth and peace, that wild beast,
which all the ordinances of God are bent
against, to restrain and subdue it. The other
kind of liberty I call civil or federal; it may also
be termed moral, in reference to the covenant
between God and man, in the moral law, and
the politic covenants and constitutions amongst
men themselves. . . , and it is a liberty to do
that only which is good, just, and honest. This
liberty you are to stand for, with the hazard (not
just of your goods but) of your lives, if need
be.[15]

Building a Republic

The attempt by Charles I to revoke the charter in 1638
was met by the formation of the Military Company of
Massachusetts. Governor John Winthrop himself served as
colonel of the 1,000-man First Massachusetts Regiment of
Militia.[16] This was the beginning of the republican militia
system that spread throughout New England—and
remained to produce the core of the Continental Army
during the American Revolution.

Two years earlier, in 1636, the General Court of
Massachusetts voted to establish Harvard College, half a
century before any other was established in America. The
1640s brought the first public system of compulsory
elementary education, and a system of publicly supported
academies for further instruction and college preparation.
On the premise of an educated citizenry, Massachusetts
adopted in 1641 a Body of Liberties, a constitutional

definition of the powers and duties of the General Court, the judiciary, and the voters and citizens. This included a criminal code that prohibited inconsistent penalties or punishments, and overturned the arbitrary use of precedent in English common law. John Winthrop cited their importance for overcoming "a great danger to our state in regard that our magistrates, for want of positive laws, in many cases, might proceed according to their discretions." Winthrop also noted that the reason such a constitution had not been put into writing, during the initial struggle to establish the colony, was the fear of prematurely challenging a provision in the charter which prohibited the enactment of laws "repugnant to the laws of England."[17]

The General Court decided that the Body of Liberties would be "audibly read and deliberately weighed" in each session for the next three years, and where not "altered or repealed" would be in force.[18] In 1646, the legislature ordered an unprecedented extension of protection to the citizens of Massachusetts. The laws were to be *printed*, despite the fact that only one press existed in the colony. A joint commission, of the magistrates of the upper house and the deputies of the lower, was appointed to examine and

> compose in good order all the liberties, laws, and orders extant with us . . . so as we may have ready recourse to any of them, upon all occasions, whereby we may manifest our utter disaffection to arbitrary government, and so all relations be safely and sweetly directed and protected in all their just rights and privileges; desiring thereby to make way for *printing* our Laws for more public and profitable use of us and our successors.

The New England Confederation in 1650

Created by John Winthrop in 1643, the New England Confederation was the beachhead of America's drive for a continental republic. The confederation linked the Massachusetts Bay, Plymouth, and Connecticut colonies for purposes of mutual assistance and defense. Massachusetts flourished under its charter's self-governing status and body of liberties, and New England as a whole was strengthened when John Winthrop, Jr. secured those freedoms in a new charter for Connecticut in 1662. Benjamin Franklin cited the New England Confederation as the precedent for the first government of the United States, established under the Articles of Confederation during the American Revolution. The design of the New England flag is also of historical interest; it consisted of alternating red and white stripes.

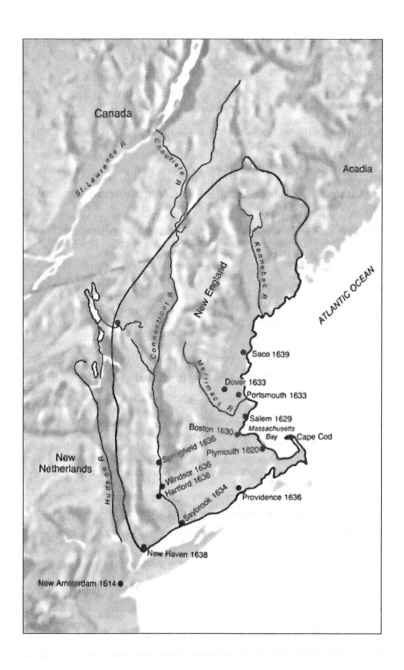

Canada

Acadia

St. Lawrence R.

Chaudiere R.

New England

Kennebec R.

ATLANTIC OCEAN

Connecticut R.

Merrimac R.

Saco 1639

Dover 1633
Portsmouth 1633

Salem 1629

Boston 1630
Massachusetts
Bay   Cape Cod

Springfield 1636
Plymouth 1620

New
Netherlands

Hudson R.

Windsor 1636
Hartford 1636

Saybrook 1634

Providence 1636

New Haven 1638

New Amsterdam 1614

The Massachusetts Bay Colony's effort to forge a constitutional republic proceeded with a specific commitment to economic and industrial development. In 1640, the General Court voted sizeable subsidies for local manufacture of textiles and, especially for outfitting a fleet, passed measures in 1641 to stimulate the production of hemp. Twenty-one-year tax exemptions were also granted for all discoverers of mines.[19]

John Winthrop, Jr., was also dispatched to England to organize and recruit skilled labor for iron manufacturing in Massachusetts. With the English Civil War under way, he secured backing from many of the bankrollers of Oliver Cromwell's New Model Army. John, Jr. returned to Boston in September 1643, with the men and equipment he had acquired to construct iron works. He received the dirigist backing of the General Court the following March, when it granted the company a twenty-one-year monopoly, necessary lands, and a ten-year tax exemption, on condition that complete facilities be developed, from blast furnaces and forges, to rolling and slitting mills. The company would only be permitted to export iron after the colony's needs were met.[20]

By 1647, the younger Winthrop's efforts led to the establishment of the Saugus Iron Works, the first automated, integrated industrial complex in the New World. Using huge water wheels, the plant featured gear-driven bellows for heating the ore and working the iron, including an automatic hammer to pound out wrought iron, and automatic rollers and slitters for turning out iron bars and rods. By the end of its first year of operation, the Saugus Iron Works was producing eight tons of wrought iron per week, far beyond the output of the best works in England.

With the disruption of Massachusetts' trade and currency flows by the English Civil War, the colony further advanced its economic sovereignty in 1652 with the creation of a mint.   Massachusetts issued its Pine Tree Shilling, redeemable only within the colony and thus secure against foreign draining of its hard currency, long into the Restoration—despite outraged protests by the monarchy.

Massachusetts' commitment to fostering a republic in the New World was never hostage to any faction in England, though it worked with friendly forces where possible.   Many Massachusetts men had returned to England to serve the Commonwealth of 1649–1653, and held some positions of influence in Cromwell's subsequent Protectorate.   But the Bay Colony refused throughout to alter its charter.   When Parliament told Massachusetts in 1651 that it should accept a new charter, under the control of Parliament, the General Court replied that it had not invoked England's authority "either in the late Kinges time or since," and "not being able to discern the need of such an injunction: These things make us doubt and fear what is intended for us."   In 1652, the General Court decreed that all inhabitants take an oath of allegiance "to the lawes of this jurisdiction," making no mention of England.

Securing the Connecticut Flank

By the time of founder John Winthrop's death in 1649, Massachusetts Bay alone had a population of more than 14,000 people, and many of its citizens had already fanned out to establish further settlements in Connecticut, though they were poorly coordinated overall.   John Winthrop, Jr., moved in 1647 to secure New England's Connecticut flank, first at Saybrook, then New London, and in 1656 to the separate New Haven colony, chiefly to oversee the establishment of iron works there.   The existing Connecticut Colony, centered around Hartford and the towns on the Connecticut River, repeatedly solicited the younger Winthrop to become its governor, electing him in absentia in 1657 and finally securing his acceptance. The necessity of establishing a viable commonwealth in Connecticut became urgent in 1658, with the death of Cromwell and the beginning of the end of the English Protectorate.[21]

Despite Cromwell's war with the Dutch, Governor Winthrop of Connecticut had opposed the Protector's war policy and complimented Peter Stuyvesant, the governor of New Netherlands, on his "Christian-like" efforts to keep the peace with New England. With the restoration of the monarchy in England and Charles II's accession to the throne, Winthrop moved to secure charter freedom for Connecticut as a whole, by improving on the early Connecticut patent obtained by the Earl of Warwick.[22]

Dispatching a florid appeal to His Majesty's "dazzling star" to "accept this Colony, your own colony, a little branch of your mighty empire," Governor Winthrop convened an extraordinary session of the legislature to draft a petition for a new charter. It called for improving upon the Warwick Patent with appropriate insertions from the Massachusetts Bay Charter, or, if the Warwick Patent were not found, to press for an entirely new document granting Connecticut control from the boundary of the Plymouth Colony to the Delaware River, "or as far as may be granted that way." Winthrop was empowered to depart from the instructions as he saw fit, during his negotiations in London.[23]

John Winthrop, Jr., was the most renowned New England intellectual of his day—a physician, astronomer, inventor, geologist, and chemist who corresponded with John Milton's inner circle, and later with the great Leibniz in Europe. Winthrop's meeting with Milton himself was undoubtedly important, but he was careful to leave no written account of their discussion.   Samuel Hartlib, a close ally of Milton's, was also Winthrop's longtime correspondent, and now became his entree to William Brereton, Robert Boyle, and the rest of the Gresham College nucleus which founded the Royal Society.[24]

After more than a year of intricate maneuvers and negotiations, Winthrop obtained a new charter for Connecticut on April 23, 1662, with almost everything he wanted. Charles II was not yet so secure, that powerful English Puritans who yielded to the restoration of the monarchy could simply be ignored. The new King was still seeking to win friends and co-opt enemies.

For Winthrop, such royal cultivation included his election on December 18, 1661 as a founding member of the Royal Society, the institution created to 'honor' intellectual achievement, while working to suppress real discovery and scientific breakthroughs. Among Winthrop's similarly targeted American successors were three other great contributors from Massachusetts to the cause of independence: Increase Mather, Cotton Mather, and Benjamin Franklin.

Notes

1. Robert C. Winthrop, *Life and Letters of John Winthrop* (2 vols., Boston, 1869), I, 17, 20.

2. *Ibid.*, 32, 47, 411.

3. *Ibid.*, 56–122.

4. *Ibid.*, 170–171.

5. *Ibid.*, 263–276.

6. *Ibid.*, 309–310.

7. Records of the Governor and Company of the Massachusetts Bay, quoted in Winthrop, *Life and Letters*, I, 342–343.

8. *Ibid.*, 345.

9. Winthrop, *Life and Letters*, 352n.

10. *Ibid.*, II, 19, 21.

11. *Ibid.*, 57.

12. Justin Winsor, ed., *The Memorial History of Boston* (4 vols., Boston, 1880), I, 338–340.

13. *Ibid.*, I, 346.

14. Winthrop, *Life and Letters*, II, 235.

15. *Ibid.*, 341.

16. *Ibid.*, 239.

17. Winsor, ed., *History of Boston*, I, 128–129.

18. *Ibid.*, 128.

19. E. N. Hartley, *Ironworks on the Saugus* (Norman, Okla., 1957), 53–54.

20. *Ibid.*, 55, 91–92.

21. Richard S. Dunn, *Puritans and Yankees*, The Winthrop Dynasty of New England (Princeton, 1962), 100–105.

22. *Ibid.*, 120.

23. For a detailed account of Winthrop' s charter negotiations, see Robert C. Black III, *The Younger John Winthrop* (New York, 1966).

24. Dunn, *Puritans and Yankees*, 130.

2

The Restoration's Assault

During war with the Dutch in 1664, King Charles II seized New Amsterdam and established New York. Connecticut's Governor Winthrop interceded, using his relations with Peter Stuyvesant to secure Dutch rights of settlement and trade, in return for the peaceful surrender of New Amsterdam.[1] But England's acquisition of a colony on New England's southern and western borders constituted a serious new threat to its independence. On April 23, 1664, Charles II issued "Private Instructions" to Colonel Richard Nicholls and the other royal commissioners for New England. The document survives, and provides an extraordinary testimonial to the monarchy's fear of New England's independent status.

The commissioners were charged with "insinuating yourselves by all kind and dextrous carriage into the good opinion of the principal persons there, that so you may . . . lead and dispose them to renew their Charters and to make such alterations as will appear necessary for their own benefit." The King had asked for a general assembly to be convened to consider the "alterations" sought by the monarchy, and he instructed the commissioners to "use your utmost endeavors privately . . . to get men of the best reputations and most peaceably inclined, to be chosen into that Assembly."[2]

The King reminded his commissioners that their basic objective was "the general disposing that people to an entire submission and obedience to our government which is their own greatest security in respect of their neighbors and leading them to a desire to renew their Charters. . . ." Charles II also warned his commissioners that the destruction of New England's sovereignty took strategic precedence over any merely material opportunities. "All designs of profit for the present seem unreasonable and may possibly obstruct the more necessary design upon their obedience and loyalty." The King noted that to the "sort of people which will be active in many projects for our profit and benefit, you must not be forwards too much, since most overtures of that kind are but airy imaginations, and cannot be put in practice by our own immediate power and authority, without manifest violation of their Charter. . ."[3]

The King's subversion campaign was complicated by England's continuing wars with the Dutch, who retook New York in 1673, only to cede it back the following year after their defeat in Europe. Charles II now determined to destroy all colonial charters, and established in 1675 a new Privy Council committee, the Lords of Trade and Plantations, to enforce looting the wealth of the colonies. But against New England, the policy called for direct military attacks as well.

The new royal governor for New York, Edmund Andros, seized the Puritan towns of eastern Long Island from Connecticut. He also informed the Hartford Assembly on May 1, 1675, that the Duke of York claimed all of Connecticut south and west of the Connecticut River, and ordered the assembly to "give present and effectual orders for my receiving, in his Royal Highnesse behalf, that part of his Territories as yet under your Jurisdiction."[4] In response to this demand for over half of Connecticut's territory, and almost all of its towns, Winthrop politely invoked the boundaries specified under the royal charter of 1664. To Andros' reply that the charter had no authority to alter the duke's claims, Winthrop and the Connecticut magistrates refused again on June 16 to surrender any territory, but suggested a "neighborly conference" if Andros remained dissatisfied.[5]

A week later, in Plymouth Colony territory bordering the degenerate colony of Rhode Island, the worst Indian war in New England history broke out. Andros informed the government at Hartford that "upon this extraordinary occasion" he was dispatching troops "to Connecticut River," citing the boundary claimed by "his Royal Highnesse."[6] More than timing suggests that Andros had encouraged the Indian hostilities. He became notorious in New England for bribing and arming the Indians to attack colonial settlements. He was officially charged with a whole list of such crimes, by Massachusetts in 1689.[7] The Indian rampage known as King Philip's War—after the Indian chief designated to lead it—laid waste to scores of towns in western Massachusetts and other outlying settlements of New England.

Governor Andros, meanwhile, took two ships of soldiers to the mouth of the Connecticut River at Saybrook, not to fight Indians, but to attack Connecticut. He had expected to seize the Saybrook fort without a fight, but found the area's militia fully turned out and massed on the shore. He sent a messenger ashore with another threatening letter asserting the Duke of York's boundary claims. The militia, meanwhile, loaded and readied the cannon in the fort. Another company of militia, dispatched by the General Assembly at Hartford, was instructed to direct Andros to the eastern shore of Naragansett Bay if he wanted to fight Indians, "for there is the seat of war." If Andros tried to land, or take any measures against the government of Connecticut, the militia commander was instructed "to declare against, oppose, and undo the same."

Stymied by this show of force, Andros blusteringly came ashore with his officers, and read the Duke of York's claims to a silent and hostile crowd. Before ordering the royal governor back to his ship, the Connecticut militia read Hartford's proclamation against him, including the directive to Connecticut citizens "utterly to refuse to attend, countenance or obey the said Major Edmund Andros or any under him. . . ." Connecticut had firmly demonstrated it would fight for its charter freedoms, and a humiliated Andros set sail for New York.[8]

New England mobilized to end King Philip's War, with no assistance whatsoever from the British crown that demanded its allegiance. In September 1675, John Winthrop went to Boston for meetings of the New England Confederation, which organized the military effort to defeat the oligarchy's surrogate warfare assault. He never left Boston. Now nearly seventy years old, he spent the winter overseeing the war effort, caught a cold leading to a long illness, and died on April 5, 1676.[9] He was buried next to his father, in the cemetery adjoining what is now King's Chapel in Boston. Increase Mather's son Cotton later wrote of John Winthrop, Jr., "A blessed land was New England, when there was over part of it a governor who was not only a Christian and a gentleman, but also an eminent philosopher. . . ."[10]

Less than two months after Winthrop's death, the monarchy launched its next attack on the Massachusetts charter. An English ship entered Boston harbor on June 10, 1676, carrying Edward Randolph, special envoy of Charles II, sent to investigate Massachusetts' violations of the Navigation Acts restricting colonial trade, especially with other European powers.[11] Randolph noted passing Castle Island, built under John Winthrop, Sr., when Charles I demanded the return of the charter in 1634, and now a bastioned stone fort with thirty-eight cannon aiming out at the channel. Among the wharves of Boston's port, Randolph also noted clusters of ships from France and Spain, trading freely with Massachusetts, without regard for the Navigation Acts. New England's trading as a sovereign power cost the crown more than £100,000 a year in customs duties alone, by Randolph's estimate, and he was determined to bring Massachusetts into line. He reported that Massachusetts had built more than 700 ships, some as large as 250 tons, under direction of thirty master shipbuilders. Massachusetts was already the leading colonial exporter of wheat and other grains, beef, pork, peas, fish, furs, and lumber products, including highly prized ships' masts.[12]

Though nominally received as an envoy from the King, Randolph was treated like a foreigner interfering in domestic affairs. After appearing before the Massachusetts Bay Council to present Charles II's demands, Randolph indignantly wrote to the King,

> I put off my hat; whereupon three of the magistrates took off their hats and sat uncovered, but the governor with the rest continued to keep their hats on. Your Majesty's letter . . . being read in my hearing, the governor told the council that the matters therein contained were very inconsiderable things and easily answered.[13]

Randolph had more than met his match in John Leverett, a testy old Puritan, now governor of Massachusetts. The royal envoy demanded "a full answer to his Majesty's letter with all convenient speed," and Leverett replied by asking "by what Order I made that demand." The apoplectic Randolph managed a meeting with Leverett a few days later, to complain that Massachusetts seemed to be violating the Navigation Act. Leverett's reply made clear the terms under which Massachusetts recognized royal authority. Leverett "freely declared to me," Randolph wrote, "that the laws made by Our King and Parliament obligeth them in nothing but what consists with the Interest of New England." Departing after six weeks of getting

Colonial Settlement by 1660

The shaded areas indicate where colonization had taken hold by the time of the Stuart Restoration in 1660. Coastal New England and the lower Connecticut River Valley were the most heavily settled regions. Their frontiers were hemmed in both north and west by mountain barriers and Jesuit-run Indian tribes, controlled from French Canada. Dutch settlements, scattered along the Hudson River from New Amsterdam to Fort Orange, controlled the only known passage through the mountain barrier—the Mohawk River Valley, which George Washington later designated for the Erie Canal. That route was also blocked by the Indian threat, and was further sealed in 1664, when England's King Charles II seized control of the Dutch colony. His royal colony of New York was established to encircle America's republican colonies—Massachusetts Bay and Connecticut. In Virginia, the only other significant area of colonization, settlements were still concentrated around the Chesapeake Bay's Tidewater plantations, and there were no plans for developing the interior.

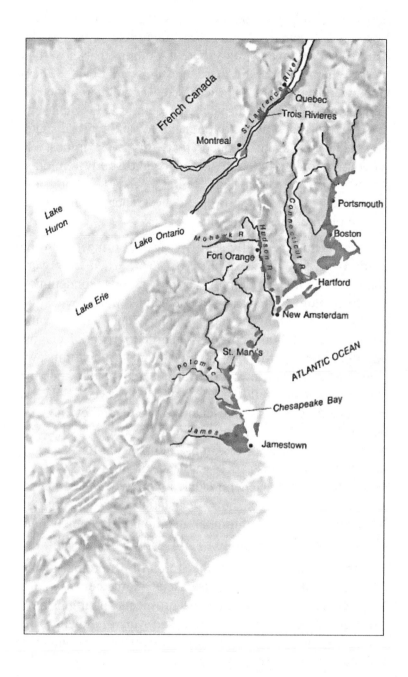

nowhere, Randolph reported that, in their final discussion, Leverett "intreated me to give a favorable report of the country and the magistrates thereof, adding, that those that blessed them God would bless, and those that cursed them God would curse."[14] The accursed Randolph returned to London, and the King dispatched orders for Massachusetts to send representatives to England to settle the dispute. Massachusetts again replied that this was impossible without action by the General Court, and subtly reminded the crown of its role in King Philip's War, by adding that the effects of the war prevented the General Court from meeting in the foreseeable future.

Massachusetts finally sent two agents to meet with the Lords of Trade in the summer of 1677, when they were confronted with Randolph's various reports condemning the Bay Colony. The King now demanded not a revocation of the charter, but a "supplementary one," that would renounce all of Massachusetts' enlarged territorial claims, beg the King's pardon for coining money, repeal all laws "repugnant" to the laws of England, and pledge that the Navigation Acts would be "religiously observed."[15] When the General Court's representatives replied they had no power to agree to any change in their charter, they were denounced for acting like "ambassadors," and for behaving like "foreigners" instead of subjects of his Majesty.   In Massachusetts, the General Court ignored all the demands, except for enacting new legislation similar to the Navigation Act, but omitting all mention of Parliament, and placing any enforcement under Massachusetts control.

In the spring of 1678, the Lords of Trade met again, resolved to deal with Massachusetts' defiance "from the Very Root," and to consider the prospects for imposing a royal governor, and for issuing a *quo warranto* against the colony's charter—a legal step toward its revocation. The General Court replied on October 2, 1678, by diplomatically belittling any conflict between crown and commonwealth. The legislature emphasized, however, that *no* English laws were legitimate, if they denied the republican mission of the founding of the colony. Massachusetts declared that it "regretted" that some of its laws were repugnant to the laws of England, but added they had not appeared so when enacted, only "different." The General Court pledged to examine the laws objected to by the crown, and to repeal any offending ones "except such as the repealing whereof will make us renounce the professed cause of our first coming hither."

The General Court further replied to charges of violations of the Navigation Act, by sending their agents in London the politic argument that Massachusetts had prevented the Dutch and the French from taking over the New World. But far greater and dearer to them than their lives, the magistrates emphasized, was the "interest of Lord Jesus, and of his churches," to be protected above all. Their "charter being under God," it was also the only security against "mutations" and subversion.[16]

The Fight to Save the Charter

Massachusetts stalled for two years, but in 1682 the crown finally brought a *quo warranto* against the colony "for usurping to be a body Politick"—an open acknowledgement of the sovereign status Massachusetts claimed for itself. The King promised that, if Massachusetts made full submission to the royal will, he would not revoke the charter, but simply regulate and alter it as he saw fit! In 1683, Edward Randolph was dispatched to Boston to deliver the King's "Declaration."[17]

Led by the Boston-area deputies of the lower house, the General Court voted to reject the King's "offer," for "it would offend God." Increase Mather followed with a pamphlet of "Arguments against relinquishing the Charter" distributed to the entire General Court, and widely circulated through the population. Mather attacked the demanded "alterations" as "inconsistent with the main end of their fathers' coming to New England. . . . Let them put their trust in the God of their fathers, which is better than to put confidence in princes. Mather declared that Massachusetts would "act neither the part of *Good Christians* nor of *True Englishmen*, if by any act of theirs they should be accessory to the Plot then managing to produce a *General Shipwreck of Liberties*."[18]

The Boston deputies called a meeting of the freemen in the Town House on January 21, 1684, addressed by Increase Mather, who told them that as to giving up the Charter "to his Majesty's pleasure, we shall sin against God if we vote an affirmative to it." Referring to the woeful condition of the colonies that were already under royal government, Mather asked, "What have they gained by their readiness to submit and comply?" One royalist left the hall, and the rest of the deputies voted unanimously to reject the King's demands.[19]

The fight to preserve the charter catapulted Increase Mather into political and intellectual leadership in New England. The son of a leading minister of the first Puritan generation in Massachusetts, Mather was educated at Harvard and at the Puritan stronghold of Trinity College, Dublin, where John Winthrop, Jr., had also studied. Deployed as a minister, organizer, and intelligence agent in England during Cromwell's rule, Mather had to flee following the Restoration. He returned to Massachusetts, and became the minister of the Second Church of Boston.

During the escalating fight for the charter, Mather founded in 1683 the Philosophical Society, the forerunner of Benjamin Franklin's American Philosophical Society.

(His son Cotton Mather later founded another institution for developing republican leadership, called "Young Men Associated," which also served as the model for Franklin's Junto in Philadelphia.) The Philosophical Society met fortnightly to confer on "improvements in philosophy and additions to the stores of natural history," and corresponded with Leyden and the circles of Leibniz, as well as with Britain's Royal Society and the Philosophical Society of Dublin. Mather's own scientific achievements include his *Kometographia* of 1683, citing Kepler as his main authority. He presented the case that comets move regularly, like the planets, in definite orbits. Mather's work appeared two years before Isaac Newton peddled his own claims in his *Principia.* As late as 1712, Mather's Philosophical Society commanded the nervous attention of the Royal Society, which also elected him as its second American member.[20]

Charles II was determined to remove New England as an obstacle to establishing a centralized imperial administration over the English colonies. The Court of Chancery, on October 23, 1684, decreed John Winthrop's charter void, and Massachusetts a royal colony.[21] Charles died the next February, and James II appointed Joseph Dudley interim royal governor for Massachusetts, New Hampshire, Maine, and the Naragansett Country (the mainland territory bordering Naragansett Bay). Dudley took office on May 14, 1686, two days after being defeated for election in Massachusetts to the Court of Assistants.[22]

Mocking the New England Confederation established by John Winthrop, the crown named Joseph Dudley "President"of the Dominion of New England. Dudley, Randolph's closest ally in Massachusetts and a recently professed Episcopalian,was given a "very remarkable" commission. The crown eliminated the representative assembly of Massachusetts, and gave Dudley the power to

rule directly through a royal council.   Edward Randolph
was given three positions, as secretary, register, and
member of the council.   Richard Wharton, married to a
daughter of John Winthrop, Jr., was appointed to the new
council, but called the change an outright "revolution."
The General Court held its final session with "many tears
shed in prayer and at parting," wrote Samuel Sewall in his
diary.[23]

But no royalist "revolution" could be effected by mere
decree, and the crown strategy was co-optation and
corruption.   Wait Still Winthrop and Fitz John Winthrop,
sons of John, Jr., were both named to the council in the
belief that they could be bought off and would add
"legitimacy" to the coup.   Randolph looked to their
brother-in-law Richard Wharton as a mainstay "insider" for
the crown, and the initial transition appeared to go
smoothly as the new council reorganized local government,
the judicial system, and the militia.[24]

Increase Mather responded to the crisis of 1686 by
publishing "The Mystery of Christ *Opened* and *Applyed*,"
expounding the doctrine of the Trinity and the task of
human perfection as revealed through Christ.   Mather
emphasized that the concept of the process of perfection
had to be instilled in the population as a whole. This could
not be done "in such a metaphysical strain as none but
Scholars should have understood anything."   Instead, the
idea would have to be presented so as "to make an *ignorant*
man understand these *Mysteries* in some good measure."
Mather added that the task "will put us to the trial of our
skill, and trouble us a great deal more than if we were to
discuss a *controversy* or handle a subtle point of Learning
in the Schools."[25]   Mather also was elected President of
Harvard College the same year, and extracted from Dudley
the title of rector, thus giving his control of the college the
added security of appointment by an agent of the crown.[26]

The monarchy soon found that Massachusetts' submission was more form than substance. In the council's reorganization of government, many of the previous officeholders were reappointed, and after only four weeks of Dudley's regime, Randolph noted that his "ally" Richard Wharton "has carried himself very oddly," blocking Randolph's nominee for commander of the fort at Castle Island. Instead Wharton got Wait Winthrop the command, as well as supervision of the Boston militia. The council reported to the Lords of Trade June 1 that the "Castle at Boston, a place of great importance *to this country*, is now put under the care and command of Captain Wait Winthrop, a person of known loyalty."[27] The council did not say to whom. Randolph was soon raving that President Dudley was "a man of base servile, and anti-monarchical principle." The council, meanwhile, refused to levy taxes without a representative assembly, leaving the crown's government in the colony with almost no funds.[28]

The appearance of pluralist contentment and cooperation in the new political arrangements was largely an illusion, as machinations against royal authority continued between the Winthrops in Massachusetts and Connecticut—whose charter was also under attack from writs of *quo warranto* secured by Randolph. Increase Mather, who directed plans for resistance, from his base as president of Harvard College, best expressed the new "toleration." Mather told his students that they were "pledged to no master; and you should moreover remember that *one* truly golden sentiment of Aristotle: 'Find a friend in Plato, a friend in Socrates.'" Mather had little use for Aristotle: "Certainly an imp would be a fine interpreter of Aristotle!"[29]

Utterly dissatisfied with the results achieved under Dudley, the crown dispatched the hated Sir Edmund Andros to take over the government of New England, which he did following his arrival in December 1686. Wait Winthrop wrote Fitz John at New London, to report that further proceedings against Connecticut's charter were scheduled, and that *quo warranto*s were out "against Pennsylvania, East and West Jersey, Carolina, etc."[30]

The English monarchy was moving to set up a centralized colonial empire in America, an impossible objective unless Massachusetts and Connecticut were subdued. In selecting Sir Edmund Andros, the crown made very clear it would use force where diplomatic co-optation failed. Andros was not only the former aggressor against John Winthrop, Jr.'s, Connecticut Colony, who armed King Philip's Indian onslaughts against New England. He was also the son of the man who drove Increase Mather from refuge on the Isle of Guernsey, at the time of the Restoration.[31] Now he would find his major adversaries in Mather and his son Cotton.

'No Taxation without Representation'

Under Andros, the council for the Dominion of New England was empowered to impose any taxes they wished, and the old English Puritan cry of "no taxation without representation" was raised, leading to the imprisonment of a number of Massachusetts Puritans. To establish Episcopalian supremacy in the colony, the Andros regime proposed to tax Congregational churches to support this Anglican suppression, and warned of dire consequences for any man who gave the value of two pence to maintain a Puritan minister. The new government ended any political restrictions for failure to meet a religious test, but denied the right to vote to all Congregational church members, the political core of the Massachusetts commonwealth. The basic institution of its local government, the town meeting, was eliminated, except for one ceremonial meeting a year, with no power to govern local affairs. Massachusetts' republican system of law was also overturned, by ending the printing of statutes and leaving the colony under the arbitrary will of the crown.

During early 1687, Andros also moved to enforce the *quo warranto* against Connecticut, sending the legislature four demands that it submit. The legislature temporized, but on October 18, Andros received orders from London to annex Connecticut, and went to Hartford and seized the government. He demanded the surrender of John Winthrop, Jr.'s Connecticut Charter, and on October 31—Halloween night—it was placed before him at a meeting with Hartford's leaders. But physical possession of the document eluded him. The candles in the room mysteriously blew out, and by the time light was restored, the document had been spirited away. Andros swore in a new government nonetheless, but named Fitz John Winthrop commander of the Connecticut militia.[32]

In Boston that same month, the Puritan ministers delegated Increase Mather to go to London, to plead Massachusetts' case with the King. News of his mission leaked out, and Edward Randolph moved to secure a warrant for Mather's arrest on December 24, charging him with sedition for accusing Randolph of forging a letter, used in a controversy over actions of the Dominion government. But with only two Episcopalians on the jury, Mather was acquitted, and went to Andros to declare his intention to go to London.[33]

In March 1688, Randolph sent a second agent to arrest Mather "on a pretended defamation." Within hours, the news spread through Boston, and his congregation advised him to stay indoors on the sabbath of March 30 "because wicked men were lying in wait to apprehend me," Mather wrote. That night, wearing a white cape, Mather slipped by the terrified royal sentry watching his house. He made his way to the Charlestown home of Captain John Phillips, father-in-law to Cotton Mather, and commander of the alerted Charlestown militia. He hid there until April 3, when he was secretly taken by boat to lie off Plymouth harbor, until the ship *President* came to take him to England.[34]

Increase Mather would not return for more than four years. His negotiations in London had to steer through Byzantine intrigues that multiplied with the approaching downfall of James II, and following the invasion of William of Orange in December 1689. His task was further complicated by the scramble to establish the new royal administration of William II. Mather's years of diplomacy in London proved a rich model, for a similar mission undertaken by Benjamin Franklin in the 1760s—also as agent for the New England colonies.

Mather was considered a man not to be reckoned with lightly. King James was informed of his arrival on May 29, 1688, and received him the next day.[35] On July 2, Mather demanded the recall of Andros and presented the King with a "Memorial of the Grievances which filled his Country with the Cry of the Oppressed." Mather attacked the "episcopal party" for suppressing public days of Thanksgiving, for imposing taxes without consent of an assembly, and for ending the printing of the laws. He called for restoring the colonists' land titles on the terms in force under the old charter, and the resumption of the traditional powers of the town meeting.[36]

To the Lords of Trade, Mather offered the inevitable concession of extending the vote to all freeholders, or property owners, as opposed to the church-member "freemen" of the old charter. He declared for "liberty of conscience in matters of religion," with each religion to support itself, and no man obliged to maintain a religion he did not profess. The Lords of Trade rejected all of Mather's proposals.[37]

New England was left with the choice of revolution or submission, and Mather intended to be fully prepared to make the most of his opportunities. Since first arriving he had met repeatedly with William Penn, proprietor of the new Pennsylvania colony. Exchanging communications carefully through intermediaries, Mather recorded that "Mr. P." assured him that "you need not doubt all things [shall be] done to your content, and that he will labor in it, but not above board." Mather also reported that "to give Mr. Penn his due," the Quaker proprietor said "that something should be sent to Andros that would settle his nose, and that if he did not comply therewith he should be turned out of his government."[38]

News of William of Orange's invasion of England reached Boston at the beginning of 1689. The Dutch seizure of the throne presented a strategic opportunity, rather than an occasion for general rejoicing. When the rumors first reached Wait Winthrop, he wrote to his brother Fitz John in Connecticut, " 'tis generally feared the Dutch are landed in England before this."[39] New England's concerns included the danger that could be posed to it, if the Dutch and English crowns were united, rather than constantly warring with one another—a division that New England had often played off successfully in the past. Wait Winthrop was suspected of plotting to strike against the Andros regime as early as January 1689. The anonymous tract *New England's Faction Discovered* reported that Governor Andros' order, for public observance of the "martyrdom" of Charles I on January 30, "was called in and suppressed by Captain *Wait Winthrop*, one of the Council, who in the Commotion appeared the chief Man and Head of the Faction against the Government. . . ."[40]

The Andros Rebellion

On April 16, Andros wrote, "There's a general buzzing among the people, great with expectation of their old charter, or they know not what."[41] Behind this buzzing was a carefully prepared conspiracy, organized by Mathers and Winthrops, to use the overthrow of James II in England as the occasion to restore the New England republic. In a desperate effort to gain control of the situation, Andros ordered a special council meeting for April 18—to try Cotton Mather for preaching sedition.

Mather later reported, in his *Magnalia Christi Americana*, on the preparations which drove Andros into a frenzy. "Some of the Principal Gentlemen in *Boston* consulting what was to be done in this Extraordinary Juncture," Mather wrote, they agreed that if necessary "to prevent the shedding of *Blood* by an ungoverned *Mobile*, some of the Gentlemen present should appear at the Head of the *Action* with a *Declaration* appropriately prepared."[42] Edward Randolph later wrote that on April 17, "this Mather had a meeting of Armd men at his house the night before they entred upon their strange worke."[43]

The "action" began on the morning of April 18, 1689— the same date as Paul Revere's midnight ride eighty-six years later to alert the militia, for the battle of Concord Bridge that launched the American Revolution. Over 1,000 Bostonians rushed to arms by beat of drum and formed themselves into companies. Militia from neighboring towns streamed rapidly in to join them, and the assembled army was placed under the command of Wait Winthrop. A royal agent reported that Winthrop "had bin with the conspirators of the North end very early that Morning."[44] The "Andros Rebellion" was carried out quickly. Boston was easily occupied, and throngs gathered outside the Town House, where the Massachusetts leadership gathered to read Cotton Mather's "Declaration" from the balcony, summarizing the charges against Andros and announcing the arrest of Edward Randolph, Joseph Dudley, and other royal officials. By evening, Andros had surrendered, and the redcoats at Castle Island followed suit the next day.

In June 1689, two months after the revolt, Cotton Mather published his *Memorable Providences*, dedicated to Wait Winthrop, "whom I reckon among the best of my friends, and the Ablest of my Readers." Winthrop was named to the Committee of Safety, established to govern while Increase Mather negotiated a charter in London with William III.[45]

In 1691, with England now at war with France and the French threatening New England from Canada, Massachusetts finally came under royal control, its governor and magistrates of the upper house henceforth appointed by the King. Despite the significant defeat represented by the imposition of the royal charter, the New England leadership had now schooled a large population in republican principles, and tested it in decades of political battle. The groundwork had been laid for the broader fight to come: establishing the nation for which George Washington gave thanks.

NOTES

1. Dunn, *Puritans and Yankees*, 154.

2. Charles II, "Private Instructions to Coll. R. Nicolls etc.," in Michael G. Hall, Lawrence H. Leden, and Michael G. Kammen, eds., *The Glorious Revolution in America, Documents on the Colonial Crisis of 1689* (New York, 1972), 14, 17.

3. *Ibid.*, 17, 18.

4. Quoted by Dunn, *Puritans and Yankees*, 182.

5. *Ibid.*

6. *Ibid.*, 183.

7. Hall, et al., eds., *Glorious Revolution*, 58.

8. Dunn, *Puritans and Yankees*, 183–184.

9. *Ibid.*, 186.

10. Robert C. Black III, *The Younger John Winthrop* (New York, 1966), 356.

11. Robert N. Toppan, *Memoir of Edward Randolph* (reprint, New York, 1967), 52.

12. Dunn, *Puritans and Yankees*, 213–215.

13. *Ibid.*, 215.

14. *Ibid.*

15. Winsor, ed., *History of Boston*, I, 366.

16. N. B. Shurtleff, et al., eds., *Records of the Governor and Company of the Massachusetts Bay in New England* (5 vols., Boston, 1853-1854), V, 198–202.

17. Kenneth Murdock, *Increase Mather, The Foremost American Puritan* (Cambridge, Mass., 1925), 152.

18. Cotton Mather, *Parentator* (Boston, 1724), 90; Murdock, *Increase Mather*, 153; Massachusetts Historical Society Collections, 3rd Series, I (1825), 74–81.

19. Hall, et al., eds., *Glorious Revolution*, 24.

20. Murdock, *Increase Mather*, 143–148.

21. Winsor, ed., *History of Boston*, I, 377.

22. Murdock, *Increase Mather*, 156.

23. Sewall, *Diary*, I, 140.

24. Dunn, *Puritans and Yankees*, 226–228, 231.

25. Increase Mather, " The Mystery of Christ *Opened* and *Applyed*" (Boston, 1686), 4.

26. Murdock, *Increase Mather*, 177.

27. Quoted by Dunn, *Puritans and Yankees*, 232.

28. *Ibid.*, 233.

29. From Cotton Mather's *Magnalia Christi Americana*, quoted by Murdock, Mather, 342–343.

30. Dunn, *Puritans and Yankees*, 238.

31. Murdock, *Increase Mather*, 158.

32. Dunn, *Puritans and Yankees*, 242–243.

33. Murdock, *Increase Mather*, 186.

34. *Ibid.*, 186–188.

35. *Ibid.*, 192–194.

36. Increase Mather, " Diary," microfilm of typescript ms., Manuscript Division, Library of Congress.

37. Murdock, *Increase Mather*, 207–208.

38. Increase Mather, " Diary."

39. Dunn, *Puritans and Yankees*, 253.

40. *Ibid.*, 252.

41. *Ibid.*, 253.

42. Quoted by Dunn, *op. cit.*, 254.

43. Hall, et al., eds., *Glorious Revolution*, 64.

44. Dunn, *Puritans and Yankees*, 251*ff.*

45. *Ibid.*

3

Corruption and Decay: Massachusetts Under Royal Rule

America's republican leadership in 1690 was still concentrated in Massachusetts, around the Puritan statesman Increase Mather and his son Cotton. They faced a desperate political and strategic situation. The elder Mather spent the years 1688–1692 in England, negotiating for a new Massachusetts charter, to restore the republican liberties the colony had lost during the dictatorial regime of royal Governor Edmund Andros.

By the time Mather returned, Boston's corrupt merchant elite had bankrolled and set in motion an antirepublican "mob"; the Jesuit-controlled Indian tribes of Canada had launched new attacks on New England; and the enemies of Massachusetts were manipulating the Salem witch trials toward a major political crisis. While the devil himself had not made an appearance, these combined assaults by the enemy were a pretty fair simulation. They were designed to crush the bold display of nation-building intentions by Massachusetts during 1689–1692.

When the Stuart monarchy was overthrown by the Dutch Prince William of Orange in 1689, Massachusetts seized the occasion to launch not only an armed revolution against the Andros regime. The patriot leaders in Boston also proclaimed an independent New England, with sovereign court systems, trade governance, coinage, and a new system of credit for productive economic improvements. News of the revolution reached Mather in London in late June 1689, and on America's subsequent independence day, July 4, he went before King William at Hampton Court, presenting the ouster of Andros as a "great service" for the new monarch, and demanding recognition of New England's "ancient rights and privileges."[1] Despite Mather's bold declaration, the Venetian-dominated financial interests behind the throne had no intention of allowing any freedom for New England that would permit real economic development.

During Parliament's debate on how to treat charters issued under the previous monarchy, a pamphlet was circulated attacking any proposals for restoring the old Massachusetts charter.   Such a decision, the pamphlet charged, would establish a virtually independent state, which would draw manufacturers and laborers from England.   With its old charter freedom, New England would develop mining and other enterprises, under its own currency and credit, free of control by English finance. Colonial trade, furthermore, would rival England's, and the pamphlet noted that republican Massachusetts had formerly taxed shipping and imports from England.[2] Fundamentally, these were the same arguments Benjamin Franklin later faced, while representing Massachusetts in London in the 1760s.

Increase Mather countered by publishing "New-England Vindicated from Unjust Aspersions," noting drily that the East India Company, an outright looting operation, had also coined its own money and been excused for doing so. As for New England's developing mining and industry, Mather declared that would be England's gain, adding that if the charter suppressed by Andros were restored, New England *would* use its own capital to develop its enterprises.[3]

While the charter issue was still being fought out in London, New England established a Committee for the Safety of the People, following the overthrow of Andros, and pursued a monetary policy aimed at economic sovereignty. Taking advantage of the hiatus in royal rule over the colony, the committee established another body in 1690 to issue bills of public credit.

To organize support for the policy, Cotton Mather produced an unsigned pamphlet in 1691, *Some Considerations on Bills of Credit*, addressed to his father-in-law John Phillips, a captain in the colony's republican army, the Company of the Massachusetts, and himself a member of the committee appointed to issue bills of credit. Also named to the Committee for the Safety of the People, Phillips served as treasurer of Massachusetts from 1692 to 1693, while the new royal government was still making short-term concessions to the Mathers.

A striking feature of Cotton's pamphlet is his reference throughout to New England as a *country*. In an able defense of the concept of public credit and the proper issuance of paper currency, he attacks "the great indiscretion of our Countrymen" who refuse to accept public bills of credit. "Now what is the *Security* of your Paper-money less than the *Credit* of the whole Country," Mather notes.

He goes further, by linking the issues of sovereignty and sound public credit, and by attacking England's oligarchical propagandist Thomas Hobbes, the tutor of Charles II. "Certainly Sir," Mather 'anonymously' tells Phillips

> were not people's heads idly bewhizled with conceits that we have no *magistrates*, no *government*, which we can call our own, I say if such foolish conceits were not entertained, there would not be the least scruple in accepting your bills as current pay.

Such foolishness, he adds, leads only to the chaos which would occur "if once we are reduced to *Hobs* his state of *Nature*, which (says he) is a *state of war*, and then the *strongest* must *sake all*."[4]

Mather's promotion of public credit foreshadows Benjamin Franklin's in Pennsylvania—and indeed the issue already involved connections between Boston and Philadelphia.   Internal references in Mather's pamphlet point to one Captain John Blackwell, a fairly recent arrival in Massachusetts, who in 1686 was the advocate of creating a new bank that would issue paper currency, to relieve the colony from an investment-strangling, fixed supply of specie under the Andros dictatorship.   Intriguingly, following the meetings between Increase Mather and William Penn in London in 1688, Penn named Blackwell governor of his Pennsylvania colony in 1689.   Blackwell sent a letter to Puritan forces in New York in late February of that year with news the Andros regime attempted to suppress— that James II was fleeing the invasion of William of Orange.[5] New York followed Massachusetts' lead in the Andros Rebellion, seizing the opportunity to carry out Leisler's Rebellion in New York.   Following Massachusetts' creation of the Committee for the Safety of the People, Blackwell returned to Boston in 1690.

Seeking Openings to the West

Within the American colonies, the loss of an independent republican base in Massachusetts raised new dangers, but even more urgency, for the task of conquering the wilderness. Only by breaking beyond the narrow band of Atlantic coastal settlements and developing the vast resources of the interior could the colonies escape the fate of becoming simply a British imperial looting ground, hemmed in by the Appalachian Mountains, French and Spanish territorial claims to the West, and hostile Indians most typically trained in barbarous rites by Jesuit "missionaries," especially out of French Canada.

The problem was compounded by the increasing introduction of English convict and African slave labor into

French-Jesuit Indian Raids on New England

Once republican Massachusetts was finally subjected to royal rule in the 1690s, both Britain and France conspired to reduce it to ruins. In 1701, England's King William of Orange signed an agreement with France, pledging Iroquois neutrality in the war about to break out between England and France. The Iroquois Five Nations, centered in northern New York, were the only significant Indian allies the American colonies had in the Northeast. With the Iroquois neutralized, the French were free to concentrate their attacks on New England, while continuing to receive supplies from Massachusetts' royal governor Joseph Dudley, the traitorous "criminal" denounced by the Mathers.

Northern tribes "converted" by the Jesuits—the Hurons, Algonquins, Penobscots, Pequawkets, and especially the Abnakis—were repeatedly hurled against the northeastern and western frontier of New England. Led by Jesuit priests, with only an occasional French officer, the Indians attacked down the Kennebec, Connecticut, and Merrimack Rivers, massacring and burning as they went. After a series of raids on the southern coast of Maine and western Massachusetts, reaching to just forty miles west of Boston, an all-out assault was launched in 1708. Jesuit tribes in Canada gathered in Montreal and marched south and east to a rendezvous with the Penobscots at Lake Winnipesaukee in New Hampshire. From there they struck Casco, Wells, Kittery, York, Kingston, Berwick, Winter Harbor, Groton, Lancaster, Exeter, Dover, Brookfield, Marlborough, and Amesbury, culminating in a major massacre at Haverhill, just thirty miles above Boston. This threat to the northeastern colonies was not removed until the American Revolution.

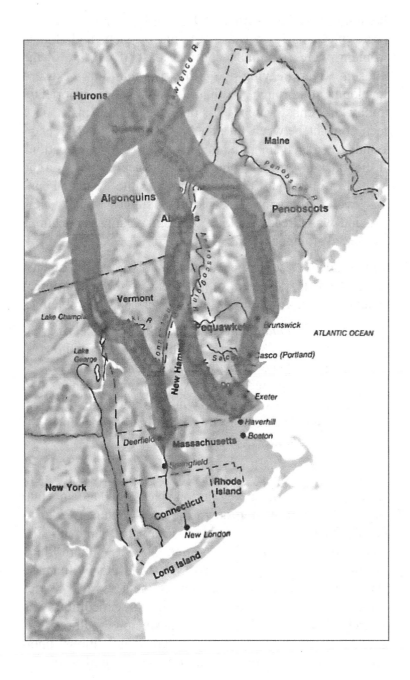

the southern colonies after 1690. New England and New York, particularly because of the French and Indian problem, were essentially confined east of the line of the Hudson River, leaving the primary route for westward development through William Penn's new proprietary colony of Pennsylvania. Historians generally insist on a deep conflict between Puritan Massachusetts and Quaker-founded Pennsylvania, due to Massachusetts' "persecution" of the Quaker terrorists who began physical assaults on the Puritan ministry in the 1660s. Yet the Mather-Penn-Blackwell coordination strikingly suggests that New England was already looking to Pennsylvania connections for the development of the West.

New England also launched a military operation against French Canada, designed to put an end to the Indian threat on its frontiers. As Cotton Mather described the problem:

> It was *Canada* that was the chief Source of *New-England's* Miseries. There was the main strength of the *French*; *there* the *Indians* were mostly supplied with Ammunition; thence Issued Parties of Men, who uniting with the Savages, barbarously murdered many Innocent *New-Englanders.* . . .[6]

Devising a strategy that was to be repeatedly employed, even in the American Revolution, New England in 1690 sent one column by ship down the St. Lawrence River to attack Quebec, and a second army by land up the Champlain Valley to strike at Montreal. Sir William Phips —soon to be chosen governor of Massachusetts by Increase Mather under a onetime concession in the new royal charter —led the expedition by sea. Phips's expedition was severely hampered, both by a suspicious outbreak of smallpox, and by impossible weather conditions upon reaching the St. Lawrence. Failure was ensured when the western army—under Connecticut's Fitz John Winthrop, son of that colony's former governor—was also stricken by smallpox, and was virtually stopped dead in its tracks when canoes to have been provided by supposedly friendly Indians did not materialize.[7]

Cotton Mather was not alone in charging sabotage by New England's "neighbors to the West," referring especially to the opposition in Albany from New Yorkers and Dutch patroons, who were happy to see New England confined by the Indians as long as they were not attacked themselves.   Otherwise, Mather noted in his currency pamphlet, "we had certainly been masters of Canada," and would have ended the threat of their "setting their *Dogs* (the *Indians*) upon us to make America too hot for us."[8]

The Devil in Massachusetts

Such adventurous efforts in republican economic and military policy, under the Committee for the Safety of the People, soon came under attack from within as well. The growing oligarchical influence among wealthy merchants and shippers, centered in Salem and Boston, was directed toward the destruction of the Mathers.

In 1692, a manipulated episode of adolescent hysteria in rural Salem Village became a full-fledged political crisis, when Salem eminences like John Hawthorne, ancestor of the nineteenth- century Transcendentalist and oligarch-worshipper Nathaniel Hawthorne, turned the witch trials into a combined assault on Puritan notions of law and religious doctrine. Far from being an expression of the character of New England Puritanism, the witch trials were designed to force the separation of law from morality, and thus destroy the republican concept of natural law upon which Massachusetts had been founded.

Under Hawthorne's "hard-line" approach, every teenage fantasy retailed in court, alleging acts of witchcraft carried out by specters to whom names would be attached, led to new accusations and arrests, finally reaching even Governor Phips' wife.   Meanwhile, William Brattle— brother of the "liberal" merchant at the top of Boston's financial heap, Thomas Brattle— propagandized against the trials, arguing, in effect, that courts of law had no business deciding between good and evil.   Witchcraft was still a long way from becoming fashionable in Massachusetts, and the only legal precedents were based in English common law. Yet Brattle pretended that the trials were an expression of an outmoded, superstitious Puritanism—a fraud historians have maintained to this day.

William Brattle was then a Harvard tutor, who had assumed the teaching of logic in 1689, after Increase Mather left for his diplomatic mission to London. Brattle introduced the dead-end, mechanistic axioms of Descartes to Harvard's curriculum, with support from the outright Aristotelian, Charles Morton.   Morton moved from England to Massachusetts in 1686, at the outset of the Andros regime. He was appointed vice-president of the college, and ran it during President Mather's absence.

Through interventions by both Increase and Cotton Mather, the witchcraft hysteria was brought to an end; but nearly a score of its victims had been put to death. The manipulators were outflanked by the elder Mather's arguments, that while charges of crimes by witchcraft had standing in the courts, the rule of law required that no "spectral evidence" be used to determine whether such acts had been committed.[9] This left the promoters of the trials in the position of having to prove acts of witchcraft scientifically.   That dilemma easily overmatched them, since they could hardly argue that they were themselves experts in the black arts.

The 'People's Party' Fraud

The trauma of the Salem witch trials was certainly destabilizing, but the more serious threat to the republican traditions of Massachusetts came in the form of plain, old-fashioned corruption—on a scale not seen during the colony's previous history under its independent charter. Increase Mather returned from London in 1692, with the best agreement he could get from the regime of King William III. The new charter conceded royal authority, but maintained some of the elected bodies and functions of the earlier government.   Soon afterward, the prototypical, oligarchically controlled "people's party" in America was founded in Boston.

This "Satanic Party," as Cotton Mather was later to brand it, was established under cover of a popular opposition to the new charter secured by Increase Mather. He was denounced for "selling out" Massachusetts to the King. This self-styled "old charter" party was headed by Elisha Cooke, who had gone to London to harass Mather's negotiations during the years 1690 to 1692, presenting himself as co-agent for Massachusetts.   After the charter agreement was reached, Cooke made a show of refusing to return to Boston with Mather, and stayed on for further instructions from the crown. Conveniently, Cooke missed all the witchcraft hysteria during the summer of 1692, while his merchant backers in Boston agitated against the Mathers.

Arriving in late October, Cooke plotted with his henchmen in the legislature to impose conditions of self-government even more restrictive than those in the agreement Mather had worked out with the crown—all in the name of democracy, of course. The key republican institution of Massachusetts— the town meeting—had blossomed without specific authority or mention under the old charter. Mather had been careful not to have it cited in the new document, for it would then exist at the pleasure of the King.

Posing as defenders of Massachusetts' republican freedoms, Cooke's cronies secured legislative passage of the Township Act in the legislature on November 18, 1692, perpetuating the structure of the town meeting under the royal charter, but now requiring its by-laws to be approved by the appointed justices of the peace of each county. Furthermore, the right to vote in annual elections was taken away from all those who did not have a "£20 rateable estate" on the tax rolls. In Boston, Cooke's swindle cut the number of eligible voters in half, and with his election as the town's tax commissioner from 1692 to 1698, his assessments of potential voters' "rateable estates" determined a substantial portion of the voting lists. Not surprisingly, the biggest gainers in electoral power under Cooke's royal democracy were the Boston merchants who controlled it.[10]

Elisha Cooke was himself the largest mill owner in Boston, and his Boston machine quickly began dominating the town's representation in the legislature.[11] The Cooke machine also sent its carpetbaggers to run as candidates from other towns, until a residency act was passed by Governor Phips and his allies in 1693. Phips also used his official powers under the royal charter to reject Boston merchant Nathaniel Byfield, a close friend of Cooke's, elected as representative from Bristol, as speaker of the house. Cooke's forces retaliated in telling fashion. They voted to cut off Increase Mather's salary as president of Harvard, then still a public institution and the only college in New England, unless he lived full-time in Cambridge, a short ride from his home in Boston's North End.

Cooke and his friends in the royal bureaucracy kept up a constant flow of public attacks and private reports to the crown, charging Governor Phips with "corruption," until, in the fall of 1694, he was recalled to England to answer charges of misconduct. Within weeks of his arrival in London, Phips died of an unnamed illness—and Massachusetts slipped further into the control of the "Satanic Party." Lieutenant Governor William Stoughton, another of the hard-line judges in the Salem witch trials, filled the office until the arrival in 1698 of the Earl of Bellomont as the new royal governor. Stoughton quickly appointed Cooke to the Council, the main arm of the executive, and even had him appointed as a judge in the Superior Court.

In Boston, Cooke's 'merchant liberation movement' moved openly into power in the wake of Phips's death. In 1696, the same Nathaniel Byfield, whose carpetbagging election from Bristol had been rejected by Governor Phips, won an assembly seat from Boston. The traditional path to the legislature, while Massachusetts had functioned as a republic, had been proven leadership as a town selectman. Now merchants with no prior elective office began regularly winning seats in the General Court. Also elected in 1696 was a small-time bureaucrat named Nathaniel Oliver. His brother Daniel earlier that year had married the daughter of Andrew Belcher, New England's largest ship owner and grain merchant. Nathaniel entered the grain business, and within months was reputed to be Boston's leading baker. He was also heavily dependent on Elisha Cooke, Boston's leading flour mill owner.[12]

In May 1698, Andrew Belcher also won election to the General Court with the backing of Cooke's machine, and the same year Belcher's son-in-law Daniel Oliver ran for Boston selectman. Daniel received the lowest possible number of votes in his first campaign, but in 1699 finished at the top of the list. The consolidation of this merchant-dominated machine, following Governor Bellomont's arrival in 1698, produced a number of sudden shifts in election outcomes. The aging Cooke henchman Theophilus Frary received a grand total of *one* vote in the elections of May 1698. Later that year, his daughter married Andrew Belcher, and in May 1699, Frary was also elected to the General Court.[13]

A Little People

The orgy of oligarchical corruption that occurred in Massachusetts following the loss of its republican charter posed a serious threat to its future. Cotton Mather sounded the alarm in 1696, in a pamphlet entitled *Things for a Distress'd People to Think Upon.* New England, Mather wrote, once abounded with heroes

> worthy to have their Lives written, as copies for future Ages to write after; *But These are Ancient Things!* A *Public Spirit* in all that sustained any *Public Office*, and a fervent *Inclination* to Do Good, joined with Incomparable *Ability* to do it, once ran through *New England*; But *These are Ancient Things!*

Massachusetts appeared no longer willing to fight for the great mission begun by its founders. Instead, Mather declared,

> There seems to be a shameful *Shrink*, in all sorts of men among us, from that *Greatness*, and *Goodness*, which adorned our ancestors: We grow *Little* every way; *Little* in our Civil Matters, *Little* in our Military Matters, *Little* in our Ecclesiastical Matters; we dwindle away, to *Nothing.*[14]

The institutions of Puritan New England, protected no longer by an independent government and under frontal attack with the imposition of royal rule, were on the verge of destruction. Republican currents among the intellectual leaders trained at Increase Mather's Harvard were increasingly being displaced, and in 1701 Mather himself was removed from the college presidency. With the aid of Thomas and William Brattle, Elisha Cooke succeeded in replacing Mather with a succession of his own henchmen, first his brother-in-law Samuel Willard, and then another brother-in-law, John Leverett, under whom Harvard degenerated further into Aristotelianism and Anglican ideology.[15]

Cooke also took a direct hand in creating an institutional opposition to the republican leaders among Boston's Congregational churches. Cooke and his merchant allies, with land donated by Thomas Brattle, moved in 1699 to establish a new church in Boston, later known as the Brattle Street Church.[16] The organizers published a three-page *Manifesto* declaring they intended to worship in conformance with the "Churches of the UNITED BRETHREN in *London*, and throughout all *England*," and claiming that they saw "cause to depart from what is ordinarily Professed & Practiced by the Churches of CHRIST here in New-England" on only a few matters.[17]

The deviations, however small they might appear today, struck at the core of Congregational worship, especially by ending the requirement that communicant status in the church be based on a public account of experiencing God's grace. This practice had been promoted to place a significant value on the individual's self-conscious grasp of the pursuit of perfection, demanded by Christ's being "the Word made flesh," as Increase Mather had emphasized in 1686. The new Brattle church decreed it would eliminate that qualification for gaining communion, and that its minister would read scripture without any explication or effort to teach its meaning.   Selection of the minister, moreover, would no longer be left to the communicants, but to all adults attending service, as long as they were baptized. [18]

These "democratizing" moves were direct steps toward the unleashing of irrationalist fundamentalism, such as has swept over American religious life ever since, substituting emotional manipulation for the enhanced powers of reason nurtured by Augustinian Christianity. Behind this scheme for the more efficient herding of sheep lay a jesuitical conspiracy, to destroy the Puritan-Congregational model dedicated to generating a republican citizenry.

Theological Subversion

New England was not unfamiliar with such assaults on reason and natural law disguised as "true religion." Against the republican morality of founding Governor John Winthrop's "On Christian Liberty," the mystic Anne Hutchinson claimed "direct revelation" from God during the Antinomian crisis.   There was no need for either education or ministerial guidance in comprehending the teachings of Christianity, she insisted. Instead, whatever "felt good" was to be regarded as truth.

Following the Stuart Restoration, Quakers were introduced to New England—in the mode of outright terrorists.   Quaker women roamed the streets naked, often with their faces painted black, and broke up congregational meetings by breaking bottles over the ministers' skulls, as "a sign" of their "emptiness." During the Cooke machine's rise to power, Samuel Sewall recorded another such disruption by Quakers, bursting into a meeting at the Old South Church—an institution which the Brattle Street Church sought to replace.[19]

By the time of the Andros dictatorship, the Jesuit threat warned of by John Winthrop, was not simply an external one in Puritan New England. The Presbyterians committed to establishing secret governance over the churches by self-perpetuating synods—beyond congregational control—were in the Puritans' minds a direct variant of Jesuit operations. Significantly, Cotton Mather compared the threat posed by the founding of the Brattle Street Church, to the hated Governor Andros' attempt to "utterly subvert our churches."[20] Andros was widely accused in Massachusetts of being a secret Papist, and a collaborator with Jesuit agents in directing Indian attacks against New England.

Increase Mather answered the Brattle *Manifesto* with *The Order of the Gospel* (1700), attacking the scheme for the ordination of ministers as threatening to "give away *the whole Congregational cause* at once." His suspicions were quickly confirmed, by the publication in London a few months later of Solomon Stoddard's *Doctrine of Instituted Churches*. The oligarchical character of the efforts to "democratize" New England's churches becomes obvious in Stoddard's arguments. A minister at Northampton in the Connecticut River valley of western Massachusetts, Stoddard had introduced irrationalist, fundamentalist methods there in 1677, in the wake of the Indian devastations of King Philip's War. He now proposed that not only should communion be automatically offered to anyone attending church, but that the ministry should regard mere participation in communion as leading to salvation—making it a mystical rite rather than an attainment of Christian self-knowledge.

Stoddard also sought to redefine the church as nothing more than a group of people assembled by God in the same place, and thus deserving no specific existence. Thus he argued that the Congregationalist church, coherent with the notion of a qualified republican citizenry, was without foundation. Instead, the churches should be subjected to Presbyterian governance, with ministers and congregations ruled by synods, which would also be free to revise doctrines as they saw fit, rather than "adopt the sayings of Ancient Fathers." The proposition sounded very much like Charles II's policy toward the Massachusetts charter.[21]

Cotton Mather confronted Stoddard at a meeting of ministers in Boston in the summer of 1700. He denounced him for advocating that the churches be ruled by synods from England, and for packing the communion table with "those that *know themselves* ungodly Wretches," in order to "make us, with our own Hands pull down our House." In print, Mather also bemoaned the appeal of Stoddard's "wretched Novelties" to a "carnal, giddy, rising Generation," and blasted "the *Presbyterianism* that runs down *Connecticut* River. "[22]

This sort of jesuitical subversion under the Presbyterian label (Mather attacked Stoddard's communion for the unregenerate as a "Popish Fancy"), was contained to a degree in Boston. Even Benjamin Colman, the first minister of the Brattle church, was brought back into uneasy alliance with the Mathers. Solomon Stoddard, however, had already established methods of breeding the frontier pestilence of backwardness and irrationalism, that would remain a crucial problem throughout America's efforts to develop its western settlements.

Stoddard's case is exemplary of oligarchical methods. Posing as a "minister of the people," he injected periodic doses of psychotic "revivalism" into the population of the Connecticut Valley. Otherwise, he basked in the society of the self-styled "river gods," the valley's feudalist landowners and trading potentates, who fostered generations of subversion and treason in America.

Stoddard brought his own grandson into the soul-saving business in 1727. He was none other than Jonathan Edwards, who used Stoddard's methods—as well as his training in Lockean psychology at Yale—to lay waste to the whole Connecticut Valley in the "Great Awakening" revivals of the 1730s. Edwards himself married into the "river gods" families, and recycled a number of his daughters through them—producing among his own grandsons the infamous traitor Aaron Burr, who later killed Alexander Hamilton, and conspired to break up the republic during the presidency of Thomas Jefferson. Another grandson was the despicable but less energetic Timothy Dwight, a leader of the treasonous Hartford Convention that sided with Britain, and advocated the secession of New England from the Union, during the War of 1812. Edwards himself, in classic Jesuit imitation, spent some of his final years as a so-called missionary to the Indians on New England's western frontier, before becoming the president of Princeton, the Presbyterian college of New Jersey.

The Threat of Utter Subjection

Besides such subversion from within, the American colonies also faced a determined threat from England to reduce them to complete economic subjugation. In 1696, the new Navigation Act was passed in Parliament. To enforce the policy of restricting trade by the colonies, the King's customs officials were given broad powers of search and seizure, and authority to prosecute violators of the act without juries. To better coordinate England's colonial looting, a new Board of Trade was established the same year—and not abolished until 1782, after the success of the American Revolution.

Appointed as one of the commissioners of trade was the wretched empiricist John Locke, the "philosopher," whom so many historians illegitimately describe as the intellectual author of American independence. Locke had returned to England from exile as part of the Venetian baggage of the Dutch invader, William of Orange. In 1701, Locke's Board of Trade called for revoking all the colonial charters in America, in order to make its lands, trade, and navigation "subject to your Majesties immediate Government." The report also charged that

> these Independent Colonies do turn the Course of Trade to the Promoting and propagating woolen and other Manufactures proper to England, instead of applying their thoughts and Endeavours to the production of such commodities as are fit to be encouraged in these parts according to the true design and intention of such settlements.[23]

The policy declared by the Board of Trade was a clear statement of intent, to eradicate America's hopes for developing the continent. The report went beyond what the crown thought could then be enforced, but more than a decade of tightening imperial rule had already led to the actual reduction of key colonial populations for the first time in their history.

The two major colonies, Massachusetts and Virginia, both declined in free population during the decade from 1690 to 1700. Including immigration, Massachusetts had grown by approximately fifty percent during each of the decades from 1640 to 1670. The rate of increase dropped to thirty-three percent during the 1670s—the period of King Philip's War. During the 1680s, when the crown launched its all-out campaign to destroy the Massachusetts charter, the growth rate fell to twenty-five percent. Following the direct imposition of royal rule in the 1690s, the population of Massachusetts declined from 49,504 to

48,517. Connecticut, while still managing a net increase in population during the 1690s, suffered the lowest rate of growth in its history.

There is a special irony in the Virginia case. After the Stuart Restoration in 1660, Virginia never reached the dramatic growth rates that Massachusetts maintained until the Andros dictatorship. During the 1680s, the free population of Virginia increased only by about seven-and-a-half percent, from 40,596 to 43,701—while slavery took hold for the first time on a major scale, with the number of slaves tripling to over 9,300. But during the 1690s—a decade typically characterized by historians of Virginia as a peaceful, unusually prosperous, and smoothly administered period—the free population *declined* three-and-a-half percent to 42,170, and slavery expanded by another seventy-five percent to more than 16,000. Presiding over this alleged upturn was Sir Edmund Andros, royal governor from 1692 to 1697, who had been reassigned to crush another colony—only three years after being driven from office in Massachusetts by force of arms.[24]

The danger of America's dwindling away "to nothing," as Cotton Mather warned New England in 1696, intensified after 1700 under simultaneous oligarchical assaults from England and France. For the existing colonies, survival required steering a narrow course between English attempts at political subjugation, and French military threats to their frontiers. In 1699, Pierre Lemoyne, Sieur d'Iberville, planted the French flag on the lower Mississippi; and within a year, the claim took on a more ominous character, when the French concluded an alliance with the Choctaw nation. With these additions to the French settlements, and Indian alliances in Canada and the Great Lakes, America's colonial frontier was now threatened along an arc running from the Gulf of Mexico, to the mouth of Quebec's St. Lawrence River.

In 1700, the colonial legislature of New York reacted with alarm to the French and Indian menace, by passing a bill aimed at Jesuit priests "who by their wicked and Subtle Insinuations Industriously Labour to Debauch Seduce and withdraw the Indians from their due obedience unto his most Sacred majesty."[25]   Their fears increased when, in 1701, the Iroquois Five Nations, previously the only significant allies among Indians of the Northeast, signed a treaty with both England and France.   Their agreement acknowledged English sovereignty in New York, but pledged the Indians to neutrality in any future Anglo-French war.   The net result gave France a free hand in launching Indian attacks against the American colonies of the Northeast, especially after England and Holland declared war on France and Spain in 1702.

The war made New England a target both from within and without.   Iroquois neutrality enabled the French to ignore New York and concentrate their Indian raids on Massachusetts.   And in 1702, the crown appointed a new governor for Massachusetts—none other than Joseph Dudley, the former servant of the hated Andros regime. French Jesuit agents incited the Abnaki Indians of eastern Maine to raid settlements as close as forty miles west of Boston.   In February 1704, the established frontier settlement at Deerfield was leveled, and over forty percent of its population taken captive to Quebec. In 1708, French Indians carried out another Deerfield-style massacre in the town of Haverhill, only thirty miles northwest of Boston.[26]

Profiteers in New York, meanwhile, used Iroquois neutrality to build up a lucrative fur trade. New Englanders charged, however, that New York provided arms and safe passage, for Indian war parties en route to attack the New England frontier.   Thomas Hutchinson, in his eighteenth-century book *The History of the Colony and Province of Massachusetts Bay*, reported that "sometimes the plunder . . . became merchandize in Albany." Governor Dudley, meanwhile, added considerably to the plundering of Massachusetts.

Following the declaration of war against France, the English government refused to deploy any significant naval forces against the French in American waters. Thus by 1705, France was able to knock out 140 ships of Massachusetts—the shipbuilding power of the American colonies.[27] Under pressure to counter such enemy attacks, Governor Dudley joined with a group of merchants in Boston to hire his own vessel, supposedly to raid French ships and carry wartime supplies. Like Captain Kidd some years before, Dudley's captain turned pirate and attacked Boston's ships and sailors. When this Captain Quelch was finally captured and taken to England for trial, Dudley pulled strings to have him pardoned.[28]

In 1706, the treasonous Dudley gave flags of truce to Boston merchant vessels, ostensibly for use on missions to exchange prisoners with the French. Instead, they were used to sell supplies and ammunition to French and Indian forces in Canada. The Massachusetts General Court convicted the merchants of "high crimes," and only under extreme pressure stopped short of charging Governor Dudley. Dudley and his son Paul, the newly appointed attorney general of Massachusetts, appealed the convictions in England, where the Privy Council threw them out on a technicality.[29]

Boston's merchants were also working against the population at home. Elisha Cooke's patron Andrew Belcher, who profiteered massively in grain sales to the Royal Navy, at the same time created an acute grain shortage for Massachusetts. In the face of popular opposition to his actions, Belcher retaliated by raising grain prices to "impossible" heights, and hoarded even more grain for profiteering.[30]   The increasing oligarchical grip over Massachusetts was also extended to its shipbuilding and ocean-going commerce—once the pride of its sovereign years.   In 1711, Elisha Cooke, Jr., heir to his father's political machine, joined with his brother-in-law Daniel Oliver, and Andrew Belcher's son-in-law Oliver Noyes, to construct Long Wharf, expanding the facilities for Boston's new breed of merchants. The Cooke machine then secured for this unholy trio exclusive rights to all the shops and warehouses on the wharf, for the next forty years![31]

In the midst of this rampage against Massachusetts, Paul Dudley began writing appeals to London, for authority to create special courts without juries, complete executive power over legislation, and a revocation of the charter secured by Increase Mather in 1692.[32] Besieged militarily, economically, and politically, New England had a growing list of reasons to concur with Cotton Mather's assessment, that it was becoming "Little every way." Without creating new institutions, to restore the minds and morality of the population, the chance of securing a whole continent for development appeared nearly—if not already—lost.

NOTES

1. Murdock, *Increase Mather*, 219.

2. *Ibid.*, 220–221.

3. *Ibid.*, 221–223.

4. Cotton Mather, *Some Considerations on Bills of Credit* (Boston, 1691).

5. Hall, et al., eds., *Glorious Revolution*, 102.

6. Cotton Mather, *Life of Sir William Phips*, Mark van Doren, ed. (New York, 1929), 67.

7. Dunn, *Puritans and Yankees*, 290–293.

8. Mather, *Some Considerations*.

9. Murdock, *Increase Mather*, 294, 299–301.

10. G.B. Warden, *Boston*, 1689–1776 (Boston, 1976), 41–44.

11. *Ibid.*, 52.

12. *Ibid.*,   51–52.   Warden' s account portrays the Cooke machine in positive terms, and finds these developments both surprising and confusing.

13. *Ibid.*, 55.

14. Quoted by Kenneth Silverman, *The Life and Times of Cotton Mather* (New York, 1984), 144.

15. Warden, *Boston*, 51.

16. *Ibid.*

17. Quoted by Silverman, *Cotton Mather*, 148.

18. *Ibid.*

19. Winsor, *History of Boston*, I, 184–185.

20. Silverman, *Cotton Mather*, 148.

21. *Ibid.*, 150–151.

22. *Ibid.*, 151–152.

23. Report of the Board of Trade, March 26, 1701, in Jack P. Greene, ed., *Settlements to Society*, 1584–1763 (New York, 1966), 222–223.

24. The above calculations are based on statistical tables printed in Greene' s documentary collection, *Settlements to Society*, 238–239.

25. *Colonial Laws of New York* (5 vols., Albany, 1894–1896), I, 429.

26. Francis Parkman, *A Half-Century of Conflict* (2 vols., Boston, 1896), I, 52ff., 92–93.

27. Douglas Leach, *Arms for Empire, A Military History of the British Colonies in North America, 1607–1763* (New York, 1973), 136.

28. Warden, *Boston*, 62.

29. *Ibid.*, 63–64; Silverman, Cotton Mather, 212–213.

30. Warden, *Boston*, 66.

31. *Ibid.*, 68.

32. *Ibid.*, 62.

4

Swift Opens the Door to the West

During the first decade of the eighteenth century, the long-cherished dream of creating an American continental republic was near to being extinguished. The colonial population was effectively confined to a strip of stagnating coastal settlements, and their former freedoms and sense of mission were rapidly eroding under increasingly corrupt oligarchical rule.

The best-kept secret of American history is that the crucial opportunity to rekindle the "beacon of hope" was provided by the brilliant satirist Jonathan Swift (1667–1745), Ireland's republican leader who transformed the political rules of the game, as the ally of Germany's Gottfried Wilhelm von Leibniz (1646–1716).

In 1710, the year that Cotton Mather launched a major republican organizing drive to uplift the American population, bold new moves were made in the American colonies to open the way for western expansion. The strategy called for seizing Canada and the Great Lakes from the French, opening western New York to settlements that could be secured for development, and linking the mid-Atlantic to the vast resources of the Middle West lying beyond the barrier of the Appalachian Mountains. The moment of opportunity was the arrival of new royal governors in New York and Virginia, allied to the faction of Queen Anne's government now guided by Jonathan Swift, whose efforts to establish a republican policy-making influence over the British crown had been closely followed by Cotton Mather since at least 1708.

By 1707, Britain and France, the principal adversaries in Queen Anne's War which continued to engulf Europe, were being drained of their real economic resources. In Britain, Venetian-Dutch banking houses, controlling the money-market district known as the City of London, were conducting a speculative orgy on top of the ruinous war costs. The Whig ministry, which to then had dominated Queen Anne's government, was largely the creation of the City of London bankers, sustaining itself through the Duke of Marlborough's military 'victories' in Europe won with Dutch and Hapsburg Austrian allies.

In France, Europe's leading power, the decaying regime of Louis XIV was similarly locked into a cycle of growing debt and destructive warfare under the dictates of its own Venetian creditors. The nations of Europe were playing out the suicidal scenario of Thomas Hobbes's *Leviathan*, the "eternal war of each against all," designed to end in an "omnipotent" world government.

In Cotton Mather's New England, the double-dealing of Governor Dudley's regime—looting the colonists under authority of the British crown, while supplying 'enemy' French forces in Canada—mirrored the depravity of the breakdown crisis in Europe. But such a crisis also provided unusual opportunities for changes in political fortunes, and in 1707 the Mathers reclaimed much of their lost ground by leading the opposition to Governor Dudley.

Positioned to intervene to end the Hobbesian nightmare unfolding in Europe were the political networks of Gottfried Wilhelm von Leibniz, the great German scientist, economist, and statesman—and the acknowledged leader of republican forces internationally. As early as 1670, while serving the Elector of Mainz, and in touch with the French nation-building forces associated with Mazarin and later Colbert, Leibniz had proposed a Grand Design for an "harmonia universalis" of sovereign republics, which included a crucial role for America.

Although historians have generally sought to minimize Leibniz's significance, and virtually obliterate his importance to America, he was no stranger to New England's leaders. Among his correspondents was John Winthrop, Jr. (1606–1676), the leading American astronomer, physicist, and industrial entrepreneur of his day. As governor of Connecticut, he secured for it the virtually sovereign status his father had established for the Massachusetts Bay Colony.

Leibniz was fully aware of the importance of America's developing a continental republic. In 1668, the German scientist, geologist, and explorer John Lederer became the first recorded white man to cross Virginia's Blue Ridge Mountains, and chart the Shenandoah River valley. His findings and maps were published in London in 1671, and were used in 1710 and again in 1716 by Virginia Governor Alexander Spotswood, in his expeditions to the Blue Ridge Mountains and across the Shenandoah River. Lederer's explorations were certainly known to Leibniz, for they were a major news item in Europe, and Lederer returned to Germany after several years' employment by Connecticut Governor Winthrop as a geological surveyor.

During the strategic crisis which unfolded after 1700, America's republican prospects depended upon defeating the British policy exemplified by Leibniz's bitter enemy John Locke. Through his position on the Board of Trade, Locke advocated the revoking of all colonial charters and the complete economic subjugation of America. Within Leibniz's networks, the leading figure inside Britain responsible for frustrating this oligarchical scheme was Jonathan Swift, the supposedly cynical gadfly of the London literary scene. It is a mark of our own cultural decay that Swift is commonly remembered today only as the author of *Gulliver's Travels*—watered down to the level of a pointless children's book. Oligarchically inspired

John Lederer's Map of 1671

The German scientist and explorer John Lederer published this map in London in 1671, following his expeditions of 1668-1669—the first to cross the Blue Ridge Mountains in Virginia and western Carolina. Commissioned by Virginia Governor William Berkeley, Lederer proved that Virginia's vast colonial claims to the West could be developed, and shattered the myth that the Blue Ridge was impassable.   Virginia's Tidewater oligarchy was determined to eliminate such prospects.   When Lederer tried to demonstrate his discovery to a "company of gentlemen," they abandoned him on the march (note No. 3 in his notes to the map) and falsely reported him dead.   Before returning to Europe, Lederer spent nearly two years working for Connecticut Governor John Winthrop, Jr., who corresponded with European republican leader Gottfried Wilhelm Leibniz.

Despite the primitive circumstances under which it was made, Lederer's map provided important new knowledge of Virginia's interior, including the upper reaches of its coastal rivers, the line of the Blue Ridge, the existence of the Shenandoah Valley beyond it (labeled "Savanae"), and the Appalachian Mountains to the west (the "Rickohockans").   Drawn from an east-to-west perspective, the map also notes (No. 6) "the head of the Rapahanock river" as its south fork.   Lederer first crossed the Blue Ridge (No. 1) just below that point—and so did Alexander Spotswood in 1716.

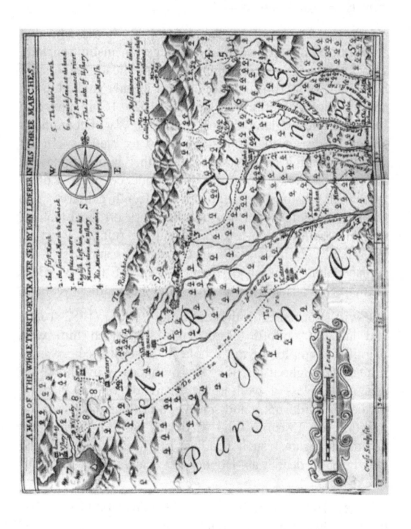

accounts of British history have also suppressed the fact that Swift was a major figure in the ruling circles of Queen Anne's government from 1710 to 1713.

The Real Jonathan Swift

Born in Dublin of English descent, Swift was educated at Dublin University's Trinity College, an institution long associated with New England's republican leadership. Both John Winthrop, Jr., and Increase Mather studied there, and Increase's older brother Samuel (1626–1671) moved to Ireland from England during the Civil War, becoming a senior fellow at the college in 1654 as well as one of Dublin's leading ministers. The Mather family remained active in Dublin, and in correspondence with Cotton Mather in Boston, well into the eighteenth century. The Puritan Samuel Mather also left his mark on local history, refusing to implement orders during the ruinous years of the late Cromwell Protectorate to suppress the (Episcopalian) Church of Ireland—which Swift served as Dean of St. Patrick's in Dublin for more than thirty years.

Swift's formal education at Trinity College (1682–1686) and later at Oxford (M.A., 1692), provided him with plentiful examples of the scholastic absurdities he was to ridicule throughout his life. But by his early manhood, he was nonetheless a well-armed champion of the Platonic method in philosophy and science, a brilliant satirist in the tradition of Erasmus and Rabelais, and a devastating polemicist against such peddlers of "Man is a beast; the Universe is dead" as Hobbes, Descartes, Newton, and Locke.

By 1697, Swift had attracted considerable attention through his satirical attacks on the degeneracy of intellectual life—the same decay in culture and morality that Cotton Mather charged in 1696 had reduced New

England to a "little" people. Two works written during 1696–1697, *A Tale of a Tub* and *The Battle of the Books*, marked Swift as a dangerous man in the eyes of those who sought to impose a cultural dark age.

A Tale of a Tub, circulated anonymously and not printed until 1704, took aim at the threat that "the wits of the present age being so very numerous and penetrating" would "find leisure to pick holes in the weak sides of religion and government," as Swift put it in his preface. Swift explains his political motive, and his choice of title, by noting

> that seamen have a custom, when they meet a whale, to fling him out an empty tub by way of amusement, to divert him from laying violent hands upon the ship. This parable was immediately mythologized: the whale was interpreted to be Hobbes's Leviathan, which tosses and plays with all schemes of religion and government, whereof a great many are hollow, and dry, and empty, and noisy, and wooden, and given to rotation: this is the leviathan, whence the terrible wits of our age are said to borrow their weapons. The ship in danger is easily understood to be its old antitype, the commonwealth. . . . [A]nd it was decreed, that in order to prevent these leviathans from tossing and sporting with the commonwealth, which of itself is too apt to fluctuate, they should be diverted from that game by a Tale of a Tub. And, my genius being conceived to lie not unhappily in that way, I had the honour done me to be engaged in the performance.[1]

Swift adds that his treatise is intended to "serve for an *interim* of some months to employ those unquiet spirits," until "a large academy can be erected, capable of containing nine thousand seven hundred forty and three persons," the number Swift cites for persons in England with "livings," or inherited wealth from feudalistic ground rent. That number, "by modest computation, is reckoned to be pretty near the number of wits in this island." The proposed "academy" is to contain the various schools "to which their genius most inclines them."

The list of "the principal schools" constitutes an attack on the degeneration of culture in England since the days of Marlowe, Shakespeare, and Milton, and especially on the imposed supremacy of Venetian-inspired oligarchical fashions from the continent:

> There is first, a large pederastic school, with French and Italian masters. There is, also, the spelling school, a very spacious building: the school of looking-glasses: the school of swearing: the school of critics: the school of salivation: the school of hobbyhorses. . . .[2]

A Tale of a Tub proceeds to satirize the cultish and irrational dogma and practices corrupting the Catholic, Anglican, and Protestant churches. In "A Digression Concerning Madness," Swift extends the same treatment to the corrupters of philosophy and science, and especially such reductionists as Descartes:

> Let us next examine the great introducers of new schemes in philosophy. . . . Because it is plain, that several of the chief among them, both ancient and modern, were usually mistaken by their adversaries, and indeed by all, except their own followers, to have been persons crazed, or out of their wits; having generally proceeded, in the common course of

their words and actions, by a method very different from the vulgar dictates of unrefined reason; agreeing for the most part in their several models, with their present undoubted successors in the academy of modern Bedlam. . . . For, what man in the natural state or course of thinking, did ever conceive it in his power, to reduce the notions of all mankind, exactly to the same length, and breadth, and height of his own? . . . Descartes reckoned to see, before he died, the sentiments of all philosophers, like so many lesser stars in his romantick system, wrapped and drawn within his own vortex.[3]

In *The Battle of the Books*, Swift delivered a devastating blow against an ongoing Jesuit-designed operation originating in France, and extended into Britain by Sir William Temple: a rigged debate over whether 'correct' knowledge was the property of the ancient, or the modern, philosophers. Besides the epistemological absurdity of the ancient-vs.-modern distinction, the 'debate' was designed to limit the choices to ancient Aristotelians or modern Aristotelians, throwing Platonic reason out the window.

In his satirical account of "the battle fought last Friday, between the ancient and modern books in St. James's Library," Swift slays Aristotelians left and right, old and new, while establishing that the actual fight is between Plato and Aristotle, and their adherents, ancient and modern. Swift emphasizes the point in a passage about Duns Scotus, the medieval Aristotelian whose name rightly served as the origin of the word "dunce":

When the works of Scotus first came out, they were carried to a certain library, and had lodgings appointed them; but this author was no sooner settled, than he went to visit his master

Aristotle; and there both concerted together to seize Plato by main force, and turn him out from his ancient station among the divines, where he had peaceably dwelt near eight hundred years. The attempt succeeded, and the two usurpers have reigned ever since in his stead: but to maintain quiet for the future, it was decreed that all *polemicks* of the large size, should be held fast with a chain.[4]

Swift's polemic was obviously not so constrained. As his mock battle unfolds, he says of "the moderns":

There came the bowmen under their valiant leaders, Descartes, Gassendi, and Hobbes; whose strength was such, that they could shoot their arrows beyond the atmosphere, never to fall down again, but turn like that of Evander into meteors, or like the cannonball into stars.[5]

Besides having the universe make the Aristotelian moderns impotent against their enemies, Swift redraws the battle lines to have the Aristotelians kill *one another*, including in his targets Sir Francis Bacon (1561–1626), the occult-worshipping "philosopher" deployed to exterminate the English Renaissance. With added irony, he has Aristotle slay Descartes accidentally.

Then Aristotle, observing Bacon advance with a furious mien, drew his bow to the head, and let fly his arrow, which missed the valiant modern, and went whizzing over his head; but Descartes it hit; the steel point quickly found a defect in his head-piece; it pierced the leather and the pasteboard, and went in at his right eye. The torture of the pain whirled the valiant bowman round, till death, like a star of superior influence, drew him into his own vortex.[6]

For such a skillful polemical warrior as Swift was, intervention directly into the political arena followed naturally, especially in an era when all camps routinely recruited literary champions. From 1701 to 1704, Swift moved steadily into the center of the leading issues in English and European politics, beginning in 1701 with his tract *On the Dissensions at Athens and Rome.* This classical parable exposed some of the Tories' 'patriotic' opposition to King William III, in support of the House of Stuart, as identical to the demagogic agitations in ancient Athens which served to cover a treasonous alliance with the Persian empire. Swift was quickly elevated that same year to the status of political prophet, when Louis XIV revealed his intentions toward England, by recognizing the Stuart pretender to the English throne, upon the death of the exiled James II in Paris.

For the next twelve years, Swift shuttled back and forth between Dublin and London, acquiring friends and enemies, both Tory and Whig, championing republican principles over party allegiances—especially given oligarchical control of leading factions in both parties.

William III died in March 1702, and Swift returned to England in April. War between England and France, to be known as Queen Anne's War, had already broken out in 1701, effectively placing control of the new Queen's government under the commander of British forces, John Churchill, first Duke of Marlborough, whose family spawned generations of everything from genocidal colonialism and international drug trafficking to Winston Churchill, that misvenerated encyclopedia of all their vices.

The new war not only threatened to reduce Europe to a pile of rubble under international oligarchical control. War further menaced the key republican flank against such a fate: the prospects for a new American nation. For the colonies, the handwriting was on the wall.   In 1701, England initiated war against France, but concluded a treaty with Paris, affirming that the only significant Indian forces in America not under French Jesuit control—the Iroquois Five Nations—would remain neutral in any conflict between Britain and France. This so-called treaty meant that, once the war was under way, French Indians out of Canada could move freely through Iroquois-controlled New York to attack the "English" colonies of New England, which received no military assistance from London whatsoever.   At the same time, new French alliances with the Choctaw and Chickasaw tribes in Louisiana and Alabama threatened the southern colonies, and the French navy began devastating assaults on New England shipping, also left unprotected by English naval forces.

The Duke of Marlborough would certainly have approved the similar oligarchical strategy of his heir Winston Churchill, who kept the United States Army idle in Britain as long as possible while the Nazis ground up Europe during World War II.

The threat to America during Queen Anne's War was a major concern of Swift's, and on several occasions he raised the idea of coming to the colonies, under his official capacity in the Episcopal Church, perhaps as Bishop of Virginia. But the prospects, both for America and for the very survival of Europe, depended upon ending the awful carnage of war. Especially after the August 1704 defeat of the French at Blenheim, where 40,000 of Louis XIV's 60,000 troops were permanently eliminated from the combat rolls, the peaceful settlement of "Queen Anne's War" became the paramount issue—and the one which on Swift's intervention would reshape the policies of Queen Anne's government.

The Worst Churchill?

John Churchill, Duke of Marlborough, was the figurehead at the center of a gargantuan financial and political swindle, imposed upon England by a Venetian-directed European oligarchy.   Since the Puritan Revolution which ended the reign of Charles I, and the foreign invasion ending the Stuart Restoration in 1688, the web of monarchical succession in England had become tattered enough to enlarge the possibilities for outright Venetian rule over the remains of Shakespeare and Milton's England —as long as a suitable "English" figurehead could be successfully installed.

The man selected to rule in Queen Anne's name was not what the oligarchy would call "well-bred," but he was the kind of dog who would respond to one master after another, as long as there was more in his bowl.   John Churchill (1650–1722) was the son of "Sir" Winston Churchill, a devoted monarchist who fought briefly against Cromwell's armies, and then fled to the protection of his mother-in-law when the Commonwealth won control of West England. While living in her house, partly ruined by a fire set by royalist troops because of her family's ties to the Commonwealth, Winston kept his options open by writing a treatise on the divine right of kings.   But even after the Stuart monarchy was returned to power, Winston was worth only a few minor offices doled out by the crown's functionaries.

His daughter Arabella led the way into more substantial royal favors, by becoming a mistress to the Duke of York, and mother of four of his bastard children.   The duke, younger brother to King Charles II and later his successor as James II, showed his gratification early, by taking on Arabella's fifteen-year-old brother John as a page in 1665. John Churchill adopted his sister's model for advancement, by having an affair with Charles II's leading mistress, Barbara Palmer, Duchess of Cleveland, and started his own fortune with £10,000 from this notorious court intriguer. Nosing his way through the young ladies-in-waiting of the King's palace, John Churchill selected his wife Sarah, who was then promoted to the inner circle of service to James II's daughter Anne, the future Queen.[7]

Sarah Jennings, the future Duchess of Marlborough, spent much of her adolescence as one of the notoriously misnomered "maids of honour" at the depraved court of Charles II. Her mother, who as a debt-ridden widow had secured lodgings in St. James's Palace to escape the law, was frequently described in pamphlets of the time as "a witch" and a "sorceress." Sarah's career of palace intrigue and sadistic manipulation might appear to be drawn from the character of Shakespeare's Lady Macbeth, except she lacked the sense of remorse. As Jonathan Swift wrote of her in 1713, after she and her Churchill had been expelled from the court of Queen Anne:

> It is to her the duke is chiefly indebted for his greatness, and his fall; for above twenty years she possessed, without a rival, the favours of the most indulgent mistress in the world, nor ever missed one single opportunity that fell in her way of improving it to her own advantage. She has preserved a tolerable court-reputation, with respect to love and gallantry; but three Furies reigned in her breast, the most mortal enemies of all softer passions, which were, sordid Avarice, disdainful Pride, and ungovernable Rage; by the last of these often breaking out in sallies of the most unpardonable sort, she had long alienated her sovereign's mind, before it appeared to the world. . . . Imagine what such a spirit, irritated by the loss

of power, favour, and employment, is capable
of acting or attempting; and then I have said
enough.[8]

Even by bestial oligarchical standards, John and Sarah
Churchill were an unlikely couple to play a major role in
the world affairs of their time.   But their unswerving,
simultaneous attention to both the highest bidder at the
time, and whoever might raise the stakes, made them the
perfect domestic vehicle for a Venetian plot to obliterate
what remained of the English Commonwealth's republican
aspirations.

After overseeing some senseless bloodbaths, during a
war between France and the Dutch in the 1670s, Churchill
was praised by his French paymasters for his mercenary
efforts in the field.   When Louis XIV's enemy, the Dutch
Prince William of Orange, invaded England in 1688 to
seize the throne from James II, Churchill promptly betrayed
the Stuart King who had bestowed a quarter-century's
patronage upon him.   He joined the armies of William, who
dispatched him to fight the French on the Rhine—and
created him Earl of Marlborough.

There was a bit more to Churchill's treason than his
general inclination to 'go with the winner.' Under the rules
of hereditary monarchical succession, even with James II's
flight to France construed as his 'abdication,' William of
Orange's only claim to be anywhere near the throne was his
marriage in 1677 to James's reluctant daughter Mary,
Anne's older sister. On the basis of Sarah Churchill's years
of ingratiating, manipulating 'service' to the younger Anne,
the new Earl of Marlborough expected even larger bowls to
be placed before him.

The rules of succession, strictly applied, would have left
the invader William with the status of 'prince consort' to

Queen Mary, who by 1689—still barren—had almost no prospect of a direct heir. In that case, Anne would be her successor upon Mary's death. But the Venetian oligarchs who bankrolled William's venture insisted on a few alterations in resolving the issue, which signaled something of the fate intended for England. William summoned a "convention" instead of Parliament, proposed himself as King, and secured approval for a joint monarchy. All administrative power would reside in his hands, and he would reign alone if Mary died before him.[9]

Princess Anne's objections that the settlement virtually entailed her waiving her right of succession were understandable. Personal entreaties from Sarah Churchill and the jesuitical Anglican leader John Tillotson were coupled with Marlborough's private assurances to all that Anne had agreed that William should rule for life, until Anne's acquiescence was a *fait accompli*. In 1691, Tillotson was rewarded by being appointed Archbishop of Canterbury.

As long as Sarah could manage Anne, the Churchills felt they could look forward to at least two reigns to build their own power. In all deals among thieves, however, there are inevitably some loose ends. Churchill's first problem was with King William himself, who was more than uneasy about a man who could so readily switch allegiances. The betrayal of James was initially quite lucrative, as Churchill was given the task of purging the Stuart army, while keeping the "vast harvest" in proceeds from the sale of new commissions, even for additional regiments created by William. William noted privately that while he approved the treason on his behalf, he disliked the traitor.

Queen Mary proved to be yet another problem. Though miserable in her marriage with William, whose reputed homosexuality was the talk of all the courts of Europe, the

Queen quickly recognized the Churchills' efforts to make Anne their own pawn, while playing her against both William and Mary.   As early as March 1690, Mary wrote privately that the new regime was threatened by a republican party and by the Jacobite party supporting the Stuarts, "and I have reason to fear that my sister is forming a third."[10]

Queen Mary's specific concerns tended to focus on such matters as Sarah Churchill's cheating Anne out of thousands of pounds at cards, as well as taking £1,000 a year from Anne's settlement as a "pension." King William had added reason to distrust the Churchills, given numerous reports that Marlborough was in secret correspondence with French plotters around James II, the deposed Stuart king, who had taken refuge in France. In January 1692, William stripped Marlborough of all of his court offices; in May, Queen Mary ordered him arrested and sent to the Tower of London, on charges of conspiring for a Jacobite invasion of England.[11]

The charges were not proven, nor were they accurate concerning the real nature of the plot Marlborough was involved in: the dismantling of what remained of the English nation-state, and converting it to a looting ground for the same Venetian-Dutch financial interests which had already invaded England.

Britain's 'Venetian Party'

The reign of King William III was totally dominated by the so-called "Court" or "Junto" Whigs, whose notorious manipulations of currency and debt instruments were such trademarks that even nineteenth-century British Prime Minister Disraeli routinely referred to them as the "Venetian party." Setting out to control both England's credit and debt, and thus its whole economy, these champions of "English liberties" and "free enterprise" soon brought a prolonged economic depression to the country.

Exemplary were the activities centering around Charles Montagu, Baron and later Earl of Halifax. The Whigs, of course, were staunch supporters of the powers of Parliament, and thus most charitably disposed toward having the House of Commons enact measures of economic ruin. As King William's Lord Treasurer, Montagu secured passage of a huge loan bill at high rates of interest, ostensibly to finance William's ongoing war in Europe, and offering future taxes as security. Simultaneously bleeding the English economy and restricting any credit for improved agriculture and manufacturing, Montagu's scheme created England's first national debt, designed to be self-expanding and permanent.

The scheme also transferred much of the country's existing wealth to a new class of speculators and money managers, who then proceeded to buy up further seats in Parliament to perpetuate the swindle. As Swift recounted later, this system was "of mighty advantage to those who were in the management of it, as well as to their friends and dependents; for, funds often proving deficient, the government was obliged to strike tallies for making up the rest." These were often sold at more than forty percent discount. Swift wrote of this arrangement:

> At this price, those who were in the secret bought them up, and then took care to have that deficiency supplied in the next session of parliament; by which they doubled their principal in a few months.[12]

By the time Queen Anne succeeded to the throne in 1702, the debt had doubled and tripled several times over. More than forty percent of the sum rolled over by her first parliament, was claimed by interest payments alone. But the same perpetrators of this swindle had by then also established a monopoly over English banking—and had imposed a vicious credit crunch as well. In 1694, Montagu oversaw the founding of the Bank of England, which soon was issuing notes against government "tallies" to repay its own loans for conducting the war in Europe.

The political heirs of the English Commonwealth Party, led by Robert Harley, had proposed in 1691 a National Land Bank to issue low-interest credit, secured by improvements of land, which could also finance trade and manufacturing. Montagu's Venetian crowd unleashed John Locke, their in-house propagandist, to counter this unwanted opposition to the 'enlightened' proposals of the Venetian 'families.' Locke's pamphlet, "Some Considerations of the Consequences of lowering the Interest and raising the Value of Money," denounced the economic development program of Harley's circle, and especially the provision that interest rates be held to four percent or less![13]

This is the same John Locke whose policies the eighteenth-century British Whig "Venetian party" tried to impose on America, as a constitutional model of "liberty." The same John Locke, as a member of King William's Venetian-reorganized Board of Trade, advocated revoking the charters of all the American colonies, a royal dictatorship over their economic activity, and a ban on their manufacturing any finished goods. The same John Locke, as an 'Enlightenment' philosopher, insisted that the human mind was nothing more than the animal register of 'sensations.'

Locke's Venetian tract against Harley's National Land Bank was complete with hand-wringing lamentation over the fate of the poor, while making clear nonetheless that his real concern was for the speculative money-managers. Rejecting any notion of investing in the production of new wealth, Locke complained that Harley's proposed four percent interest rates would harm

> widows and orphans, and others uninstructed in the arts and management of more skillful men, *whose estates lying in money*, they will sure, especially orphans, to have no more profit of their money, than what interest the law barely allows [emphasis added].

The charter for Montagu's Bank of England, smuggled through Parliament under the guise again of financing the war against France, indebted the government to the Venetian-controlled money managers at the doubled, "moderate" rate of eight percent interest. But this newly licensed looting agency had bigger things in mind. Once Montagu secured appointment as Chancellor of the Exchequer, he moved to impose a further credit crunch by cutting the amount of circulating coinage virtually in half. He appointed, as the appropriate instrument for such economic carnage, a new Warden of the Mint in 1695, the Aristotelian plagiarist and devoted student of the occult, Sir Isaac Newton. The pathetic Newton, who had tried to steal a little scientific credibility by claiming Leibniz's invention of differential calculus as his own, gratified his patron Montagu by supplying him a mistress, Newton's own niece and adopted daughter.

In 1696, Newton oversaw the "Great Recoinage," under which all English coins shaved or "clipped" at their edges for their metallic value—a centuries' old practice would no longer be accepted as legal tender. Nor would they be redeemed for their face value, even though they had circulated as such. Instead they were to be turned in, to be replaced at a later, unspecified date, for face-value coins equal to the total metallic weight of the old coins. By contemporary estimates, this removed over £2,700,000 of specie from circulation in 1696, a figure more than a third larger than the entire crown debt at the end of James II's reign. Meanwhile, Montagu had cranked up the national debt to over £20 million.[14]

By 1697, the Venetian coup inside England was nearly total. Montagu was appointed that year prime minister, succeeding his crony Lord Sidney Godolphin (1661–1715). Godolphin was already an intimate, with Sarah Churchill's help, of Princess Anne, and also served as lord treasurer during King William's reign. In 1698, Godolphin's son married one of Churchill's daughters, and during the Duke of Marlborough's perpetuation of "Queen Anne's War," Godolphin's control of the Treasury ensured the continual flow of funds into the bottomless pit of Marlborough's campaigns in Europe.

Also in 1697, Robert Spencer, Earl of Sunderland, was named Lord Chamberlain, temporarily elevating the power of another Venetian conspirator who had helped arrange William's seizure of the English throne. Sunderland's son Charles married Churchill's second daughter, and extended the Venetian "family" system of control upon becoming Secretary of State, from 1708–1710, for the Whig Junto then ruling Queen Anne. Charles Montagu, Baron Halifax, was appointed in 1707 by the same Junto to an even higher position—ambassador to Venice.

The Leibniz Card

In 1700, shortly after Montagu's mission to Venice as "special plenipotentiary" for King William, a new twist was added to the Venetian party's scheme to assume complete control over England.

Queen Mary's death from smallpox in 1694 had placed Princess Anne next in line to succeed William on the throne, to be followed in turn by her son, the Duke of Gloucester, the only one of her eighteen children to survive infancy. In 1698, Marlborough was appointed as governor to the young duke, and the Churchills' hold on the future favors of the crown seemed secure indeed.

But in 1700 the eleven-year-old Duke of Gloucester died suddenly of smallpox, leaving no automatic solution to the question of a successor, especially in light of Anne's recent string of miscarriages. Political realities ruled out the return of the Catholic exile James II or his heirs. Both Whig insistence on a Protestant succession, and Tory defense of the hereditary monarchy, now converged upon a plan first mooted when William of Orange seized the throne in 1689: Anne's successor would be the Electress Sophie of Hanover (1630–1714), the granddaughter of James I.

The arrangement satisfied the dictates of royal genealogy, but from the oligarchical standpoint, there was an enormous complication. Sophie's court at Hanover was the focal point of influence of the great republican leader, Gottfried Wilhelm von Leibniz, who first arrived there in 1679 at the age of thirty-three, already a major figure in international scientific and economic policy making. In 1701, when the English Parliament approved the Act of Settlement determining the Hanoverian succession, Leibniz was officially a privy counsellor to Sophie, and an assistant in the Court of Chancery.

Succeeding William to the throne in 1702, the new Queen Anne quickly became the center of one of the fiercest struggles between oligarchism and republicanism since the fight for the English Commonwealth. From the oligarchy's standpoint, the battle plan required intensifying

John Winthrop (1588–1649), founder and first governor of the Massachusetts Bay Colony. The 19th-century statue of Winthrop formerly stood in Boston's Scollay Square.

The 1629 Charter of the Massachusetts Bay Company. Under Winthrop's leadership, the self-governing powers smuggled into the charter were used to establish a Puritan republic in America. (Courtesy of the Massachusetts Archives)

John Winthrop, Jr. (1606–1676), united the early settlements of Connecticut under a new charter in 1661, with sovereign powers much like those his father had established for Massachusetts. (clipart.com)

In the 1640s, the younger Winthrop also established the first automated industrial complex in America—the iron work at Saugus, Massachusetts, a water powered factory producing wrought iron, automatically rolled and cut into iron rods and bars. (Courtesy of H. Graham Lowry)

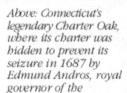

Above: Connecticut's legendary Charter Oak, where its charter was hidden to prevent its seizure in 1687 by Edmund Andros, royal governor of the Dominion of New England. Right: the Massachusetts Bay Charter, revoked in 1684, remained a symbol of independence even at the time of the American Revolution. Here Sam Adams defiantly points to the historic document, in a portrait by Copley, painted following the Boston Massacre in 1770. (Prints and Photographs Division, Library of Congress)

England's King Charles II (1630–1685). Tutored in his youth by the bestial Thomas Hobbes, Charles II made the Stuart Restoration synonymous with depravity and corruption. He spent the last decade of his reign attempting to destroy the charter freedoms of the American colonies. (clipart.com)

Increase Mather (1639–1723), the Puritan philosopher, scientist, and statesman, who led the fight to restore the Massachusetts charter. As president of Harvard, he promoted Plato and Kepler, against Aristotle and Descartes.

Sir Edmund Andros

The bloodless coup which overthrew the Andros regime in 1689 was announced in Boston by this handbill, ordering the governor to surrender peacefully.

Cotton Mather (1663–1728), the son of Increase, and the most prolific intellectual figure in colonial America. His 445 published works included treatises on philosophy, religion, ancient languages, history, politics, economics, physics, astronomy, biology, botany, geology, the art of singing, and the only medical guide for American physicians at the time.

The title page of Mather's 'Bonifacius,' which he published anonymously in 1710. Generally known as 'Essays to Do Good,' it was cited by Benjamin Franklin as the major influence on his life, and was widely reprinted in America—as late as the 1860s, during the Civil War.

BONIFACIVS.

AN ESSAY
Upon the GOOD, that is to be
Devised and Designed,
BY THOSE
Who Desire to Answer the Great END
of *Life*, and to DO GOOD
While they *Live*.

A BOOK Offered,
First, in General, unto all CHRISTIANS,
in a PERSONAL Capacity, or in
a RELATIVE.
Then more Particularly,
Unto MAGISTRATES, unto MINISTERS,
unto PHYSICIANS, unto LAWYERS,
unto SCHOLEMASTERS, unto Wealthy
GENTLEMEN, unto several Sorts of
OFFICERS, unto CHURCHES, and
unto all SOCIETIES of a Religious
Character and Intention. With Humble
PROPOSALS, of Unexceptionable
METHODS, to *Do Good* in the World.

Eph. VI. 18. *Knowing that whatsoever Good thing any man does, the same shall he receive of the Lord.*

BOSTON in N. England: Printed by B. Green, for Samuel Gerrish at his Shop in Corn Hill. 1710

Gottfried Wilhelm von Leibniz
(1646–1716)

Jonathan Swift
(1667–1745)

The brilliant satirist Jonathan Swift directed the republican networks of his time in England, Scotland, and Ireland. Working in alliance with Leibniz, the leader of republican forces internationally, he played a decisive role in freeing Queen Anne from the Duke of Marlborough, and helped launch America's initial breakthroughs toward becoming a continental nation. For both Leibniz and Swift, the point of reference dated back to the battle between Plato and Aristotle. Raphael's Renaissance painting of 'The School of Athens' emphasized the distinction between the two outlooks. In the painting's central figures, Plato, pointing heavenward, is portrayed on the left; Aristotle, on the right, is gesturing downward, clutching his immoral Ethics.

Raphael, 'The School of Athens.'

Thomas Hobbes
(1588–1679)

René Descartes
(1596–1650)

Isaac Newton
(1642–1727)

John Locke
(1632–1704)

A Rogues' Gallery of Aristotelians.
All of them promoted the ideology of an oligarchical world
order, based on the evil notions that man is a beast, and the
universe is dead. All of them were sponsored through the
Venetian controllers of European finance, and were identified
as enemies of mankind by Leibniz, Swift, and the Mathers. The
deceitful plagiarist Isaac Newton, for example. prostituted his
own niece to the head of the Bank of England; and John Locke
advocated seizing all land titles in America in the name of the
King.

The Duchess of Somerset (1667-1722). A Marlborough ally and enemy of Swift, she facilitated the Venetian Party's coup against the dying Queen Anne. (National Portrait Gallery, London)

John Churchill (1650–1722), Duke of Marlborough. Brother of the royal prostitute, Arabella, he was admitted to court as a page boy. He followed his sister's example as best he could, becoming a plaything for the mistress of the Duke of York (later King James II).

Sarah Jennings Churchill, Duchess of Marlborough (1660–1744). The 'Lady Macbeth' behind her husband's dreams of power. Her mother, a palace servant, was suspected of witchcraft. (National Portrait Gallery, London)

the grip of John and Sarah Churchill over the counsels of the Queen, isolating her from Leibniz's political influence, and ensuring that Sophie never ascended the English throne —for then Leibniz would acquire direct policy-making authority at a level which might tilt the balance in favor of republicanism internationally.

The enormity of the Leibniz threat in the eyes of the oligarchy ironically left a crucial opening on another flank: the control over Queen Anne herself. As long as Anne reigned, Sophie could not succeed to the throne. The fact that Anne was thirty-six years old in 1702, and Sophie twice that age, gave Anne a certain freedom she may only partially have grasped. As long as Sophie were alive, any oligarchical inclinations to terminate the reign, of even a rebellious Queen Anne, would be held in check by the 'Leibniz card.'

In the meantime, every effort was made to keep Anne under the sway of the Churchills, and—looking past the day of Sophie's death from old age—to ensure control over the next Hanoverian in line, Georg Ludwig, the Prince Elector (the future George I). Sophie herself seems to have entertained little hope of becoming Queen of England, though Leibniz and his friends in England made several unsuccessful attempts to secure official residency for her there. Upon news of the Act of Settlement in 1701, Sophie told John Tolland, envoy to Hanover for Robert Harley, the Speaker of the House of Commons:

> She was afraid the nation had already repented
> their choice of an old woman, but she hoped
> none of her posterity would give them any
> reasons to grow weary of their dominion.[15]

In the case of her son Georg Ludwig, such a cautiously guarded statement proved more than justified. Already nineteen years old when Leibniz arrived in Hanover in

1679, the Prince Elector had chosen the pathetic Dutch Prince William of Orange as his idol, and hunting as his avocation. Following the Act of Settlement, the oligarchy's interest in this potential monarch became effusive. Both Charles Montagu, the Venetian-run powerbroker billed as Baron Halifax, and the model hireling, John Churchill, personally devoted considerable time and prodigious sums of money throughout Anne's reign, to keep the Elector in the oligarchs' camp. Their efforts were successful. The Elector openly opposed the peace plan for Europe which Leibniz and Swift steered to the negotiating table after 1710. In 1714, as King George I, he appointed Montagu to the highest post in his cabinet, First Lord of the Treasury, and upgraded his feudal looting title from Baron to Earl of Halifax. Venice was well pleased.

While this rigged game of the Hanoverian succession was being played out, the republican moment of opportunity was increasingly limited to winning the support of Queen Anne, before her 'insurance policy' ran out. As long as Sophie lived, the 'Leibniz card' remained in force, and Queen Anne's remaining on the throne was the 'lesser of two evils,' from the oligarchs' standpoint, even if she were induced to break substantially with their policies.

Whatever her deficiencies, Anne was not exactly unaware that machinations at court historically involved larger stakes than one might imagine. She was the great-granddaughter of Mary, Queen of Scots; she was the daughter of James II, deposed by William of Orange with the crucial assistance of John Churchill. But from adolescence—ignored as a daughter of the royal family with only the most remote prospects of becoming Queen— she had developed a fixated dependence on the 'friendship' of Sarah Jennings, the enraged, manipulative maid-of-honor in the Stuart stable who married John Churchill.

Marlborough's Coup

Once Anne was on the throne, the Churchills' power grew enormously. Within five days, Marlborough was named captain general of the army, master general of ordnance, ambassador extraordinary to Holland, and a member of the Queen's cabinet council. Sarah became the Queen's first lady at court as groom of the stole, and soon was named ranger of the Great Park at Windsor for life, a nicely salaried position to which was added possession of the royal lodge. Officially, Sarah's appointments were worth £5,600 per year, and her husband's nearly £60,000. Profiteering in commissions, contracts and soldiers' pay added far greater sums to the Churchill fortune.

On May 4, 1702, Queen Anne issued an official declaration of war against France. Days before Marlborough sailed for Holland to take command in the field, the Queen granted his "urgent request" that Godolphin be named Lord Treasurer, the highest post in the cabinet. By the end of 1702, Marlborough had been elevated to duke; and following his victory at Blenheim in 1704, the Queen announced she would build the Palace of Blenheim for the Marlboroughs, on the scale of Louis XIV's Versailles.

Especially with such lavish backing from the Queen, the "conquering hero" Marlborough was, to all appearances, the most powerful man in England by 1705. But except for his military reputation (a dubious one, in the eyes of many of his officers), his influence derived mainly from the machinations of his 'Lady Macbeth,' Sarah, Duchess of Marlborough, and her irrational sway over Queen Anne. As long as Marlborough held such favor with the Queen, the oligarchical cabal around him seemed assured of success.

Though Leibniz's Electress Sophie was the acknowledged successor in line for the throne of England, relations with Hanover were largely under the control of Marlborough and his Venetian party cronies. Anne herself was persuaded that Sophie would be a threat to her authority were she granted residence in England.

Both the High Tories and the Junto Whigs were committed to keeping the 'Leibniz card' out of play, and as the 'right' and 'left' of the oligarchy's forces, staged operations to prevent such opportunities. On November 15, 1705, Tory Lord Haversham proposed, in his annual State of the Nation address to the House of Lords with the Queen in attendance, that Anne invite Sophie to come to England to live. Public pressure in that form could only embarrass the Queen, and gave the Whig lords the opportunity to demonstrate their 'loyalty' by defeating the measure.

The maneuver was also designed to drive Queen Anne into the clutches of the Whig Junto, and greater reliance on the Marlboroughs. That same night following the vote, the Queen wrote to the Duchess of Marlborough:

> I believe dear Mrs. Freeman [as Anne called her in their correspondence] and I shall not disagree as we have formerly done, for I am sensible of the services those people have done me that you have a good opinion of, and will countenance them, and am thoroughly convinced of the malice and insolence of them, that you have always been speaking against.[16]

Queen Anne also wrote to the Duke of Marlborough, who was to visit Hanover early in 1706, concerning "the disagreeable proposal of bringing some of the house of Hanover into England" and urging him "to set them right in notions of things here."[17]

By the time Marlborough arrived in Hanover in February, Sophie had written a carefully worded letter to the Archbishop of Canterbury expressing her desire to come to England. That same month, her letter appeared *as a pamphlet* in London, bound with a second letter, addressed to a Whig lord, from an English agent in Hanover, suggesting that the opposition to inviting Sophie to England originated with "Jacobites." The second letter was signed by Sir Roland Gwynne, a former Whig Member of Parliament who had worked to ingratiate himself with the Electress Sophie since coming to Hanover in 1703.

Gwynne's letter was subsequently attributed to Leibniz, but bears all the earmarks of a Junto Whig black operation. Invoking the Jacobite specter of Catholic-Stuart-French plots against England's Protestant monarchy was the Whigs' standard tack against any serious opposition—and the same one they used against Swift and his allies. Publishing the letter with Sophie's own could only intensify Queen Anne's hostility to any further machinations aimed at bringing Sophie (and thus Leibniz) to England. And the Duke of Marlborough's actions in Hanover conform to a classic 'cover' operation to place his own apparent role beyond suspicion.

Besides making clear to a compliant Elector George that a visit to England by his mother Sophie was ill-advised, and might work against his own interests, Marlborough warned him that Gwynne must be denied any further access to the Hanoverian court. Gwynne then retired to Hamburg —until Sophie's death.

Marlborough also promised George that Parliament would enact further legislation to guarantee the Hanoverian succession, and made him a private loan of £20,000 in exchange for a blank commission from George giving the duke supreme military command upon Anne's death. The arrangements omitted any consideration that Sophie would become Queen of England.

During the same month, with Queen Anne's consent, the bills promised by Marlborough passed both houses of Parliament, by initiation of the Whigs. The key piece of legislation was the Regency Act, establishing a commission of regents to rule England upon Anne's death *until her successor could arrive from Hanover.* The very premise of the bill carried the not-so-subtle implication that the Electress Sophie would never reside in England during Anne's lifetime, and the regency commission itself was designed to ensure that the Venetian party would have all necessary powers of state to impose their own policies— and also their anticipated pawn, King George I.

Manipulated into embracing her own worst enemies, Queen Anne now fulfilled her promise to the Duchess of Marlborough, to "countenance" those "that you have a good opinion of." On April 5, she agreed to name Charles Montagu, Baron Halifax, as Special Envoy to Hanover to convey the Act of Regency. Montagu, the longtime leader of the Whig Junto, also delivered to the Electress a list of twenty-one candidates picked by the Junto to serve as Lord Justices to administer the regency. In response to this pretense of consultation, Sophie struck seven names from the list—including Montagu's own.

Sophie's gesture did not alter the fact that the Junto had succeeded in their Regency Act maneuver. The best that could be said was that the Hanoverian succession had been reaffirmed, but the 'Leibniz card' would have to be played covertly, through intermediaries, and in Queen Anne's own court, before the end of Sophie's life. Pierre de Falaiseau, Hanoverian agent in London from 1705 to 1707, informed Leibniz that Parliament's actions were the most convenient means to succeed in this affair without shocking the Queen, and I can tell you frankly that those who believe that the goal could have been reached by any other means or highhandedly, know neither the Queen, who is very opinionated and quite ferocious, nor England.[18]

The entire episode, moreover, demonstrated conclusively that the key obstacles, to weakening the oligarchy's grip on Queen Anne, were Sarah's insidious influence and the Duke of Marlborough's powers of blackmail as England's 'indispensable' commander in the war with France. The Venetian cabal, with renewed confidence in both assets, then proceeded to overplay its hand.

The 'Secret Springs'

Swift's own first-hand judgment of Queen Anne's reign emphasized the extraordinary degree of conspiratorial activity behind the official exterior. "I am deceived," he wrote, "if in history there can be found any period more full of passages which the curious of another age would be glad to know the secret springs of."[19] On many important details, our curiosity remains, because Swift himself could not risk committing them to paper during his lifetime. Much of the story can be reconstructed nevertheless, though reporting it fully would go beyond the scope of the present work.

Despite Queen Anne's blind favoritism regarding the Marlboroughs, she had struggled from the beginning of her reign to keep her government from outright domination by any one faction, and to check the influence of both the High Tories and Junto Whigs. Marlborough and Godolphin, for example, she believed to be mild Tories. Until 1706, she excluded the Junto Whig lords from her cabinet, and in 1704 she replaced the High Tory Secretary of State Nottingham with Whig moderate Robert Harley. If Sarah Churchill were to lose her role as inside controller, alternatives to Venetian policy could be brought to the close attention of the Queen—including those originating with Leibniz himself.

Harley was one such channel, and the most significant among the official cabinet members. He had maintained some direct liaison with Leibniz since the late 1690s, and his fight against the Bank of England demonstrated that the two identified some enemies in common. But Harley's political inputs varied in quality, for as Leibniz later observed of him, he was too prone to 'back room' dealing in pursuit of his objectives.

Among members of Queen Anne's personal household, an important positive influence was the Scottish doctor John Arbuthnot (1667–1735), who began attending the Queen in 1703 and was appointed her physician extraordinary in October 1705. Arbuthnot had studied with Christiaan Huygens in Paris, at the academy Leibniz had once directed under the patronage of Colbert. He became one of Swift's closest lifetime friends and co-conspirators, a poet and a polemicist, a collaborator of the composer Handel in England, a member of the Royal Society, and a leading political confidant of Queen Anne. In 1710, a court observer noted that Arbuthnot was "a very cunning man, and not much talk't of, but I believe what he says is as much heard [by the Queen] as any that give advise now."[20]

Personally closest to the Queen was Abigail Hill Masham (1670–1734), who was to drive Sarah Churchill to distraction, and replace her as the Queen's favorite personal attendant. Abigail was ironically one of Sarah's cousins, but she was also second cousin to Robert Harley, for whom she provided steady access to Queen Anne, and was a ready ear for Jonathan Swift.   Her husband, Samuel Masham, whom she married secretly in 1707 in Arbuthnot's chambers with the Queen present, became a member of "the society" or "Brothers Club" which served as Swift's secret council within Queen Anne's government from 1711 to 1713.   Abigail's brother John, promoted through army ranks by the Queen herself, commanded the British-American expedition against Quebec in 1711.

When the Marlboroughs and their Junto allies made their drive for absolute power in 1706, they discovered more obstacles in their way than were thought to exist—and than Sarah could even locate.   Once their headlong rush was outflanked, the advantage in the battle for Queen Anne's government began shifting to a new combination of forces —marginally, but crucially, strengthened by the 'Leibniz card.'

In February 1706, while the Junto was settling the matter of the Regency Act, Queen Anne was persuaded by the same crowd to begin formal proceedings for the Act of Union between England and Scotland.   Though the two kingdoms had long recognized the same crown, the Venetian cabal, for its own purposes, now wanted them fully administered as one.   From Hanover, the Elector George announced on cue that he regarded the measure as the greatest proof of Anne's support for the Hanoverian succession.   For public consumption, such reasoning stressed the value of adding so many Protestant subjects to the future Hanoverian kingdom.

In the Junto's private reckoning, the merger had best be done while the Scottish Stuart Queen Anne were still on the throne. The reign being designed for George I, whom the Jacobites would scornfully refer to as "the wee bit German lairdie," was not expected to be an attractive replacement for what remained of Scottish independence. Nor was the Swiss-Venetian cabal centered in Edinburgh yet sufficiently accepted to ensure Scotland's consent to the union, without an appeal for the full measure of its loyalty to Queen Anne.

Even that was not enough. Scottish opposition proved intense, and by the fall of 1706 the possibility of an uprising against the Act of Union was real. It was prevented only by the decisive intervention of Lord George Hamilton, Earl of Orkney, the leader of the Scottish nationalists, and originally an opponent of the act. He was also a cousin to the Queen, who saw that his services were well rewarded. The Act of Union, ratified in 1707, removed the prohibition against Scots holding major political posts under the crown, and Orkney was named governor of Virginia.

Though he never saw the colony he governed in name only until his death in 1737, two of the Scottish lieutenant-governors he chose in his stead created crucial openings for America's emergence as a continental republic—with benefit, as we shall soon see, of passages for which Jonathan Swift knew the 'secret springs.'

The Junto did not detect in 1706 this disaster developing on the flank of its annexation of Scotland, but its drive for greater power soon encountered frontal resistance from Queen Anne herself. In July of that year, Louis XIV of France made his first serious overtures for peace. The Queen's Secretary of State, Robert Harley, advised her to enter into negotiations to end the ruinous war which the oligarchy was determined to perpetuate. Harley later noted that "from this time, the D:[uke] of Marlboro & My Lord Godolphin projected the ruin of Mr. H:[arley] upon a Jealousy that the Queen had too great a regard for me."[21]

Utterly confident of their political position, the Junto lords now determined to replace Harley with one of their own, the young Earl of Sunderland, who was also the Churchills' son-in-law. They were astounded when Queen Anne refused to even discuss the matter. Sarah at first chose tactically to stay out of the controversy, but she complained in a letter to Marlborough of a "secret influence" on Anne which she could not identify. By late August, the Marlboroughs were openly pressuring the Queen to appoint Sunderland. Godolphin was coupling threats of resignation with more menacing ones, telling her in writing on September 25, "You have an opportunity of making your Government strong, which you will never have again." The next day, Sarah wrote Anne a similar threat, also probing for a clue to the unknown influence at work on the Queen, and touting her husband and Godolphin as unparalleled servants of their country:

> by all one hears [the next parliament] is likely to bee a sessions soe criticall that in all probability your future happynesse & the nations depend upon it . . . the only fear I have is that there is somebody artfull that takes pains to mislead Mrs. Morley [Sarah's private name for Queen Anne] for otherwise how is it possible that one who I have formerly heard say, she was not fond of her own Judgment, could persist in such a thing soe very contrary to the advise of two men that has certainly don more services both to the Crown & Country than can be found in any history.[22]

On the same day that Godolphin wrote to the Queen, Harley presented his own arguments to her against yielding to the outrageous demands of the lord treasurer and captain general. Harley urged Queen Anne to "relieve therefore those who are gone too far," but instead she wrote twice to Marlborough appealing for his support of her decision to reject Sunderland.   The duke refused, at the same time suggesting that her opposition to the Junto Whigs merely strengthened the hand of France. In his reply on October 13, Marlborough openly defended their program of endless war. Without the Whigs' support, he asked, "How is it possible to obtain near £5,000,000 for carrying on the war with vigour, without which all is undone."[23]

Harley, meanwhile, attempted to organize a new ruling coalition, among moderate Tories and non Junto Whigs. But Anne was confronted with Marlborough's "diplomatic" blackmail, with the Junto's threat to deprive her of a parliamentary majority, and with sufficient hints that Marlborough would resign his military command unless she yielded on the Sunderland appointment. In November, the duke returned to London to personally ensure the defeat of Harley's coalition scheme, strong-arming wavering Whigs into line.   Grudgingly Queen Anne accepted Sunderland into her cabinet, but she retained Harley as Secretary of State, and assigned the Churchills' son-in-law to a lesser position.

Jonathan Swift also returned from Dublin to London in November, staying this time until May 1709. Despite the Junto's ostensible victory on the Sunderland question, it soon became apparent that all their pressure on the Queen had produced quite contrary, and longer-term results. Anne now regarded the Marlboroughs and Godolphin as hostile to her interests.   Sarah's own manipulative power was definitively broken, and Abigail Masham replaced her in the Queen's trusted inner circle.   Harley, with obvious support from the Queen, moved more determinedly toward assembling a new government, in which he himself would become head of the cabinet as lord treasurer.

On February 6, 1708, her forty-third birthday, Queen Anne sent a letter to Marlborough informing him she intended to replace Godolphin. Sensing that the Queen was still not prepared to risk the dismissal or resignation of her captain general in the midst of the war, Churchill pulled out all the stops. The duke and duchess, with Godolphin, demanded an audience with the Queen on February 8. First Godolphin, and then Sarah, offered their resignations unless Anne would dismiss Harley from the cabinet, but the Queen only gave them "leave to retire as you desire." Marlborough then railed against having to contend with "so vile a creature" as Harley, and announced he must surrender his commands, while warning the Queen that he feared "the Dutch would immediately on the news make a peace [with France] very injurious for England."

Queen Anne replied, "And if you do, my Lord, resign your sword, let me tell you, you will run it through my head."[24] Marlborough refused to attend that evening's meeting of the cabinet; the next day the corrupt Parliament rallied to the duke. The Queen summoned him to inform him she would dismiss Harley, who resigned a day later, along with three ministers loyal to him. Marlborough's blackmail had again succeeded, but now for the last time.

Godolphin stayed on, and the drains at the British treasury were opened anew for Marlborough's war.   In early March, their friends in the French oligarchy assisted with a crudely rigged show of an invasion of Scotland, under the name of the Stuart pretender to the throne. Marlborough and the Whig Junto were then able to play patriots, mobilizing against the expedition a week before it even sailed, and pledging an anxious and grateful Queen Anne their fullest support. Sarah later wrote of this episode, "Such sort of frights would work upon Her Temper, when better arguments had no manner of force."[25]

Deciphering 'Isaac Bickerstaff'

The Junto's ousting of Harley, who was replaced as Secretary of State by Sunderland, coupled with the Anglo-French oligarchy's refueling of Marlborough's war machine, marked a dangerous escalation by the Venetian party to extinguish any republican prospects during Queen Anne's reign. Though she now recognized some of her domestic enemies more clearly, they still held the upper hand. Internationally, the threat was even greater, for France's King Louis XIV was slipping further under the control of the Jesuits, the murderous cult created by the Venetians themselves to eliminate the apostolic authority of the Catholic Church.

Jonathan Swift responded to the crisis by publishing one of the most explosive counterintelligence documents in modern history, *Predictions for the Year 1708, . . . by Isaac Bickerstaff, Esq.* Generally known today only to literary specialists, and acknowledged simply as a gentle spoof of astrology, Swift's intervention under his "Bickerstaff" pseudonym was a brilliant, preemptive assault, exposing some of the foul Venetian plots then ongoing—and threatening retaliation should they proceed.

The political significance of Swift's Bickerstaff operation was broadly recognized by leading circles of the time, including those fighting for an American republic. In Massachusetts, Cotton Mather paid the extraordinary tribute of copying all of Swift's "predictions" into his diary, otherwise entirely reserved for his own words and thoughts.[26] His protégé Benjamin Franklin would later launch *Poor Richard's Almanack* (1733) in deliberate imitation of the *Bickerstaff Papers*, as would numerous pamphleteers during the American Revolution.

The *Bickerstaff Papers* cannot be deciphered today without reconstructing the strategic and political map of the time, *from the vantage point of a republican conspirator* on the inside. To the extent that task can be accomplished here, Swift provides important clues to the inner workings of the process which led to the founding of the United States.

For such republican leaders as Leibniz and Swift, the strategic situation demanded strengthening the nation-building factions of both Britain and France. The same two monarchies held competing titles to the territory the colonies needed for a republic in North America, and together had worked to constrain their growth, below the threshold required for defensible independence. Should both crowns fall firmly under the dictates of Venetian policy, their potentials for internal economic development might be eliminated, along with any tolerance for such progress in the American colonies. The republican task was to revitalize the seventeenth-century nation-building tendencies of the Commonwealth party in England, and the more successful programs of Mazarin, Richelieu, and Colbert in France. As shifting circumstances required, the strategy also entailed playing one government off against another, as Franklin himself would in steering America's course for independence.

By 1708, the situation in France was grim. The country was sliding into economic ruin; peasant revolts and urban bread riots spread, as taxes rose with the spiraling war debt. Yet Louis more tightly embraced the policies destroying his country. It was widely rumored that he had become a Jesuit affiliate in 1705; in 1709, the fanatic Jesuit Le Tellier officially became his confessor. Early in 1707, Louis banned a book urging economic reform by the aging Marquis de Vauban, the brilliant military engineer whose fortifications stopped Marlborough's advance toward Paris that same year, even though constructed a generation earlier.

Of Louis' oligarchic tax policy, Vauban wrote, "It is certain that the evil has been pushed to excess, and that if no remedy is applied, the people will fall into such destitution that they will never recover." Instead, Vauban proposed taxing the income of the feudalist landowners at five to ten percent, while abolishing existing taxes on workers and farmers, substituting a tax of no more than three and one half percent on their earnings. It was this "lower class of the people," Vauban emphasized, "which, by their labor and industry, and their contributions to the royal treasury, enrich the sovereign and his realm." Yet under prevailing policies, he added, "it is that class which now, through the demands of war, and the taxation of its savings, is reduced to living in rags and crumbling cottages, while its lands lie fallow."[27]

Vauban's fortification designs, modeled after those of Leonardo da Vinci, would later protect key coastal cities of the young American republic against British attacks.

But by March 1708 (the beginning of the New Year, by the "Old Style" calendar still in use in Britain and its American colonies), the threat within France had been compounded by the Venetian party's success in depriving Harley of his ritual "staff" of office. Harley surrendered his staff on February 10. Swift's *Predictions* thus refers to the "bickering" over the "staff"—the battle for political control.

Swift's literary device in the *Bickerstaff Papers* is to present himself as the author of a new almanac, competing against the cultish astrologers who dominated the field. He adds in the subtitle, "Written to prevent the People of England from being farther imposed on by vulgar Almanack-Makers," whom he denounces as

> mean, illiterate traders between us and the stars;
> who import a yearly stock of nonsense, lies,

folly, and impertinence, which they offer to the world as genuine from the planets, although they descend from no greater a height than their own brains.[28]

Under this satirical guise, however, Swift delivers what amounts to an open letter to the inner elite of the oligarchy, announcing republican preparations for deadly warfare. The nature of the battle is first established symbolically, and historically:

> My first prediction is but a trifle, yet I will mention it, to show how ignorant those sottish pretenders to astrology are in their own concerns: it relates to Partridge the Almanack-maker; I have consulted the star of his nativity by my own rules, and find he will infallibly die upon the 29th of March next, about eleven at night, of a raging fever; therefore I advise him to consider of it, and settle his affairs in time.[29]

Swift's prediction of the death of Partridge, a widely read astrologer of the time, is only "a trifle" because he is actually aiming at a higher level of evil: the still-existing cults of ancient Babylon and Syria, the "Magi" or Magicians, the Satan-worshiping astrologers of the oligarchy. Swift identifies the world-historic magnitude of the battle by twice invoking Socrates, the ancient Greek philosopher who established that the power of human reason is based on the principles originating in the divine Creator of the Universe.

For thus offending the cult of irrationalism, upon which oligarchic power is based, Socrates received a "prediction" of his own violent death. It was delivered by one of the Syrian Magi, and was fulfilled by an act of juridical murder, when Socrates was executed by order of the cult's

Athenian followers, for the crime of "impiety." To the Venetian descendants of the Whore of Babylon, Swift's prediction of the astrologer Partridge's death sent a message unmistakably clear. So did his satiric pledge to "restore" astrology to the level of science— in other words, to replace it with the laws of the universe:

> For example: a man may, by the influence of an overruling planet, be disposed or inclined to lust, rage, or avarice, and yet by the force of reason overcome that evil influence. And this was the case with Socrates. . . .[30]

Beyond foretelling the death of Partridge, Bickerstaff's first prediction seems curious at first glance: "On the 4th [of April] will die the cardinal de Noailles, Archbishop of Paris."[31] Cardinal de Noailles was one of France's leading republican figures, and a member of one of its most influential political families, which later provided crucial support for the American Revolution. The daughter of the later Duke de Noailles, Adrienne, became the invaluable wife of the Marquis de Lafayette.

Cardinal de Noailles was also the foremost protector in the church of two major Catholic republican factions: the Oratorians, and the wing of the Jansenists associated with the great Blaise Pascal. As such, he was bitterly hated by the Jesuits, who at one point plotted to kidnap him, and repeatedly sought his removal as archbishop of Paris.[32]

Swift follows his prediction of de Noailles' death with a host of others, including the deaths of the French Dauphin, of Louis XIV, and of Pope Clement XI (himself a frequent tool of the Jesuits), plus a series of catastrophes and upheavals, such as the burning of the Paris suburbs and "an insurrection in Dauphiné, occasioned by the oppressions of the people, which will not be quieted in some months." He also warns that "a shameful discovery will be made of a French Jesuit, giving poison to a great foreign general; and when he is put to the torture, will make wonderful discoveries."[33]

Immediately following the *Predictions for the Year 1708*, Swift published another piece which made it clear that the first one was designed as a preemptive intervention *in defense* of Cardinal de Noailles and his circle, coupled with a series of warnings to the enemy, conveyed in the other predictions. The second piece, in the form of an anonymous letter "to a Person of Honour," reports the death of Partridge, within four hours of the time Bickerstaff predicted. (Swift's little game with Partridge proved so successful that the astrologer was at first denied permission to further print his almanac—on the grounds that he was dead!) The letter concludes as follows:

> But whether he [Bickerstaff] hath not been the *cause* of this poor man's death, as well as the predictor, may be very reasonably disputed. . . . I shall wait with some impatience, and not without some expectation, the fulfilling of Mr. Bickerstaff's second prediction, that the Cardinal de Noailles is to die upon the 4th of April; *and if that should be verified as exactly as this of poor Partridge, I must own I should be wholly surprised, and at a loss, and infallibly expect the accomplishment of all the rest* [emphasis added].[34]

The threatened "accomplishment of all the rest," if anything should happen to de Noailles, drove the Jesuits berserk.   Swift noted in his 1709 "Vindication of Isaac Bickerstaff" the fact that the Inquisition in Portugal "was pleased to burn my predictions, and condemn the author and readers of them."[35] He also then identified the political forces in Europe which lent substance to his warnings as the circles of Leibniz. Bickerstaff reports "near an hundred honorary letters from several parts of Europe" praising his 1708 predictions, and cites the following as his very first example: "The most learned Monsieur Leibniz thus addresses me in his third letter:—*Illustrissimo Bickerstaffio astrologiae instauratori, &c.* ["most illustrious Bickerstaff, restorer of astrology"].[36]

As for de Noailles, Swift's "Vindication" cited the supposed report

> of a Frenchman, who was pleased to publish to the world, that the Cardinal de Noailles was still alive, notwithstanding the pretended prophecy of Monsieur Biquerstaffe: but how far a Frenchman, a Papist, and an enemy, is to be believed in his own cause, against an English Protestant, who is true to the government, I shall leave to the candid and impartial reader.[37]

The ironic joke intended in this passage, concerning the credibility of those "true to the government," is directed at the fact that the ministry run by Marlborough's cronies Godolphin and Sunderland, repeatedly collaborated with England's supposed enemies in the French oligarchy. The political impact of the *Bickerstaff Papers* derived from Swift's redrawing the battle lines on their real basis: the fight between republicanism and oligarchism.

Included in the specific targets of Swift's Bickerstaff operation was another instance of precisely this sort of Anglo-French oligarchical collaboration. At the time Swift published the *Predictions for the Year 1708*, his good friend Colonel Robert Hunter, appointed governor of Virginia in April 1707, was being held as a prisoner of war in France!

On the British side, the leading party to the scheme was none other than the Duke of Marlborough.

Breaking Venice's Grip on America

Even while the battle over policy-making control of Queen Anne's government still raged, Harley's tenure as secretary of state from 1704 until his ouster in early 1708 marked the beginnings of improving prospects for America. A significant break occurred when the Scottish Earl of Orkney was granted the title of governor of Virginia following the 1707 Act of Union with England. After decades of evil administration by the crown's colonial officials in America, Orkney's appointment led to the installation of two of the most extraordinary royal governors in our history, Robert Hunter (1666–1734) and Alexander Spotswood (1676–1740).

An intriguing pattern of evidence establishes that the 'secret springs' for this remarkable opening were triggered throughout by Jonathan Swift. Orkney's wife was a very dear friend and admirer of Swift, who called her the wisest woman he ever knew, and frequently got Harley to seek her political advice. Orkney's own role in securing the Act of Union gave him considerable influence with Queen Anne, sufficient to see that the lieutenants he chose to govern in Virginia, could override the veto power on colonial appointments, held by the Duke of Marlborough and the Whig Junto.

Both Hunter and Spotswood were Orkney's friends and fellow Scots, and served as senior officers under him in Marlborough's European campaigns. Hunter was the first of them named lieutenant governor of Virginia, by which time he was also an open opponent of the Duke of Marlborough. After nearly two decades of loyal military service, and a promotion to full colonel after the battle of

Blenheim, Hunter intervened against incompetent orders issued by Marlborough at Ramillies in May 1706. The duke took a general's revenge by bringing Hunter's military career to a dead end, and Hunter resigned from the army when the campaign broke for the winter.[38]

There was much more to Hunter than the typical career officer of Marlborough's day, and the keys to his future were not all in Marlborough's hands. He had grown up in Ayrshire, a hotbed of resistance in the Scottish Lowlands to the degenerate reign of Charles II, whose corrupt court first bestowed favors on the Churchills. The Scottish school system of his youth was then one of the best in Europe, and, unlike England's, was strongly influenced by continental learning. Proficiency was required in Greek, Latin, Italian, French, and Dutch, as well as history, geography, philosophy, mathematics, and music. Hunter himself became a poet, playwright, and political satirist, and his 'literary' friends included not only Swift but Arbuthnot, Queen Anne's personal "physician extraordinaire."

Hunter's friendship with Swift most probably began between 1699 and 1702. During those years, Hunter was stationed at the English garrison in Dublin, as a major in the Irish Dragoons. In the summer of 1699, Swift was named domestic chaplain to the lord lieutenant of Ireland, Lord Berkeley; and the following year he became prebendary of Dublin's St. Patrick's Cathedral. After his journey to England in 1701, when he published his classical parable attacking the oligarchy's Anglo-French collaboration (*On the Dissensions at Athens and Rome*), Swift returned to Dublin to complete work on his Doctor of Divinity degree, conferred in February 1702 by Trinity College.

News of Hunter's appointment as lieutenant-governor of Virginia did not sit well with Marlborough.   Should Virginia break out from the oligarchy's Anglo-French containment, the threat of America's emergence as a republican superpower would become quite real.   The colonial charter of Virginia claimed a territory so vast as to astound most Americans today, including the current states of West Virginia, Kentucky, Indiana, Illinois, Ohio, Michigan, Wisconsin, and the portion of Minnesota east of the Mississippi River.   (The armies of the American Revolution, in fact, organized the territories of the first four states listed, as counties of Virginia.)

Marlborough signaled something of his intentions regarding the Hunter appointment by preventing him from selling his officer's commission—a market in which the duke otherwise assiduously profiteered.   Hunter overcame this unusual bit of financial harassment, but the next move against him was intended to be more decisive.   After setting sail from England to assume the governorship, Hunter was captured by French "privateers," apparently off Virginia's coast, on August 12, 1707, and taken to Paris as a prisoner of war.[39]   Marlborough had routinely arranged prisoner exchanges for officers in a matter of days, but Hunter's final release was not secured for over a year and a half.[40]

Hunter's status as a British royal official, as well as his previous military rank, entitled him to confinement under simple house arrest, and also to parole for a number of months during 1708 back to England.   Marlborough, of course, guaranteed his return to the French.   While in London, Hunter met repeatedly with Swift, and the two men corresponded while Hunter was in French hands, within the restrictions of censorship and interception of their letters by both sides.   Even the caution necessitated by such enemy scrutiny did not prevent Swift from stressing the importance of their Virginia project.   Writing to Hunter on January 12, 1709, Swift declared his hope that Hunter "make haste over and get my Virginian bishopric."[41] Whether Swift actually hoped for such a post in the Episcopal Church, or whether he raised it to symbolize his political mission, the reference is significant in either case.

His next letter to Hunter never got through. Swift wrote again on March 22: "I imagine my former letter was intercepted by the French court. . . ." Again he stressed "that all my hopes now terminate in my bishopric of Virginia." Under the pretense of a "prodigiously witty" joke about the weather interfering with Marlborough's movements, Swift also hinted that Hunter would soon escape the duke's clutches:

> The Duke of Marlborough has at length found an enemy that dares face him, and which he will certainly fly before with the first opportunity, and we are all of the opinion it will be his wisest course to do so.[42]

Hunter was released a week or so later, at the beginning of April 1709.[43]

Hunter landed in England on April 24, reentering a political war that had grown even more intense during his imprisonment. The Junto Whigs had followed up their 1708 ousting of Harley, by further pressing Anne that spring to name another of their own, Lord Somers, as President of the Queen's Council. Anne had informed Marlborough it would "be utter destruction to me to bring Lord Somers into my service . . . it is what I can never consent to."[44] Sarah Churchill worsened matters at the same time by trying to extort a promise that her daughters would assume her own lucrative positions upon her retirement. By the spring of 1709, Marlborough himself sensed that their hand was overplayed, and that Queen Anne was on the verge of seeking to crush the Junto. Yet he played further into the hands of "the enemy that dares to face him," by asking the Queen to make him captain general for life. Swift reported that Anne reacted "as if she apprehended an attempt upon the Crown."[45]

Harley all the while, though out of office, had maintained a secret correspondence with Abigail Masham. Along with Swift's and Hunter's friend John Arbuthnot, Mrs. Masham had replaced Sarah Churchill in Queen Anne's inner circle, and was working to change the pattern of "backstairs" access to the royal chambers. When Queen Anne rejected Marlborough's 'Roman-general' demand, as she had Sarah's 'hereditary-priestess' ploy, the duke accused her of acting simply on the peevishness of Mrs. Masham—a 'mere servant,' who was now hostile and ungrateful to Sarah, her former 'benefactor.'

Anne's reply disturbed both duke and duchess:

> I saw very plainly your uneasiness at my refusing the mark of favour you desired, and believed from another letter I had from you on the subject you fancied that advice came from Masham, but I do assure you you wrong her most extremely, for upon my word she knows nothing of it, as I told you in another letter. What I said was my own thoughts. . . . You seem to be dissatisfied with my behaviour to the Duchess of Marlborough. I do not love complaining, but it is impossible to help saying on this occasion I believe nobody was ever so used by a friend as I have been by her ever since my coming to the Crown.[46]

Though the Queen still felt she could not dispose of the captain general, until other arrangements for ending the war were in place, the tide was running against the Venetian party.

Marlborough and Godolphin were still determined, however, to do everything in their power to prevent any actual development of the American colonies. Just as they refused to allow Robert Hunter to become the instrument for making Virginia the gateway to the West, so they worked to perpetuate the Jesuit-run Indian attacks out of Canada against New York and New England. This particular piece of Anglo-French oligarchical collusion was the subject of mounting concern and bitter resentment in America.

After the Haverhill massacre in 1708, upon personal appeal from American colonial leaders, Queen Anne had ordered an expedition against French Canada to root out such terrorism. A British naval squadron, with five regiments of army regulars, was to proceed to Boston by the middle of May 1709. An additional 2,700 colonial troops were to be raised by New England and New York, to take part in a combined attack against Quebec and Montreal. New England militiamen waited month after month at Boston, but there was no sign of the British fleet. Word finally arrived in the fall, that the expedition intended for America, had been ordered to Portugal!

Not only was Marlborough still commander of the army. His brother, George Churchill, was also first lord of the admiralty, in effect the chief of British naval operations. And besides Godolphin's powers as lord treasurer to intervene in military matters by controlling expenditures, the disposition of naval resources was also under the immediate control of the treasurer of the navy, Robert Walpole, whose career as a powerful enemy of America would stretch all the way into the 1740s.

After the sabotage of the 1709 attempt to break the French stranglehold on the colonies, an intercolonial assembly met in Rhode Island, and appealed again for an attack on Canada, to take place in the spring of 1710. Queen Anne gave her approval. But once more the plan was sabotaged, and finally reduced merely to an attack on Port Royal, Nova Scotia, opposite the northern coast of Maine. A largely New England force seized it on September 24, 1710, and renamed it Annapolis for the Queen.

Even this token effort was more than Marlborough and Godolphin had planned. Word had reached London in August 1709 of the death of Lord Lovelace, just recently appointed governor-general of New York. Godolphin proposed a new scheme, to finish off Hunter's governorship of Virginia—and perhaps Hunter himself. The lord treasurer wrote to Marlborough that he wanted

> to join the two governments of New York & New England into one, to give these to Coll: Hunter, if you approve the Scheme & the person & to send him thither immediately with instructions to raise about 1500 men in those governments and transport them to Jamaica.[!]

The 'battle plan' for the American militiamen who were to be dragooned into this operation, was to invade the French and Spanish colonies in the West Indies![47]

With New England literally up in arms over the French menace in Canada, Godolphin's murderous plan never got off the ground. Even to the most rabid of the Venetian party, it must have appeared politically deranged. No further details are provided by available sources, but, in a matter of days, Marlborough replied, informing Godolphin that he had approved Hunter's appointment as governor-general *of New York and New Jersey!* Queen Anne informed Hunter she had confirmed it on September 6, 1709, and Hunter accepted.

What had happened? Whether Marlborough and Godolphin fully realized it or not, an in-depth coup was under way against them. Though Sarah Churchill was still in place as their palace guard, the 'secret passages' to the Queen were opening wide to their enemies, and planning was again under way for a new government to be headed by Harley. Within a year, first Sunderland, Churchill's son-in-law, and then Godolphin himself would be out of office, and in 1711 Swift would personally lead the final onslaught against Marlborough.

Godolphin's scheme for dealing with Hunter was judoed beyond anything the plotters could have imagined. When Hunter sailed for America to assume the governorship of New York, he convoyed the largest single migration in our colonial history, nearly 3,000 German settlers from the Rhenish Palatinate, refugees from Marlborough's war in Europe. Armed with both civil and military powers, Hunter was also charged with preparing a full-scale invasion of Canada, to be conducted both by land and sea. And the lieutenant-governorship of Virginia, left vacant by his new appointment, was filled by Alexander Spotswood, who would open the gateway to an American continental republic so wide it would never be closed again.

NOTES

1. Jonathan Swift, *A Tale of a Tub*, in Thomas Sheridan, ed., *The Works of the Reverend Jonathan Swift, D.D.* (24 vols., London, 1803), III, 50–51.

2. *Ibid.*, 51–52.

3. *Ibid.*, 149–150.

4. Jonathan Swift, *The Battle of the Books*, in Sheridan, ed., *Works of Swift*, III, 207–208.

5. *Ibid.*, 217–218.

6. *Ibid.*, 223–224.

7. George Malcolm Thompson, *The First Churchill: The Life of John, 1ˢᵗ Duke of Marlborough* (London, 1979), 16–19, 24–25.

8. Jonathan Swift, *History of the Last Four Years of the Queen,* in Sheridan, ed., *Works of Swift* (London, 1758), VII, 27–28.

9. Edward Gregg, *Queen Anne* (London, 1980), 68–69.

10. Quoted in Gregg, *Queen Anne* (London, 1980), 79.

11. Thompson, *First Churchill,* 76–79.

12. Swift, *History,* 102.

13. Philip Valenti, " The Political Economy of Leibniz' s English Allies" (unpublished ms., 1978).

14. The above account of the bank fight and recoinage scheme is based on the Valenti manuscript.

15. Quoted by Philip Valenti, "The Politics of the Newton-Leibniz Controversy" (unpublished ms., 1977), 43.

16. Quoted by Gregg, *Queen Anne*, 212.

17. *Ibid.*, 211.

18. Falaiseau to Leibniz, March 19, 1706, quoted by Waltraut Fricke, *Leibniz und die englische Sukzession des Hauses Hannover* (Hildesheim, 1957), 64.

19. Jonathan Swift, *Memoirs Relating to the Change in the Queen's Ministry*, in Sheridan, ed., *Works of Swift*, VI, 264.

20. Peter Wentworth to Lord Raby, August 25, 1710, quoted by Gregg, *Queen Anne*, 234.

21. *Ibid.*, 218.

22. *Ibid.*, 226.

23. *Ibid.*, 226–227.

24. This account of the confrontation, based on Godolphin's, is from a letter of Sir John Cropley to the Earl of Shaftesbury, February 19, 1708. Quoted by Gregg, *Queen Anne*, 258–259.

25. Sarah Churchill, "The Character of Princes," 1715, 110.

26. Worthington Ford, ed., *The Diary of Cotton Mather* (2 vols., from Massachusetts Historical Society *Collections*, 7th series, VII–VIII, 1912), I, 600.

27. Quoted by Will and Ariel Durant, *The Age of Louis XIV* (New York, 1963), 709.

28. Jonathan Swift, *The Bickerstaff Papers*, in Louis A. Landa, ed., *Jonathan Swift, Gulliver's Travels and Other Writings* (Boston, 1960), 381.

29. *Ibid.*, 384.

30. *Ibid.*, 384.

31. *Ibid.*, 384.

32. M. MacDermot Crawford, *Madame de Lafayette and her Family* (New York, 1907), 62–63; Alexander Sedgwick, *Jansenism in Seventeenth Century France* (Charlottesville, 1977), 188–192.

33. *Bickerstaff Papers*, 384–386.

34. *Ibid.*, 391.

35. *Ibid.*, 393.

36. Ibid., 393.

37. Ibid., 394.

38. Mary L. Lustig, *Robert Hunter, New York's Augustan Statesman* (Syracuse, 1983), 35–37.

39. Lustig, *Hunter*, 48.

40. *Ibid.*, 37.

41. Swift to Robert Hunter, January 12, 1709, in Harold Williams, ed., *The Correspondence of Jonathan Swift* (5 vols., London, 1963–1965), I, 120.

42. Swift to Hunter, March 22, 1709, *Correspondence*, Williams, ed., I, 132–134.

43. Lustig, *Hunter*, 37.

44. Quoted by David Green, *Queen Anne* (New York, 1970), 190.

45. Green, *Queen Anne*, 184, 213, 213n., 214.

46. Quoted by Green, *Queen Anne*, 214.

47. Lustig, *Hunter*, 59.

5

The Republican Offensive of 1710

While Jonathan Swift and his circle were dramatically reorienting the government of Queen Anne, preparations were under way in America to seize the opportunity for nation-building. America's republican leaders were embarking on a renewed drive to rekindle the sense of moral purpose among its citizens, to accomplish the great and daring task of developing the continent. That world-historic mission, first undertaken by John Winthrop's republican Massachusetts Bay Colony in the 1630s, was about to be resumed after a quarter-century of dwindling away.

In 1710, Cotton Mather published one of the most important books in American history, *Essays to Do Good*, as it was generally titled in editions widely published as late as the 1860s. Its full, original title unfurled the banner of Socrates and Plato, of St. Augustine and Nicholas of Cusa—and of Leibniz, whose associates Mather corresponded with frequently: *Bonifacius, An Essay Upon the Good, that is to be Devised and Designed, by Those Who Desire to Answer the Great End of Life, and to Do Good while They Live.* Published anonymously to reduce the danger of suppression, Mather's book became a rallying cry for the American Revolution—for the task of creating a republic based on natural law, in which each citizen could realize his potential for good, and his immortality, through his contributions to posterity.

As Mather wrote in *Bonifacius*,

> It is an invaluable *honor*, to do *good*; it is an incomparable *pleasure*. A man must look upon himself as *dignified* and *gratified* by God, when

an *opportunity* to do *good* is put into his hands.
He must embrace it with *rapture*, as enabling
him to answer the great End of his being.

Against the decay of Massachusetts since the loss of its
charter, Mather's polemic was clear. "*Government* is
called, the *ordinance* of God," he wrote. Thus "it should
vigorously pursue those noble and blessed *ends* for which it
is *ordained: the good of mankind.*" After years of
corruption in the hands of the Cookes and the "Criminal
Governor" Joseph Dudley (as Mather branded him in a
1707 pamphlet), New Englanders had no trouble
identifying the evil that Mather attacked:

> *Rulers* who make no other use of their higher
> station, than to swagger over their neighbors,
> and command their obsequious flatteries, and
> enrich themselves with the spoils of which they
> are able to pillage them, and then wallow in
> sensual and brutal pleasures; these are, the
> *basest of men.*[1]

The indictment was meant just as clearly for America's
enemies in Britain, the wretched Venetian party led by
Marlborough and Godolphin.

Essays to Do Good was but one of 455 works Mather
published, an astonishing output encompassing religion,
philosophy, politics, economics, physics, astronomy,
botany, the art of singing, and the only comprehensive
medical textbook in America in his time. This particular
little book, cited by Benjamin Franklin as the foremost
influence on his life, was Mather's handbook for organizing
a republican movement. He had already initiated a
network of voluntary associations, toward forming a
political machine to overcome the corruption of official
institutions. In Boston, under such names as "Associated

Families" and "Young Men Associated," Mather nurtured a new political force through his "reforming societies," establishing the model that Franklin subsequently employed in organizing the city of Philadelphia.

Reviewing his activities for the year prior to the publication of *Essays to Do Good*, Mather noted in his diary, "I proposed a Method that every person in the *Reforming Societies*, might be obliged in their Turn, to mention some thing, that be a Proposal of Consequence to the main Intention." The 'main intention' of *Essays to Do Good* was to establish the concept of republican citizenship, even for specific modes of practice, by doctors, lawyers, merchants, clergymen, educators, and family members.   The popularity of the book was undoubtedly enhanced by Mather's humor, including his knack for punning. In one passage he proposes that a good way to begin to do good, is to improve the lives of one's relatives. He then adds, "One great way to prove ourselves *really good* is to be *relatively good*."

Yet there was another, more immediate task which *Essays to Do Good* was designed to promote, revealed in the book's preface, for those who were meant to see it. Mather declares that he is

> very strongly persuaded, there is a day very near at hand, when books of such a tendency as this, will be the most welcome things imaginable, to many thousands of readers, and have more than one edition. *Yea, great will be the army of them that publish them!*

He then adds a most extraordinary statement, which previous historians have routinely ignored:

> A vast variety of *new ways to do good* will be lit upon; *paths* which no fowl of the best flight

at noble designs has yet *known*; and which the
vulture's most piercing eye has not yet seen,
and where the *lions* of the strongest resolution
have never passed.[2]

In 1710, a two-pronged offensive got under way to open
a new path to the West, when New York's Governor Robert
Hunter began preparations to strike at the French Jesuit
"vulture" in Canada, and Governor Alexander Spotswood
of Virginia sent his rangers to find a pass through the Blue
Ridge Mountains, beyond which the British "lion" had
never extended its power, West of the Blue Ridge lay the
Shenandoah Valley, a protected natural highway stretching
to the borders of what became Kentucky and Tennessee—
and still hidden from the "piercing eye" of the Jesuit
command posts of Canada and the Great Lakes.

An American New York

With the arrival of Governor Hunter, New York for the
first time since becoming an English colony in 1664 was no
longer in enemy hands. Its feudal system of land tenure in
the Hudson River valley had served as a barrier to
westward development.   For nearly a decade prior to
Hunter's arrival, the 1701 Anglo-French agreement on
Iroquois neutrality had again permitted the tribes of French
Canada to move freely through northern New York en route
to murderous assaults on New England towns. As might be
expected, New York's colonists had not fared well under
such administrations either.

From 1701 to 1708, the combined governments of New
York and New Jersey had been in the hands of one of
Marlborough's longtime allies, Lord Cornbury, described
by one historian as "a drunkard, a spendthrift, a sexual
pervert, a grafter, and a vain fool."[3] Though today's New
Yorkers are accustomed to perverts in high places, it was

then considered a bit much to have a transvestite for governor. Local citizens were shocked to discover him parading on the porch of his New Jersey home in women's clothing, even on the morning of his wife's funeral! The New York assembly watched £1,500, appropriated for the colony's defense, go instead to build a "pleasure palace" for sexual perversion on Nutten (now Governor's) Island. Upon Cornbury's removal from office by Queen Anne in 1708, the Council of New Jersey gave thanks for "her princely care in putting an end to the worst administration New Jersey ever knew."[4] When Hunter arrived in 1710, Cornbury was in debtors' prison in Manhattan, now sporting the Dutch fashions still popular among the island's women. Hunter paid off the remaining £200 of Cornbury's debts and packed him off to London, where he assumed his place in the House of Lords as the Earl of Clarendon and worked feverishly against Hunter's administration.[5]

Governor Hunter came with plans for bringing much more than a breath of fresh air to the colonies in his charge. The ten ships in his convoy bearing German Palatine refugees added population equaling nearly half the size of New York City at the time. Hunter himself had officially proposed their mass migration, which would also end their months of suffering in refugee camps in England. The Junto accepted the plans, but added the provision that the Palatines be put to work producing British naval stores, to repay the costs of resettling them. Hunter nonetheless intended them to help break the feudal grip of the Hudson Valley landowners and open New York's route to the West: the Mohawk River passage through the mountains west of Albany, leading to the shore of Lake Ontario. Hunter planned to implement Queen Anne's prototype "Homestead Act," by giving each Palatine immigrant forty acres of land, free from taxes and quitrents for seven years, if they would settle the areas leading to the West.

Any success for such a scheme depended, of course, on putting an end to the danger of Indian raids from French Canada. The Godolphin ministry by 1709 was losing its hold on Queen Anne, and his proposal to use Hunter for a New York-New England assault on the West Indies had fallen flat.   Hunter, then in close contact with Jonathan Swift, followed up with a proposal to Secretary of State Sunderland, Marlborough's son-in-law, drily noting something he had learned while Marlborough had left him in prison in France. Hunter reported that he had "heard some of good sense and Interest at that Court Say that Canada was no otherways worth their care than it was a thorn in our Side." Hunter therefore proposed a strong attack against Canada from New York and New England, backed by a major British expeditionary force, which he believed "might meet with a prosperous Issue."[6] Queen Anne approved. Hunter was given personal command of New York's 400-man garrison of British troops, and a captaincy of one of the colony's four militia companies. He was also granted authority to draft two additional companies, each one hundred men strong, to be supplied with British arms and ammunition.   Imagine the joy in New York, among Lord Cornbury's opponents, in having a real defense budget, instead of having appropriations stolen for a palace of sexual perversions. But there was no joy in Marlborough's camp. The captain general of the British army had demanded in 1709 that Queen Anne confirm his rank as supreme commander for life. He had done his utmost to crush Robert Hunter, ever since his former colonel had exposed his military incompetence at Ramillies in 1706. Yet the commission from Queen Anne, granted to Hunter before he sailed for America, appointed him governor-in-chief and *captain general* of New York and New Jersey. The expedition against Canada was initially set for the spring of 1710, and Hunter completed his military preparations in England by February.[7]

While Hunter made ready, Marlborough was in England, during the usual winter recess of his military campaigns in Europe. The timetable for the Canadian expedition was again set back, just as the Allied invasion of Europe during World War II was repeatedly delayed by Sir Winston Churchill, Marlborough's admiring heir. Queen Anne was increasingly determined to remove her captain general, yet just as strongly wanted arrangements to end the war in place before doing so. She now undertook a series of moves to attain both objectives, and worked privately with Robert Harley toward forming a government-in-the-wings to implement the peace.

Politically, the moment was ripe. The Venetian party's financial swindle of England had produced growing suffering among the population as a whole, which worsened under the awful costs of war. On top of soaring taxes, declining trade, and a dwindling supply of specie, grain prices in London reached an all-time high by January 1710. Economic collapse had all but stifled the organized cheering for Marlborough's supposed military victories. Herding more and more unwilling subjects into the army, for his repeatedly stagnating campaigns, had added to popular resentment; and his gargantuan, personal profiteering from the war left an open flank which Swift would soon attack.

Queen Anne's moves against Marlborough were worked out secretly with Harley, though not without some difficulty, as Swift informs us, with the "duchess of Marlborough, by her emissaries, watching all the avenues to the back stairs." Harley persuaded the Queen that "she ought gradually to lessen the exorbitant power of the duke and duchess of Marlborough, and the earl of Godolphin, by taking the disposition of employments into her own hands," thus breaking the patronage machine that had been so politically and financially lucrative for them. "Her majesty, pursuant to Mr. Harley's advice, resolved to dispose of the first great employment that fell, according to her own pleasure, without consulting any of her ministers."[8]

That opportunity was first presented on January 10, 1710, with the death of the Earl of Essex, who held both the lieutenancy of the Tower of London and a regimental colonel's command. Swift reports, "It was agreed between the queen and Mr. Harley," that Lord Rivers, one of Harley's closest allies, "should go immediately to the duke of Marlborough" to seek his endorsement for lieutenant of the tower. Expecting to settle the matter privately with the Queen, Marlborough replied he had no objections. When the duke took his own recommendation for the post to Queen Anne on January 13, she informed him she had already appointed Rivers, who had assured her that Marlborough "had no objection to him."[9]

No sooner was the outraged Marlborough out the door, than Anne also sent him a written order to appoint Abigail Masham's brother, Captain John Hill, to Essex's other command as colonel of a regiment. Sir Winston Churchill, in his 1930s biographical attempt to deify his ancestor, wrote, "It was obvious that an insult of the most carefully studied character was intended by the Queen's secret advisers."[10] Though Marlborough did block this particular appointment for Hill, Queen Anne drove home her point further by promoting him to brigadier general, and by adding Abigail's husband, Samuel Masham, to the list of colonels. Marlborough then angrily ordered Robert Walpole to strike both names from his list of promotions presented to the Queen.

Queen Anne did not draw back. She ordered Marlborough to Holland, to attend peace negotiations between the Dutch and the French—a vital step toward ending Britain's own decade-long involvement in the war.

She flatly rejected a speech, prepared for her by Godolphin, praising Marlborough "as God Almighty's chief instrument of my glory[!]" Upon her refusal, Godolphin complained that she must be guided by "secret advisers." Marlborough's son-in-law, Secretary of State Sunderland, wrote him in February warning that "none of our heads is safe, if we can't get the better of what I am sure Mrs. Morley [Queen Anne] designs.[11]

That same month, Hunter made a farewell visit to Queen Anne to discuss the governorship he was about to assume for New York and New Jersey. Marlborough's power to undo his mission was waning, and Sunderland's concerns proved accurate. With Marlborough out of the country, Hunter sailed for America on April 10. On June 14, the day Hunter landed in New York, Sunderland was forced to resign as secretary of state. Marlborough was also forced to yield in June on the military commissions for Masham and Hill. In 1711, General Hill would command the British army regulars deployed for the attack on Quebec, which his friend Robert Hunter was preparing for.[12]

Upon arriving in New York, Hunter was greeted by the city's leaders and its militia, and led them in marching order to what was then Fort Anne at Battery Park. There his commission from the Queen as captain general and governor-in-chief was read to the assembled public. His first concern was for the convoy of Palatine immigrants he had brought to the New World, many of whom had begun the voyage sick and malnourished from their internment in England. During the two-month voyage, 470 of the 2,814 who sailed with Hunter had died. He seized the island Governor Cornbury had used for his palace of perversions and built temporary homes and hospitals to care for the Palatines. Anticipating that British military backing for a strike against Canada would soon be ordered, Hunter made plans to resettle them in forward positions for opening the West.

The first site he chose was near present Schoharie, about thirty miles west of Albany along the Schoharie River, which flows north from there into the Mohawk—the natural highway to western New York and the Great Lakes —at a point still named Fort Hunter. The scheme was abandoned, however, because of the requirement that the Palatines initially produce naval stores—ship's masts and spars, pitch and tar, from pine trees, which were too scarce along the Schoharie. In late September 1710, the Palatines were instead settled along the Hudson River, about one hundred miles north of New York City, on the west bank near the present town of Catskill, and on the east near present Hudson.

Not all New Yorkers welcomed their new governor, nor his plans for opening the colony's western lands to settlement.   The New York City merchant oligarchy and the great landowners of the Hudson Valley were the political combine which had sustained Lord Cornbury. They now threw their weight in the Assembly against Hunter, on everything from paying his salary to the collection of public fees.   They also blocked a naturalization bill Hunter proposed to enable the Palatines to enjoy the colony's legal and voting rights, even though many other European-born immigrants desired it as well. Governor Hunter was taking on the same New York forces, which bitterly hated the republicanism of New England, and had worked long and hard to contain the influence of such leading figures as Cotton Mather.

Mather himself made a good-humored reference to their common problem, in one of his letters to Hunter during the governor's early years in New York. Hunter had printed a piece written by Mather, to intervene in a New York political fight, which had omitted the standard salutations for referring to a governor. Mather told Hunter that he had done so only out of regard for

Your Excellency's repose, inasmuch as your *Cornburian* crew might improve it unto your disadvantage for Your Excellency to have been known corresponding with a person of my well-known circumstances. And indeed, besides Your Excellency I am not aware of any one person in your city whom I can suppose to have any other sentiments of me but such as are full of contempt, and the greatest aversion.[13]

Hunter's own problems in establishing his political authority proved far greater than he anticipated. The difficulties of colonial service included delays of four months or more in communicating back and forth with London. Whatever the developments there, most of the burden rested on his shoulders. Sometimes the news was worth the wait. On August 8, 1710, Lord Treasurer Sidney Godolphin, bankrupter of Britain and bankroller of Marlborough's endless wars, was forced to resign when Queen Anne demanded he return his staff of office. In an infantile rage, Godolphin broke the staff instead, and threw it into the fireplace.

Jonathan Swift, old "Isaac Bickerstaff," could not resist sticking the knife a little deeper into the ancient oligarchical enemy. He wrote a poem, anonymously circulated as a political broadside, entitled "The Virtues of Sid Hamet the Magician's Rod." Deftly deflating "our great magician, Hamet Sid," Swift presented him as the ludicrous heir of the evil cult of the Magi:

> Sid's brethren of the conjuring tribe
>
> A circle with their rod describe,
>
> Which proves a magical redoubt,
>
> To keep mischievous spirits out:

Sid's rod was of a larger stride,

And made a circle thrice as wide;

Where spirits thronged with hideous din,

And he stood there to take them in.

But, when the enchanted rod was broke,

They vanished in a stinking smoke.[14]

Nearly all of the Venetian party's leaders vanished with Godolphin, when on September 20 Queen Anne dissolved Parliament and ordered new elections, which produced a landslide against the Junto.

Against the oligarchy, however, real political war fighting has only partly to do with elections, especially in countries without republican institutions. In Hunter's case, though buffered by distance from his enemies in Britain, he could still expect no miracles. His project to make the Palatine Germans pioneers of New York's westward development was unacceptable to his opponents on both sides of the Atlantic, and they made no effort to conceal the fact. In late 1710, Hunter was already looking beyond the period of the Palatines' indentured service for producing naval stores. To sustain them during the period required to clear and settle new lands on the frontier, Hunter requested a budget of £15,000 per year for 1711 and 1712. When Britain's Board of Trade took up his proposal in January 1711, the fact that Harley's new ministry was in power had little effect.

The board solicited the "opinion" of the transvestite Lord Cornbury, the deposed New York governor who now paraded as the Earl of Clarendon. Cornbury not only opposed the appropriations Hunter had requested; he recommended canceling the entire Palatine project, declaring that they should simply be sent out to fend for themselves. Even though Cornbury's scheme must have been appealing in its genocidal simplicity, the Board of Trade felt politically compelled to endorse Hunter's request, especially since it cost them no more than the gesture. No additional British government funds were ever expended on the Palatines, even though their migration to New York was undertaken as government policy. They were sustained instead out of Hunter's own pocket, at an expense of over £21,000.[15]

A few years later, following Queen Anne's death and George I's accession to the throne, Hunter wrote of his difficulties to the new secretary of state, Joseph Addison. Swift and Addison had repeatedly crossed paths as literary propagandists before 1710, and then broke when Addison continued to champion the Junto Whigs. In a diplomatic letter strengthened by a personal touch, Hunter assured Addison that generally he had

> suffered beyond the force of human nature without having received the least answer to my enumerable complaints during the whole course of the last administration.   Tho' your old acquaintance the Tale of a Tub [Swift] who it seems had power with the ruin'd faction [under Queen Anne] was pleased to interpose in my favour. . . .[16]

Not only Hunter's Palatine project, but his governorship itself was under attack from the outset. As the correspondence between Cotton Mather and Hunter suggests, the new governor did not undertake his assignment without benefit of some political map of the territory. He began even in 1710 to build a political machine against the "Cornburian crew," recruiting from among its enemies an important ally in Lewis Morris, who had been driven from his post as a New Jersey councillor.

Born in New York City in 1671, Morris was the son of a captain in Cromwell's army, and had inherited 2,000 acres in Westchester County, New York, as well as 3,500 in Monmouth County, New Jersey. With the downfall of the Godolphin ministry in London, Hunter pressed the Board of Trade to restore Morris to the New Jersey Council. Hunter soon urged Morris to run for the New York Assembly as well, and he was elected in 1710 as representative from Westchester.   In 1715, Hunter appointed him chief justice of the New York Supreme Court.[17]

Hunter's efforts to enhance his political control over the colony were also spurred by the coming expedition against Canada. At Albany, he met with leaders of the Iroquois and the Algonquins, seeking their participation in the attack. The year 1711 began with still no word from London; in Boston, Cotton Mather noted in his diary fears of "a destructive Invasion from the French."[18]

Virginia: The Second Front

While Governor Hunter made his political and military preparations in New York, the crucial second front in the republican offensive for America was established in Virginia.   On June 10, 1710, a few days before Hunter landed in New York, Alexander Spotswood sailed into Hampton Roads at the mouth of the James River, bringing little more than his commission from Queen Anne, as the Earl of Orkney's lieutenant-governor of Virginia. At the age of thirty-three, he already had behind him a sixteen-year career in the military, earning the permanent rank of colonel. He was also a *commander*, of the highest order, and a true pioneer, whose dedication to America's development over the next thirty years molded a whole generation of nation-builders.   Without him, a successful American Revolution would be hard to imagine.

The Virginia colony in 1710 was, quite simply, a disaster area. Its intensely rural, backward, stagnant society was by 1700 entirely dominated by production of a single, soil-depleting crop—tobacco. Tobacco-growing's enormous consumption of land and cheap labor reinforced an oligarchical system of control, dominated by the large plantations of the coastal tidewater lands, worked increasingly by black African slaves. Of the American colonies in 1710, Virginia had the largest population, over 78,000, but outranked Massachusetts only by the inclusion of 23,000 slaves in that figure. Over the previous thirty years, Virginia's "free" population had increased by a total of only thirty-five percent, while the number of slaves increased by 670 percent! The colony had no industries, no cities, and almost no towns, even around its numerous coastal and riverfront loading sites for shipping its tobacco. Public education—three-quarters of a century old in Massachusetts—was unknown in Virginia. What little there was of private education was generally restricted to the sons of wealthy planters, and usually conducted by itinerant tutors of dubious competence.

Though Virginia's earlier colonists had included some with republican aspirations, such hopes were virtually extinct by the time Spotswood became governor. The death knell had been sounded in 1676, as a result of Bacon's Rebellion. That wretched, anarchist uprising—still celebrated by most American historians as a prelude to the American Revolution— was led by Nathaniel Bacon, an oligarchical landholder whose lineage traced to Sir Francis Bacon, the occult-worshiping enemy of the English Renaissance. The Virginia Bacon, while pretending to champion the settlers and small landholders who had pushed inland from the Tidewater, was opposed to any further development of the frontier. His so-called remedy established the model that the British oligarchy repeatedly used against America's westward development until the end of the nineteenth century. Bacon launched murderous attacks on the Indian tribes with whom Virginia had peaceful relations, to ensure their hostility to frontier settlers. Then, in the ensuing bloodbath, he turned the settlers against the 'corrupt' and 'indifferent' colonial government, for failing to protect them! Bacon's supposed contributions to America's democratic tradition culminated in his leading a rebel mob to burn the colonial capital at Jamestown to the ground.

Bacon's opponents left a far greater legacy. Among them was Colonel Thomas Fairfax, cousin to the father of Lord Thomas Fairfax. Lord Fairfax became the republican developer of Virginia's Northern Neck Proprietary, and lived to see the British defeated at Yorktown in 1781. Another of Bacon's foes was John Washington, the great-grandfather of the first commander-in-chief of the United States.

No such promise for the future was identifiable when Spotswood arrived in 1710. Yet the hopes of America's colonies under British rule depended entirely on Virginia, whose acknowledged colonial boundaries extended on the south all the way to the Mississippi River, which bounded its western line northward through Minnesota, and back along the Great Lakes to the western border of Pennsylvania. This awesome expanse, encompassing all the land west of Virginia through Kentucky, and virtually the entirety of what President George Washington would later designate as the Northwest Territories, offered enormous opportunities for development.

But to think in those terms, in the oligarchical mud-hole of Virginia in 1710, went far beyond the bounds of common sense. Virginia's claims were acknowledged by the oligarchy because they existed only on paper. The ruling planters of the Tidewater lost little sleep thinking of a wilderness stretching more than a thousand miles away, when their subjects were confined to within fifty miles of the coast. Within generally one hundred miles of that constricted frontier, the supposedly "impenetrable" line of the Blue Ridge Mountains ended all prospects for western colonialization—at least in the minds of slumbering planters. Spotswood's arrival was a rude awakening.

Spotswood had a clearly defined mission in mind. He intended to break the oligarchy's financial and political control over the colony, create a citizenry committed to developing Virginia's vast potential, generate real industrial and agricultural production, establish a functioning militia and system of defense, and push the frontiers of settlement all the way to the Mississippi and the Great Lakes! Had he announced plans to put a man on the moon, he could hardly have more astounded Virginia's degenerate elite.

Governor Spotswood wasted no time before signaling his intentions. He convened a meeting of the Council, a ruling body of twelve men appointed by the crown, though usually on recommendation of the governor. The Council liked to play House of Lords as against Virginia's "Commons," the elected House of Burgesses. The Council was completely dominated by the leading oligarchical families—the Byrds, the Carters, the Blairs, the Ludwells. The Byrd then ruling the roost, William Byrd II, in fact had sought the governorship for himself before Spotswood's appointment, and would so again. Spotswood presented his commission from Queen Anne, designating "our trusty and well beloved Alexander Spotswood" to govern the colony for "our right trusty and right well beloved cousin George Earl of Orkney." He then submitted the list of council members confirmed by the Queen. Lo and behold, it contained only eleven names; William Byrd's was missing. Pending "clarification" from London, the other members added Byrd provisionally; but Spotswood had made his point.[19]

In his first legislative session, in the fall of 1710, Spotswood dropped a bombshell. For the members of the House of Burgesses, representing the freeholders of their districts in typically a feeble show of opposition to the great planters, their first encounter with their new governor was memorable indeed.   The gossip radiating from Williamsburg had already spread some colorful stories, including one about the cannon-ball Spotswood brought to Virginia which had shattered his ribs and collarbone at the Battle of Blenheim.[20] But nothing matched the impact of what the governor now proposed: legislation destroying Virginia's oligarchical system of land tenure, and making the *cultivation* of new lands a legal requirement for ownership.

Spotswood's unprecedented scheme struck at one of the oligarchy's main barriers against the development of Virginia's frontiers. During the 1690s, Virginia's "land rights" system had been revised along lines that might have been designed by today's World Wildlife Fund, appropriately headed by Britain's Prince Philip. The policy was prescribed then by Governor Edmund Andros, the former would-be dictator of New England, overthrown in 1689 in a coup led by Cotton Mather, and reassigned by William of Orange to Virginia. Though royal revenues from colonial lands were based on "quitrents" paid by persons granted title to the land, Andros permitted speculators to gobble up tracts as large as 20,000 acres— *and pay no quitrents if the land remained wild!*

Not surprisingly, during the 1690s Virginia's free population actually declined. Hundreds of thousands of acres were kept forcibly undeveloped. Speculators like William Byrd and Robert "King" Carter bought up vast

Boundaries of Virginia's Colonial Claims

The full extent of Virginia's original grant of 1609 included most of what is the United States today, at a time when nearly all of the territory was unknown in England. This visionary paper claim, however, proved materially important to Virginia's leading role in breaking through the eastern chain of the Appalachian and Allegheny Mountains. It provided a legal basis for Governor Alexander Spotswood's proposals, beginning in 1710, to extend Virginia's settlements west to the Mississippi River and north to lake Erie. Given Spotswood's nation-building momentum, the Virginians who followed him laid the basis for a continental republic: George Washington, from the Ohio River to Lake Erie, during the French and Indian War, George Rogers Clark, to Kentucky and Illinois as far as the Mississippi, during the American Revolution; William Clark (the younger brother) and Merriwether Lewis, from the Mississippi to the Pacific Ocean, after Secretary of State James Monroe negotiated the Louisiana Purchase in 1803.

When George Washington became the first President of the United States in 1789, the state of Virginia included all of present Kentucky and West Virginia. The states of Illinois and Indiana were first organized, like Kentucky, as counties of Virginia, by its militia during the American Revolution. Virginia's claims north of the Ohio River, between the Mississippi and the Great lakes, were ceded to the new American government in 1784, and then became the Northwest Territory. The Northwest Ordinance of 1787 ensured the development of the entire region, which produced the additional states of Ohio, Michigan, Wisconsin, and the eastern half of Minnesota. Approximately 55 million Americans live within those boundaries today, nearly one fourth of the United States population.

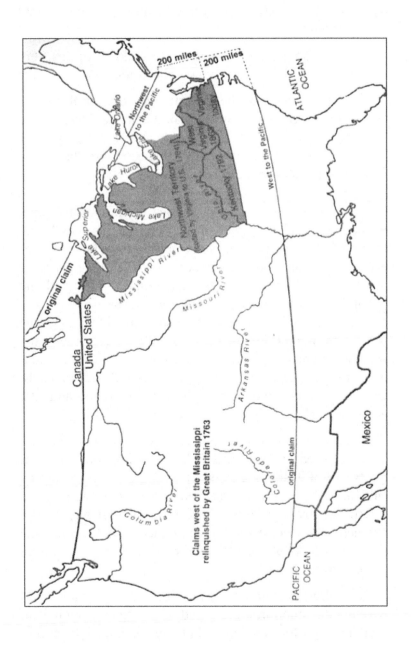

tracts of wilderness, and key river frontages, forcing settlers deep into the colony's unprotected frontiers if they would have any land at all.

Spotswood presented measures to undo all of this. On December 8, 1710, he issued a proclamation

> to the End that the Industrious Poor of this Colony & others who Shall Come to Dwell here may not want Land whereon to Imploy their Industry whilst others possess more than they are able to Cultivate.

Citing his royal instructions from Queen Anne, Spotswood declared that future land grants would be restricted to tracts that were to be cultivated. Three acres of every fifty would have to be planted within three years, or the land would revert to the government. To end the oligarchical practice of removing vast areas of land from any prospect of development, he also decreed that no grants would be issued for more than 400 acres, unless the applicant personally satisfied the governor that he could improve a larger tract. Finally, he declared that all lands, cultivated or not, would be subject to quitrents, and title would be forfeited if payments were three years in arrears.

The quitrent provisions passed the assembly, despite opposition led by William Byrd. From London, however, the Board of Trade overruled Spotswood's plan to enforce cultivation by executive fiat, and ordered that the issue be determined by legislation. The bill which finally passed retained the cultivation requirement, but with the significant loophole that it could be met simply by turning cattle onto the land.[21]

Toward establishing a productive economy which could develop the interior, Spotswood also began planning an iron industry for Virginia. Initially he hoped to secure

legislative backing and subsidies for iron manufacturing—
as John Winthrop, Jr., had done during the early years of
the Massachusetts republic. By September 1710, he was
energetically putting his case forward, as William Byrd
noted in his secret diary.[22] Before the fall session of the
assembly convened, Spotswood had also begun touring the
colony to inspect and drill its militia, which he found to be
utterly unprepared for combat. That too he determined to
change.

Governor Spotswood's official correspondence during
1710 confirms that he came to Virginia in full knowledge
and expectation of the ongoing coup against the
Marlborough regime, which Swift and Harley had
launched. Word reached him in December that Lord
Dartmouth had replaced Sunderland, Marlborough's son-in-
law, as secretary of state in Queen Anne's reorganized
cabinet. Spotswood replied to Dartmouth, "It is with great
Satisfaction that I am able to acknowledge the honor of
your Lordship's of the 31st of July last, which brought me
the agreeable news of your Lordship's promotion to the
office of Secretary of State."[23] With this happy
confirmation, Spotswood wrote the same day to the Board
of Trade, laying out his plans for conquering the West.

Mindful of the plans for an expedition against Canada,
Spotswood presented his argument in terms of military
necessity:

> Whereas the French are endeavouring to settle a
> communication between Canada and their late
> Settlements on [the lower] Mississippi by way
> of the [Great] Lakes, our people would, by
> pushing on their settlements in one straight
> Line along the banks of James River, be able to
> cut off that communication and fix themselves
> so strongly there that it would not be in the

> power of the French to dislodge them,
> especially considering how much further they
> must travel than we to come at the place.

Imagine how astounding this proposal seemed in its time, for a colony which had not developed its interior as far as the Blue Ridge, let alone the Appalachians and Alleghenies, to extend its settlements through hundreds of miles of uncharted wilderness, all the way to the banks of the Mississippi River! Yet Spotswood proposed this massive undertaking, with a full system of fortifications as well.

He also reported his own preliminary feasibility study. That all this could be done, he told the Board of Trade,

> seems to be manifest by the Discoverys which I
> have encouraged to be made this fall by a
> Company of Adventurers, who found the
> Mountains not above a hundred miles from our
> Upper Inhabitants, and went up to the top of the
> highest Mountain with their Horses, tho' they
> had hitherto been thought to be unpassable, and
> they assured me that the descent on the other
> side seemed to be as easy as that they had
> passed on this, and that they could have passed
> over the whole Ledge (which is not large) if the
> season of the year had not been too far
> advanced before they set out on that
> Expedition.

In this same letter, Governor Spotswood reported that he had already put his proposals for iron manufacturing before the House of Burgesses. But their narrow economic thinking, enveloped in a cloud of tobacco smoke, and the hostility of the Tidewater oligarchy, had blocked his scheme for public support of the enterprise. Given the change in the Queen's ministry, he now appealed for direct assistance from the crown:

> [My original] design did not meet with the countenance which was expected from the House of Burgesses, it being the temper of the people here never to favor an Undertaking unless they can see a particular advantage arising to themselves, and these Iron Mines, lying only at the Falls of James River, the rest of the Country did not apprehend any benefit they should reap thereby.

Like the American System which the Revolution would later establish, Spotswood's plan called for directing public revenues into projects promoting the general welfare. He asked the Board to consider

> whether it might not turn to good account if her Majesty would be pleased to take that work into her own hands, sending over workmen and materials for carrying it on, and imploying therein the Revenue of Quitrents which would be a sufficient fund to bring it to perfection.[24]

Just three days earlier, Spotswood had celebrated his thirty-fourth birthday by treating the members of the Virginia Council to a party. In just six months, he had moved Virginia into a role on the center stage of world history. His uneasy Council members were not in a position to fully appreciate what was unfolding, but William Byrd, for one, had already begun recording strange dreams in his diary:

> I dreamed last night that the lightning almost put out my eyes, that I won a ton of money and might win more if I had ventured, [and] that I was great with my Lord Marlborough.[25]

The Republican Offensive in Britain

Jonathan Swift returned to England at the end of August 1710, after a stay in Ireland of sixteen months. During the month following his return, Queen Anne and Robert Harley worked jointly to clean out the rest of the Godolphin ministry. The Queen's proclamation dissolving Parliament was issued on September 20, and most of the Whig ministers resigned the following day.[26] The resulting elections, as Harley expected, smashed the power of the Junto. Harley and the Queen next concentrated their efforts on reducing the Duke of Marlborough's control over the army, and on getting rid of the evil Duchess of Marlborough.

That same month, Secretary of War Adam de Cardonnel, who was also Marlborough's personal secretary, was replaced by George Granville, an open enemy of the duke. Three more Marlborough protégés—Generals George Maccartney, Thomas Meredith, and Philip Honeywood— were dismissed by Queen Anne in December for damning the new ministry while drinking public toasts.[27] Even more devastating was the barrage of public ridicule trained on Marlborough by Jonathan Swift, now serving as the chief polemical propagandist of Harley's new government.

The ousted Junto was still pinning its hopes for a return to power on Marlborough's supposedly indispensable position as captain general of the army. The Junto's own scribblers had been busy denouncing the Queen's change in ministers as a monstrous show of ingratitude toward Britain's great hero. In the November 23 issue of *The Examiner*, the official newspaper of the Harley government, Swift shattered that ploy once and for all:

> If a stranger should hear these furious outcries
> of ingratitude against our general, without
> knowing the particulars, he would be apt to

enquire where was his tomb, or whether he
were allowed Christian burial, not doubting but
we had put him to some ignominious death. . .
. as the prince seized on his estate, and left him
to starve?. . . Have neither honours, offices,
nor grants, been conferred on him or his
family?. . . Is it not at the same time notorious
to the whole kingdom, that nothing but a tender
regard to the general was able to preserve that
ministry so long, until neither God nor man
could suffer their continuance?[28]

Swift proceeded to draw up a comparison, in equivalent
monies, of the costs of a typical 'triumph' rewarding a
conquering Roman general, with the grants, salaries, and
rewards bestowed on the Duke of Marlborough, mentioning
"nothing which hath not been given in the face of the
world." The resulting "Bill of Roman Gratitude" (£4.10
"for frankincense and earthen pots to burn it," £8 for "a bull
for sacrifice," £500 for "a triumphal arch," etc.) came to
£994 and 11 shillings. The "Bill of British Ingratitude"
(£200,000 expended so far on Blenheim Palace, £100,000
for "employments," £60,000 for "pictures, jewels, &c.")
came to £540,000.

Here is a good deal above half a million of
money, and I dare say, those who are loudest
with the clamour of ingratitude will readily own
that all this is but a trifle in comparison with
what is untold.[29]

The outraged Duchess of Marlborough complained that
"to be printed & cry'd about the country for a common
cheat & pickpocket is too much for human nature to
bear."[30] Her response was typically "Churchillian." She
threatened to blackmail the Queen, by publishing old

personal letters from Anne from the time she had been under Sarah's sway, including one from 1702 promising the duchess an annual pension of £2,000. Sarah demanded payment for the last nine years, totaling £18,000. After two weeks of deliberation, Anne consented— but on January 17, 1711, she rejected a personal appeal from the duke to let Sarah retain her offices. He grudgingly surrendered her gold key the next day. In the end, Sarah Churchill proved to be a rather *un*common cheat; one modern historian has calculated that she pocketed "£32,800 above and beyond her normal salary and prerequisites."[31] In a final display of her "ungovernable rage," as Swift once put it, she stripped her apartments in St. James's Palace of every fixture she could remove, down to the mantelpieces and the doorknobs!

Disposing of the Duke of Marlborough was still complicated by the delicate nature of the Queen's private negotiations for a peace with France. Since the beginning of 1710, French republican circles had been continually informed of the ongoing coup against the Marlborough-Godolphin regime, through the Abbé François Gaultier, a Catholic priest who served as the London agent for the Marquis de Torcy, the nephew of Jean-Baptiste Colbert.[32] It had been through the surviving political circles of Colbert, the former nation-building policymaker for Louis XIV, and leading patron of the young Leibniz, that Leibniz and Swift ran their 1708–1709 "Bickerstaff" operation.[33] Through Gaultier, Harley had begun peace negotiations for Anne with de Torcy, even before Godolphin's dismissal in August 1710.

Against these efforts, Marlborough continued to work for war at any price. As Swift wrote to Esther Johnson ("Stella"), his great love and confidante in Dublin,

He is covetous as Hell, and ambitious as the Prince of it: he would fain have been general for life, and has broken all endeavours for Peace, to keep his greatness and get money. He told the queen, he was neither covetous nor ambitious.   She said, if she could have conveniently turned about, she would have laughed, and could hardly forbear it in his face.[34]

Though Queen Anne was rid of Sarah, nearly a year was to pass before she removed Marlborough from command—and then only after Swift's devastating indictment of Marlborough's plotting to prolong the war, with his pamphlet *The Conduct of the Allies* (1711).   In the meantime, Swift joined the innermost circles of Harley's counsels, working to bring what political coherence he could, to the pragmatically compromised coalition of the new ministry.

Ostensibly as an emissary of the Church of Ireland, Swift had begun meeting with Harley in October 1710, on roughly a weekly basis, seeking improved funding for the church's operations. Far more important issues, however, soon dominated their discussions. Harley assured him, "That it should be his particular care, to establish me here in England, and represent me to the queen as a person they could not be without."   Besides serving as the new ministry's leading propagandist, Swift was informed by Harley "that he had other and greater occasions for me."[35] By December, Swift was attending the weekly meetings of Harley's 'kitchen cabinet':

It was Mr. Harley's custom, every Saturday, that four or five of his most intimate friends, among those he had taken in upon the great change made at court, should dine at his house;

and after about two months acquaintance, I had the honor always to be one of the number. This company, at first, consisted only of the lord keeper Harcourt, the earl Rivers, the earl of Peterborough, Mr. secretary St. John, and myself; and here, after dinner, they used to discourse, and settle matters of great importance.[36]

The plain truth that Swift operated at the center of policy making during the Harley ministry is voluminously documented. His own correspondence, *Memoirs, Journal to Stella, and History of the Last Four Years of the Queen* are among the major repositories of first-hand accounts of the inside workings of Queen Anne's government, during especially the years 1710–1713. Swift's role is extensively corroborated by the writings and correspondence of other leading principals of the time: Robert Harley himself, Henry St. John, Erasmus Lewis, John Arbuthnot, Samuel and Abigail Masham, Sir William Wyndham, Lord Peterborough, Lady Orkney, John Gay, and Alexander Pope, to name a few. Swift's political prominence is beyond question. His enemies at the time raised a constant hue and cry over it; yet their heirs among the oligarchy's historical and "literary" apologists hysterically deny it.

What dark secret is supposed to die, concerning Swift's life as he really lived it? Why are the vast majority of his works, among the greatest in the English language, not even in print today? Why, indeed, are *all* the other reigns from Henry VIII through Queen Victoria, better known than the reign of Queen Anne? On one level, some of the answers lie in simply turning these questions around: If Swift and his allies had not existed, what would have stood in the way of a complete triumph for Marlborough and the Venetian party—and of the defeat of America's republican hopes?   Or step back to consider the standard accounts of an earlier battle, during the English Civil War, and ask why so little attention is paid to the fact, that the secretary of state for the republican Commonwealth, was the great poet John Milton.

From this standpoint, it becomes clear why Swift's role simply as an "insider" of Queen Anne's government, has so continuously alarmed his oligarchical opponents.   That such a principled man of reason, should ever get so close to making policy for the British monarchy, is bad enough. That his republican energies helped promote the founding of the United States, is even worse!   That he was operating beyond the bounds of mere politics is certain.

Swift's Fight for Republican Culture

Swift had long made his broader purposes known.   As early as 1696–1697, when he wrote *A Tale of a Tub* and *The Battle of the Books*, he had gone to war against the cult of the Venetian 'Enlightenment,' against the denial of human reason being imposed by Descartes and Locke. With the allied efforts of Leibniz's circles in Europe, Swift's return to London in 1710 signaled a major offensive against oligarchical policies—and, inseparably, a stepped-up fight for republican culture.

Swift set up his command post that September at the Smyrna Coffee House, on the north side of Pall Mall, appropriately opposite Marlborough House.   The Smyrna was a political hotbed.   A small notice had appeared the year before in the *Tatler*, one of the papers of the time funded by the Duke of Marlborough, inviting all those desiring "to be instructed in the noble sciences of music, poetry, and politics" to repair to the Smyrna.[37]   Before Swift began his meetings with Harley, he revived Isaac Bickerstaff, his fictional correspondent with Leibniz from 1708, in the pages of the *Tatler* of September 28.

Bickerstaff was now pleased to publish an anonymous letter addressed to him, urging that something be done about the "continual corruption of the English tongue . . . by the false refinements of twenty years past."[38] It was a call to arms against the degradation of the English language under the Venetian 'Enlightenment' ushered in with William of Orange. It was an opening salvo against such notorious cultural degenerates as the members of the Kit Kat Club, the treasonous Bank of England's 'literary' project to turn out 'educated' men as babbling idiots. The Kit Kat's luminaries included Ambassador to Venice Charles Montagu, the Duke of Marlborough, and Sir William Temple, one of the targets of Swift's *Battle of the Books*.

The anonymous appeal to Bickerstaff begins:

> There are some abuses among us of great consequence, the reformation of which is properly your province; although as far as I have been conversant in your papers, you have not yet considered them.   These are the deplorable ignorance that for some years hath reigned among our English writers, the great depravity of our taste, and the continual corruption of our style.

As an example of the "late refinements crept into our language," the writer encloses a letter from "a most accomplished person in this way of writing," which begins:

> SIR, I *cou'dn't* get the things you sent for all *about Town.—I thot to ha'* come down myself, and then *I'd ha' bro't 'um;* but I *ha'n't don't,* and I believe I *can't do't,* that's *pozz—*

Bickerstaff's correspondent asks, "If a man of wit, who died forty years ago, were to rise from the grave on purpose, how would he be able to read this letter? And after he got through that difficulty, how would he be able to understand it?"[39]

In 1711, Swift published his *Proposal for Correcting, Enlarging, and Ascertaining the English Tongue*, modeled in method on Leibniz's earlier treatise, *On the Cultivation of the German Language*. Swift presented his program for a cultural revival as a formal letter to Robert Harley, then at the head of Queen Anne's cabinet. He called for the establishment of an "academy of poets," to overcome the mind-deadening doggerel of the Venetian party's print media, and to restore all English vocabulary lost since the reign of Queen Elizabeth—the age of Shakespeare and of Marlowe.[40]

To this crucial task of fostering a new English renaissance, Leibniz also contributed directly on the issue of music. He succeeded in 1710 in arranging a visit to England for the great German composer at the Court of Hanover, George Frederick Handel. For the first time since Sir Francis Bacon burned the compositions of the exiled John Bull a century before, England had a real composer, one who had mastered the science of well-tempered polyphony.

In 1712, Handel moved permanently to England, taking up residence near Picadilly at Burlington House. This was the headquarters of the Scriblerus Club, founded by Swift in 1711 to expose "false and pedantic learning." Handel's earliest musical settings of English poetry were to pieces by Arbuthnot and John Gay, both members of Swift's Scriblerus Club. His English debut—the première of his opera *Rinaldo* in February 1711—was commissioned by the new Haymarket Theater, founded by Aaron Hill to counter the Venetian favorite, Drury Lane. The pattern of political coordination was unmistakable, even in the case of

Aaron Hill: his sister was Abigail Masham, who replaced the Duchess of Marlborough as the first lady of Queen Anne's personal household; his brother was General John Hill, promoted to that rank by the Queen, over the Duke of Marlborough's personal objections.

These signs of a cultural resurgence did not go unnoticed by the Junto. Handel's *Rinaldo* was denounced in the *Spectator*, the Junto Whig organ run by Joseph Addison and Richard Steele. The London *Journal* informed its readers that Handel's music was not for them, since the purpose of music for Englishmen was to "chase away ennui, and relieve clever men from the trouble of thinking."[41] The level of concern among these "clever men" was more clearly registered, however, by the sudden decision of the Royal Society, in the fall of 1710, to move from its historic headquarters at Gresham College. It now took up residence at Crane Court, within the confines of the financial district known as the City of London.

Though primarily functioning as a society for the prevention of progress, the Royal Society's 'watchdog' functions necessitated the inclusion of some actual scientists among its members. It kept a particularly close eye on any threats of scientific 'breakout' in the colonies. Both Increase and Cotton Mather were members; John Winthrop, Jr., had been recruited by its founders. Even Marlborough's nemesis, Robert Hunter, had been elected in 1710, apparently with the sponsorship of Dr. John Arbuthnot. But the controllers of the Royal Society, including its president, Sir Isaac Newton, were now poring over the files of a much more disturbing case: the dreaded playing of the 'Leibniz card.'

Swift's reappearance as Isaac Bickerstaff, the establishment of his close political relationship with Harley, and the arrangement to bring Handel to England, were certainly grounds to suspect that Leibniz had opened up much wider avenues of influence into British affairs. The Junto Whigs had been swept from power; the foolish notions of the Marlboroughs, that the "secret influence" over Queen Anne could simply be attributed to Abigail Masham's petty jealousies, had been thoroughly discredited. The political coup of 1710, moreover, had been carried out while Anne's acknowledged successor to the throne, Leibniz's own Electress Sophia of Hanover, had still not granted the Junto the courtesy of dying of old age. The oligarchy therefore determined to mount a campaign to discredit Leibniz, the greatest genius of his time, by any means possible.

'The Art of Political Lying'

By the fall, the Junto's rumor mills and propaganda machinery were running at fever pitch against the new government. Whig journalists, like their latter-day heirs at the *New York Times* and *Washington Post*, were constantly striving for new levels of the art of sheer fabrication. In early November, Swift struck back in the pages of the *Examiner*, employing the highly unusual device of calling a spade a spade. He published a brilliant dissection of "the Art of Political Lying"—the principles of which, unfortunately, are still all too familiar today.

Directly invoking Milton's *Paradise Lost*, Swift begins by noting that Satan himself is the father of lies, "and which is more, his first essay of it was purely political, employed in undermining the authority of his Prince, and seducing a third part of the subjects from their obedience." Swift adds, however, that the Devil seems,

> like other great inventors, to have lost much of
> his reputation, by the continual improvements

that have been made upon him. . . . the moderns have made great additions, applying this art to the gaining of power, and preserving it, as well as revenging themselves after they have lost it. . . . Accordingly we see [the art of political lying] hath been the guardian spirit of a prevailing party for almost twenty years. It can conquer kingdoms without fighting, and sometimes with the loss of a battle: it gives and resumes employments; can sink a mountain to a mole-hill, and raise a mole-hill to a mountain; [and] hath presided for many years at committees of elections. . . . This goddess flies with a huge looking-glass in her hands to dazzle the crowd, and made them see, according as she turns it, their ruin in their interest, and their interest in their ruin. . . . Here, has this island of ours, for the greatest part of twenty years lain under the influence of such counsels and persons, whose principle and interest it was to corrupt our manners, blind our understandings, drain our wealth, and in time destroy our constitution both in Church and State; and we at last were brought to the very brink of ruin; yet by the means of perpetual misrepresentations, have never been able to distinguish between our enemies and friends.[42]

The Junto suffered no such inability to distinguish Leibniz as their enemy; but given the trend at court, they also had to acknowledge him to be a powerful one. Given the added consideration that his ally Jonathan Swift was the confidant of Queen Anne's chief minister, even the masters of political lying proceeded with some caution. The Royal Society's unexpected relocation to the City of London caused quite a stir, but its officials were careful to keep the motives hidden.

Some suspicions were raised in a pamphlet which appeared in London on November 22, presenting "an account of the surprising convulsions that have lately happened in the Royal Society." The author suggested that things were not as they seemed, by noting that "the real causes that have produced these odd effects are buried too deep for me to reach." The decision to transfer its headquarters to the City of London had been opposed by a majority of the Society's fellows. Their president Isaac Newton, however, "was not prepared (or, perhaps, not instructed) to enter upon that debate: but freely (though methinks not very civilly) replied, that he had good reasons for their removing, which he did not think proper to be given there." The pamphlet further charged that the acting secretary, Sir Hans Sloane, helped sway the members' decision by reporting that one of their officers had "asked him (not long ago) why the Royal Society did not remove from Gresham College? Since the City had several times sent their warnings to that purpose. . . ."[43]

The unstated purpose of this high-handedness concerning the affairs of the Royal Society soon became evident. It had been ordered to forget any scientific pretensions, and to launch a campaign of 'political lying' directed at Leibniz. There shortly appeared in the Society's *Transactions* a paper by one John Keill, containing the wild lie that Leibniz, the inventor of the differential calculus, had plagiarized his work from Newton—who still did not even understand Leibniz's method! Keill's paper purported to draw upon

> that very celebrated arithmetic of fluxions [the calculus, which without any doubt Dr. Newton invented first. . .; yet the same arithmetic afterwards, under a changed name and method of notation, was published by Dr. Leibniz in the Acta Eruditorum.[44]

Appropriately, Keill's hoax was written to Halley, who himself plagiarized the work of the astronomer Flamsteed to foist the name "Halley's Comet" upon posterity. Keill's political motivations were further underscored by the fact that his paper had been written in 1708, the year Queen Anne had first determined to remove Godolphin and place Harley at the head of her government. The Duke of Marlborough's political blackmail and threatened resignation as captain general, defeated the Queen's intentions at the time; and Keill's attack on Leibniz was then left on the shelf.

Its publication now commenced a three-year propaganda assault on Leibniz's scientific authority, during which the British oligarchy rallied around "our beloved Newton"— who in 1710 still held the post at the Treasury he had obtained by prostituting his niece to Charles Montagu. In 1712, a special committee of the Royal Society rejected Leibniz's demands for a retraction of the fraudulent charge of plagiarism. The society published a report upholding Keill and Newton, with a conclusion written by Newton himself.

Sabotage and Assassination Attempts

The Royal Society's attack on Leibniz identified the source of the Venetian party's worst fears, but they did not ignore the danger posed by Harley himself, a well-intentioned patriot whose direct relationship with Swift was a subject of grave concern. Though Harley tolerated a number of incompetents (and worse) in the cabinet, in two areas of policy his commitment was a matter of principle. As Swift reported in his Memoirs,

> Mr. Harley, to give credit to his administration, resolved upon two very important points: first, to secure the unprovided debts of the nation; and secondly, to put an end to the war.[45]

The Bank of England's swindle, in creating a national debt while crushing productive activity needed to pay it, had also built up a "floating" debt of over £10 million, with no tax revenues even legally assigned to meet it. Harley had prepared a plan to retire the debt by attracting investment into a new government corporation, which would pay six percent annual interest from the proceeds of development-oriented trade and colonization in the "South Seas." On hearing of the plan, Leibniz wrote to one of Harley's supporters,

> Your new ministry disabused those foreigners who had doubted if it would contribute, as it has, to the general situation. For one can say that it surpasses its predecessor, not only in paying the costs of the present, but also in making good those of the past, and satisfying the debts of the nation.[46]

Swift's *Memoirs* suggest that the decision to try to break the stranglehold on the British economy was sufficient grounds for an attempt on Harley's life, on March 8, 1711:

> I shall only observe, that while he was preparing to open to the house of commons his scheme for securing the publick debts, he was stabbed by the marquis de Guiscard, while he was sitting in the council chamber at the Cockpit, with a committee of nine or ten lords of the cabinet, met on purpose to examine the marquis, upon a discovery of a treasonable correspondence he held with France.[47]

Guiscard had formerly been a paid agent of Britain, ostensibly to provide intelligence concerning the designs of France. The Duke of Marlborough had also employed him as military captain of a unit of French Huguenots.[48] No clear case has been established as to who was behind the attempt. Some suspicions have been raised, especially by modern apologists for Marlborough, implicating Secretary St. John, who was also a slanderer of Leibniz.

Swift was distraught, and grew more so as Harley's recovery from his wounds seemed unusually prolonged. Swift confided to Stella, "we fear by the caprice of Radcliffe [Harley's physician], who will admit none but his own surgeon, he has not been well lookt after."[49] With a poem, he issued a public warning:

> To Mr. Harley's Surgeon
> On Britain Europe's safety lies,
> And Britain's lost if Harley dies:
> Harley depends upon your skill,
> Think what you save or what you kill.[50]

Harley did not recover until May, when a vastly relieved Queen Anne made him lord treasurer and Earl of Oxford. During his lengthy convalescence, Swift reported, "All things [were] at a stop in parliament for want of Mr. Harley; they cannot stir an inch without him in their most material affairs.[51] Yet during this time of crisis and confusion, the decision to attack Quebec in force was finally made, at the instigation of St. John, and over the objections of Harley.

The moment so long awaited in America, especially in New England, and for which Governors Hunter and Spotswood had energetically prepared, was at hand. The expedition's timing and surrounding circumstances, however, as well as the manner in which it unfolded, suggest a built-in will to fail.

The Quebec Campaign of 1711

Secretary of State Henry St. John had persuaded Queen Anne, during the first two weeks that Harley lay incapacitated, to authorize a British naval squadron and 5,000 army regulars to mount an attack against French Quebec. The Duke of Marlborough, and his cronies in the former ministry, had repeatedly sabotaged earlier plans for such an expedition. Though he still held the title of captain general, his authority had been curtailed, and the Queen was determined to remove him. At the cabinet meeting of March 25, she announced her approval of St. John's plan, and ordered him to present the details.[52] Harley suspected that St. John had worked secretly with Marlborough from the beginning of the new ministry, although the secretary's Quebec proposal certainly had all the earmarks of an "anti-Marlborough" operation.

Five regiments of Marlborough's troops in Flanders were to be withdrawn from his command and placed under Abigail Masham's brother General John ("Jack") Hill, now designated to head the land forces for the Quebec campaign. The naval component was to be commanded by Hovenden Walker, newly knighted and promoted to rear admiral for the occasion. Neither officer had command-level experience for an undertaking of this magnitude, and their preparations were apparently carried out with something less than military precision. Swift wrote to Stella on April 30,

> Our Expedition Fleet is but just sailed: I believe it will come to nothing. Mr. secretary . . . hopes great things from it, though he owns four or five princes [of Europe] are in the secret; and, for that reason, I fear it is no secret to France.[53]

Swift's fears were well founded. French intelligence networks had been continually apprised of any British schemes concerning Canada. There were, however, two distinct operational levels in French Canada. The higher, more significant one was the thoroughly evil Jesuit element, a Venetian-created cult operating without regard for any particular national interest. The second was the French military and civil authority, whose inclinations were not automatically identical to the objective of the Jesuits, which was to lay waste to New England's republican forces below the border.

The official channels of the French government, for example, were fully aware that the previous schemes of Godolphin and Marlborough for New England were hardly benign. Godolphin's 1709 plan to use the New England militia as cannon-fodder, for an imperial war of conquest in the Caribbean, was a case in point. The French colonial minister wrote to the governor of Quebec in 1710, that the chief object of the armament made by the English last year was to establish their sovereignty at Boston. . . . the people of these provinces having always maintained a sort of republic, governed by their council, and having been unwilling to receive absolute governors from the kings of England. . . . it is much to be wished that the Council at Boston could be informed of the designs of the English court, and shown how important it is for that province to remain in the state of a republic. . . . The matter is of the greatest importance, but care is essential to employ persons who have the talents necessary for conducting it, besides great secrecy and prudence, as well as tried probity and fidelity.[54]

There was a marked difference between such 'diplomatic' approaches to French policy making, and the typically Jesuit version. An anonymous memorandum in the French archives, dating from the period when Harley was consolidating his coup against the Godolphin ministry, proposed to deal with the New England problem in more straightforward terms.   There was great danger in any British attack on Canada, this *Mémoire sur la Nouvelle Angleterre* warned, especially if it were to succeed:

> There is an antipathy between the English of Europe and those of America, who will not endure troops from England even to guard their forts. . . . Old England will not imagine that these various provinces will then unite, shake off the yoke of the English monarchy, and erect themselves into a democracy.

The *Mémoire* singled out Massachusetts as the greatest menace, and appealed to God for a massive onslaught, by land and sea, against Boston:

> When Boston is reduced, we would call together all the chief men of the other towns of New England, who would pay heavy sums to be spared from the flames. As for Boston, it should be pillaged, its workshops, manufactures, shipyards, all its fine establishments ruined, and its ships sunk.[55]

To date, it has taken the oligarchs nearly three centuries, by economic rather than military means, to accomplish that end.   At the time, the best they could do was forestall a republican victory in a much larger war.

The degree of commitment by the British expedition of 1711, to remove the menace in Quebec, was questioned in Massachusetts from the outset. First word that such an expedition even existed reached Boston on June 8, barely two weeks before the fleet. Sir Francis Nicholson, the former royal governor of a number of colonies, arrived with orders to requisition supplies for ten weeks, for an expeditionary force which would total, with colonial troops, nearly 12,000 men! Beyond meeting this staggering logistical demand on such short notice, Massachusetts was also required to finance the entire venture. The ruined British treasury had not supplied any funds to sustain the expedition beyond getting it to Boston. The Massachusetts legislature had to issue bills of credit totaling £40,000. Additional credit was voted by Connecticut, and by New York and New Jersey, the two colonies governed by Robert Hunter.[56]

There were some rude surprises for Hunter as well. He was returning down the Hudson from Albany to New York, after another meeting with Iroquois chieftains confirming they would join the attack on Canada. Hunter was intercepted by a messenger from Nicholson, with orders that he convene the New England governors and immediately prepare the invasion. He had nine days' notice to organize provisions for three months for a 5,000-man force, and to raise 2,000 colonial troops who would march on Montreal from Albany. The operation against Montreal was to be commanded, not by the veteran field officer Hunter, but by Nicholson, "who if I be not mistaken," Hunter complained later, "had never seen troops in the field in his life."[57]

There were suspicions in Massachusetts that the demands for provisions, nearly impossible to meet on such short notice, indicated something less than total sincerity on London's part. There were also fears that Massachusetts was to be the scapegoat, should the expedition fail for lack of supplies.[58] Governor Dudley, already accused by Cotton Mather of treasonous collaboration with the French, was in no position to sabotage anything this time. The General Court proceeded to impose virtual martial law, to ensure that every British demand for the expedition was met or even exceeded.

On June 24, Nantasket Roads, the approach to Boston Harbor, was filled with British ships—fifteen men-of-war and forty transports, bearing over 10,000 men. Beside the sailors, there were seven army regiments (about 5,500 men) and 600 marines.[59] The batteries of Copp's Hill and Fort Hill fired salutes welcoming Admiral Walker and General Hill, met by a full muster of the Boston militia. The General Court had frozen prices for provisions and other needed supplies, at the levels prevailing before any word of the fleet's approach. From Massachusetts, Her Majesty demanded 1,000 militiamen; the General Court ordered 1,160 to be raised at once. They were to be quartered by the citizens of Boston, as ordered, at the rate of eightpence a day per man. Mechanics and laborers required for mounting the expedition were drafted, to work even on Sundays if need be. So were ship's pilots, and virtually every seaman in New England who had ever seen the St. Lawrence River, through which the attack on Quebec would be made. Stringent acts were passed against harboring deserters, and many of the leading citizens resolved to live on their existing stores of salt provisions, to provide more fresh food for the army.[60]

New York's Governor Hunter, still irked by the selection of Francis Nicholson to lead the attack on Montreal, nonetheless energetically mobilized the needed manpower and supplies. On appeal from Hunter, Virginia's Governor Spotswood scoured the countryside to commandeer barrels of salt pork for the expedition. One week after receiving Nicholson's message, Hunter convened the council of war at New London, Connecticut, with the governors of Massachusetts, Connecticut, and Rhode Island, to set their quotas for the contingent to be raised at Albany.[61]

Within a month, New England had completely reprovisioned the fleet at Boston, for the massive undertaking against Quebec. Backed up by twenty more ships of Massachusetts bearing troops and supplies, the expedition set sail on July 30. To navigate the unfamiliar channels of the St. Lawrence, Admiral Walker had employed a most unusual pilot. One of his warships, the *Chester*, had been dispatched from England ahead of the fleet, on a mission to the Gulf of Mexico! There it supposedly captured a French vessel, whose captain happily agreed to pilot the attack on Quebec, France's only stronghold in the New World, for a mere 500 *pistoles* (Spanish currency).[62]

The departure of the column at Albany was delayed almost three weeks, anxiously awaiting the arrival of 800 Iroquois Indians, and then arming them for the attack on Canada. Hunter had promised this undertaking would be no mere gesture, like those of the past. Understandably, the Iroquois were unwilling to violate the "neutrality" treaty between Britain and France in a losing cause, since they faced reprisals from the Jesuit-run tribes of Canada. They had been reassured by four of their chiefs who had visited London in the spring, and by their delegation sent to Boston to view the fleet.

The French governor at Quebec had intelligence reports of the impending attack, two weeks before the expedition entered the St. Lawrence River.[63] He mobilized the priests and nuns, together with the Indians and what little militia he had. From a military standpoint, he was totally outgunned. At Montreal, the local candidate for sainthood, the recluse Mademoiselle Le Ber, made a flag embroidered with a prayer to the Virgin Mary. The ladies of the outpost "bound themselves by oath to wear neither ribbons nor lace, to keep their throats covered, and to observe various holy practices for the space of a year."[64]

None of these powers to defend French Canada were ever called upon. On August 22, the expeditionary fleet encountered strong winds, at a point where the St. Lawrence is seventy miles wide. Admiral Walker later claimed that he believed he was steering a course along the river's south shore, and on an imagined sighting of land, turned the fleet northward away from it. He then retired to his cabin, and dismissed a report shortly delivered to him that the fleet was surrounded by breaking surf on all sides. The fleet held to its northward course until a second, panicked report finally brought the admiral on deck. Some ships nearby were already being driven on the rocks, and when the French pilot was finally located, he declared that the coast before them was the *north* shore.

Though all of the fleet's warships escaped destruction, eight transports and two supply ships were lost, along with over 700 men. After two days of indecision, while rescue operations proceeded, Admiral Walker transferred to General Hill's ship, where a council of war was convened. Discussing whether to proceed or abandon the expedition, Walker harped on the difficulties of navigating the St. Lawrence. They had not deterred the New England expedition of 1690, piloted with even less knowledge, under Massachusetts Governor William Phips, whose journal of the voyage Walker had with him. Walker asked the commander of the New England militia, Samuel Vetch, if he would pilot the fleet to Quebec. Vetch's answer, as recorded in his journal, and confirmed by the report of the war council, was that

> I never was bred to sea, nor was it any part of my province; but I would do my best by going ahead and showing them where the difficulty of the river was, which I knew pretty well.[65]

The British naval captains, however, insisted that the navigational hazards made it impossible to continue to

Quebec.   Faced with Walker's concurrence, Jack Hill accepted the decision to abandon the attack. Years of hope and preparation were wiped out, by an incident which had still left the expeditionary force at over 90 percent of its original strength—not counting 2,300 men proceeding up Lake Champlain from Albany.[66]

The following day, Vetch sent an indignant letter to Walker protesting the decision, and clearly implying his suspicions of the admiral's treacherous collusion with his French 'pilot':

> The late disaster cannot, in my humble opinion, be anyways imputed to the difficulty of the navigation, but to the wrong course we steered, which most unavoidably carried us upon the north shore. *Who directed that course you best know*; and as our return without any further attempt would be a vast reflection upon the conduct of this affair, so it would be of very fatal consequence to the interest of the Crown and all the British colonies upon this continent.[67]

Admiral Walker wisely waited until 1720 to publish his own defense, since in England the Whig Junto laid all blame on General Hill, in an effort to discredit Queen Anne's new inner circle. If anything, Walker's account damns him further.   Citing tales fed him by his French 'pilot' of the awful Canadian winter, Walker made his August voyage to Quebec, sound like a January mission to the North Pole. He confirmed that he never intended to reach Quebec in the first place,

> because, had we arrived safe at Quebec, our provisions would have been reduced to a very small proportion, not exceeding eight or nine weeks at short allowance, so that between ten

and twelve thousand men must have been left to perish with the extremity of cold and hunger. I must confess the melancholy contemplation of this (had it happened) strikes me with horror; for how dismal must it have been to have beheld the seas and earth locked up by adamantine frosts, and swoln [sic] with high mountains of snow, in a barren and uncultivated region; great numbers of brave men famishing with hunger, and drawing lots who should die first to feed the rest.[68]

Besides his diseased vision of cannibalism, Walker's "apology" offered the insane premise, that nearly 15,000 men would storm Canada, with no hope of early victory, nor of being resupplied from America. His account was otherwise entertaining, no doubt, to the year-round residents of Quebec.

The retreating fleet dispatched a frigate to Boston, with news of the expedition's ignominious result. Having worked so hard to ensure its success, the people of Massachusetts were not likely to forget their original suspicions. Word was sent urgently to the colonial army advancing north toward Montreal, since the retreat from Quebec had left Nicholson's force in a possibly fatal trap. Nicholson's reaction was dramatic enough. According to a New York militia officer at his camp, he flew into a rage, tore off his wig, and stamped it into the ground, while shouting "Roguery! Treachery!" Nicholson then burned the forts the militia had built, marched back to Albany, and disbanded the army.[69] Robert Hunter's efforts to build a working relationship with the Iroquois were the most serious casualty.

In Virginia, Alexander Spotswood had anxiously awaited the news of the conquest of Quebec. Should the

French barrier be removed, he was prepared to sweep aside all opposition to opening up the continent's interior. William Byrd, his leading oligarchical foe, had kept his own vigil. Just a year before, when Spotswood first informed him of his plans for iron manufacturing, Byrd had dashed off an alarmed letter to his ally in Massachusetts, Joseph Dudley.[70] After word was received of the aborted expedition against Canada, Byrd tersely noted in his secret diary, "the Governor [Spotswood] told me that our design upon Canada had miscarried by the fault of the Admiral." [71]

The 'new paths' to a continental republic had not been decisively established, as their designers had hoped. America's enemies took comfort, from the disaster of the expedition against Quebec, and now prepared their own assault against Queen Anne, to eliminate the nation-building trend of her policies.

NOTES

1. Cotton Mather, *Bonifacius, An Essay upon the Good* (Cambridge, Mass., 1966), 92.

2. *Ibid.*, 15.

3. Frederick B. Tolles, *James Logan and the Culture of Provincial America* (Boston, 1957), 38.

4. Lustig, *Hunter*, 75; memorial of New Jersey Assembly, quoted by Green, *Queen Anne*, 188.

5. Lustig, *Hunter*, 75.

6. Quoted by Lustig, *Hunter*, 61.

7. Lustig, *Hunter*, 61–70, *passim*.

8. Swift, *Memoirs*, in Sheridan, ed., *Works of Swift*, VI, 273, 275.

9. *Ibid.*, 275–276.

10. Gregg, *Queen Anne*, 300–301; Sir Winston Churchill, *Marlborough, His Life and Times* (4 vols., London, 1933–1938), quoted by Green, *Queen Anne*, 216.

11. Gregg, *Queen Anne*, 311, 304–305; Sunderland to Marlborough, February 21, 1710, quoted by Gregg, 305.

12. Lustig, *Hunter*, 63–64; Gregg, *Queen Anne*, 311, 314.

13. Mather to Hunter [undated, late 1713-early 1714?], in Kenneth Silverman, *Selected Letters of Cotton Mather* (Baton Rouge, 1971), 147.

14. Jonathan Swift, *The Complete Poems*, Pat Rogers, ed. (New Haven, 1983), 110, 111.

15. Lustig, *Hunter*, 158.

16. Hunter to Addison, November 8, 1714, in Walter Graham, ed., *The Letters of Joseph Addison* (Oxford, 1941), 493.

17. Lustig, *Hunter*, 78.

18. Cotton Mather, *Diary*, II, 166.

19. Walter Havighurst, *Alexander Spotswood, Portrait of a Governor* (New York, 1967), 10–11.

20. *Ibid.*, 3.

21. R. H. McIlwaine, ed., *Executive Journals of the Colonial Council of Virginia* (Richmond, 1928), III (May 1, 1705 to October 23, 1721), 580–581. Hereafter referred to as Jour. Coun. Va.

22. William Byrd II, *The Secret Diary of William Byrd of Westover, 1709–1712*, Louis B. Wright and Marion Tinling, eds. (Richmond, 1941). This is one of a series of Byrd' s diaries, deciphered by the

editors from his coded shorthand. With a personal life as disgusting as Byrd' s, it is clear why he kept his diary in code, as we shall elaborate later.

23. Spotswood to Lord Dartmouth, December 15, 1710, *The Official Letters of Alexander Spotswood* (2 vols., Richmond, 1882–1885), I, 43. Certain of Spotswood's abbreviations, such as " y' r Lo' p' s" for " your Lordship' s," have been filled out by the author.

24. Spotswood to the Council of Trade, December 15, 1710, *Letters*, I, 41–42.

25. Byrd, *Secret Diary*, 223–224.

26. Gregg, *Queen Anne*, 322.

27. *Ibid.*, 327.

28. *The Examiner*, No. 16 (November 23, 1710), in Swift, *Writings*, Landa, ed., 407–409.

29. *Ibid.*, 409–410.

30. Sarah Churchill to Sir David Hamilton, November 28, 1710; quoted by Gregg, *Queen Anne*, 325–326.

31. Gregg, *Queen Anne*, 329.

32. *Ibid.*, 300*n.*, 334–335.

33. *Cf. Supra*, chapter 4, 98–104.

34. Jonathan Swift, *Journal to Stella*, Harold Williams, ed. (2 vols., London, 1948), I, 145 (December 31, 1710).

35. Swift, *Memoirs*, 284.

36. *Ibid.*, 284–285.

37. Swift, *Journal to Stella*, I, 60-61*n* .

38. *The Tatler*, No. 230, September 28, 1710.

39. *Ibid.*

40. Dana Arnest, "Handel, Swift, and the Cultural War for the New World, Part I," *New Solidarity*, February 28, 1985; Kathy Wolfe, " Handel and the Cultural War for the New World, Part II," *New Solidarity*, March 6, 1985.

41. Quoted by Dana Arnest, "Handel, Swift and the Cultural War for the New World."

42. *The Examiner*, No. 14, November 9, 1710.

43. Valenti, " Newton-Leibniz Controversy." The author's first appreciation of the Royal Society' s attack on Leibniz, as a response to his expanding influence over Queen Anne' s government, was entirely due to Valenti's researches.

44. Quoted by Valenti, " Newton-Leibniz Controversy."

45. Swift, *Memoirs*, 288.

46. Quoted by Valenti, " Newton-Leibniz Controversy."

47. Swift, *Memoirs*, 288.

48. Green, *Queen Anne*, 243.

49. Swift, *Journal to Stella*, I, 225.

50. Swift, *Poems*, 115.

51. Swift, *Journal to Stella*, I, 224–225.

52. Gregg, *Queen Anne*, 337.

53. Swift, *Journal to Stella*, I, 257.

54. Ponchartrain to Vaudreuil, August 10, 1710, quoted by Francis Parkman, *Conflict*, I, 151–152.

55. *Mémoire sur la Nouvelle Angleterre*, Archive de la Marine, quoted by Parkman, *Conflict*, I, 154–155.

56. Parkman, *Conflict*, I, 158–163.

57. Hunter to the Earl of Stair, October 18, 1714, quoted by Lustig, *Hunter*, 92.

58. Hutchinson, *History*, II, 173.

59. Parkman, *Conflict*, I, 159, 163*n* .

60. *Ibid.*, I, 161–163.

61. Lustig, *Hunter*, 91*ff.*

62. Parkman, *Conflict*, I, 163–164.

63. *Ibid.*, I, 171.

64. Quoted by Parkman, *Conflict*, I, 172.

65. *Ibid.*, I, 169.

66. *Ibid.*, I, 165–169.

67. Vetch to Walker, August 26, 1711, quoted by Parkman, *Conflict*, I, 169–170.

68. Sir Hovenden Walker, *Journal of the Canada Expedition* (London, 1720), Introduction, 25.

69. Lustig, *Hunter*, 95; Parkman, Conflict, I, 170–171.

70. Byrd, *Secret Diary* (September 24, 26, 1710), 235–236.

71. *Ibid.* (October 23, 1711), 426.

6

A Bloody Time of Peace

The period of Queen Anne's reign, following her dismissal of Marlborough's son-in-law in 1710, lasted barely more than four years. It was never a period of political tranquility; Marlborough and his Venetian party allies worked constantly to undo her. Especially from 1710 on, against the perceived growth of Swift and Leibniz's republican influence, the oligarchy resorted to increasingly —and literally—murderous measures. The battle had tremendous significance for America, and forced the final determination that its aspirations must never be left dependent on monarchical favor.

After the unsuccessful attempt to assassinate Robert Harley in 1711, he nonetheless proceeded immediately, upon his recovery in May, to secure passage of the South Sea bill, designed to break the destructive grip of the 'Venetian' Bank of England over the nation's economy. Endorsed by Leibniz, the plan provided for restructuring the ruinous war debt, while providing credit for colonial economic development. By the end of May, Harley was made chief minister as lord treasurer, and raised to the peerage as Earl of Oxford. He was now in position to consolidate political control, and to proceed toward his other major objective—an end to the war with France.

The Duke of Marlborough and his backers were determined to destroy any chance for a peace negotiated on the two countries' mutual, long-term interests. For ten years, Marlborough had instead deliberately fought a war of mutual attrition, confined largely to the fields of Flanders. Now, in 1711, the propagandists for the 'indispensable' captain general projected a triumphant march on Paris, *for the following year*, after Marlborough's 'allied' army seized the town of Bouchain on September 12. The attack had begun in August, while Swift's friend Matthew Prior was in Paris, on private instructions from Queen Anne, negotiating terms of peace. During the siege of Bouchain, Marlborough puffed up his new 'war-winning' pose by sending an official communique´ to London— and a secret one to Elector George of Hanover— announcing plans to establish winter quarters for the army directly along the borders of France.[1] On September 26, Queen Anne wrote to Lord Treasurer Oxford that the

> Duke of Marlborough shows plainer than ever
> by this new project his unwillingness for a
> peace, but I hope our negotiations will Succeed
> & then it will not be in his power to prevent it.[2]

Was the great general poised for military victory? Even by the fawning account of a recent British biographer, his capture of Bouchain was merely the alternative to outright retreat:

> there was no possibility of challenging [French
> general] Villars to battle. The Frenchman had
> seven thousand more men than he had and had
> drawn them up in a position of great natural
> strength. In these circumstances, Marlborough
> decided to content himself with besieging
> Bouchain, a fortress beyond which there was
> open country all the way to Paris.
>
> The siege is something of a military
> curiosity, for the French army was as close to
> Marlborough as he was to the fortress and the
> entrenchments he dug to hold off a relieving
> party were thirty miles long. It was a situation
> of some delicacy.[3]

Marlborough's military 'breakthrough' was pure sham; but Britain's Whig press, so accomplished in the art of political lying, declared without blushing that Queen Anne's peace proposals would give away an allied triumph. Swift wrote to Stella on October 26, "We have no quiet with the Whigs, they are so violent against a Peace; but I'll cool them, with a vengeance, very soon."[4]

Swift's Conduct of the Allies

Four days later, Swift's draft of *The Conduct of the Allies* was at the printer.[5] It was a devastating exposė of the international oligarchy's conduct of the war, as a deliberate effort to grind up the populations and economies of Europe, in order to remove all obstacles to a Venetian-Dutch financial dictatorship. In great detail, Swift also reviewed the policies and motives of the Venetian financiers of the City of London, as well as the Duke of Marlborough's part in the conspiracy to prolong the war. The pamphlet's publication was delayed until November 27, again as an anonymous work, for the Junto still controlled the courts of law. Near the conclusion of the piece as printed, Swift hinted that the delay also involved the setting of a trap.[6] The Duke of Marlborough, for one, walked right into it.

Faced with the dramatic turn in Queen Anne's government, the Whig Junto had begun preparations for a possible coup, to be staged as a patriotic upsurge under the banner of the Duke of Marlborough. The Royal Society was already waving the British flag for the 'great' Sir Isaac Newton, against the 'foreign' political-intellectual influence of Leibniz. The Junto now chose the date of Queen Elizabeth's birthday, November 17, for mass demonstrations against Queen Anne's pursuit of a peace with France, which she hoped would free both nations from the policy of mutual destruction. On the appointed day, Marlborough landed at Greenwich, accompanied by the

Elector George of Hanover's right-hand man, Baron von Bothmer. The Bank of England's Kit-Kat Club had spread the word, and greased the necessary palms, for 'spontaneous' outpourings of welcome for the returning captain general—complete with burnings-in-effigy of the Pope and Lord Oxford, head of the Queen's cabinet.[7]

Swift reports that such lavish preparations did not go undetected:

> From the several circumstances of the expense of this intended pageantry, and of the persons who promoted it, the court, apprehensive of a design to inflame the common people, thought fit to order, that the several figures [effigies] should be seized as popish trinkets; and guards were ordered to patrol, for preventing any tumultuous assemblies.

Due to the preemptive measures ordered by the Queen, the scheme proved "wholly abortive," as Swift put it, but he noted two features of the plan suggesting "it had a deeper meaning." One was the role of Marlborough, who had always avoided public demonstrations even when returning from his triumphs of the past:

> therefore, so very contrary a proceeding at this juncture, made it suspected as if he had a design to have placed himself at their head.

As for the second,

> if what was confidently asserted to be true, that a report was to have been spread at the same time of the Queen's death, no man can tell what might have been the event.[8]

The failure of the November 17 plot left Marlborough rather indecently exposed. His fate was sealed during a private meeting with Queen Anne at Hampton Court on November 23, when he refused to support her measures for peace. A parliamentary investigation into his personal profiteering from the massive war expenditures was already under way.[9] The Junto had assured him of support by a majority of the House of Lords, and Marlborough

> therefore boldly fell, with his whole weight, into the design of ruining the ministry . . . . He was at the head of all the cabals . . . . [and] fell into all impotences of anger and violence, upon every party debate . . . .[10]

When Swift's *Conduct of the Allies* was finally released on November 27, it "exploded in the reader's mind with the power of a bomb," as a recent British biographer of Marlborough has put it."[11] The pamphlet was an instant best-seller. A thousand copies sold in the first two days— and Swift was evicted from his lodgings. Three more editions appeared within ten days; seven were printed in London by April 1712, and it was also published in Dublin and Edinburgh.[12] Within weeks of the pamphlet's original release, the publisher was hauled before the lord chief justice, the Whig Thomas Parker.[13]

Marlborough's part in prolonging the war was the least crime Swift had exposed, as far as the Junto was concerned. Far worse was his demonstrating that the Junto's objective was not victory over France, but the ruin of Britain *and* France, as prescribed by the Junto's Dutch and Hapsburg allies. When France had made peace overtures before, during Godolphin's 'Venetian' ministry, response from London consistently provoked continuing hostilities. In one such negotiation, Swift noted in *Conduct of the Allies*, the concessions demanded from France "were so extravagant, that in all human probability we could not have obtained them by a successful war of forty years."[14]

Marlborough's "passing rivers, and taking towns" in Flanders may have been "attended with many glorious circumstances," but had "no other end than to enlarge the territories of the Dutch, and to increase the fame and wealth of our general."[15] A ten-year effort to conquer Flanders (part of Belgium today) demonstrated no intention to defeat France militarily.   Of the allied campaign, Swift said, "Give me leave to suppose the continuance of the war was the thing at heart among those in power, both abroad and at home."[16]

What reason could there be for a policy of endless war? Swift asked:

> we are destroying many thousand lives, exhausting our substance, not for our own interest, which would be but common prudence; not for a thing indifferent, which would be sufficient folly; but, perhaps, to our own destruction, which is perfect madness.[17]

The decade of carnage had been perpetuated by

> that set of people, who are called the monied men; such as had raised vast sums by trading with stocks and funds, and lending upon great interest and premiums; whose perpetual harvest is war, and whose beneficial way of traffick must very much decline by a peace . . . .[18]

> It is the folly of too many to mistake the echo of a London coffeehouse, for the voice of the kingdom. The city coffeehouses have been for some years filled with people, whose fortunes depend upon the Bank [of England), East-India, or some other stock. Every new fund to these, is like a new mortgage to a usurer . . . .[19]

Swift's exposé of how the "monied men" had deliberately bankrupted the nation had a tremendous political impact. A modern British biographer of Queen Anne, though devoting only one paragraph to it, simply describes *The Conduct of the Allies* as "the most powerful pamphlet ever known in Britain."[20] Swift summarized the economic toll of ten years of war in stark terms. All but £2.5 million of Britain's annual revenues were "mortgaged to pay interest for what we have already borrowed," yet war expenditures averaged £6 million per year. By 1711, interest payments on this ever-growing debt were "a million more than all the funds the parliament could contrive," and £12 million had to be cut from the government's operating budget.

> If the peace be made this winter, we are then to consider what circumstances we shall be in toward paying a debt of about fifty millions, which is a fourth part of the purchase of the whole island if it were to be sold.[21]

Swift did not mince words in detailing "a conspiracy on all sides to go on with those measures, which must perpetuate the war . . . ." He recounted the continual efforts of the Marlboroughs and the Junto to manipulate, strong-arm, and blackmail the Queen, adding that

> nothing is so apt to break even the bravest spirits, as a continual chain of oppressions; one injury is best defended by a second, and this by a third. By these steps . . a general during [the Queen's] pleasure might have grown into a general for life, and a general for life, into a king.

Swift appealed to his readers to think like citizens, and emphasized that he expected to have little influence on those, whose particular ends or designs of any sort lead them to wish the continuance of the war: I mean the general, and our allies abroad, the knot of late favorites at home, the body of such as traffick in stocks, and lastly, that set of factious politicians, who were so violently bent, at least upon clipping our constitution in church and state. Therefore I shall not apply myself to any of those, but to all others indifferently, whether Whigs or Tories, whose private interest is best answered by the welfare of their country.[22]

The day after *The Conduct of the Allies* was published, the Elector George of Hanover provided an efficient demonstration of whose interests he served. His ambassador, Baron von Bothmer, lately at Marlborough's side during the threatened coup against Queen Anne, delivered a memorial containing the Elector's formal protest against the preliminary articles of peace. Then, on December 6, the day before the opening session of Parliament, the Whig press published Bothmer's memorial, to arm their allies against the proposed treaty. The session began with the address by the Queen, who drove the conspirators into a frenzy:

I am glad that I can now tell you that notwithstanding the arts of those who delight in war, both place and time are appointed for opening the treaty of a general peace.[23]

The "monied men," however, had done their work. The Junto carried a resolution in the House of Lords designed to sabotage key points of the preliminary agreements between Britain and France. Marlborough worked openly against the peace. Oxford's ministry struck back, with proceedings in the House of Commons against the Duke, for siphoning off enormous sums from the army payroll for his personal enrichment.   On December 22, the Junto's forces managed to adjourn the House before the government's charges could be debated.   The maneuver did not stay the Queen's hand, however, in stripping Marlborough of all of his offices and commands.   Her letter of dismissal was delivered on December 29; and with a traitor's rage, Marlborough threw it into the fire.[24]

Sabotaging the Peace

The removal of Marlborough did not end the "conspiracy" against the peace which Swift had exposed. The charade was over, however, that peace must await a military victory over France that was just around the proverbial corner.   During   subsequent   stages   of negotiations, in fact, the Duke of Ormond, Marlborough's replacement as captain general, was under orders from the Queen merely to maintain his lines, and to avoid inflicting any further damage or casualties upon France. The Whigs, naturally, denounced this reasonableness as "cowardice." For the Venetian party factioneers on both sides, the game now shifted from managing the war, to ruining the peace— especially one which might permit both nations to turn their energies toward renewed economic development.   The stakes were enormous: if 'Venetian' policies were to dominate   postwar   Europe,   hopes   for   an   American continental republic would appear dim indeed.

Soon the streets of London by night became the stalking grounds of a new breed of terrorist thugs—self-styled "Mohawks," who assaulted pedestrians as the "punkers" of their day. Queen Anne's ministers warned the public that the Whig Junto was planning riots to overthrow the government.   Bothmer reported to George of Hanover that plans had also been made to kidnap the Queen and assassinate members of her cabinet. Additional security measures were taken, including strengthening the Queen's guard and moving Lord Oxford, her chief minister, into the royal palace of St. James.[25] Harley (now Lord Oxford) had narrowly survived a previous assassination attempt.

The peace conference at Utrecht opened on January 18, 1712, but the negotiations were soon complicated by a rapid series of deaths among the heirs of France's ruling House of Bourbon. Louis XIV was now seventy-three years old, and his only legitimate son had died the previous year. One week after the talks began, the wife of Louis's grandson, the Duke of Burgundy and next in line for the throne, was stricken with "a burning fever and suffered from violent pains in the head." It was believed she had scarlet fever, which develops as a rampant streptococcal infection through the bloodstream; there were "whispers, at the same time, of ugly symptoms." She was dead in a week, at the age of twenty-six. Her husband soon followed her, taken to bed two days after her death, *declaring himself to be poisoned.* He died four days later, at the age of twenty-nine, reportedly of scarlet fever. From the same sort of infection, his older son, age eight, died barely two weeks after his father.[26] In the direct male line of succession to Louis XIV, only Burgundy's infant son, who was also stricken, survived— though in an extremely weakened state.

Such wholesale reduction of the French royal heirs aroused considerable suspicion, directed particularly at the Duke d'Orléans, the Venetian party's favorite among the nobility. Should the surviving infant die, and thus extinguish the direct line of succession, his older uncle, the Duke de Berri, would become king. The next claimant, the younger uncle, was King Philip V of Spain, who two months later renounced his rights to the French throne. The title would next fall to the Duke d'Orléans, a grandson of Louis XIII who had married a daughter of Louis XIV.

Robert Harley, Earl of Oxford (1661–1724), an early opponent of the 'Venetian' regime established under King William, led the fight against the ruinous policies of the Marlborough gang, and in 1711— with the help of Jonathan Swift— became the head of Queen Anne's cabinet. (National Portrait Gallery, London)

Above: Princess Anne in 1689, after her father James II had been driven into exile in France, by the invasion of William of Orange. The coup was ensured when John Churchill betrayed King James, and joined the invading army. (National Portrait Gallery, London)

Left: Queen Anne (1665– 1714) succeeded to the throne on the death of King William in 1702. Manipulated from adolescence by Sarah Churchill, she was expected as Queen to remain a puppet of the Marlboroughs. (National Portrait Gallery, London)

A contemporary portrait of the Duke of Marlborough, brazenly displaying his own imperial ambitions. (National Portrait Gallery, London)

Blenheim Palace, constructed by order of Queen Anne following Marlborough's victory at Blenheim in 1704. Built on the scale of Louis XIV's Versailles, this royal gift to Marlborough amounted to more than £200,000 in construction costs by 1710.

Lord Sidney Godolphin (1645–1712). The key 'Venetian' controller of Queen Anne's cabinet, until his dismissal in 1710. As Lord Treasurer, he imposed economic ruin on Britain, and bankrolled Marlborough's policy of endless war. (National Portrait Gallery, London)

Charles Talbot, Duke of Shrewsbury (1660–1718). The Jesuit-linked Shrewsbury played the key role in the final destruction of Queen Anne's government in 1714, and arranged for her enemies' return under George I. (National Portrait Gallery, London)

Thomas Malthus (1766–1824), the population-control propagandist for modern genocide. He was the great-grandson of Daniel Malthus (1651–1717), the royal apothecary at the time of Queen Anne's death under mysterious circumstances.

Rear view of the main hall of the College of William and Mary, reconstructed in classical proportions by Spotswood.

Alexander Spotswood (1676–1740), governor of Virginia, 1710–1722. Founder of the republican faction which produced George Washington, Spotswood made Virginia the spearhead of America's drive to develop the vast continent beyond the Appalachian mountains.

Below: Bruton Church, Williamsburg, Virginia. A cruciform structure designed by Spotswood in 1711, demonstrating the principles of geometric construction by circular action. (Prints and Photographs Division, Library of Congress)

The official governor's residence at Williamsburg, designed and built by Alexander Spotswood. Spotswood's architectural contributions to Virginia's colonial capital were a significant part of his efforts to uplift the former backwater.

Right: Spotswood's expedition crossed the summit of the Blue Ridge at this point in 1716, opening the way for the colonization of the West. (Courtesy of H. Graham Lowry)

Below: The site of Spotswood's home at his frontier settlement of Germanna, where he established Virginia's first iron industry with

(Right) William Byrd II (1674–1744), the degenerate leader of Spotswood's opposition, among the great slaveowners, fur traders, and land speculators of Virginia. (Colonial Williamsburg Foundation) (Left) Robert 'King' Carter, one of Byrd's leading allies, laid claim to huge tracts of land to keep Virginia's frontier a feudal domain. (Shirley Plantation in Charles City, Virginia)

The Shenandoah River Valley, west of the Blue Ridge Mountains. Thanks to Spotswood, Fairfax, and Washington, it became a strategic corridor for developing the American continent. (Courtesy of H. Graham Lowry)

Robert Walpole (1676–1745) presided over an orgy of corruption in Britain, as prime minister from 1721 to 1742. A devotee of the Satan-worshipping circles of the Hell-Fire Club, he is best remembered for coining the phrase, 'every man has his price.' (National Portrait Gallery, London)

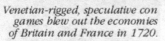

Venetian-rigged, speculative con games blew out the economies of Britain and France in 1720.

Below: Ruined investors assemble in panic in Paris, over news of the collapse of the Mississippi Bubble, a nation-wrecking scheme run by the Duke of Orléans and Venetian agent John Law (right).

Three views of Walpole's 'Hell-Fire' regime, by the English artist William Hogarth, an ally of Jonathan Swift.

Left: The painting 'Sir Francis Dashwood at his Devotions,' commenting on the pornographic rituals of the head of the Hell-Fire Club. (Courtesy of a private collection)

Right: A scene from 'The Beggar's Opera' (1728). The highwayman Macheath is in jail, flanked by his two wives, who plead with their nderworld fathers to save him. Hogarth puts the audience itself inside the prison. (clipart.com)

Below: Hogarth's cartoon 'The South Sea Scheme' (1721), portraying the bestial nature of the swindle that brought Walpole to power.

The Duke d'Orléans was widely accused of having poisoned the Duke and Duchess of Burgundy, and their eldest son: "people called to mind his taste for chemistry and even magic; his flagrant impiety, his scandalous debauchery. . . ."[27] Autopsies were performed on the three victims, but the physicians were "divided" on whether the cause of death was poison.[28] Little more than a year later, there were new grounds for suspicion. On May 4, 1714,[29] the Duke de Berri died, at the age of twenty-seven, "of a disease which presented the same features as the [previous cases of) scarlet fever . . . ."[30] Now only the *enfant*, the King's ailing great-grandson, stood in the way of Orléans' seizing the throne.

But another death in the royal line might have stretched suspicions too far, and the risk was not worth it in any case. Louis XIV had been under the spell of his Jesuit confessor, Le Tellier, since 1709, to the point of reluctantly absolving Orléans of suspicion in the deaths of Louis' grandson, granddaughter, and great-grandson in 1713. The King remained in good health until August 12, 1715, when "sores broke out on his leg." Whatever treatment was provided, he was soon dying of gangrene.

His Jesuit 'guardians' now inducted him as a full member of their Venetian-run order. As he weakened, a new codicil to his will was "wrung from him" on August 25, appointing the Duke d'Orléans ruler of France, as the head of the regency for the *enfant* until he became of age.[31]

To the surprised French magistrates who received this alteration in the King's will, Louis said,

> I have made a testament; they insisted that I should make it. I had to purchase my own repose; but as soon as I am dead it will be of no account.[32]

On August 31, Louis received the final sacraments. Le Tellier and his fellow Jesuits hovered about his bedside, and heard some unwelcome words from the dying King:

> I call you to witness that I have done nothing therein but what you wanted, and have done all that you wanted; it is you who will answer before God for all that has been done.[33]

A different reckoning took precedence for the moment. Even before Louis expired, his courtiers flocked to pay homage to the new dispenser of royal favor, the Duke d'Orléans. At the end, "some Jesuits gathered around the corpse and performed the ceremonies for one who had died in their order."[34]

The negotiations begun at Utrecht in 1712 soon faced a lethal counter-assault within Britain as well. Orders were given in May to the new captain general of the British army, the Duke of Ormond, to refrain from further offensive actions against France. The policy was privately communicated to the French government. Britain's Dutch and Hapsburg 'allies' determined to continue the conflict nonetheless. Marlborough's Junto friends, led by the Bank of England's Lord Halifax, demanded in the House of Lords that the Queen direct Ormond "to prosecute the War with the utmost vigour."[35] The Whigs attempted to portray Ormond as a cowardly betrayer of the allies, for attempting to establish a cease-fire during the peace negotiations. A supporter of the government responded that Ormond's courage compared favorably "with the conduct of 'a certain general' who had deliberately led his troops to the slaughter so that he could fill his pockets by disposing of the commissions of officers killed in action."[36] The desperate Duke of Marlborough challenged his critic to a duel, but backed down upon an order from Queen Anne.[37]

Dutch and Hapsburg mercenaries continued military actions aimed at destroying the negotiations at Utrecht, but suffered a crushing defeat in July by French forces under Marshall Villars. By the fall of 1712, Villars had driven them out of their key remaining positions on the chessboard, including Marlborough's last prize, Bouchain.[38] Dutch opposition to the peace now collapsed, and Queen Anne began making arrangements to put postwar relations between Britain and France on a positive footing.

As ambassador to France, she named the Duke of Hamilton, brother of the Earl of Orkney, and one of the circle at court with whom Jonathan Swift had established some influence, especially through Hamilton's sister-in-law, Lady Elizabeth Orkney. On the eve of Hamilton's departure for Versailles in late November 1712, he was murdered, following a duel, by one of Marlborough's thugs —the cashiered General Maccartney. The challenger was Lord Mohun, whom the Duke of Marlborough had earlier named as his second in the duel prevented by Queen Anne.[39] As Swift reported,

> The Duke [of Hamilton] was preparing for his journey, when he was challenged to a duel, by the Lord Mohun, a person of infamous character. He killed his adversary on the spot, though he himself received a wound; and, weakened by the loss of blood, as he was leaning in the arms of his second, was most barbarously stabbed in the breast by Lt. Gen. Maccartney, who was second to Lord Mohun. He died a few minutes afterward in the field, and the murderer made his escape.[40]

So did the Duke of Marlborough, who fled to Holland nine days later, and did not return to Britain until August 1, 1714 — the day Queen Anne died.[41]

While this deadly mode of political realignment continued, the Venetians in all camps, especially among the Junto in Britain, repeatedly delayed the concluding of a treaty of peace. In January 1713, in a special appendix to yet another edition of his *Conduct of the Allies*, Swift lashed out at the "unreasonable clamours of an insolent faction" for bringing about "the present stagnation of affairs."[42] He also identified the motive for their obstruction, in declaring that "our happiness will not be put off till they who have ill-will at us can find time and power to prevent it." The "whiggarchy," as Swift called them now, had added to its repertoire of political lying the charge that the French negotiators were reneging on the initial agreements:

> but the authors of this forgery know very well I do not miscall it; and are *conscious to the criminal reasons* why it is with so much industry bandied about. France rather enlarges her offers, than abates or recedes from them: so happy are we in finding our most inveterate and ungenerous enemies within our own bowels! [Emphasis added.][43]

Swift's justifiable outrage, however, also carried a hint of desperation. He concluded this "appendix" with a violent denunciation of the lies and machinations of the Whigs against the peace:

> But these artifices are too thin to hold: they are the cobwebs which the faction have spun out of the last dregs of their poison, made to be swept away with the unnecessary animals who contrived them. Their tyranny is at an end; and their ruin is very near: I can only advise them to become their fall, like Caesar, and "die with decency."[44]

Death Stalks Queen Anne

During the early months of 1713, Queen Anne's government did succeed in moving the allies, except the Hapsburg emperor, toward acceptance of the preliminary terms negotiated between Britain and France. Though the Dutch had agreed, the Duke of Marlborough sent a personal emissary in March to persuade them to sign at a later date, to make the treaty

> at least have the appearance of a separate peace [with France), and oblige their British friends, who knew how to turn so short a delay to very good account . . . .[45]

A Dutch representative told Queen Anne's ambassador at The Hague that

> the same person employed by the duke [of Marlborough] was then in conference with the magistrates of Rotterdam (which town had declared for the continuance of the war) to assure them, if they would hold off a little, they should see an unexpected turn in the British parliament: That the duke of Marlborough had a list of the discontented members in both houses, who were ready to turn against the court; and to crown all, that his grace had certain intelligence of the queen being in so ill a state of health, as made it impossible for her to live above six weeks.[46]

During this period, rumors of the Queen's impending death, were as common as Whig tirades against her policies. She had survived seventeen pregnancies, eleven of them ending in miscarriage. Periods of fever, or weakness of the limbs, were attributed routinely to gout, a

disease rare in women.   Yet even during the months
preceding her brief, fatal illness in July 1714, she remained
remarkably active, riding at a fast pace as much as twenty
miles a day.   On Christmas Eve, 1713, she was seized by a
violent fever, from which she recovered.   Yet soon the
Junto's rumor mills were again grinding away, this time
with the report that she was dead.   There was unfeigned joy
among the Whigs, and a speculative rise in the stock market
in anticipation of renewed war.

In response, Swift oversaw the production of another
biting satire, "A Modest Inquiry into the Reasons of the Joy
Expressed by a Certain Set of People, upon the Spreading
of a Report of Her Majesty's Death."[47]   The Peace of
Utrecht, proclaimed with popular rejoicing on May 5, 1713,
had intensified the rage among that "set of people" who
were determined to erect a new feudal empire, upon the
ruins of Britain and Europe.   It was no secret that they
wished the Queen dead.

Swift retorted that the

> Almighty Being . . . will not shorten the
> period of her life one moment, for all the
> impatient curiosity of those people who are
> daily inquiring, "When will she die?" *So long
> as they keep off their hands*, let them wish as
> much as they think fit: and, when it shall
> please God to give her the happy change of an
> earthly for a heavenly crown, let this be written
> upon her tomb: "That, in compassion to the
> miseries of Europe, and the sufferings of her
> own subjects, after a bloody and expensive war,
> which had lasted twenty years, she concluded a
> peace: and, that she might transmit the liberties
> of her people safe to posterity, she disbanded
> her army: by which glorious achievement, she

acquired the hatred of a faction, who were fond of war, that they might plunder their fellow subjects at pleasure; and of an army, that they might do this with impunity."[48]

Until May 28, 1714, Venetian party temptations to shorten the life of Queen Anne, were held substantially in check, by their remaining fears of the 'Leibniz card.' On that date, the Electress Sophie of Hanover collapsed and died, following a walk in her garden at Herrenhausen, at the age of eighty-four.[49]   Since the Act of Settlement in 1701, she had been next in line for the British throne in the event of Queen Anne's death. Had Anne died before Sophie, the British monarchy might have been guided by Leibniz, the leader of republicans internationally, and Sophie's longtime adviser. Thus, while Sophie lived, Anne held a substantial insurance policy against not-so-accidental death at the hands of her enemies.

There was no doubt that her enemies were now *politically* moving in for the kill. At the end of May, Queen Anne received a death threat in an anonymous letter, and temporarily relocated from Kensington to St. James's Palace.[50]   Oxford and Henry St. John, now Viscount Bolingbroke, were at one another's throats, in a political feud which had been worsening since the period of Oxford's recovery from an assassination attempt in 1711. Swift had repeatedly tried to reconcile the two ministers, but by the middle of May 1714, decided that the situation was beyond repair, and withdrew from the court. The Elector George of Hanover, now the immediate heir to the throne, awaited the selection of a British ambassador. The Queen backed Bolingbroke's choice over Oxford's, and on May 26 named the Earl of Clarendon, the former Lord Cornbury, transvestite governor of New York and New Jersey, and a personal enemy of Oxford's. The Elector emphasized his own ties to the Junto by naming Baron von Bothmer ambassador to Britain, a move which also revived fears of the Duke of Marlborough's plotting against the Queen.[51]

In early June, the Duke of Shrewsbury, the arch-manipulator and political intriguer of the Whig oligarchy for more than twenty years, returned to court after a stint as lord-lieutenant of Ireland. Nominally a Catholic turned Protestant, the "King of Hearts" had had an unusual career after helping establish the Bank of England in 1696. In and out of various ministries and government posts, he had also sojourned in Europe, as they say, from 1700 to 1705. His major stops were five months in Geneva in 1701, followed by three-and-one-half years in Rome, where he frequented the English Jesuit villa. (He had no children, and upon his death left his estate to his cousin, Gilbert Talbot, a Jesuit priest.) Shrewsbury's intervention into the court of Queen Anne was certainly Jesuitical. Upon the Queen's request that he seek to reconcile Oxford and Bolingbroke, Shrewsbury encouraged each to oust the other, initially pressed Anne to dismiss Bolingbroke and then to get rid of Oxford, and held a dinner party for both ministers on the pretense of reuniting them.[52]

Rumors were flying that Queen Anne's government would soon collapse. On June 17, Marlborough informed the court of Hanover from Antwerp, "My best friends think my being in England may be of much more use to the service than my continuing abroad."[53] Soon the Elector George also had reports that Shrewsbury had persuaded the Queen to remove Oxford, and was securing an invitation for Marlborough to return to England. A Hanoverian agent in London reported on June 22 that one of Marlborough's men knew *"from the Queen herself,* that *My Lord Duke* would be *welcome."*[54] On June 25, Ambassador Bothmer arrived in London, and met with Shrewsbury after word was out that Oxford would be dismissed.   Shrewsbury "politely regretted the fact that Oxford had fallen and showed some anxiety at the prospect of Bolingbroke at the helm, but the real purpose of his visit was to assure Bothmer that he, Shrewsbury, had already enjoyed the best of relationships with Bolingbroke's new ally, Marlborough.[55]

During this period, Abigail Masham, who had replaced the Duchess of Marlborough as controller of the back stairs, also turned against Oxford. She told him early in June that she would no longer carry his messages to the Queen.[56] Jonathan Swift, who had withdrawn for security reasons to the English countryside, implored his friend, Dr. Arbuthnot, to make a greater effort to inform Abigail of the deadly game being played at Queen Anne's court. Arbuthnot still had access to the Queen's personal household as one of her physicians, though the Whig-Doctor David Hamilton now had the inside track to the Queen. During the last month of Anne's life, Arbuthnot kept Swift informed of the deteriorating situation in London. On July 24, he reported that Abigail, in a rage, had denounced him for supporting Oxford even if it meant the Queen's ruin. Arbuthnot ended his letter with the guarded suggestion that Dr. Hamilton was cutting off his medical attendance upon the Queen ("but mum for that").[57]

Three days later, on July 27, Hamilton came to the Queen's chambers for a lengthy visit. According to his own diary, as he later reconstructed the meeting, Queen Anne now experienced a remarkable change of heart, and declared an extraordinary breach of protocol, on the issue of permitting a visit to England by the Hanoverian heir to her throne. The Whig Junto had continually manipulated her against allowing such a visit during the Electress Sophie's lifetime, in order to keep Leibniz out of Britain. Now her successor would be George I, who had already eliminated Leibniz's salary as adviser to the court of Hanover. Queen Anne was also fully aware that George had backed Marlborough's efforts to destroy the peace and overthrow her government. Yet the Whig-Doctor Hamilton would have us believe, that during their meeting, Queen Anne entrusted *him* with a secret mission to Hanover, to deliver an appeal to George:

> He was to ask leave to come over to pay a visit to her for three or four weeks, by which means he would have entire satisfaction and she quiet, she resolving to put it upon him *to make changes.* This confidence affected me even to tears . . . but sudden death coming in prevented her going on; for she told me Lord Oxford would be out that night. . . . [emphasis added][58]

The Queen did indeed summon Oxford that night, having held a cabinet meeting that afternoon, apparently without Oxford, to announce that she was dismissing him from office.   He had headed her government as lord treasurer for more than three years; he had put together the coalition which ousted the Godolphin-Marlborough regime, established measures for economic recovery, and brought an end to the ruinous war.   Shrewsbury had tilted the final balance against him, though the Queen had also declared that she would not entrust her government to Bolingbroke either. Between 8 and 9 p.m., Oxford came to surrender his white staff of office, and also to warn her against the Duke of Marlborough.   The duke's planned return to England, Oxford told her, was the central feature of a plot to undo her and plunge the country into civil war. "The Queen said very little to this," Oxford reported afterward, yet their meeting lasted over two hours.[59]

Available accounts of the events which followed are often conflicting, contradictory, and byzantine.   Any evaluation is complicated by the fact that one crucial source, Swift himself, was operating at his country refuge some distance from the scene, with the added restriction of having to rely almost exclusively on covert channels of communication.   It is essential to proceed first from a chronology of the events which culminated in the death of Queen Anne, at 7:45 a.m. on Sunday, August 1.

Sometime between 10:30 and 11:30 on the night of July 27, following her private meeting with Oxford, Queen Anne reconvened the cabinet, *with Oxford in attendance.* The lord treasurer whose dismissal she had declared that afternoon was not only present, but was permitted to make a "violent" speech to the cabinet. Veiled accounts suggest that Oxford thundered against "disloyalty" and "treason," directly attacking Bolingbroke.   The meeting was ostensibly held to appoint a group of commissioners to assume the functions of Oxford's office.   He left following his speech, and the meeting dragged on until 2 a.m., adjourning without agreement on whom to nominate.[60] Legally, Oxford was still lord treasurer, as long as no replacement were named.

Queen Anne, "silent and seemingly withdrawn," remained throughout the meeting, and then retired "in a distraught state" to her bedchamber, where she reportedly wept through the night.[61] The next day, July 28, the royal apothecary Daniel Malthus recorded, "Her appetite was quite lost and Her Spirits sunk:"[62] This was the first report of a change in the Queen's condition.   Throughout these final days before her death, Malthus had continuous access to Queen Anne.[63]   The same day, Dr. John Shadwell, Shrewsbury's agent among the Queen's physicians,[64] reported to him that her pulse rate was quite abnormal.[65] Another cabinet meeting, with the Queen present, but reportedly saying little, again failed to agree on a

replacement for Oxford—by one account, because no final decisions could be made without the Duke of Marlborough!
[66]

Bolingbroke held a dinner party that night for some of the Whig leaders who were *already planning a coup* against the Queen's government, to restore Marlborough to power if she lived. Bolingbroke is alleged to have offered them posts in a new government he would form, but their plans were already too advanced to include such a deal. The most significant dinner guests were General Cadogan, one of Marlborough's former commanders, and James Stanhope, the close friend of Marlborough's ally Sidney Godolphin, the former lord treasurer. Stanhope had previously commanded British forces in Spain as a leading figure in Marlborough's 'endless war' faction.[67] Plans for the coup included Cadogan's seizing control of the Tower of London, and Stanhope's ensuring the arrest of Marlborough's leading opponents, who would be branded as 'Jacobite' enemies of George I's succession to the throne. During this unusual dinner party, Stanhope told Bolingbroke that he would be on the list to die, unless he agreed to the following terms: Marlborough would resume command as captain general, and install one of his own as admiral of the fleet. "Bolingbroke could keep his ministerial posts for his friends until the Queen died."[68] The party was over, and Stanhope told Bolingbroke as he left,

> you have only two ways of escaping the gallows. The first is to join the honest party of the Whigs; the other to give yourself up entirely to the French King and seek help for the Pretender [the son of the Stuart King James II, in exile in France]. If you do not choose the first we can only imagine that you have decided for the second.[69]

The 'honest' Whigs had just given Bolingbroke a choice, between two acts of treason against Queen Anne.

Early the next morning, July 29, the Queen's physicians were summoned, for her condition was much worse. Dr. Hamilton, the Whig, recorded that she "had a trembling in her hands, a pain and heat in her head, with sleepiness, and a little bleeding at the nose."[70] Malthus added that she was "flushed and Her Head full." A scheduled meeting of the cabinet, which had still not resolved on a successor to Oxford, was postponed until the Queen were well enough to preside.[71]

At his retreat in Berkshire fifty miles from London, Swift was now deluged with urgent appeals for his services. Even before Oxford surrendered his staff to the Queen, he had written to Swift of his intention to resign on July 28. Swift wrote to Ireland on July 29

> of my Lord Oxford's laying down; he was to do it yesterday. He has sent to desire I would stay some time with him at his house in Herefordshire, which I am not likely to refuse, though I may probably suffer a good deal in my little affairs in Ireland by my absence . . . . I believe you will reckon me an ill courtier to follow a discarded statesman to his retirement, especially when I have always been well with those now [remaining] in power, as I was with him. But to answer that would require talking.[72]

He wrote to another Irish correspondent the same day, "I shall lose all favour with whose now in power by following Lord Oxford in his retreat. I am hitherto very fair with them, but that will be at an end."[73]

Also on July 29, Lady Masham wrote urgently to Swift, bitterly denouncing Oxford for not having listened to

Swift's advice when the ministry was collapsing, and imploring him to come to Queen Anne's aid with his counsels now:

> will you, who have gone through so much, and taken more than anybody pains, and given wise advice, if that wretched man had had sense enough and honesty to have taken it, I say, will you leave us and go to Ireland? No, it is impossible; your goodness is still the same, your charity and compassion for this poor lady [the Queen], who has been barbarously used, would not let you do it . . . . Pray, dear friend, stay here; and do not believe us all alike to throw away good advice, and despise everybody's understanding but their own. I could say a great deal upon the subject, but I must go to her, for she is not well.
>
> This comes to you by a safe hand, so that neither of us need be in any pain about it.[74]

Swift's close friend John Barber was to have delivered the letter the next day, but his "safe hand" was stayed by another worsening turn of events. Queen Anne was unable to sleep during the night, and was seized by an attack of vomiting at three in the morning. Malthus had again remained at her bedside. Around 7 a.m. on July 30, after a few hours' sleep, she awoke and attempted to rise for the day. At 9 a.m., she experienced the first of two "violent convulsions, one after the other, which lasted from nine until eleven o'clock."[75] The Duke of Ormond's wife, a lady of the bedchamber, quickly summoned him from Whitehall, where he and the other cabinet ministers were about to meet. They all came running; her doctors rushed to her side. The Queen was unconscious for about an hour, and then "could not speak beyond answering 'yes' or 'no.'" "One of Oxford's enemies, Lord Chancellor Simon Harcourt, burst in upon the Queen, and thought she was "dead in her chair."[76] If Queen Anne were dying, destroying her by an outright military coup would become superfluous —and potentially dangerous to those whose preparations for such treason were no longer secret.   There is no satisfactory record available, of what Oxford had warned her of during their meeting on July 27, nor of what he said at the cabinet meeting later that night.   But suspicions that Marlborough and his allies plotted to overthrow her were longstanding, and were not allayed by reports that he planned to return to Britain, with or without an invitation from the Queen.   Such fears had increased in mid July, when Marlborough moved to the Belgian port of Ostend, the embarcation point for ships sailing to Dover.   One of Swift's correspondents at court wrote him on July 22, "The Duke of Marlborough is expected here every day . . . . The Whigs are making great preparations to receive him."[77] The Venetian party alternative to such a coup, was the death of the Queen, a neater resolution once the Electress Sophie's death had removed the 'Leibniz card,' and ensured the succession of their own asset, the Elector George of Hanover.   By the terms of the Junto's earlier Act of Regency, Queen Anne's death would give all power to a committee designated by the Hanoverian heir to the throne, until the coronation of the new monarch took place.   With a dead queen, all of the objectives of a military coup could be accomplished without an open fight.

But on the morning of July 30, one definite complication remained.   Despite all the gaps in the available historical record, one thing is clear.   Following her meeting with Oxford on the evening of July 27, Queen Anne did not impose a new lord treasurer upon her cabinet members, nor could they agree on his replacement, while she was in attendance. Were she to die without designating a new head of her government, Oxford would still hold his rank. But Harcourt's fears that the Queen was "dead in her chair" were relieved: "he went close up to her, look'd in her face & touch'd her hand without her showing the least knowledge of him."[78] He quickly returned to the lords of the Privy Council assembled outside her chambers, who had been joined by the Dukes of Somerset and Argyll, former cabinet members who had been ousted for their opposition to the peace. Argyll reportedly proposed that they all agree to put forward the Duke of Shrewsbury, as the new lord treasurer to the dying Queen. Harcourt endorsed the proposal, and so apparently did Bolingbroke, with great anxiety.[79]

The Duchess of Somerset, the enemy of Swift, who, as a lady of the bedchamber, had maneuvered her way into substantial control of the back stairs, was asked to go to the Queen and tell her that the lords wished to "propose something of great moment to her." Shrewsbury, Somerset, Argyll, and Harcourt went in. It is unclear who else accompanied them. The Queen was conscious, but unable to speak. "So weak was she that Harcourt had to direct her hand as she gave the Staff to the Duke of Shrewsbury." In this condition, she signed the royal warrant appointing Shrewsbury as lord treasurer.[80]

Shrewsbury had already held the position of lord chamberlain before his appointment as lord-lieutenant of Ireland. Now, on the afternoon of July 30, he became lord treasurer and chief minister as well. The first phase of the inside coup was complete, and the "principal statesmen" soon gathered at the house of Baron von Bothmer, the Elector's ambassador to London.[81] The cabinet now assumed emergency powers as a Privy Council "in defense of the realm," issuing a series of unanimous decrees obviously aimed more at domestic than foreign enemies.

All of Britain's lords lieutenant were ordered to seize the arms and horses of Roman Catholics and "to watch suspected persons." The ports were closed, a number of army regiments were called to London, and preparations were made to transport additional British forces from the southern Netherlands.

At four in the afternoon, some of the Queen's physicians informed the Privy Council that she would be dead within twelve hours. An official communiqué was dispatched to Hanover to assure the Elector she would not live.[82]

At some point during the day, Bolingbroke told John Barber, who had still not left London to bring letters and news to Swift, that he would "reconcile" Swift and the Duchess of Somerset,

> and then it would be easy to set you right with
> the Queen, and that you should be made easy
> here, and not go over [to Ireland]. He said
> twenty things in your favor, and commanded
> me to bring you up, whatever was the
> consequence.[83]

Whatever the intent of such desperate schemes, the time for them was fast running out. By the evening of July 30, the Queen no longer knew what was happening around her. She had experienced terrible head pains and was believed to be dying of "gout in the head." Before 9 a. m. on July 31, the word at the palace was that she was "just expiring," one of Swift's correspondents reported to him.

> That account continued above three hours, and
> a report was carried to town, that she was
> actually dead. She was not prayed for, even at
> her own chapel at St. James's, and what is more
> infamous, stocks arose three per cent. Upon it
> in the city . . . . This morning the Hanoverian
> envoy was ordered to attend with the black box,

containing the names of the lords justices chosen by the Elector to rule as regents.[84] One physician called in late on the case, Dr. Richard Mead, informed a visitor at court that afternoon "that any body wou'd have been in her condition, if they had had the gout in their head six & thirty hours, without anything done to them."[85] She lingered through the night, slipping into a coma before dawn, and was dead at 7:45 a.m., August 1.[86]

The Queen's Privy Council immediately convened in the palace to open the "black box." Only one of her ministers, the Duke of Shrewsbury, found his name among those designated by the Elector George to serve on the regency council, until his coronation as King of England. That afternoon, his proclamation as George I began at St. James's Palace, and the Duke and Duchess of Marlborough landed at Dover. Britain's first Hanoverian King refused to attend any funeral for Queen Anne, and announced he would not set foot in his new kingdom until she was buried. Her estate was seized by the crown, for she had died without a will. Her body rotted in the palace for more than three weeks, until finally, preparations for a funeral, with a certain amount of pomp and ceremony, were made. There was no public lying-in-state.[87]

Queen Anne was buried at night, privately, in Westminster Abbey on August 24, 1714. The Duke of Shrewsbury supervised the proceedings. Her coffin was lowered into a vault beneath the tomb of Mary, Queen of Scots, her great-great-grandmother, in the chapel of Henry VII. No monument, no stone, no tablet has ever marked her resting place. In the entire abbey, only a small plaque on a distant wall mentions her name. It was presented, ironically, by New York's Trinity Church in 1966, noting the grant it received during her reign of "the Queen's farm and garden on Manhattan Island."

Was Queen Anne Murdered?

On the morning of her death, the Whig head of St. John's College at Oxford ordered prayers for "King George" for the morning services at the town's Christ Church. Few yet knew of Queen Anne's fate; and the canon of the church, William Stratford, objected that she might not be dead. (Stratford had been a friend and mentor of Robert Harley, Lord Oxford, since his college days, and had hosted a private meeting between Swift and Harley's brother Edward in late July, to discuss the crisis at court.) The answer to the objection, Stratford wrote Edward Harley the next day, was "'Dead,' says he, 'she is as dead as Julius Caesar.' "[88]

Was Queen Anne, like Caesar, murdered? If the ministry which Swift had influenced had already been politically broken, why were Marlborough and his Venetian allies preparing a coup, until the fatal illness which suddenly struck her? What had the Queen concluded from Lord Oxford's warnings against Marlborough, during their two-hour meeting on July 27, and during the address she permitted him to make to the cabinet following it? Why did Oxford, even before his final audience with Queen Anne, and expecting his removal from the government, write urgently to Swift requesting a meeting at Oxford's country home, *following* his assumed dismissal? Had Anne lived, was there still time, or still someone besides Swift, to expose the planned coup, and thus give the Queen room to resume the policies which threatened the oligarchy's control over Britain and Europe? Was it merely coincidental that the Queen's symptoms only appeared the day after the dramatic political events of July 27? Was there also a political reason, regarding the Queen's health, that Swift's friend and physician to the Queen, Dr. John Arbuthnot, had increasingly restricted access to her chambers preceding and during the period of her final illness?

From available evidence, none of these questions can be definitively answered. What is clear from the historical record, however, is that preparations for a coup against the Queen's *government* were rapidly put into place, following the death of the Electress Sophie of Hanover on May 28. With her died the threat of her succeeding Anne as Queen of England, and bringing Leibniz directly into British policy making. Her son George was already Venetian property, so there was no longer any reason to postpone taking over the throne. Political realities, moreover, had changed during the period that Swift and Leibniz had influenced Queen Anne's cabinet. There was a significant tide of support running in favor of new prospects of economic development, in the wake of the peace with France. Swift's pamphlets had forever eliminated the Duke of Marlborough's dreams of becoming once more a popular hero—no matter how much the Bank of England spent to promote him.

Any coup involving Marlborough, against Queen Anne's personal support for policies the Bank of England hated from their beginning, could not be expected to succeed merely by imposing a new cabinet upon the Queen. During the months preceding the Queen's death, the news of Marlborough's planned return was coupled with widespread anticipation of civil war.[89] Thus, there was no safe plan, without *precalculating* the exercise of dictatorial powers in support of the plot. Only Anne's death, and such regency powers as the Venetian party required to impose their creature George I upon Britain, uniquely met the conditions of a successful coup.

There were no public charges at the time that Queen Anne died from anything but natural causes. Certainly Marlborough and his cronies *wished* her death, and on several, premature occasions had predicted and even declared it. Even Swift, on the record at least, indicated *afterward* that her illness during Christmas 1713, made him fear she would not live long. Yet all observers reported her to be in excellent health during the spring and summer of 1714. For Queen Anne's enemies, her sudden demise could not have been better timed. Political dividends were amassed at a prodigious rate. There was now a Venetian party regency in Britain to link imminently with one in France. The suspected poisoning of three successive heirs to the French throne, had ensured the regency of the Duke d'Orléans, upon the death of Louis XIV. Queen Anne's reported symptoms are virtually identical to those reported in the deaths in France, and are summarized in modern terms by one of her biographers as "intense local inflammation of the skin and subcutaneous tissue, caused by a hemolytic streptococcus."[90]

There was, of course, no medical knowledge at the time of streptococci or any other bacterial forms of disease. In all four cases, however, the symptoms described also fit those resulting from a class of chemical poisons, producing hemorrhaging throughout the system, which were well known at the time. Was Queen Anne poisoned? If she were, only those directly involved in the crime might have reported it, if assured it would remain a 'family secret.'

There are several clues worth considering. One comes from a modern biographer of the Duke of Marlborough, who served as personal secretary to Lord Beaverbrook, during Sir Winston Churchill's World War II government in Britain. He offers the following report of the period prior to the Queen's death:

> Although, in the spring of 1714, Queen Anne's health made a spectacular recovery, it was plain the improvement was not likely to last [?]. It was a time when Royal mortality had a disturbing effect on political calculations. King

Louis' son died in 1711; his grandson died in
1712; his great-grandson, a weakly infant, was
now heir to the throne of France.   It was an
extraordinary Royal holocaust . . . . Now it
seemed that another Royal death, that of Queen
Anne, would at any moment [?] bring new
anxieties to a troubled world.   *With that in
mind*, Marlborough moved to Ostend in the
middle of July and let it be known that he
meant to cross over to England [emphasis
added].[91]

Besides the casual reference to a "Royal holocaust," as
though it were simply an unusual turn in the weather, this
account is remarkable for reporting that Marlborough's
plans were based on the presumption of Anne's imminent
death, at a time when she showed no signs of ill health.
Did Marlborough's biographer learn some Churchill
'family secrets'?

If the amazing political timing of Queen Anne's death
were determined by poison, another clue may lie in the
unusual career of her royal apothecary, Daniel Malthus
(1651–1717), who reported the Queen's earliest signs of
illness and had continuous access to her until her death.
Malthus had been certified as an apothecary in London in
1688, the year William of Orange invaded England to seize
the throne for himself and the Venetian party.   He had
studied under the renowned Thomas Sydenham (1624–
1689), who studied at Oxford and in France and became the
foremost authority on smallpox, *scarlatina* (scarlet fever),
and gout.   For unspecified services rendered, Malthus
amassed quite a fortune for an apothecary (or anyone else)
by 1691, for that year he was able to purchase a manor
from the estate of the Earl of Suffolk for over £5,500.   He
was appointed apothecary to Queen Anne in 1704, with an

annual salary of £115, and a medical expense budget of £205 and 5 shillings.

By 1712, Daniel Malthus was the central figure, with a unique degree of access to the Queen, in an intermarried set of families who controlled the preparation of all of Queen Anne's food, drink, and medication. His son, Sydenham Malthus, was married that year to Anne Dalton, whose father Richard was gentleman yeoman of the wine cellar. Dalton's other son-in-law, James Eckersall, from 1711 on supervised the preparation of royal meals.

All of them prospered rather nicely after Queen Anne's death, remaining in service to King George I. Daniel Malthus prepared the anointing oil for the new King's coronation, and envisioned a little dynasty of his own to retain oligarchical favors. He was royal apothecary to King George until 1717, and on his death was replaced by Thomas Graham, his sister's husband. Their son was named Daniel Graham, who succeeded his father as apothecary to George II and continued under George III. Sydenham Malthus was groomed for the legal profession; his son Daniel Malthus II (1730–1800) was partly placed in service to Jean Jacques Rousseau (1712–1778), the lunatic Swiss 'philosopher' of the French Enlightenment, who also served for a time as secretary to the French embassy in Venice. So stark, raving mad that at various times even his oligarchical patrons kicked him out of Venice, Switzerland, France, and Britain, Rousseau is still celebrated for his so-called modern notion that the purest ideas are those of an infant, whose simple nature should be left uncorrupted by books or other forms of contact with civilization.

Daniel Malthus II married Daniel Graham's daughter, and was also the executor for whatever Rousseau left in his will. Such inbreeding produced an infamous case of oligarchical overkill. Their son, Thomas Malthus (1766–

1834), was born deformed, with a hare lip and cleft palate. His education was left to his Rousseauvian father, which should certainly have guaranteed his dying in pathetic obscurity. No doubt in acknowledgement of his family's generations of willing dirty work, Thomas Malthus was instead promoted as a model of so-called 'natural' ideas. While the decadent salons of Britain and Europe laughed privately and in the face of their plaything, whose mere speech could not be understood, Thomas Malthus was allowed to put his name to the bible of modern genocide and environmentalism—the 1798 *Essay on the Principle of Population*.[92]

At that time, the ancient, oligarchical rationale, that poverty was necessary for all but a few, was such obvious quackery that only a freak could be assigned to promote it. Denying human creativity, scientific progress, and the history of the world, Malthus argued that food supplies could only increase arithmetically, while populations increased geometrically. Therefore, the only cure for poverty was war, famine, and disease. The argument was especially aimed at America, where the new republic of the United States was already on its way to becoming the largest population in the western world, while helping to feed much of the world besides.

Considerations for America

The degeneracy promoted during the reigns of Britain's Hanoverian kings provided an obvious lesson for America's patriots. Republican aspirations for developing the American continent could expect nothing but hostility from the British monarchy. During a few, brief years at the end of Queen Anne's reign, Swift and Leibniz had temporarily routed the Venetians in a major battle. That moment of opportunity was not lost. But the accession of George I unleashed a bloody purge, designed to eliminate any future breach of oligarchical control over royal policy.

Nearly a month after Queen Anne's burial, King George arrived in London on September 18. All of the Queen's ministers, except the Duke of Shrewsbury, were dismissed the next day. New elections for Parliament restored the Whig Junto to power, as expected. The Whigs awaited only the King's signal to launch their vendetta, against the ministry which had allowed Jonathan Swift to enter its doors, and had imposed peace upon Europe. When King George opened the new session in March 1715, he denounced the Peace of Utrecht as the "fatal cessation of arms."[93] General Stanhope, one of Marlborough's minions in the House of Commons and a leader of his planned coup, unblushingly charged Queen Anne's peace ministry with being "the most corrupt that ever sat at the helm," and threatened criminal proceedings against her cabinet members.[94] Presaging the British-supported Jacobin Terror which later destroyed American hopes for the French Revolution, a Committee of Secrecy was established April 9, to root out 'traitors' who had supported the peace. Its chairman was Robert Walpole, the future prime minister, whom Swift continued to battle throughout his life. "The slightest criticism of the government was enough to bring threats of the Tower."[95]

The Committee of Secrecy presented its report to the House of Commons on June 9. Thomas Harley and Matthew Prior, one of Swift's associates who had played a key role in the peace negotiations, had already been arrested. Bolingbroke had fled to France only ten days earlier. On June 10, Walpole took the easy route, charging Bolingbroke with high treason. One of his protégés followed him by impeaching Robert Harley, Lord Oxford, on the same charge. Despite popular demonstrations of support, Oxford was taken to the Tower of London to await trial. The Duke of Marlborough was restored as captain general; his successor, the Duke of Ormond, who had enraged the Junto by preserving a cease-fire during the final peace negotiations, was also charged with treason. Ormond too fled to France, and took the Hanoverian opposition's bait, by taking part in the Stuarts' Scottish uprising of 1715 against George I.[96]

Ormond survived the misadventure in exile. The rebellion had been encouraged by the French oligarchy, with promises of military support—never delivered—for the Stuart claimant to the throne, Queen Anne's half-brother James. Legitimate opposition, to George I's Venetian coup, went down with these manipulations of pathetic Scottish loyalty to the Stuart royal heirs. Among those heirs, ironically, had been Leibniz's patron, the Electress Sophie of Hanover, granddaughter of James VI of Scotland and I of England.

But of all the Stuarts on the throne of England, only the last one, Queen Anne, deserves to be remembered. For all her faults, and for all her compromises with the evil around her, she nonetheless mustered the will to do good during her lifetime. Yet for all her willingness, during her final years, to oppose the monstrous policies earlier controlling her reign, she had no citizenry to appeal to. She had only British subjects, and the rules of court were defined without them. Jonathan Swift had learned the rules, and knew there was no hope without changing them.

Many years later, in a poem written in 1731, Swift reviewed those last years of Queen Anne:

> And oh! How short are human schemes!
>
> Here ended all our golden dreams.
>
> What St. John's skill in state affairs,
>
> What Ormond's *valour*, Oxford's cares,
>
> To save their sinking country lent,

Was all destroyed by one event.

Too soon that precious life was ended,

On which alone, our weal depended.[97]

During the first year of George I's reign, London was an unpleasant place. Numerous public sites were adorned, week after week, with the severed limbs and rotting heads of those executed on charges of participating in the Scottish Jacobite rebellion. The orgy of revenge finally proved so sickening to the population, that those still awaiting death were spared for lesser sentences. One of them made it to Virginia, with the help of Alexander Spotswood, and taught the young George Washington the science of surveying.

Jonathan Swift returned to Dublin, and began the task which Leibniz had never accomplished—the building of a mass republican movement. His eye was on America, for there were no prospects simply of influencing courts, and Leibniz's own death in 1716 left him no choice. Swift's short-term protection was that he was dean of St. Patrick's Cathedral, but as he reported himself, his position offered no real sanctuary:

> Upon the Queen's Death, the Dean returned to live in *Dublin*, at his Deanry-House: Numberless Libels were writ against him in *England*, as a Jacobite; he was insulted in the Street, and at Nights he was forced to be attended by his Servants armed.[98]

Perhaps then he wished again for his bishopric in Virginia. His more urgent task, however, was to politically arm sufficient forces to protect America against the mad vengeance of the new regime in Britain.

NOTES

1. Gregg, *Queen Anne*, 338, 340, 343; Swift, *Journal to Stella* (August 24, 1711), 339.

2. Quoted by Gregg, *Queen Anne*, 343.

3. George M. Thomson, *The First Churchill, The Life of John, 1ˢᵗ Duke of Marlborough* (New York, 1980), 265.

4. Swift, *Journal to Stella*, 395.

5. *Ibid.*, 397.

6. Swift, *The Conduct of the Allies*, in *Works*, Sheridan, ed., V, 310.

7. Swift, *History*, 51–52; Green, *Queen Anne*, 259.

8. Swift, *History*, 52.

9. Gregg, *Queen Anne*, 345.

10. Swift, *History*, 53.

11. Thomson, *First Churchill*, 271.

12. Swift, *Journal to Stella* (November 27–29, 1711), II, 422–423, 422*n*.

13. Ibid. (December 13, 1711), II, 437, 437*n*.

14. Swift, *Conduct*, 305.

15. *Ibid.*, 272.

16. *Ibid.*, 306.

17. *Ibid.*, 272.

18. *Ibid.*, 297.

19. *Ibid.*, 310.

20. Green, *Queen Anne*, 259.

21. Swift, *Conduct*, 311.

22. *Ibid.*, 300–301.

23. Gregg, *Queen Anne*, 346; Green, *Queen Anne*, 260.

24. Gregg, *Queen Anne*, 347–348.

25. Gregg, *Queen Anne*, 354. Only by a footnote citation does Gregg reveal that the documentation for all of these lurid particulars comes from Bothmer's communique´s.

26. F. Guizot, *History of France* (8 vols., London, 1872), IV, 459–461; Durant, *Age of Louis XIV*, 716.

27. Guizot, *History*, 461.

28. Durant, *Age of Louis XIV*, 716.

29. April 23, by Britain's Old Style calendar.

30. Guizot, *History*, 461.

31. *Ibid.*, 461–462; Durant, *Age of Louis XIV*, 718; Henri Martin, *The Age of Louis XIV* (2 vols., Boston, 1865), II, 540*n*.

32. Martin, *Age of Louis XIV*, II, 539.

33. Quoted by Durant, *Age of Louis XIV*, 718.

34. Durant, *Age of Louis XIV*, 719.

35. Motion of Halifax in the House of Lords, May 28, 1712, quoted by Gregg, *Queen Anne*, 357.

36. Thomson, *First Churchill*, 280. In his "acknowledgements," Thomson states, "Much of the shape and substance of this book is inspired by the monumental work of Sir Winston [Churchill]." Such charges against Marlborough, Thomson adds, were "preposterous."

37. *Ibid.*, 280.

38. Gregg, *Queen Anne*, 358.

39. Thomson, *First Churchill*, 282.

40. Swift, *History*, 203.

41. Thomson, *First Churchill*, 282; Gregg, *Queen Anne*, 394, 397.

42. Swift, *Conduct*, 327, 328.

43. *Ibid.*, 328.

44. *Ibid.*, 329.

45. Swift, *History*, 213.

46. *Ibid.*, 213–214.

47. Printed February 4, 1714; Swift, *Works*, Sheridan, ed., VI, 109–128.

48. *Ibid.*, 127–128.

49. On June 8, by Europe's "New Style" calendar, in universal use today.

50. Green, *Queen Anne*, 311.

51. Jonathan Swift, "Verses on the Death of Dr. Swift," with notes by the author (Dublin, 1739), in Carl van Doren, ed., *The Portable Swift* (New York, 1948), 596, 596n.; Green, *Queen Anne*, 310–311; Gregg, *Queen Anne*, 384–385.

52. Dorothy H. Somerville, *The King of Hearts, Charles Talbot, Duke of Shrewsbury* (London, 1962), 204–205, 208–213, 357; Green, *Queen Anne*, 312–313; Gregg, *Queen Anne*, 388–389.

53. Quoted by Green, *Queen Anne*, 313.

54. Gregg, *Queen Anne*, 389.

55. *Ibid.*

56. Arbuthnot to Swift, June 12, 1714, in Swift, *Works*, Sheridan, ed., XIV, 35.

57. Arbuthnot to Swift, July 24, 1714, *ibid.*, 71; Green, *Queen Anne*, 314–315.

58. Hamilton's diary, mss., quoted by Green, *Queen Anne*, 317.

59. Erasmus Lewis to Swift, July 27, 1714; Gregg, *Queen Anne*, 391–392.

60. Swift, *Correspondence*, Williams, ed., II, 201*n.*, editor's note; Green, *Queen Anne*, 319.

61. Green, *Queen Anne*, 319; Gregg, *Queen Anne*, 392.

62. Quoted by Gregg, *Queen Anne*, 392.

63. Patricia James, *Population Malthus* (London, 1979), 5.

64. Gregg, *Queen Anne*, 371.

65. Somerville, *King of Hearts*, 331.

66. Green, *Queen Anne*, 319; Gregg, *Queen Anne*, 392.

67. Thomson, *First Churchill*, 291; Gregg, *Queen Anne*, 256, 258.

68. Thomson, *First Churchill*, 291. Thomson reports these monstrous doings without comment, as though he had just noted the weather.

69. Quoted by Green, *Queen Anne*, 319. Green reports nothing else about what transpired at the dinner.

70. Hamilton's diary, quoted by Green, *Queen Anne*, 320.

71. Quoted by Gregg, *Queen Anne*, 392.

72. Swift to Joshua Dawson, July 29, 1714, *Correspondence*, II, 204.

73. Swift to Archdeacon Walls, July 29, 1714, *Correspondence*, II, 204.

74. Lady Masham to Swift, July 29, 1714, *Correspondence*, II, 201.

75. Gregg, *Queen Anne*, 392.

76. *Ibid.*

77. Charles Ford to Swift, July 22, 1714, *Correspondence*, II, 193.

78. Quoted by Gregg, *Queen Anne*, 392.

79. Somerville, *King of Hearts*, 331–332.

80. *Ibid.*, 332.

81. *Ibid.*

82. Gregg, *Queen Anne*, 393–394.

83. John Barber to Swift, August 3, 1714, *Correspondence*, II, 212–213.

84. Charles Ford to Swift, July 31, 1714, *Correspondence*, II, 208.

85. Quoted by Gregg, *Queen Anne*, 394.

86. Green, *Queen Anne*, 323; Gregg, *Queen Anne*, 394.

87. Somerville, *King of Hearts*, 333; Gregg, *Queen Anne*, 397–398; Green, *Queen Anne*, 327.

88. William Stratford to Edward Harley, August 2, 1714, quoted by Gregg, *Queen Anne*, 395; Swift to John Arbuthnot, July 22, 1714, *Correspondence*, II, 190, 190*n*.

89. Gregg, *Queen Anne*, 380.

90. *Ibid.*, 392.

91. Thomson, *First Churchill*, 290.

92. James, *Population Malthus*, 2*ff.* And genealogical tables; *Dictionary of National Biography; Columbia Encyclopedia.*

93. Somerville, *King of Hearts*, 342.

94. *Ibid.*

95. *Ibid.*, 343.

96. *Ibid.*; Gregg, *Queen Anne*, 399.

97. Swift, "Verses on the Death of Dr. Swift," in Van Doren, ed., *Portable Swift*, 596–597.

98. One of Swift's own footnotes to his poem, "Verses on the Death of Dr. Swift," *ibid.*, 597.

7

Alexander Crosses the Euphrates

The Duke of Marlborough's sabotage of the British expedition against Quebec in 1711 had severely undermined American hopes for opening the West. French outposts, stretching from Quebec to the Great Lakes, still supported the threat of Jesuit-run Indian warfare against the northern frontiers of New England and New York. The Mohawk Valley route through the mountains remained closed. France retained control of Cape Breton Island, guarding the strategic entrance to the St. Lawrence gulf and river. Louis XIV now determined to close off that line of attack as well, by ordering the construction of a vast, fortified city on Cape Breton. Erected on a design of Vauban's, the fortress at Louisbourg was one of the largest ever built, and upon completion by 1740 was considered impregnable by all the powers of Europe.

Virginia's colonial claims to the West, reaching to both the Mississippi River and the Great Lakes, were now the primary avenue to the potential for a continental republic. By the spring of 1713, the peace treaty signed at Utrecht between Britain and France, removed the possibility of ending French containment by an act of war. The major responsibility for America's future prospects now fell upon Virginia's Governor Alexander Spotswood.

The Spotswood family was accustomed to being in the center of significant historical events. Alexander's great-grandfather John Spottiswoode (1565–1639), an opponent of John Knox's Calvinist "reformation" in Scotland, had served as archbishop of St. Andrews and lord high chancellor of Scotland. Upon his death, Charles I ordered that he be interred with full ceremony in Henry VII's chapel in Westminster Abbey. In 1644, his younger brother James was also buried in Westminster, having served in the court of King James I, from 1621 to 1642 as bishop of Clogher in Ireland.

Alexander's grandfather, Sir Robert Spottiswoode (1596–1646), son of the lord high chancellor, was a member of James I's privy council, and the author of "Practicks of the Law of Scotland." Under Charles I, he was appointed lord president of the College of Justice and, in 1636, secretary for Scotland. In 1646, during the Civil War, he was executed by order of the Presbyterian-controlled Parliament.[1]

Such family lore Alexander Spotswood knew. But by the time of his birth in 1676, under the abysmal Stuart Restoration, his own father lived under much humbler, if only marginally safer, circumstances. Trained in medicine, Robert Spottswood, third son of the beheaded secretary for Scotland, held an appointment as physician to the English governor and garrison at Tangier, North Africa. He died when Alexander was eleven; his wife Catherine Elliott, now twice widowed, took their only son to live near her relatives in Ireland. Her son by her previous marriage entered a career in the military, and as General Elliott, later commanded the cavalry at the Battle of Blenheim.[2]

Fatherless and "without prospects," as the phrase of the time put it, Alexander Spotswood also entered the military. Like his fellow Scot Robert Hunter, his competence in the field won him promotion in the ranks. Despite a year's convalescence in London, after nearly being killed by a cannonball at Blenheim in 1704, Lieutenant Colonel Spotswood returned to the army, fighting with Hunter alongside the Earl of Orkney, who was soon to become governor of Virginia. In 1708, while Hunter, Orkney's appointee to govern Virginia, remained a prisoner of

France, Spotswood's horse was shot out from under him at the Battle of Oudenarde. The French took Spotswood prisoner also. The Duke of Marlborough negotiated his exchange much more rapidly than he had done for Hunter. Perhaps he was mindful of Swift's *Bickerstaff Papers*.

Yet Spotswood similarly found his military career to be at a dead end under Marlborough. Although a full colonel and aide-de-camp to the captain general at the time of his capture, Spotswood was reassigned to the role of assistant quartermaster general for Scotland.[3] In 1709, Spotswood also resigned from the army, and returned to London. Following Hunter's appointment as governor of New York and New Jersey, Spotswood was named governor of Virginia by his old commander, General George Hamilton, Earl of Orkney.[4]

Transforming Virginia

When Spotswood took office, the capital at Williamsburg was little more than a rude village, surrounding a cluster of taverns. At one end of its main street, a single wall stood amid the charred ruins of the College of William and Mary, destroyed by fire in 1705. Construction of a governor's residence had been authorized in 1706, but virtually nothing had come of it. Except for the Capitol, neither public buildings nor private homes suggested that anything of positive significance was ever expected to transpire there. Williamsburg's location, not far up the peninsula between the James and the York rivers, was convenient enough for the Tidewater oligarchy. Many of their plantations were within a comfortable day's ride. If the ritual of conducting public affairs required staying overnight, the town offered sufficient 'pleasures' for the likes of William Byrd, whose diary catalogued the prostitutes of his favorite taverns.[5]

For the Tidewater planters, Williamsburg simply existed as part of their own feudal domain. In Massachusetts, the coastal capital at Boston was connected to scores of towns of the interior by both postal service and an extensive system of roads. In Virginia, when Spotswood took command, there was no post office, and the roads varied from miserable to nonexistent. The bold agenda of economic development and western colonization he had presented in 1710, required transforming its tidal backwater as well.

During his governorship, Spotswood rebuilt the College of William and Mary, from the ruins of the original structure erected after a design of Sir Christopher Wren, the architect of St. Paul's Cathedral in London. With only the front wall to work from, the college's main hall was "rebuilt and nicely contrived, altered and adorned by the ingenious Direction of Governor Spotswood."[6] Nothing matched it in America at the time. In restored form, it is still in use today. In its original banquet hall, a large portrait of Queen Anne hangs fittingly in the place of honor.

Spotswood was renowned for his abilities in geometry and mathematics, which were the bases for his accomplishments in architecture. Under his direction, Williamsburg soon became the most beautiful capital in colonial America. Spotswood was also the architect of Virginia's first Governor's Residence, a magnificent building which served as the model for the best architecture in the Mid-Atlantic colonies for decades to come. The success of his designs was entirely lawful, for he based them on principles of classical constructive geometry— circular action and the Golden Section.

Early in 1711, Governor Spotswood presented his design for a new church for Williamsburg's Bruton Parish.

Reconstruction of Gov. Alexander Spotswood's Geometry in the Design of Bruton Parish Church, Williamsburg

Given: Only line AB (see diagram), from folding a circle with a radius of 33 ft. (half the length of a surveyor's chain).

Procedure:

1) Fold the half-circle with diameter AB against itself again, to establish focal point C.

2) Construct circles with an 11 ft. radius from both points A and B. The 11 ft. radius is the first division of the Trinity or one-third of 33 ft. At the 'folded' right angle to Line AB, establish points D and E where the new circles intersect those radii in the same direction. This creates lines AD and BE.

3) Construct circles with a 22 ft. radius from both points D and E. The 22 ft. radius represents the second division of the Trinity or two-thirds of 33 ft. Establish points F and G where these circles intersect line AB.

4) Also construct circles with a 22 ft. radius from points F and G. In the same direction as lines AD and BE, establish a point H where the circles from G and E intersect.

5) The points created now establish lines HI, FH and GI. Establish point J, at the intersection of extended lines BE and HI.

6) Return to original focal point point C, and generate a circle of radius JC (thus reaching to the farthest point from C created so far). The new circle will also intersect point K which was created in an identical manner.

7) Extend Lines FH and GI in both directions to their points of intersection with the new circle, establishing points L and M along the original 'forward' direction, and points N and O where the lines intersect the new circle in the opposite direction. The new points establish lines LM and NO.

The original floor plan of Spotswood's church is now exactly revealed by the sequence of parallel and perpendicular outside lines. HLMI defines the apse, or altar end of the church; FAJH and GBKI the wings of the transept; and FNOG the nave, the section for the pews. The entire cruciform structure is circumscribed by the *one* circle whose radius is greater than all preceding circles, and is derived from the geometric transformations generated by them.

The "Three-in-One" theme of the design is also reflected by the resulting equilateral triangles (FDH and GEI) in each wing of the transept. The classical proportions of the Golden Section, the characteristic pattern of development in living processes, also emerge in the internal dimensions of the church. The area common to both the length and breadth of the church (FGIH), known as the crossing, is the Golden Section ratio to the area of the apse (HLMI). Finally, of course, the original focal point (C) is equidistant from all points of the cross, except A and B, which it lies midway between.

Using standard graph paper, you can easily duplicate the design yourself. Plot the length of the 66 ft. surveyor's chain, Line AB, as 18 spaces. That establishes a scale of 3 spaces = 11 ft., which is convenient for the division Spotswood employed.

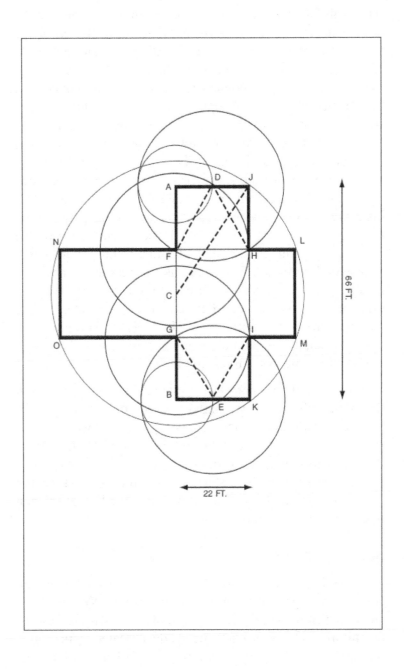

Although no record survives recounting the method he employed, the dimensions of his plan, for a church in the shape of a cross, point to a classical geometric approach. The author set out to reconstruct Spotswood's method, and found it to be a pedagogical expression of the concept of the Trinity as well. Adopting the standard length of a surveyor's chain (sixty-six feet), Spotswood generated the outlines of his cruciform church by circular action, using radii representing divisions of the Trinity. From the thirty-three-foot radius of the surveyor's original circle, each side of the church is determined by one rotation of a radius one-third the original, and two rotations of a radius two-thirds the original. To express the nonlinear significance of the Trinity, as being greater than the mere sum of its parts, Spotswood derived a further radius from a new dimension, created by the previous actions based on the Trinity's divisions. The circle defined by the greater radius circumscribes the entire church. The accompanying diagram (page 207) and explanation will enable the reader to reproduce the procedures involved.

The church still stands in Williamsburg today, although for politically imposed, budgetary reasons, Spotswood's original breadth for the transept (sixty-six feet) was reduced in 1712 by six feet, six inches on each side. In the 1750s, the apse was extended to equal the length of the nave—thus destroying the cruciform shape of the church. In 1768 the decision was made to add a steeple, much higher than Spotswood's original belltower.

Securing the Frontiers

While seeking to instill the principles of republican culture, through transforming the capital at Williamsburg, Governor Spotswood constantly looked westward, toward the future. On horseback, he made repeated expeditions throughout the colony, exploring its inland waterways, selecting routes for new roads and sites for future towns and forts. Knowing the need for colonial industry, he searched for deposits of iron ore and locations for forges. To ensure a network of communications for extending the colony's frontiers, he also established the first postal system in Virginia.[7]

In 1711, expecting the long-delayed British attack on Quebec, Spotswood had to devote considerable attention to military matters. He concentrated initially on the threat of attack by the French fleet, and in August fortified Old Point Comfort, guarding the entrance to Hampton Roads at the mouth of the James River. Batteries of up to sixteen guns were deployed to guard the entrance of the other major rivers along the coast as well. Spotswood ordered a general muster of all the county militias, and began centralizing them under his command. He informed the Council of Queen Anne's instructions to Governor Hunter in New York, that a general state of readiness throughout the colonies be maintained "from the time the Squadron and Land forces shall proceed to the River Canada for the Reduction of that Colony."[8]

Spotswood soon discovered that the danger was not merely external, when the Virginia assembly returned its thanks, but not the money he had advanced for the colony's defense.[9] The nature of this internal threat became clearer when hostilities actually broke out in 1711 not with the French, but with the Indians. A new German-Swiss settlement in North Carolina, near Virginia's southern border, was attacked by Tuscaroras. Sixty people were massacred and scores taken prisoner, including the settlement's founder, Baron de Graffenreid. Virginia's major fur traders, led by William Byrd, had armed many of the tribes to the south and west, and there were fears of a wider uprising. Upon receiving the news, Spotswood immediately mobilized the militia under his personal command, and marched to the various Indian towns of Virginia to ensure that they would not join the Tuscaroras. He prohibited all trading with the Indians, who already had more ammunition than the militia, secured an alliance with the Nottoways, and led an expedition against the Tuscaroras which secured the release of de Graffenreid and his fellow survivors.

Spotswood concluded a peace treaty with the eight Tuscarora towns who had not taken part in the massacre. They were to send hostages to Williamsburg as proof of their good faith. The governor now began to implement a much broader Indian policy, however, aimed at educating and integrating the tribes of Virginia, while ensuring both their security and the colony's against any hostilities emanating from beyond the areas of settlement. The measures Spotswood sought to institute were much like those initiated by the New England Puritans in the 1630s, including a plan to provide college education for leading Indian youth, as Harvard College had done as early as 1638. For the fall session of 1711, Spotswood recruited the sons of the tribal leaders of the Nansemonds, Nottoways, Meherrins, and Pamunkeys to attend the College of William and Mary, and secured them comfortable housing nearby. His plan succeeded so well, that soon the Indians were sending twice the number of students than existing funds could provide for. His appeals for financial support to various 'Christianizing' agencies in Britain—the bishop of London, archbishop of Canterbury, and the Church of England's Society for the Propagation of the Gospel—fell on deaf ears.

But from William Byrd and his cronies in the Virginia assembly, Spotswood's program to ensure peace on the frontiers provoked a most definite response. The House of Burgesses disowned the governor's policy entirely, and virtually attempted to raise the spirit of Nathaniel Bacon from hell. The House demanded a war against all Indians, friend or foe. That Byrd should be at the center of such a criminal scheme was entirely appropriate. His father, William Byrd I, had been the leading oligarchical backer of Bacon's rebellion.[10]

Spotswood held firm against the lunacy which had overtaken the assembly. He knew that any such barbarous policy would also destroy his plans for opening the West, in the ensuing conflagration. The governor insisted that his treaty with the Tuscaroras be observed, and reminded the assembly that the hostages the Indians had pledged were due to arrive in Williamsburg on November 20. When the date passed with no sign of their arrival, the same House of Burgesses which had refused to spend a penny for defense of Virginia's coast, now voted £20,000 for all-out Indian warfare—half the sum Massachusetts raised for the 12,000-man expedition against Quebec! Two weeks later, hostages arrived, having been delayed by sickness and bad weather. But William Byrd, if not "great with my Lord Marlborough," was just as dedicated on this occasion to 'war at any price.' The burgesses now demanded a declaration of war against the Tuscaroras, to be financed by a 10 percent excise on all *imports*.[11] Since Virginia produced nothing but tobacco, even the funding scheme would be a severe blow to the colony, except for those great planters and land speculators who could comfortably survive it.

Spotswood heatedly rejected the entire proposal, and struck at its backers by observing that a tax of even half a penny per acre on Virginia landholdings would yield more. On Christmas Eve, he recessed the assembly for a month, and then dissolved it on January 31, 1712, after a week of further stalemate. Only one new measure was passed, giving the governor power to appoint rangers to patrol the frontiers. The plot to foment the bloodbath of Indian warfare was stymied. Throughout the session, however, the House of Burgesses had obstructed virtually every measure Spotswood intended for the welfare of the colony, while advancing some which might have plunged it into ruin. Spotswood had no patience with the posture adopted by some of the members, as champions of the people against the arbitrary will of a royal governor.

In an address delivered January 29, 1712, he put forth his own credentials as a Virginia patriot:

> Mr. Speaker and Gentlemen of the House of Burgesses: He that acts honestly may always act boldly, and 'tis not the possessing the minds of the Populace with your being the only true Defenders of the poor that will deter me from Showing my Dislike of Some of your unwarrantable proceedings. I came hither with a resolution to be as great a Patriot to this Country as any one of you can pretend to—and I will stand in the Gap—to Stop all measures that may injure the people . . . . I should be glad in respect to Several wise and honest Gentlemen of your House, who with Concern behold the present Confusions in your Counsels to find an Excuse for the Irregular proceedings of the Session, and cannot tell how to account for the Same—otherwise than by believing a rumour now abroad that Some Crafty and ambitious persons, to accomplish their Sinister ends, have led you into an abundance of these Irregularities with an intent to dissolve this Assembly. . . .
>
> Let the Consequences be what they will, I shall have this to Comfort me, that I have done my duty, and having the whole Council and my

own Conscience witnesses of my deliberated Actions and Disinterested Intentions, I can boldly stand the Strictest Scrutiny into my Administration . . . . And I Do assure you that I shall readily yield to whatever you can with reason and Justice Demand.[12]

Following the Peace of Utrecht in 1713, Spotswood renewed his drive to implement his policies for stabilizing relations with the Indian tribes of Virginia. The greatest danger to the peaceful development of the colony's western lands, however, came not from the Indians as such, but from the interference of the major land speculators and Indian traders, led by William Byrd. Spotswood knew he had to deal with that menace as well. At Williamsburg in February 1714, Spotswood concluded treaties with the chiefs of the Nottoways, Saponis, and Tuscaroras, granting them six-mile tracts to build fortified towns. Each town would have a trading post, supervised from Williamsburg, and a church and school for the education of Indian youth. The town's defense would also be strengthened by a garrison of twelve rangers and a commanding officer.[13]

Spotswood's rangers had discovered iron ore during one of their frontier patrols, below the south fork of the Rappahannock River.[14] Spotswood wrote to Baron de Graffenreid, who had returned to Europe after being freed from the Tuscaroras, requesting him to recruit German miners for a project to develop a Virginia iron industry. In the spring of 1714, twelve families, totaling forty-two persons, arrived from the towns of Siegen and Meusen in Nassau-Siegen. Spotswood paid their ship captain £150 for their passage, and then led them to the frontier site he had selected for the new mining settlement.

He named it Germanna, honoring both the new colonists' origins and Queen Anne, who directed the

Alexander Spotswood's Virginia

When Alexander Spotswood became governor of Virginia in 1710, the colony was a stagnant backwater. What there was of an economy consisted almost entirely of feudalist plantations producing tobacco for export. The colonial capital at Williamsburg featured only one building of significance—the legislature—and a few taverns and boarding houses. There were no industries, no cities, and almost no towns; the population was huddled along the lower Chesapeake Bay and the tidewater sections of the York and James Rivers.

Under Spotswood's direction, Williamsburg became the most beautiful colonial capital in America. A road system was begun to provide access to the interior, and a postal service was established for the first time. In 1712 he established a fortified town, complete with Indian school, at Christanna on the Meherrin River, along Virginia's southern frontier. In 1714, with a body of German mine-workers and their families, he established another fort and settlement at Germanna, above the fork of the Rappahannock, where he founded Virginia's first iron industry. His dream of colonization beyond the "impassable" Blue Ridge Mountains took shape in 1716, when he led an expedition through Swift Run Gap and into the Shenandoah Valley. During the 1720s, the interior west of Germanna grew more rapidly in population and cultivated acreage than any other part of Virginia, paving the way for settling the West.

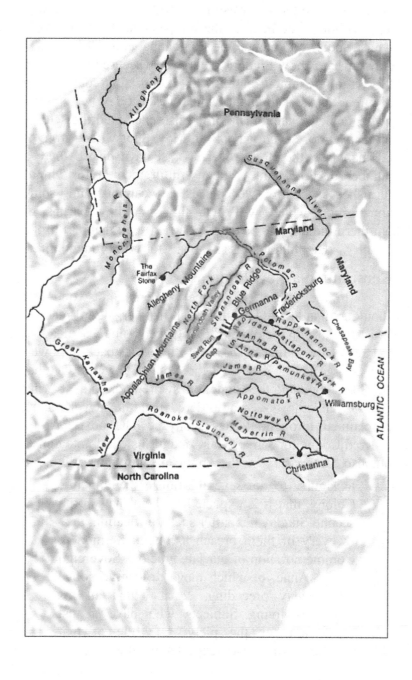

governor by letter to furnish them with land. The site was along a horseshoe bend of the Rappahannock's south fork, which Spotswood named the Rapidanna, about thirty miles above what is now Fredericksburg. He secured an order of the Virginia Council on April 28, authorizing construction of a road to the settlement, which was to be protected by a pentagonal stockade. The order also exempted the settlers from taxes for seven years.[15] In May, Spotswood wrote of Germanna to the Board of Trade, "I have placed there a number of Protestant Germans, built them a fort, [and] furnished it with two pieces of cannon and some ammunition which will awe the straggling parties of Northern Indians and be a good barrier to all that part of the country." He did not stress his plans for iron production.[16]

Confronting a New Regime

In the fall of 1714, the burdens Spotswood had shouldered suddenly became much heavier. Word reached Williamsburg on October 18 that Queen Anne was dead, at the age of forty-nine. The Whig Junto was back in power, and George I was King. At the Council meeting October 19, Spotswood and the councilors swore their oaths to King George, and the governor ordered that the new King be proclaimed throughout the colony. The next day, he ordered Councilor James Blair, one of his chief antagonists but also commissary for the Anglican Church in Virginia,

> to signify to the several Ministers within this Colony, that it is expected of them that on the second Sunday next after such notification, they & every of them preach a funeral Sermon in Commemoration of our late gracious Sovereign Queen Anne, of which they are to give notice the Sunday preceding, & at which all his Majesties living Subjects who have a just veneration for the piety & virtue of that excellent Princess are expected to attend.[17]

Certainly Queen Anne's memory was better honored in Spotswood's Virginia than in Britain. Besides Queen Anne County, Spotswood saw to it that her name endured in a long list of inland waterways leading to the West—the rivers North Anna, South Anna, Rivanna, Rapidan(na), and Fluvanna (for which the county was also named)—as well his forts on the frontier, Christanna and Germanna.

The accession of George I clearly threatened Spotswood's mission in America. But the governor still had some maneuvering room. It would take some time for the new regime to establish itself in Britain, and still more for it to extend its sway to America. King George also had to proceed with a degree of caution. The faction supporting him was detested among all ranks of the population. The Act of Union between England and Scotland, which George himself had demanded, had been ratified only with crucial assistance from the Scottish Earl of Orkney. Spotswood served in Virginia as Orkney's lieutenant, and the earl retained his title to the governorship of Virginia for life, by appointment of Queen Anne.

Spotswood had also made headway in the House of Burgesses. The body elected in 1712 was about to sit for its third and final session. In 1713, it had been the most supportive of any during Spotswood's term of office. By a special British law, no colonial assembly in existence at the death of Queen Anne could remain in session longer than six months—then to be replaced by an assembly selected under the new regime of King George. Spotswood determined to make the most of the time remaining.[18]

He decided to escalate his campaign to open the West. In his address on November 16 to open its final session, Governor Spotswood focused the agenda of the House on the frontier. The legislative program he outlined was soon passed by the burgesses, despite opposition from the minions of William Byrd. Spotswood's policies had pacified the colony's borderlands, and he announced that the cost of their defense had been reduced by two-thirds, due to his success in establishing a fortified town for the friendly Indians to the south. He had named it Christanna, for Queen Anne, and maintained it with only a token deployment of rangers. In time, he added, no soldiers would be needed, because the Indians had agreed to receive the benefits of education at a school at Christanna.

Control of Virginia's southern frontier was especially important for Spotswood. This was the nexus of William Byrd's opportunities to both arm and make trouble with the Indians, through his fur-trading operations. It was thus the most dangerous flash-point for instigating hostilities throughout the interior. Spotswood's other fort at Germana, where he had settled the German ironmakers, already guarded the northern frontier and key routes to the West along the Rappahannock River, and its south fork, the Rapidan. He now presented to the House of Burgesses an "Act for the better regulation of the Indian Trade," designed to crush Byrd's southern flank.

Spotswood's Indian Act confined all trade south of the James River to the post established at Christanna, under the control of a new state-chartered enterprise, the Virginia Indian Company. The company would be responsible for building a schoolhouse for Indian children, and for assuming the costs of defense of the fort within two years. Another provision, designed as a safeguard against legislative sabotage of the colony's defense, mandated the construction of a magazine at Williamsburg, with half the cost to be borne by the Virginia India Company. Spotswood himself designed the octagonal brick structure, which initially housed a large supply of arms and ammunition sent to Virginia by Queen Anne, shortly before her death. He placed it at a prominent point along

Williamsburg's main thoroughfare, not far from where the new governor's mansion was being constructed.[19]

Spotswood signed the bill and adjourned the assembly again on Christmas Eve, 1714. That same day, he began organizing the Virginia Indian Company, seeking £4,000 initial capitalization. He sought support of men who had established some interest in the colony, but he was determined to exclude control by the great oligarchical landholders. Shares in the company were thus limited to no less than £50 and no more than £ 100. The new charter company's monopoly over Virginia's southern Indian trade, especially on these terms, drove William Byrd into absolute frenzy. He had been the leading Indian trader for years, with his pack trains carrying arms and supplies as far as the Cherokee and Catawba camps in South Carolina.[20] Spotswood had not only defeated his scheme for turning all the Indian tribes into a ring of fire along the colony's frontiers. The governor now threatened to put Byrd out of business altogether.

Through his longstanding power on the Council, Byrd had maintained the office of receiver general, overseeing the collection of government revenues—most importantly, the quitrent taxes on land holdings. Spotswood had discovered massive irregularities in the accounts of these collections, and had ordered Byrd and auditor Philip Ludwell to correct the problem. He suspected Byrd and his crony of lining their own pockets. Spotswood was certainly not surprised when they offered no remedy, and in November he had introduced a new system of revenue collection, which the Council passed despite strenuous objections from Byrd. A year after Spotswood's plan had been in force, he reported that merely a third of the lands subject to quitrents had yielded more revenue than Byrd had reported for all of them the previous year.[21]

Byrd Plots in London

Following the enactment of Spotswood's Indian trade legislation, Byrd soon departed for England, where he was to spend nearly five years seeking personal support from the Hanoverian Whigs. He tried to overthrow Spotswood's entire program, and dreamt of replacing the governor himself. Byrd's secret diaries for the years of Spotswood's governorship were brought to light during the 1940s and 1950s. No better record is needed to measure the private thoughts and personal life of such a pathetically empty, perverted soul, whose only devotion was to pursue the favors of his oligarchical masters. The monotony of Byrd's daily accounts of life on his estate at Westover—taking his morning milk, dancing by himself, eating his meals, and noting the weather—varies in only a limited way. Regular variations include the occasions when he cheated his wife at cards, spread her upon his billiard table for sexual gratification, or whipped her female slave himself. During his years in London, his diary's basic format showed little change, except more frequent entries detailing his sexual adventures.

While courting favor with George I's regime, Byrd made the rounds of all the leading brothels, slept with both women and men, took opium to overcome his "weakness," and impotently solicited prostitutes and the maids at his lodgings, so that he could "commit uncleanness" or "spill his seed," as he generally put it. The reader should be spared further details. When he could, Byrd carefully recorded the list of 'influentials' who accepted his company. These included the Duke of Argyll, a former member of Queen Anne's cabinet, whom she had dismissed for his opposition to the peace, and who had forced her deathbed appointment of the jesuitical Duke of Shrewsbury as lord treasurer. Another was Lord James Stanhope, from whom Byrd sought a place on the Council of Trade, the body which attempted to dictate American colonial affairs. Stanhope was one of Marlborough's former generals, who had played a leading role in the planned coup against Queen Anne in July 1714—a crime made unnecessary by her 'timely' death. Lord Islay, the Duke of Argyll's brother, was another object of Byrd's strange attentions, whom he reported "received me very kindly and advised me to bribe the German [King George's adviser, Baron von Bernsdorff] to get the governorship of Virginia and told me he would put me in the way."[22] This gaggle of Byrd's associates in London, like all his other 'regulars,' hated Jonathan Swift.

William Byrd II is still celebrated in nearly every published history of Virginia, and is favorably mentioned in most modern American history surveys. Alexander Spotswood remains virtually unknown. Let us give Byrd his due, in his own words, on one of his better days, when he had more name-droppings:

> I rose about 7 o'clock and read a chapter in Hebrew and some Greek in Lucian. I said my prayers, and had milk for breakfast. The weather was cloudy and cold, the wind east. About nine I paid Mr. H-l-n twenty-five pounds for my coach. Then I danced my dance and wrote a letter to my Lady Mohun [wife of Marlborough's thug, Lord Mohun, who had tried to assassinate Queen Anne's ambassador to France]. About eleven I went to Lord Islay's who told me the King's going to Hanover was a great hindrance to my affairs. Then I went to the Duke of Argyll's and from thence to my Lord Percival's, who was from home. Then to visit Mrs. Southwell, where I drank a dish of chocolate. Then I went home where Sir Wilfred Lawson [crony of Lord Stanhope] came to see me and we went to

Pontack's [tavern] to dinner and I ate some
boiled beef.   After dinner we went to my
milliner's [women's   hatmaker] and from
thence to Crane Court where we stayed till 5
o'clock and then we went to Mrs. Pierson who
was from home.   Then we went to Kensington
Garden where we walked till 8 o'clock and then
I returned and I went to see my French whore
where I supped and ate some fricassee of
chicken.   I gave the whore two guineas and
committed uncleanness and then went home in
the chair and said my prayers.[23]

While Byrd thus danced to the tune of the new regime in
London, Spotswood pressed forward in Virginia. The other
Indian traders allied to Byrd refused to subscribe to the new
Virginia Indian Company, but the governor enlisted enough
councilors, burgesses, and merchants to get the venture
started.   Spotswood invested £100 of his own, and the
subscribers chose him as governor of the company. With
an eye toward developing the frontier, he promptly
presented plans for new roads, bridges, and warehouses to
facilitate the 'Indian commerce.'[24] He also accelerated his
project at Germanna, to bring iron production on line.

A Messenger from Ireland

Alexander Spotswood already had very definite ideas on
what had to be done to pursue the goal of a continental
republic.   But with Queen Anne's death and the Venetian
party's return to power under George I, the task was far
more complicated than simply outflanking his opposition in
Virginia.   He now held the forward line in the entire
campaign, and urgently required some degree of broader
strategic coordination.   While Jonathan Swift had held a
position of influence within Queen Anne's government,

there had been significant opportunities to meet that need. But no longer; Swift was not even in England, and now operated from his more isolated—but safer—base in Ireland. His friend, Robert Hunter, was still the governor of New York and New Jersey, but Hunter's choice of initiatives remained limited. He was hemmed in by Jesuit-directed Indian containment of New York's western frontiers, especially since the disaster of the Quebec expedition of 1711.

Even during Queen Anne's reign, any political communication between Swift and his allies in America had to be undertaken with extreme caution, and almost always through intermediaries. In the face of the murderous band licensed by George I, the difficulties were even greater. Today, more than two-and-a-half centuries later, the search for any historical evidence of their concerted plans would seem to confront overwhelming obstacles. One of the biggest is the fact that for more than 150 years, historians have denied that the American colonies *ever had* republican aspirations. They insist that we merely sought to 'preserve our rights as Englishmen,' and busily sweep away all the decisive evidence to the contrary. Happily, there is a method to overcome the madness of such historians.

Take the case of Jonathan Swift, concerning his political role during a thirty-year period beginning in 1707. To put the matter simply, imagine that Swift was constructing a secret tunnel, for use by persons who shared his objective. We can document that the tunnel's entrance and exit are of the same design. We can also prove that persons he admitted to its entrance, later emerged at his objective. We may not discover everything they were doing down there, but we certainly know where they were going!

In 1715, once Spotswood was apprised of the ugly public scene in London, his most crucial decision was whether to proceed at that time with an expedition upon which America's future might depend: crossing the still unbroken line of the Blue Ridge Mountains, to open up the West. Early in June, a messenger arrived from Dublin to help him seek the answer. His name was John Fontaine, the Irish-born son of a Huguenot refugee from France. His journal of his trip to America was preserved by the descendants he left here, and was published as part of a family history in the mid-nineteenth century. Genealogies have a funny way of yielding buried historical truths, if one knows what to look for. In this case, the journal preserved by the Fontaine family provides a rare glimpse into Swift's 'secret tunnel.'

The father of John Fontaine had been awarded a pension from Queen Anne, for mobilizing his neighbors to beat back a French raid on the eastern coast of Ireland. The episode was certainly celebrated enough for Jonathan Swift to have known of it. John Fontaine's life story is only dimly reported, except for his own journal's account of his trip to America. What is known, however, before his departure from Ireland in November 1714, is that on two occasions he left his father's home for extended stays in Dublin, the center of Swift's own political networks. The first of these lasted from July 7, 1713, until the end of March 1714, the period of deepening crisis while Swift maintained intimate access to the cabinet-level workings of Queen Anne's government. Fontaine returned to Dublin in June, shortly after Swift had removed himself from the doomed court of Queen Anne, to a temporary base in the English countryside, fifty miles from London. While Swift weighed the political possibilities during the period just preceding and following the Queen's death, Fontaine remained in Dublin, and was there when Swift returned in August.[25]

About three months later, on November 9, 1714, John Fontaine left Dublin bound for America. He stopped first at Bideford, down the Irish Sea on the west coast of England. There, he says he received "a letter of introduction for Boston" from the local Presbyterian minister, William Bartlett. From Massachusetts, Cotton Mather maintained a regular correspondence with ostensible Presbyterians in England, Scotland, and Ireland, often through networks centered around his own family's relations. Daniel Defoe, another of Mather's occasional correspondents, and a propagandist for Robert Harley in the fight against the Venetian party's Bank of England, mentions William Bartlett as "a very valuable Man."[26] While waiting through the depths of winter to set sail, Fontaine stayed in nearby Barnstable with a fellow Huguenot, Dr. Louis Mauzy, who had close ties to Boston. Mauzy's wife was the daughter of Edward Hutchinson, who had two cousins in Massachusetts, born in the 1670s, who knew Cotton Mather well. The daughter of one of them married Cotton's son Samuel, who lived to proclaim America's Declaration of Independence from his pulpit in Boston in 1776. During Fontaine's stay with the Mauzys at Barnstable, he was also given letters of introduction to the Hutchinson relatives in Boston.[27]

On February 28, 1715, Fontaine sailed for Virginia, and reached the Potomac by the end of May. During a stopover there, he was invited to dinner by Mrs. Mary Hewes, whose daughter would marry Augustine Washington and become the mother of the first President of the United States. Fontaine proceeded to the capital at Williamsburg, arriving there on June 3. His journal for June 7 records,

> I waited on Governor Spotswood and he assured me of all he could do and after I had been with him some time I took my leave of him. He invited me to dinner which I accepted.[28]

Fontaine offers no details concerning this discussion, nor of many more that would follow. His journal carefully avoids substantive references, except to his seeking and receiving Spotswood's help in purchasing a tract of land. What is clear, however, is that Fontaine spent the next year-and-a-half obtaining an extraordinary education from Spotswood himself, on the subject of developing the West.

In November, Fontaine journeyed to Germanna, Spotswood's frontier outpost and ironmaking center, above the fork of the Rappahannock River. The following spring, "the Governor proposed a journey to his settlement, on the Meherrin river called Christanna." They left together on April 13, and returned April 22. Not long after this second frontier expedition, on June 12, 1716, Spotswood informed the Virginia Council that his rangers had found a pass over the Blue Ridge.[29] The gateway to a continental republic was about to be opened.

Spotswood had long waited for this moment. He wished to forever dispel the oligarchical myth that settlement beyond the mountains was impossible. After years of exploratory patrols, his rangers had found a mountain gap where passage was not limited to daring adventurers, traveling with only the barest necessities. They had instead discovered one suitable for easy crossings with supply trains, and Spotswood determined to demonstrate that feasibility himself. During the summer of 1716, he recruited a "company of gentlemen" for an expedition beyond the Blue Ridge. Many of them came from families already looking to the West, whose sons and grandsons became prominent figures of the future American republic.

Among these was George Mason, whose son became a member of the Ohio Company, organized to promote settlement in that region before the French and Indian War of 1754–1763. The younger Mason later succeeded George

Washington, as a delegate to the Virginia convention, at the outset of the American Revolution, and designed much of the constitution of the new state of Virginia.   Others included James Taylor, ancestor of Presidents James Madison and Zachary Taylor; Robert Brooke, whose grandson of the same name became governor of Virginia in 1798; and Thomas Todd, whose family later helped secure Kentucky against the British during the Revolution.[30] Another of Spotswood's companions, once again, was the visitor from Dublin, John Fontaine, whose journal provides the only detailed account of the expedition.

Across the 'Euphrates'

Spotswood led his party out of Williamsburg on August 20, and thence to rendezvous at Germanna with two companies of rangers.   There he had a surprise in store, of tremendous symbolic and practical significance. Virginia's first iron works were now operational, and Spotswood ordered that both pack and riding horses be equipped with iron horseshoes for the journey over the mountains.[31] The horseshoes were something of an innovation for Virginia. The lack of domestic iron, and the colony's gentle terrain in the Tidewater region, had long accustomed Virginians to riding their horses unshod. Spotswood's point was that an American iron industry was essential, not only for crossing the Blue Ridge mountains, but for the economic development of all that lay beyond. Without iron, there would be no wheel rims, barrel bands, woodsaws, axes, stove pots, rifles, hoes, and plows. Without iron, there could be no republic.

Spotswood had no titles to bestow, but those who accompanied him beyond the Blue Ridge became known as the Knights of the Golden Horseshoe, for he later presented them miniature golden horseshoes to commemorate the historic occasion.   Spotswood had inscribed them, "Sic juvat transcendere montes" ("Thus we crossed the mountains").[32] The mountain pass lay roughly fifty miles west of Germanna, but was still the end of the earth for Virginia. Yet, within thirty years of America's Declaration of Independence, two of Spotswood's political heirs in Virginia—Merriwether Lewis and William Clark—would plant the flag of the United States on the shores of the Pacific Ocean, at the mouth of the Columbia River in Oregon.

Spotswood knew he was making history. When he led his company out of Germanna, along the south fork of the Rappahannock which he had named the Rapidanna River, he camped the first night by a stream he named Expedition Run. On September 5, he camped by a stream just below the summit of the Blue Ridge, in the pass his rangers had charted. Even today, the site suggests Jonathan Swift's contributions to America. Fontaine's journal, perhaps for understandable reasons, records no ceremonial naming by Spotswood in this case. Yet on any detailed road map of Virginia, one can still find Swift Run Gap, where U.S. Highway 33 crosses the Blue Ridge, heading west to Harrisonburg. It could be argued that any stream descending a mountainside might be named descriptively a "swift" run. But only this one bears such a name along the Blue Ridge, and no stream's natural attributes are known to have earned the name "Expedition."

On the other side of the Blue Ridge, Alexander Spotswood found a major inland river. He led his expedition across it in triumph, and named it the Euphrates. He thus invoked the bold venture of Alexander the Great, who on behalf of Plato's Academy in ancient Greece, led his city-building forces beyond the barbarian boundaries of the Persian Empire. In today's Middle East, the Euphrates River still bears its ancient name. In Virginia, the river Spotswood crossed has long since been known as the

Shenandoah—an Indian name meaning "daughter of the stars." Its long valley, running southwest between the Blue Ridge and the Appalachian Mountains, became a strategic corridor for the American Revolution.   Spotswood's company reached the west bank of the Shenandoah on September 6, 1716—and changed the course of history.[33]

Spotswood had come prepared for a major celebration. At a feast that evening along the river, the glasses were raised for toast after toast, punctuated by volleys of musket fire, as his party drank imported burgundy, claret, "Virginia red wine and white wine, Irish usquebaugh, brandy shrub, two sorts of rum, champagne, canary, cherry, punch, cider, etc.," as Fontaine somehow managed to record in his journal. They broke camp the next day and began their return trip, reaching Spotswood's base at Germanna on September 10. There, the expedition disbanded, but the Governor and John Fontaine remained for three more days before making for Williamsburg. Certainly Spotswood was already planning how to follow through on his opening of the Shenandoah Valley, but Fontaine's journal is again discreetly silent.

We do know that Governor Spotswood quickly determined to build up the iron operations at Germanna. Colonial land records show that on October 31, 1716, not long after his return to Williamsburg, a grant of 3,229 acres of land was made to William Robertson, Clerk of the Virginia Council.[34] Robertson was also a Knight of the Golden Horseshoe; one month later he transferred the land title to Spotswood. Apparently the first land Spotswood owned in America, the tract was located along the Rapidan River, adjoining the Germanna site.[35] In 1717, he brought in eighty more German immigrants— twenty Lutheran families recruited in Alsace and the Palatinate, who were originally to have been settled in Pennsylvania.   That course of German emigration to America, interestingly enough, was generally directed for William Penn by August Hermann Francke, who had worked with Leibniz and maintained an extensive correspondence with Cotton Mather in Boston.[36] Their change of destination, following Spotswood's opening of the Shenandoah, is suggestive of the sort of coordination involved. This new contingent of Germans also arrived penniless. Spotswood again paid the passage money, and indentured them to his own service for work in his iron enterprise.   They may have been employed in developing his Tubal Furnace near La Roche Run, about thirteen miles from the first settlement at Germanna.[37]

Beyond building up the economic machinery required for colonizing the West, Spotswood confronted major, unresolved strategic issues. His objective had never been the Shenandoah Valley itself, except as a vital corridor for conquering the vast wilderness that lay beyond it. As he later informed the generally hostile Board of Trade in London,

> The Chief Aim of my Expedition over the great Mountains in 1716, was to satisfy my Self whether it was practicable to come at the [Great] Lakes. Having on that occasion found an easy passage over the great Ridge of Mountains which before were judged Unpassable, I also discovered, by relation of Indians who frequent those parts, that from the pass where I was It is but three Days' March to a great nation of Indians living on a River which discharges itself into Lake Erie.[38]

Even if allowances are made, both for Spotswood's habit of making the most difficult task seem easy, and for imprecise intelligence received "by relation of Indians," his report is still credible. From the camp he made on the banks of the

Shenandoah, it is less than a hundred miles to the Monongahela River, in present West Virginia.   The Monongahela flows north into the junction of the Ohio and Allegheny Rivers, at the point which became the center of America's giant steel industry— Pittsburgh, Pennsylvania. George Washington, on a mission in 1753 to assess the French military buildup in the West, moved north from there up the Allegheny River, to its junction with French Creek at Venango (later renamed Franklin, Pennsylvania), sixty miles south of Lake Erie. He followed French Creek forty miles north to the French outpost at Fort Le Bouef, not far from the stream's origin less than ten miles from Lake Erie.

Spotswood had told the Board of Trade in his report,

> I have often regretted that after so many Years as these Countrys have been Seated, no Attempts have been made to discover the Sources of Our Rivers, nor to Establishing Correspondence with those Nations of Indians to the Westward of Us, even after the certain Knowledge of the Progress made by [the] French in Surrounding us with their Settlements.[39]

He continued to press for settlements in the West:

> To prevent the dangers which Threaten his Majesty's Dominions here from the growing power of these Neighbors, nothing seems to me of more consequence than that now while the Nations [Britain and France] are at peace, and while the French are yet uncapable of possessing all that vast Tract which lies on the back of these Plantations, we should attempt to make some Settlements on the Lakes, and at the

The Ohio River System—
Strategic Highway to the West

From its origin in the junction of the Allegheny and Monongahela Rivers (at Pittsburgh), the Ohio River winds its way westward for 921 miles, flowing into the Mississippi at the southern tip of Illinois. No river was more vital to America's developing beyond the eastern mountain barrier. Except for a short stretch west of Pittsburgh, the entire length of the Ohio lay within Virginia's colonial claims. Alexander Spotswood stressed the Ohio's strategic significance as early as 1720, by which time he already had a surprisingly accurate map of its course to the Mississippi. In the 1740s, Virginia surveyors for Lord Fairfax plotted the feeder streams into the Youghiogheny and Monongahela Rivers, as routes to the Ohio. The Virginia-based Ohio Company, whose founders in 1748 included George Washington's two older brothers, was organized to begin settlement of the upper Ohio River Valley. During the American Revolution, the Ohio River provided the logistical capability for Virginia militiamen, led by George Rogers Clark, to defeat the British in the crucial battle for the West.

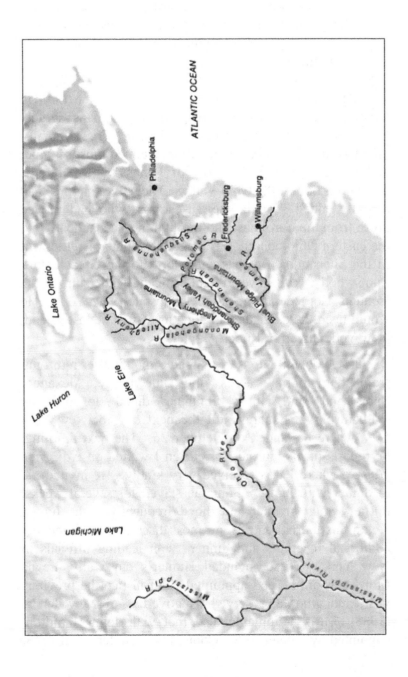

same time possess our selves of those passes of
the great Mountains, which are necessary to
preserve   a   Communication   with   such
Settlements.[40]

The routes to the Great Lakes in 1716 ran through
territories only sparsely inhabited, by Indians largely
hostile to the Jesuit-run tribes of Canada. These Indians,
allied as the Iroquois Confederation, claimed most of upper
and western New York, most of Pennsylvania, and the
eastern portion of the Ohio Valley. Their five 'nations' had
recently added a sixth, the Tuscaroras, who had moved
north from the Carolinas, and through the Shenandoah, into
the eastern Ohio country. To negotiate rights of settlement
in the Shenandoah, or passages north to the Great Lakes,
Spotswood would have to deal with the leadership of the
Iroquois Confederation, based in upstate New York. He
would need the assistance of Jonathan Swift's close friend,
New York Governor Robert Hunter.

On October 14, 1716, less than a month after returning
from their journey across the Blue Ridge, Alexander
Spotswood and John Fontaine dined together in
Williamsburg. Fontaine left the next day for New York
City, where he landed on October 26. The next morning,
he reports in his journal, "at eleven I waited on *Governor
Hunter*, where I was received very kindly. He invited me
to dinner with him."[41] Fontaine stayed for several weeks,
during which he met and dined frequently with Hunter.
Again, his journal entries are most discreet, but he records
additional meetings and dinners with leading officials in
New York. These included Hunter's close ally, Lewis
Morris, whom he had appointed chief justice the previous
year, and who later served as governor of New Jersey
(1738–1746). Fontaine also met with John Hamilton,
appointed by Hunter to the Council of New Jersey in 1713,

who was now postmaster general in the colonies. As such, Hamilton controlled not merely the mail, but the only efficient intelligence service existing in the American colonies as a whole. Later, with Jonathan Swift's help, Spotswood himself became colonial postmaster, in 1730. Fontaine left New York for Virginia in mid- November, and, on December 1 "at eleven came to Williamsburg.   I went and visited the governor."[42] Meanwhile, from New York, Governor Hunter began issuing a steady flow of proposals to the British government, for new settlements and outposts on Lake Ontario in western New York. Fontaine remained in Virginia until 1719, the year Robert Hunter returned to London to coordinate yet another phase of America's struggle. The young Irishman secured lands in Virginia for his son, who lived to support the cause of American independence.   Fontaine returned to Dublin, perhaps to report to Jonathan Swift, on December 5, 1719.[43]

NOTES

1. Cf. Charles Campbell, *Genealogy of the Spotswood Family in Scotland and Virginia*, (Albany, N.Y., 1868).

2. *Ibid.*

3. Walter Havighurst, *Alexander Spotswood, Portrait of a Governor* (Williamsburg, 1967), 5.

4. *Ibid.*, 4, 5.

5. William Byrd II, *The Secret Diary of William Byrd of Westover*, 1709–1712, Louis B. Wright and Marion Tinling, eds. (Richmond, 1941), almost anywhere.

6. Hugh Jones, *The Present State of Virginia* (London, 1724), 28.

7. Armistead C. Gordon, *Men and Events, Chapters*

of Virginia History (Staunton, Va., 1923), 117–137.

8. R. H. McIlwaine, ed., *Journal of the Colonial Council of Virginia* (Richmond, 1928), III, 282–283. Hereafter referred to as *Jour. Coun. Va.*

9. Havighurst, *Spotswood*, 26.

10. Wilcombe E. Washburn, *The Governor and the Rebel* (New York, 1957), 29–35.

11. Havighurst, *Spotswood*, 28–33.

12. R.H. McIlwaine, ed., *Journals of the House of Burgesses of Virginia, 1702–1712* (Richmond, 1912), 354–355. Hereafter referred to as *Jour. Burgesses*.

13. Havighurst, *Spotswood*, 44.

14. W. David Lewis, *Iron and Steel in America* (Meriden, Conn., 1976), 21.

15. *Jour. Coun. Va.*, III, 371.

16. James Roger Mansfield, *A History of Early Spotsylvania* (Orange, Va., 1977), 23–24.

17. *Jour. Coun. Va.*, III, 379–380.

18. *Jour. Burgesses*, 1712–1726, xxv.

19. *Ibid.*, xxv–xxxvii.

20. Havighurst, *Spotswood*, 49ff.

21. Louis B. Wright and Marion Tinling, eds., *William Byrd of Virginia, The London Diary and Other Writings* (New York, 1958), 25.

22. Byrd, *London Diary*, 259, 259n. Byrd' s repeated associations with Argyll, Stanhope, and Islay are itemized in the index to the " London Diary." His wretched sexual activities are documented

throughout; *cf.*, for example, his entries for November 22–December 4, 1719, 344–348.

23. *Ibid.* (November, 1719), 263.

24. Havighurst, *Spotswood,* 50.

25. John Fontaine, *The Journal of John Fontaine,* Edward P. Alexander, ed. (Williamsburg, 1972), introduction.   Alexander notes only Fontaine's movements.

26. Daniel Defoe, *Tour Through Great Britain,* I, 261.

27. Fontaine, *Journal,* February 23, 1715; Esther Forbes, *Paul Revere and the World He Lived In* (Boston, 1942), 105.

28. Fontaine, *Journal,* 82.

29. *Ibid.,* 90; *Jour. Coun. Va.,* III, 428.

30. Gordon, *Men and Events,* 152*ff.*

31. Mansfield, *Early Spotsylvania,* 28.

32. Gordon, *Men and Events,* 152.

33. Havighurst, *Spotswood,* 68–70; Matthew Page Andrews, *Virginia, The Old Dominion* (2 vols., New York, 1937), I, 186; Fontaine, *Journal.*

34. Mansfield, *Early Spotsylvania,* 41.

35. *Ibid.*

36. *Cf.,* Kuno Francke, *Cotton Mather and August Hermann Francke* (New York, 1897).

37. Mansfield, *Early Spotsylvania,* 41–42.

38. Spotswood to the Board of Trade, August 14, 1718, *Letters,* II, 295.

39. *Ibid.*

40. *Ibid.*, 297.

41. Fontaine, *Journal*, October 14, 26, 27, 1716.

42. *Ibid.*,   October   28–November   30,   *passim*;
December 1, 1716, 122.

43. *Ibid.*, December 5, 1719.

8

The Power Struggle Over the West

It was not long before Spotswood's enemies attempted to strike back against his plans for the West. Whatever detailed arrangements they may have known, they had no doubt of his intentions. They also knew that Spotswood's Virginia Indian Company was his key agency for controlling and financing any westward moves, since these depended on positive relations with the tribes of the interior. It had been the passage of the Indian Act in late 1714, following news of Queen Anne's death, that drove William Byrd to London to seek Spotswood's removal as governor. Once word of the expedition of the Knights of the Golden Horseshoe reached London, Byrd's two years of wheedling, bribery, and debauchery seemed to open new doors.

Early in 1717, Byrd was able to present a petition, signed by himself and thirteen of his merchant and landowner allies in Virginia, to King George's Board of Trade. The petition demanded that the crown revoke Spotswood's Indian Act, as well as his legislation regulating the corrupt tobacco trade. The King was only too happy to comply, and Spotswood had to inform the Council on November 12 that His Majesty had ordered both laws "repealed and made void." Byrd gloated in a letter to Philip Ludwell that his own machinations had defeated Spotswood's policies. He began lobbying with greater frenzy to be appointed to replace Spotswood as governor—when he was not too busy chasing prostitutes.[1]

Spotswood had already stretched his royal authority to the utmost, having dissolved the assembly elected in 1715, after a session of only one month. As he had expected, his

enemies enjoyed far greater leverage following the death of
Queen Anne. Byrd and Ludwell had reversed the majority
he had built in the Council, and now controlled eight of the
twelve seats. His ally Peter Beverley, speaker of the
House, fell victim to a massive campaign run by Byrd's
corrupt machine, which defeated him for his seat in the
House and installed its own speaker.[2] Spotswood had
convened this new assembly on August 3, 1715, only to
deal with measures to respond to an all-out Indian assault
on South Carolina. He was especially concerned with
upgrading the Virginia militia in the face of such imminent
danger—something which his enemies had blocked
throughout his governorship. The assembly not only
refused to respond to the governor's emergency requests,
but turned itself into a parliamentary sham, hearing only
contrived 'grievances' down to the most trivial level. They
might have continued until the colony were in flames, but
Spotswood would have none of it.

On September 7, declaring the assembly dissolved,
Spotswood addressed the House of Burgesses:

> It has been Practiced by former Assemblys, at
> the Close of a Session, to give a Summary of
> their Proceedings; but as I question whether
> you have truly Considered what you have been
> doing, I Judge the Task would be too difficult
> for you to undertake, or too ungrateful for your
> Speaker to Deliver. I shall therefore Spare you
> the Confusion of telling your own Actions, and
> Shall Sum them up for you, with Such
> faithfulness as may be proved from your
> Journals, with Such Resentment as becomes a
> Governor who has at heart the Safety and
> Honour of his Province, and with Such
> Boldness as he may Venture who no ways
> apprehends a Charge of One unjust, Illegal or
> Corrupt Act during his whole Administration.

Spotswood reminded them that he had convened the assembly "to provide for the Security of the Country, in a most perilous Juncture, and that you might upon that Point consult the People you Represent."

Byrd's henchmen brought no such matters before the attention of the people. This assembly, Spotswood charged, instead adopted "the Giddy Resolves of the illiterate Vulgar in their Drunken Conventions," many of them circulated "in the hand writing of your Members . . . at Election fields, Horse Races and other drunken Meetings." By such means, 'popular' demands had appeared for the repeal of the same measures opposed by William Byrd, especially Spotswood's reforms of quitrent collections and the Indian trade. Regarding the latter policy, as Spotswood summarized it for them, the Burgesses had demanded that

> the Act for Regulating Trade and Propagating the Christian Faith among the Indians Shall be abrogated, the School for teaching their Children be Demolished, and the Gentlemen at whose charge it was Erected, be Banished out of America, and their Estates Confiscated.

The entire legislative program put forth by "the Seditious and ignorant Vulgar," Spotswood declared, was "to Reverse Such Laws as the last Assembly raised upon the Basis of Religion, Justice or Honour . . . ." Though Byrd's machine had presented this package as representing the will of twenty-three counties, Spotswood retorted that

> 'tis evident all the Subscribers will not make up half a County: nor shall a Seditious Paper Signed by five obscure Fellows, who must have a Scribe to write all their names, ever pass with me for a County Grievance.

He cited a long list of the assembly's acts of immorality in legislative affairs. Among them,

> to Shew the Regard you have for Religion; you at first Sight Rejected a Proposal for Christianizing your Slaves, but at the same time another Proposition for Discouraging the Propagation of the Gospel amongst the Indians, was Referr'd to your Grand Committees Consideration, as if Preaching the Gospel to the Heathen were a Crime which ought to be Restrain'd by Law . . . .

> You fain would pass for Patriots who Strive to Indulge the poorer Sort of People, yet have you refused to Ease them of a Burthen which they very unjustly bear, for certainly the charge of Securing a Country ought to be laid proportionably to the Estates that are to be defended: And upon this Maxim did I form my Scheme for providing the poor with Arms, and paying them by the Rich, whenever they were called from their homes to Musters or other Publick Services. But you have chosen rather to keep your old Militia Law, which obliges the men who have generally the least Stakes in the Country to be at the Expense of Arms and Ammunition, and at the trouble of Attending Musters; while the wealthier Sort contribute not One farthing thereto, nor are under any Penalty for non Attendance.

Having reviewed the record, Spotswood declared:

> I cannot but Attribute those Miscarriages to the Peoples Mistaken Choice of a Set of Representatives, whom Heaven has not

generally endowed with the Ordinary
Qualifications requisite to Legislators . . . .
And to keep Such an Assembly on foot, would
be Discrediting a Country that has many able
and Worthy Gentlemen in it; and therefore I
now Dissolve you.[3]

Spotswood did not call the House of Burgesses into
session again until April 1718. In the meantime, he took
his own case to the people, by word and deed, especially
around his 1716 expedition beyond the Blue Ridge. He
maintained the colony's affairs through the Council, and
prepared for the opportunity to outflank the Byrds and
Ludwells.

Spotswood's transgressing the line of the mountains was
a criminal offense in the eyes of the British oligarchy and
its Virginia branch. Byrd's cronies soon issued wild
slanders against the governor, to pave the way for his
dismissal. A ridiculous set of charges was *anonymously*
sent to London, with a list of fifteen "queries" for
investigating Spotswood's conduct. In today's American
media, they would undoubtedly appear as front-page
stories, under such headlines as "Spotswood Charged with
Extortion, Implicated in Murder." His enemies actually
made such allegations, but Virginians at the time could not
be persuaded that reality had ceased to exist.

On January 16, 1717, Spotswood wrote his official reply
"To the Lords Commissioners of Trade and Plantations":

I am charged in plain words as Guilty of breach
of Trust, breach of Oath, breach of the King's
instructions, breach of Faith in my publick
Contracts, of tricking an Assembly out of
£1,350, of Extortion, of Murder, of stirring up
Sedition and Rebellion &c.[4]

He devastated his accusers with detailed, point-by-point refutations of their charges, some of which say more about his enemies' character than they may have realized.

Take, for example, the "8ᵗʰ Query: Whether the Governor [was] commanding the Attorney General to prosecute a Woman contrary to Law, for the Death of her slave under a very Moderate Correction .   .   .   ." Spotswood replied:

> I readily acknowledge that I countenanced the Prosecution of a Woman for Whipping her Slave to death, and though the Querist can, with a barbarous unconcern, call it a very moderate Correction under which an hail Negro gave up the Ghost, Yet when a Coroner's Jury have gone and taken up a Body that has been suddenly and secretly buried, and returned upon their Inquisition a Verdict of Murder, I think it is indispensably my Duty to take care that such Proceedings be not stifled, but that a legal Trial do ensue thereupon. For how unpopular soever the Doctrine may be in this Country , . . . the king may lawfully bring to Trial all Persons here, without exception, who shall be suspected to have destroyed the Life of his Subject.[5]

Spotswood's outrage over this obscene complaint may not have been shared by the court of George I, then busily engaged in building up its loot from the Royal African Company's slave trade.

Though the charges by Spotswood's anonymous accusers were ridiculous, the political fight was deadly serious. The "11ᵗʰ Query" charged the governor with "high Crimes and Misdemeanors," against the King and the laws of Virginia, for his proposals to reform the militia system.

If Virginia were to lead the way in opening the West, it would require an effective colonial militia.   Not coincidentally, Spotswood was accused of the same 'crime' that the slave-trading interests attributed to George Washington during the American Revolution: creating a standing army to impose his own dictatorship.

In his response to the Lords of Trade, Spotswood reminded them "that even though your Lordships might condemn the Measures I proposed," not even in Britain were the burdens "of defending the Estates of the Rich" so unequally imposed "upon the Poor" as in Virginia.   The existing regulations were so full of loopholes, that incentives existed for an officer not to muster his men at all.   Even if he did,

> it is to no manner of purpose, there being not one Officer in the Militia of this Government that has served in any Station in the Army, nor knows how to exercise his Men when he calls them together.   This is the State of the Militia under the present Law, and therefore I could not imagine that my endeavouring a Reformation thereof would be imputed to me as a Crime.[6]

Spotswood had proposed measures to produce a fully trained fighting force, while *reducing* the economic burdens on the average citizen, and *increasing* the circulation of money and credit available to productive labor.   The ironmaker was determined to end the dictatorship of Virginia's one-crop, tobacco-export economy.   Instead of a 'paper militia' of 11,000 infantry and 4,000 cavalry, mustering five times a year and ineffectively at best, Spotswood proposed an active militia of "3,000 Foot and 1,500 Horse," mustering ten times a year.   His enemies charged that this would "be more a Standing Army" for Spotswood "to govern Arbitrarily," and that doubling the number of musters would be a greater burden on the colony. Spotswood retorted that mustering 4,500 men ten times a year consumed far fewer days of labor, than turning out 15,000 men five days a year,

> unless the Querist has found out a new kind of Arithmetick, or that he looks upon the Labour of those People who are now obliged to Muster to be of no value.[7]

Under the new regulations, a man could still hire someone to serve in his place, but the "Querist" complained that the sums expended for replacements might exceed the equivalent of 600,000 pounds of tobacco. Spotswood answered:

> far from granting that such a Charge must be to the entire Ruin of the Country, I apprehend that it must be rather a benefit to the Publick by the Circulation of Money and Credit that would be increased thereby, and this circulation would be more just and beneficial, seeing the Payments would generally happen to be made by the Richer to the Poorer sort. It is true, that by my scheme Persons of Estates would not come off so easily as they do now. They must have contributed to the Arming as well as the Paying the Men who were to be train'd up for the defence of their Estates.[8]

In the eyes of William Byrd and his kind, Spotswood's plan amounted to forcing them to underwrite the nurturing of a republican militia. Worst of all, Spotswood would personally see to their training, reproducing his own military expertise through designated "Adjutants" from all parts of Virginia:

These Adjutants were proposed to be of the Inhabitants of the Country who were first to be exercised and instructed by me in Military Discipline, and afterwards to go into their respective Countys to teach the Officers and Soldiers.[9]

His enemies charged, Spotswood reported, that the Adjutants were intended

to huff and Bully the People. This, I am sure, was never intended as any part of their Office in my Scheme, nor am I apt to believe the House of Burgesses, to whom it was referred, would readily have given them such an authority.[10]

While continuing to fend off the attacks of his opponents, Governor Spotswood concentrated his efforts on securing a treaty with the Iroquois nations that would ensure Virginia's rights of settlement in the strategic Shenandoah Valley. That could be effected if the Iroquois would yield their claim to any lands south of the Potomac River, which continues west from its junction with the northern end of the Shenandoah, on the western side of the Blue Ridge Mountains. The tempo of activity on the Iroquois question increased markedly in 1717.

The House of Burgesses remained dissolved, but even the Council began to budge when a party of Mohawks attacked Fort Christanna in the spring. Spotswood wrote to Governor Hunter in New York, proposing they negotiate "suitable reparations" and better defined provisions for peace. Hunter met with the Five Nations at Albany in the middle of June, and secured a confession and an apology, but nothing else of substance.[11]   In August, the Virginia Council endorsed a proposal by Spotswood "for making a

Settlement and erecting a Fort at the late discovered Passage over the Great Mountains," and appealed to King George "to give such directions." The wording of their address undercut Spotswood on a key point, however, by proposing that the Five Nations and their allies be "restrained from passing Potomack River *on this side [of] the great Mountains* [emphasis added]."[12]   Such an arrangement would have left Virginia shut off from the Shenandoah, but in any case King George ignored the entire proposal.   Yet the Indian threat was growing. Governor Keith of Pennsylvania soon reported that a large body of northern Indians was marching towards Virginia.[13]

The Pennsylvania Case

In September 1717, Spotswood set out for New York, to pursue the Indian question directly with Hunter.   He stopped on the way at Philadelphia, however, to meet with the new governor, William Keith.   Keith was another fellow Scot, originally appointed to colonial service by Queen Anne in 1714, as Surveyor General of Customs for the southern colonies.   His official relationship with Spotswood dated from that time.   Keith was removed from that office in 1716, during the Whig Junto's vengeful purge of the dead Queen's appointees.   He was accused, like Jonathan Swift and so many of Swift's friends from Robert Harley's ministry, of being a Jacobite sympathizer.   Yet, Keith returned to London, and in less than a year became Pennsylvania's governor.   The full details of this remarkable development remain unknown today, but the circumstances surrounding it provide some very important leads.

First, it is necessary to recall some historical background.   From the early American vantage point, Pennsylvania is appropriately known as the "Keystone State."   Geographically, its western extent is the keystone for an arch bridging Massachusetts and Virginia, the colonies which provided the primary foundations for the American Revolution. Following Charles II's revoking the Massachusetts Bay Charter in 1684, the newly founded Pennsylvania colony acquired greater political and strategic significance to America's hopes of becoming a continental republic. Its *potential* for such a role lay in the fact that it had been chartered in 1681 as a proprietorship, rather than as a royal colony. Its governors would be appointed by the proprietor, rather than by the crown, and the colony might thus enjoy some degree of protection from the looting policies typically pursued by the English kings of the seventeenth and eighteenth centuries.

Any such margin of freedom depended, of course, upon having a proprietor who wished to promote it. In the case of Pennsylvania, Charles II imagined no such threat when he granted William Penn the proprietorship for his Quaker "Holy Experiment" in America. At the time, Charles II was bent on revoking all the charter freedoms which remained in the English colonies. While he had no use for Quakers inside his kingdom, he had applauded their American debut in the 1660s, when they served as an anarchist battering ram against the republican institutions of Massachusetts. Granting them a colony of their own seemed like a stroke of shrewd management.

But just as the demanding realities of organizing a society in the wilderness outstripped the Quaker creed, Pennsylvania's strategic significance also attracted numerous republican efforts to transform its purpose. In 1688, New England's republican leader Increase Mather was in London, seeking to negotiate a new charter for Massachusetts. On May 30, only days after his arrival, Mather obtained an audience with James II. That same evening, he met with William Penn at his house.[14] Mather recruited Penn as his behind-the-scenes ally in the charter fight, and his diary records six more meetings with Penn during the next six weeks.[15] Mather also supplied Penn with a Boston militia officer to serve as governor of Pennsylvania, during the period through the Andros Rebellion in Massachusetts, led by Mather's son Cotton in 1689. To Pennsylvania's hard-core, pacifist, Puritan-hating Quakers, Penn's choice for governor was proof enough that other influences were at work on the colony.

The key figure behind the republican influences on Pennsylvania was the movement's international leader, Gottfried Wilhelm von Leibniz, whose circles included the Mathers.   William Penn's recruiting agent for German immigrants to Pennsylvania was August Hermann Francke, an associate of Leibniz's who also organized much of the faculty which later founded Gottingen University, the foremost center of learning in eighteenth-century Germany. In 1699, Penn returned to his struggling colony with a new personal secretary, the Scots-Irishman James Logan (1674– 1751), who became the leading Leibniz scholar of his time in America, and the dominant intellectual and political figure in Pennsylvania for much of his life there. Logan's writings include a defense of Leibniz against Isaac Newton's absurd claims of inventing the calculus, which Sir Isaac had incompetently plagiarized from Leibniz. The Newton-Leibniz controversy of 1711–1713 had been faked by the Whig Junto to discredit Leibniz's growing influence in Queen Anne's cabinet—then headed by Robert Harley, who brought Leibniz's ally Jonathan Swift into its inner circle.

During that same period, William Penn was also a welcome figure at Whitehall and at the court of Queen Anne.   During Swift's first recorded discussion with Harley, at a small party Harley gave on October 7, 1710, Swift was introduced to, "among others, Will Penn the quaker: we sat two hours drinking as good wine as you do," he wrote to Stella, "and two hours more he [Harley] and I alone."[16] In January 1712, Swift referred in another letter to Stella to "my friend Penn."[17] Penn's health was declining, and that fall he suffered an incapacitating stroke. In the will he had drawn up in the same year, the government of Pennsylvania was left in the care of two trustees in the event of his death. One of them was Robert Harley.[18] Penn survived until 1718; early in 1717, as one of his last acts as proprietor, he signed the commission appointing William Keith as governor of Pennsylvania.[19]

Keith was the sort of bold, self-assured man that Spotswood liked. He had been impressive enough in his customs post to receive a unanimous recommendation from the Pennsylvania Council for the governorship of the colony, when he returned to England in 1716. Pennsylvania was anxious to replace the wretched Governor Charles Gookin, who had become notorious for his stupidity, jealousy, greed, and "recurrent fits of insanity." [20] Prior to Keith's appointment, in fact, the colony had in general been badly governed. Keith was soon being praised by Logan and others for his "skill and good genius" for government, his "humanity and freedom of access," and his "professed good will to the people of this province."[21] He would later play a significant role in promoting America's development beyond the mountains, in concert with Spotswood, Swift, and Benjamin Franklin.

Pennsylvania was a necessary component in the treaty arrangements Spotswood sought with the Iroquois Five Nations. It was through Pennsylvania that they made their incursions into western Virginia, from their strongholds in New York, and many of the Pennsylvania tribes were themselves tributaries of the Iroquois. With Keith in command at Philadelphia, and Hunter in New York, a comprehensive settlement at last seemed attainable. Following Spotswood's meeting with Keith in September

1717, the two governors proceeded to New York, accompanied by Logan, who had formed a close friendship with Governor Hunter.[22]   There they worked out two preliminary articles of agreement which the Iroquois were to consider: that they would remain west of the mountains, and not cross the Potomac. It was upon Spotswood's return from these negotiations in New York, that he learned that King George had annulled the Indian Act, raising once more the threat of chaos on the frontier.[23]

Fort Christanna itself was in jeopardy. The fort and its garrison had been maintained by the Virginia Indian Company, now dissolved by the repeal of Spotswood's legislation.   He persuaded the council to permit Fort Christanna to continue operations until a new assembly could be convened in 1718, to determine how to maintain it for the future. Beyond the question of the fort, Spotswood was deeply concerned over the threat to the entire protective screen of Virginia's friendly Indians.   For Virginia to pull out of Fort Christanna, at a time when its Indian allies were being menaced by the powerful tribes of the Iroquois, "may be attended with ill Consequences," Spotswood told the new assembly, "and from the Strictest Friends may make those Indians our most dangerous Enemys."[24]

Spotswood's own political enemies now recognized a danger of a different sort.   The continuous arc of the western frontier, from upper New York to the Shenandoah Valley, lay within the governments of three men whose political careers traced back to the circles of influence of Jonathan Swift, during the reign of Queen Anne. Governor Hunter of New York, who continued to correspond with Swift, was pressing for the establishment of a fort on Lake Ontario.   Governor Spotswood was making plans for an expedition to Lake Erie, to secure the opening phase of a colonization drive as far as the Mississippi River.

Governor Keith of Pennsylvania was now in a position to link the efforts of the other two and turn them into reality. He would soon lend official support to Spotswood's proposal for a fortified settlement on Lake Erie.

Spotswood Forces the Hand of the Burgesses

The drive to open the West was rapidly gaining momentum. In 1718, there was a full-scale confrontation over this issue, and Alexander Spotswood was at the center of it. Greeting Virginia's new assembly on April 24, Spotswood presented only one item to the members for their consideration: the need for a new treaty with the Iroquois. His language was mild; he had been ordered by the Lords of Trade, of all people, to show more respect to the House of Burgesses, after he dissolved the session of 1715 with a blunt portrayal of their actions. Spotswood nonetheless reminded them of an earlier session, in 1711, "when a Bill was formed to raise Twenty Thousand pounds" for all-out warfare against the Indians of Virginia:

> Reflect who restrained you then from that violent proceeding. And if I have procured your welfare by other measures, and Saved you an Expence of Blood and Treasure, they must be Strangely perverse who can continue to Clamour when their Country prospers, merely because it has not been rescued after their fancies.

He directed their attention to the Iroquois, the "five United Nations to the Norward," who now showed "a Disposition to break with us and the Indians under the Protection of this Government." Spotswood informed the assembly of his mission to New York the previous fall, and of the preliminary articles under negotiation with the Iroquois "which shall be laid before you." He would leave it to the assembly "to determine whether any further measures shall be taken to preserve those Peoples Friendship," but added that if any treaty were to be negotiated, "the Indians insist upon having it carried on at Albany." He concluded with a diplomatic appeal for funds to be appropriated for the peace conference, since no "reasonable man [could] think it Just that the many Expensive and fatiguing Expeditions I have undertaken purely for the Country's Service should be defrayed by my own private Purse."[25]

The warlike 'disposition' of the Iroquois, against the American colonies, was not self-determined. From Pennsylvania, James Logan confirmed that same year that the French were "using their utmost endeavors to bring over all the Indians into their interest." Their special target was the Iroquois Five Nations, who formerly "stood chiefly in their way, but by their Jesuits and other means they daily debauch them from the English."[26] Logan estimated that 700 Iroquois warriors were already under Jesuit control, while only 2,000 remained friendly to the American colonies. As for the tribes to the west of the Iroquois, French Jesuit control was complete, all the way to the Mississippi.[27] Without a treaty of friendship with the Iroquois, American hopes for developing the West might be speedily terminated.

Spotswood's determination to settle the Iroquois question forced the hand of his opposition. That spring, the entire Council boycotted his party for the King's birthday, given as a matter of protocol. Instead, the councilors caroused in the Hall of Burgesses with their leading agents in the House, while dispensing large quantities of liquor and sedition to a mob gathered outside. The burgesses replied to Spotswood's address by rejecting any appropriation for negotiations with the Iroquois, and declaring that the additional expenses he had incurred on behalf of the colony, justified "the salary allowed by his Majesty" King George.[28] On May 24, they adopted a resolution that "keeping up and guarding fort *Christanna* is not any Service or Security to this country."[29] Both the Council and the House passed a bill intended to cripple Virginia's postal service, Spotswood's vital communications link with the northern colonies. It so flagrantly violated the barest standards of credibility, as well as royal instructions dating back to Queen Anne, that it never saw the governor's desk.[30]

On May 29, Byrd's gaggle of hirelings in the House turned their assault directly against Spotswood. They voted to repeal the previous assembly's authorization for completing construction of the governor's official residence under Spotswood's direction, and the measly £250 appropriated for him to do so. (Perhaps he reflected upon Swift's sarcastic "Bill of British Ingratitude" regarding the Duke of Marlborough, who had extorted more than £200,000 from Queen Anne for Blenheim Palace, as a private residence for himself and his heirs.) Instead the Burgesses decided to appropriate funds for an ornate marble tomb over the simple grave of Edward Nott, who had briefly served as an utterly forgettable royal governor before his death in 1706. He had been buried in the graveyard of Bruton Parish Church, since rebuilt according to Spotswood's classical design. The burgesses now commended Nott for his "prudent and Easy Administration."[31] Lest there be any confusion over the source of these measures, the burgesses added a resolution designating William Byrd as the colony's official agent in London.[32]

Spotswood adjourned the assembly the next day. He knew that its obstruction of his efforts to secure a treaty with the Iroquois originated among Byrd's henchmen on the Council.   In refusing to appropriate funds for the negotiations, the House of Burgesses had left the matter to "the Determination of the Governor & Council." Spotswood summoned the councilors the following morning, and asked for their recommendation. Of the eight members present, seven had already sided with Byrd. Led by Philip Ludwell, "King" Carter, and James Blair, the councilors replied that "there doth not appear an immediate necessity for entring into any New Treaty."[33]

Byrd's seven dwarves, plus another absent on this day, had signed a letter to the Board of Trade in March, attacking Spotswood's "new measures." They claimed to have "complied as far as possible with his desires in everything; but had they gone intirely [sic] into all the new measures that have been proposed to them and prest upon them," they believed that "the Consequences would have been very bad." Spotswood had obtained a copy of the letter at the time, and demanded an immediate explanation. His accusers had replied, "that this Question being unexpected, they did not think proper to give an immediate answer," and had stalled ever since.[34] With the House now adjourned, the signers still maintained "that it is not proper to meddle with that Letter without directions from their Lordships" of the Board of Trade.[35]

Spotswood then announced that he would put the matter "in a fuller light than they have set it forth," and ordered that the following entry be made in the Council journal for May 31, 1718:

> The aforenamed 8 Councilors secretly combined to draw up a charge against the Lieut. Governor, and privily sent it away to the Right Honorable Lords Commissioners for Trade, Complaining therein of his proposing and pressing them into New and pernicious Measures . . . . And now fourscore days after,

seven of them come and declare against explaining themselves unless they are first directed from England to do so.

Spotswood further declared for the record "that he took their Evasive Answers, to be a Plain Confession that they knew their Accusation is Groundless," and he would have nothing more to say about it.[36]

In New York, Governor Hunter was under a similar attack. Though the Duke of Marlborough had been incapacitated by a stroke in 1715, his ally General Stanhope, the treacherous plotter against Queen Anne, became the head of King George's cabinet in 1716. Hunter's enemies in New York were soon lobbying in London for his removal—and perhaps his death. An intercepted letter from one of them boasted that

> Coll. Hunters interest is intirely sunck at Court .
> . . . Even Parliament men [Whigs] wonder how a Province of freeborn Englishmen could beare to be kept under soe much tyrany and oppression without serveing him even as the people of Antigua served Generall Parkes . . . .[37]

The reference was to Daniel Parke, former governor of the Leeward Islands, murdered by islanders in 1710. Hunter read it as an assassination threat, and reported it as such to the Board of Trade. He also continued to maintain a personal guard of two companies of armed soldiers.[38]

Like Spotswood, Hunter was continually the target of fraudulent petitions and baseless charges against his governance of New York and New Jersey. Even if such complaints came from "Criminals" and "common disturbers of the publick peace," as he wrote to the Board of Trade in 1718, they always found a hearing in London. Hunter challenged the board, however, to "look back into the affairs of this Province . . . & compare the former confusion with the present happy tranquility." [39] Considering the bizarre state of affairs under his predecessor, the transvestite Lord Cornbury, Hunter's point could not be dismissed out of hand by the Lords of Trade. They reported that Hunter's enemies had not submitted proof of their charges, so no proceedings against him could be recommended. [40]

Showdown with Byrd

Spotswood's confrontation with Byrd's followers on the Virginia Council also dictated a showdown with the Board of Trade in 1718. He wrote to his old commander, the Earl of Orkney, who was still the official governor of Virginia. The councilors could largely ignore popular opposition, for they were appointed by the crown, under authority generally vested in the Lords of Trade. Spotswood urged Orkney to go before the board, to demand the removal of four members of the Virginia Council: William Byrd, Philip Ludwell, James Blair, and John Smith. Blair had been acting lieutenant-governor before Spotswood's arrival, and continued as a powerful enemy as president of the Council. Spotswood also recommended four replacements for them: Peter Beverley, Cole Diggs, John Robinson, and Edward Hill. [41]

He informed Orkney that the opposition "party" not only sought to remove Spotswood, but to secure the revocation of Orkney's title to the governorship as well. Spotswood did not mince words about the character of the opposition:

> I take the power, interest and reputation of the
> King's governor in this dominion to be now

reduced to a desperate gasp, and if the present
[efforts of the country] cannot add new vigor to
the same, then the haughtiness of a Carter, the
hypocrisy of a Blair, the inveteracy of a
Ludwell, the brutishness of a Smith, the malice
of a Byrd, the conceitedness of a Grymes, and
the scurrility of a Corbin . . . must for the
future rule this province.[42]

Orkney took Spotswood's case before the Board of Trade
on August 19, 1718, and urged a change in the Council. He
offered to propose new councilors if the board desired, but
received no immediate response.[43]

From Virginia, Spotswood continued to press his own
case. On August 14, he wrote the Board of Trade of his
own bold plans (cited earlier) for establishing a settlement
on Lake Erie. The French, he emphasized, from their ring
of outposts stretching from the St. Lawrence River all the
way to Louisiana,

may, when they please, Send out such Bodys of
Indians on the back of these Plantations as may
greatly distress his Majesty's Subjects here.

That threat could be cut off by the settlement he proposed
on Lake Erie, which his discoveries beyond the Blue Ridge
had proven to be entirely feasible:

We are nearer to Support than they to attack.
As this Country is the nearest of any other to
Supply such a Settlement, and as I flatter my
Self I have attained a more exact knowledge
than any other Englishman Yet has of the
Situation of the Lakes, and the way through
which they are most accessible over Land, I
shall be ready to Undertake the Executing this

project if his Majestie thinks fit to approve of
it.[44]

The costs for such an expedition, Spotswood added
pointedly, could entirely be met from Virginia's revenue
surplus from quitrents—thanks to his having ended the
swindle under the former collectors, William Byrd and
Philip Ludwell.[45]

Spotswood's reports of France's growing designs on the
West at last provoked some genuine alarm in London. The
Board of Trade wrote to Governor Keith in Pennsylvania,
requesting his own estimate on the extent of the French
threat, and any measures he might recommend to deal with
it. Keith asked for a preliminary report from James Logan.
Logan not only had nearly twenty years' experience in the
colony, but had built up an extensive fur trade as well, with
a number of French traders on his payroll. The fur trade
was a generally nasty business, as Spotswood had learned
in Virginia. In New York, Hunter had found that the
Albany traders were more interested in supplying the
French and their Indians than in the safety of the colony.
But Logan insisted that the only way to hold the Iroquois
was to expand the British fur trade and undercut the
French. He also suggested, however, that the Lords of
Trade approve Spotswood's proposal "to extend
[Virginia's] settlements beyond the mountains" and place
forts upon Lake Erie. Keith incorporated nearly all of
Logan's report in his own reply to the Board of Trade.[46]

Spotswood's hand was strengthened, but the tribes of the
Iroquois were once more menacing Virginia. In September,
he wrote again to the board, pressing for reviving the
policies of his vetoed Indian Act, and for a showdown with
Byrd's opposing faction:

> It was in August, 1714, that I began to build the
> fort of Christanna, and to form a Scheme for the
> better defending the Frontiers. From that time

The Threat of French Encirclement

During the early 18th century, the American colonies faced a dual threat. Neither Britain nor France supported any significant development of the continent's potential, since the oligarchies of both kingdoms feared the possibility of a New World republic. By British agreement, violated only during the last years of Queen Anne, the French were licensed to ensure the subjection of Britain's own colonies. Virginia's Governor Alexander Spotswood (who served from 1710 to 1722) constantly advocated extending American settlements to the Mississippi and the Great lakes, to break the grip of French encirclement. Following Queen Anne's death in 1714, his warnings became more urgent; but with George I on the throne, the French buildup proceeded unchallenged. With the partial exceptions of Quebec, Montreal, and New Orleans, French outposts had simply been military chokepoints against America's western expansion, with no serious intent at colonization. Typically, they were also garrisons to protect Jesuit "missions" among the Indians, designed to replace primitive tribal beliefs with murderous, pseudo-Christian rituals.   After 1715, French operations in North America expanded from the lower Mississippi into Alabama, from Quebec down to the southern stretches of Lake Champlain, and from the Great lakes deep into Indiana and Ohio. The map indicates French forts and command posts established by 1735.

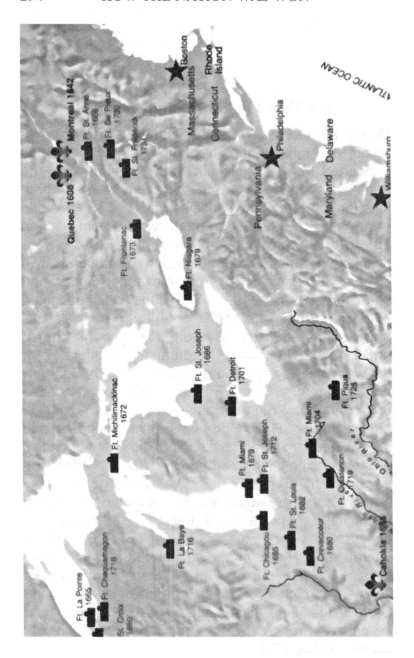

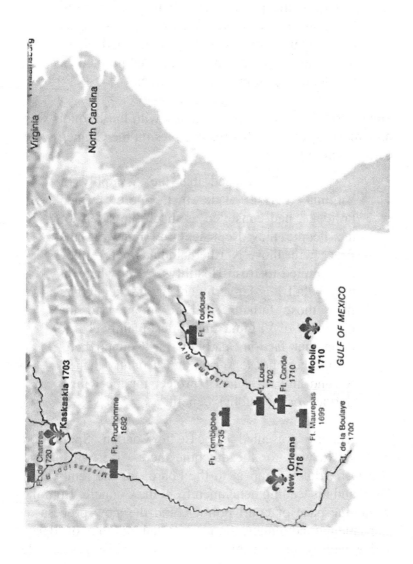

to the dissolution of the late Indian Company,
and that the Assembly refused to keep up that
Fort, there was not so much as one Alarm from
any foreign Indians, nor occasion for ordering
out the Militia for defending the Frontier, as
had been the practice for many years before.
But now the Northern Indians and Tuscaroras
begin again their usual Incursions, and about
the beginning of last Month committed a
murder at one of our out Plantations.

Spotswood warned that a new treaty with the Iroquois was
now most urgent, but that his enemies on the Council were
determined to prevent it:

It were to be wished that the Assembly of
Virginia, laying aside their more refined
Politicks, had consulted as much the safety of
the People they Represent, by renewing the
Peace with those Northern Indians before they
are tempted to fresh Hostilitys.   But whatever
may befall this Government or its Neighbours
from those Indians, will be imputed to the
obstinacy of Virginia, and I must plainly charge
it on that factious party in the Council here,
who rather choose to ruin their Country than to
Second any Measures I project for the King's
Service, or the publick benefit.[47]

Having presented his case to London, Spotswood
resolved to wait for the outcome there.   He still had no
word of Orkney's appeal to the board, for the removal of
Byrd and his leading henchmen from the Council. Both the
byzantine pace of court politics, and the slow process of
transatlantic communications, dictated months of delay.
On November 11, he convened the House of Burgesses. He

presented no opening address, but merely sent a message through the clerk that he had nothing to lay before them, and that they should proceed with whatever routine matters of business that had been certified by the counties for their consideration.[48] The burgesses generally expected a short and uneventful session— even more so as Byrd's committee chairmen and floor managers began tabling even minor items and deferring them to the next assembly. By November 20, nearly a third of the members were at home in their districts.   Most of them were supporters of Spotswood, and knew that he planned nothing of significance for this session.[49]

That same day, under the guise of winding down to adjournment, Byrd's lackeys in the House made their move. Controlling slightly more than a third of the total House, but with approximately a three-fifths majority of the members still in attendance, they passed an address to King George, charging Spotswood with

> the Subversion of the Constitution of our Government, the depriving us of our ancient Rights & priviledges and many hardships which he daily exercises upon your Majestys good Subjects of this Colony . . . . And therefore we humbly hope your Majesty will be graciously pleased to receive some particulars from the Honourable William Byrd Esq. Whome we have desired to appear in behalf of your oppressed Subjects of this Colony. . . .

A list of fourteen instructions to Byrd, "Agent for the Colony of Virginia," was then presented for adoption, headed by the direction that he present the charges against Spotswood to the King, "and to the utmost of your power endeavour his Removal" as governor. The burgesses loyal to Spotswood were able to force a debate on the instructions, however, and secure a continuation to the following day.[50]

The plotters' attempted parliamentary coup against Spotswood blew up in their faces. Enough of his supporters were rallied to reduce the bill of particulars against the governor to an impotent gesture. Eight of the fourteen charges were voted down outright, including such absurdities as "he hath intirely [sic] neglected the Militia." Only two of the original complaints passed, dealing with disputes over the burgesses' salaries and expenditures for the governor's residence. Three more were amended, into insignificant challenges to Spotswood's interpretations of minor laws and royal directives. And in the remaining, leading instruction to Byrd, the language calling for Spotswood's removal was stricken.[51]

The degenerate William Byrd, waiting in London for news of his minions' expected success, would have to confront a new reality. Through Spotswood's leadership, a republican movement had taken hold in Virginia. More than the governor now stood in the way of the feudal empire he sought. In a losing effort, Byrd had also publicly surfaced all of his agents, both in the Council and in the House.

Spotswood did not hesitate to press this advantage. When he prorogued the assembly on December 1, he directed his remarks at the burgesses who had conspired with Byrd. "Far from being disturbed at your violent Impeachments," he declared, "I take this to be an happy Crisis, when the Country will be no longer imposed upon by malicious Whisperers, Clandestine Informers, and Anonymous Libellers of Government." [52] Spotswood's own supporters could now meet the enemy on an open field. Twenty-one of Virginia's twenty-five counties passed resolutions condemning the "general and hasty" charges against the governor. The colony's clergymen, meeting in convention, commended him for his "just and wise government." The grand jury lodged a formal protest against the rump proceedings in the House.[53] Of the plotters among the burgesses, Spotswood noted later, "Scarce one of them would ever be chosen burgess again were it not for the awe that the discontented Councillors carry."[54]

Deadlock over the Treaty

Spotswood's defeat of Byrd's faction in the House turned the political calculations of London's oddsmakers into so much rubbish. The governor's support among the Virginia population also left the Board of Trade with no pretext to act on the remaining shreds of the burgesses' address to the King. His Majesty's government, however, was determined to delay action as long as possible on the crucial issue of the Virginia Council. Without the Council's consent, Spotswood could not negotiate a treaty with the Iroquois, to open the way for settlements beyond the Blue Ridge. Byrd controlled eight seats on the twelve-man body; but if the Board of Trade granted Orkney's request, to replace four of them with supporters of Spotswood, the situation would be reversed. In the meantime, the Governor of Virginia was forced to operate under the Council's absurd restriction, that no treaty could be proposed to the Iroquois, until *after* they had attacked Virginia.[55]

Spotswood's patience was wearing thin, but there was no response from the Board of Trade on the Council issue during the entirety of 1719. It was a year of more intrigue than usual at the court of King George. The Venetian party's Bank of England and East India Company had just taken over the South Sea Company, and were preparing a blowout of the British economy. Robert Harley's South Seas Act of 1711, for restoring the nation's credit, had been turned by the Junto Whigs into an insiders' orgy of speculation, from which Robert Walpole would soon emerge as the ruler of Britain for the next two decades. Britain had also declared war with Spain; and from Dublin, Jonathan Swift again detected the foul odor of his enemies run amuck.

In the spring of 1719, Swift's old friend Robert Hunter, in communication with Spotswood and Keith, decided to make the difficult voyage to London to assess the political situation at first hand.[56] His departure was delayed by sudden displays of warlike intentions among the Iroquois tribes, ultimately aimed at Virginia. Given the growing influence of the Jesuits within the Five Nations, this development was hardly coincidental. With the threat of impending attack, Spotswood decided not to convene the House of Burgesses, and rarely called a meeting of the Council. When he did, it was to confront their idiotic policy of 'no peace without war.' He met with them on May 28 to report that the Senecas, one of the Iroquois Five Nations, had raided a plantation in Essex County, not fifty miles north of Williamsburg, and that 350 more of them "were encamped at the foot of the great Mountains."

With bitter irony, Spotswood informed the councilors he had taken no action, because of their resolution to do nothing until the Iroquois "should Commit actual Hostilitys on the Inhabitants of this Colony, and he did not know whether the Gentlemen who were of that Opinion then, would judge the Plundering [of] a House such an Act of Hostility."[57] He next summoned the Council on June 26, to inform them of petitions from the outlying inhabitants of nearby New Kent and Henrico counties, "representing the great and eminent Danger they apprehended themselves exposed to by the frequent marches of the Northern Indians through their Plantations," and "praying such Measures may be taken as may protect them in their Lives and estates. . . ." The Iroquois invasions of these counties threatened to isolate the capital at Williamsburg, located on the peninsula between the York and James rivers. Spotswood also read a letter from Pennsylvania Governor William Keith,

> giving an account that a great Body of the said Northern Indians . . . are marched away towards Virginia, privately declaring That they intend to Try the Strength of the English at the fort of Christanna.

The combined assault could "cut off and destroy" the Sapponi Indians, the only significant tribe still allied to Virginia.[58]

All of these moves by the Iroquois violated the preliminary articles of agreement negotiated by Spotswood, Keith, and Hunter, by which they would not cross the Potomac or the Blue Ridge. But the "obstinacy of Virginia," as Spotswood had warned regarding Byrd's faction on the Council, had given the Jesuits a free hand. Keith's letter to Spotswood also reported that the Cayugas of western New York, another tribe of the Five Nations, had "plainly declared That they expected a Free recourse for their People through the English Plantations while they were making War on their Enemys."[59] After presenting this entire intelligence picture, Governor Spotswood

> was pleased to ask the Advice of the Council what measures they Judged proper to be taken for the Protection of the Inhabitants of this Colony, seeing . . . that the Council hath heretofore declined entering upon any Terms with these Indians until actual Hostilitys should be Committed.[60]

Spotswood was fully aware of the potential trap before him. If he took the bait of the Iroquois incursions, and responded militarily on his own authority, Byrd's henchmen might charge him with initiating an Indian war which could devastate the colonies from New England to the Carolinas.   Beyond the carnage, such an outcome might entirely close the door to the West.   Spotswood coolly reminded the Council, that the last assembly had done nothing to compensate for the safeguards lost by the King's veto of the Indian Act. He then declared

> that if this Board can take a more Effectual
> Course for the Defence of the Country than
> what he hath hitherto proposed, he shall readily
> follow their Advice.[61]

He thus placed the burden of the Iroquois threat upon his enemies on the Council; and they choked accordingly, while considering the least measures they dared recommend.

In the event of an attack on Fort Christanna, the Council advised that the "Governor order out the Militia of the Adjacent Countys to relieve that place and to repell the said Indians by force." Incursions by the Iroquois on "their way to the Southward" should be met by armed militia under orders not to fight unless attacked. The Indians should be informed "in a friendly manner" that they were not to pass through Virginia's settlements, but if they refused to comply, the commanding officer should immediately notify the governor "of the rout the said Indians intend to take." The governor should also order Virginia's tribes to no longer allow "any of their Indians to be employed as Guides to the Northern Indians."

To this blueprint for defeat, the Council added a final recommendation that Spotswood write to Governor Hunter, urging him "to use his authority and interest to restrain the five Nations under his Government from passing through the Inhabitants of this Colony." This last advice from Byrd's cronies on the Council, strongly suggested their desire to tie down Hunter as well, who was about to sail for England. Spotswood shot back that

> he had already writ in the most pressing Terms he could to the Governor of New York on that Subject, and could add nothing more to prevent those dangers which apparently threaten our Frontiers by the marches of the Five Nations.[62]

Governor Hunter's Legacy

On June 24, 1719, just two days before Spotswood's confrontation with Byrd's allies on the Virginia Council, Robert Hunter addressed a joint session of the New York legislature. He was fifty-two years old, but recently stricken with severe arthritis. His wife had died in 1716, at the age of thirty, leaving him with four children. He announced that in consideration of his health and his "little family," as well as "private affairs on the other side," he was returning to England. Hunter emphasized that he held "a firm resolution to return to you again," but if he could not, he pledged to "be watchful and industrious to promote the interest and welfare of this country, of which I . . . account myself a countryman. "[63]

He was never again to set foot in New York, but he could be proud of his political legacy. Upon his arrival, the deliberative functions of provincial government had resembled a clogged sewer, full of factional waste piled up since the defeat of Leisler's Rebellion against Francis Nicholson, following the Andros Rebellion in Massachusetts. The leaders of the Anglican clergy operated simply as agents of Lord Cornbury, and had worked to remove Hunter as an "enemy of the church." Hunter had been protected at first, by Swift's influence at the court of Queen Anne. In January of 1712, the same month that the Duke of Marlborough was removed from all his offices, Hunter had been promoted from colonel to brigadier general.[64]

The accession of George I, however, set off a new round of attacks on Hunter, of much the same sort as were aimed at Spotswood. Hunter was not reappointed governor until January 25, 1715, and Cornbury's ally Nicholson waited in Boston until March, for word he might be named to replace Swift's friend. As in Virginia, the New York assembly of 1715 proved more obstructive than usual, under the influence of the powerful New York merchants Jacobus Van Cortlandt and Stephen DeLancey[65]—whose descendants joined the British against the American Revolution. Governor Hunter combatted his enemies in Swiftian fashion, with the first play written in America—a political satire which made them the laughingstock of New York.

Weaving together actual characters and events in both the New York and New Jersey assemblies, Hunter's Androboros exposed the plotters against him to devastating ridicule. The title role represented Francis Nicholson, "Old nick-nack, who had paganized himself with that Name," reports the play's court jester, "Tom o'Bedlam." The name Androboros "signifies a Man-Eater. He is now very far gone indeed." Other plotters featured in the play include "Lord Oinobaros" ("the sot," Lord Cornbury); the "Speaker" (New York assembly speaker William Nicoll); "Coxcomb" (Daniel Coxe, a New Jersey councilor who was lobbying for Hunter's removal in London); "Fizle" (Anglican minister William Vesey, an agent of Cornbury's); and "Flip" (Adolph Philipse, a major New York merchant, landholder, and member of the Council).

Hunter himself is cast as the "Keeper," supported by "Solemn" (his friend Lewis Morris, expelled from the New York assembly in 1710 for defending the legal powers of the governor); "Aesop" (David Jamison, chief justice of New Jersey and attorney general of New York); and the "Deputy" (George Clarke, secretary and auditor of New York).

The "Senate" is waiting for Androboros to bring "some mighty Deliverance" from the rule of their Keeper. Meanwhile, they pass a resolution not to be "bound by any Laws, Rules or Customs, any Law, Rule or Custom to the Contrary Notwithstanding." When Solemn objects to this wild doctrine, the Speaker informs him that "for *Reasons* best known to our selves, you are Expell'd." Androboros is ushered in and congratulates the Senate for expelling Solemn, "that wandring Plague, that Kibes in the Heels and Piles in the Posteriors of Mankind." Androboros has been appointed general to lead an expedition against the Canadian possessions of France's Louis XIV. He pompously vows "not to pare these Nails, wash this blew Visage, or put off this speckled *Shirt* Until I have made that Haughty Monarch Confess himself, in all his Projects for Universal Dominion, my Inferior."

The Senate immediately passes a resolution commending Androboros for his "Courage, Conduct, and Prudence" on the expedition which has not yet begun. When he finally departs, the Keeper is informed of the Senators' actions. In disgust he declares, "To your Kennels, ye Hounds," and dissolves the session. Fizle, Flip, and Coxcomb then plot to have the Keeper removed as governor, and to reinstall Lord Oinobaros, who has orchestrated "secret Representations and Remonstrances" against the Keeper. Coxcomb demands that additional charges be faked immediately, in the name of the "Consistory" (the Anglican clergy), and put in the form of an address to Lord Oinobaros. Meanwhile Androboros, like Nicholson in 1711, has returned without a fight from his "expeditious Expedition." He declares that there is no need for a conquest of Canada.

Hunter's emphasis on the Quebec issue in *Androboros* underscored the importance he attached to opening the West. The Peace of Utrecht in 1713 was followed by the disintegration of Queen Anne's government, and her death the following year. Especially following the Jesuit-Orleanist coup in France, the French and British monarchies were again allied on the issue of containing the American colonies. Hunter still chafed under the restraint, and he loathed the arrangement which required him to treat the French foe in Canada, as a peace-loving neighbor.

In Hunter's play, Androboros reports that "our Reputed [French] Enemies" are "our good and faithful Friends and Allies." As proof, he announces that the French even made concessions on trade, "generously resigning and yielding to us that of the two Poles, reserving to themselves only what may lie betweeen 'em." In a comic battle of wit against witlessness, Hunter ("the Keeper") and his friends foil a plot by Fizle and Flip to assassinate the Keeper and install Androboros as governor. Their plot to kill him, by placing his chair over an unbolted trap door, is overheard by the Keeper's friend Tom. Androboros remains ignorant of the scheme, and in the play's climax, rushes to the vacant chair to assume the governor's office. Fizle and Flip attempt to restrain him, and all three conspirators fall to their deaths. The playwright added this concluding thought:

> Like the everlaughing Sage
>
> In a Jest I spend my Rage
>
> (Tho' it must be understood,
>
> I would hang them if I could.)[66]

Androboros did more than provide Hunter with an opportunity to let off steam. The play had a tremendous impact on New York politics, and Hunter could soon take satisfaction that his enemies "were so humorously exposed that the laugh was turned upon them in all companies, and from this laughing humour the people began to be in a good humour with their Governour."[67] By 1719, as he prepared for his mission to England, he could also point to a distinguished set of political leaders he had helped establish for the future.

Hunter's friend "Solemn," Lewis Morris, became the first governor of New Jersey, when that colony came under separate rule in 1738, and remained its head until his death in 1746.   His son, Robert Hunter Morris, became chief justice of New Jersey, and then governor of Pennsylvania from 1754 to 1756, during the crucial first phase of the French and Indian War.   In 1756, to rally Pennsylvania settlers against devastating Indian attacks to the north of Philadelphia, he gave Benjamin Franklin the first military assignment of his career, and then appointed him Colonel of the Regiment of Philadelphia.   Grandson Lewis Morris became a leader of New York's forces for independence during the American Revolution, a signer of the Declaration, a member of the Continental Congress, and a brigadier general in the Continental Army.

Another of Robert Hunter's protégés in New York was James Alexander, heir to the Scottish earldom of Stirling, who was deported to America for his part in the Jacobite rebellion of 1715.   Hunter had known his family in Scotland, and the young Alexander soon became one of Hunter's most trusted friends, and remained his personal agent in New York following Hunter's departure.   Hunter appointed him to several offices in New York and New Jersey, and Alexander later served on the councils of both colonies and as attorney general of New Jersey.   Trained in mathematics and surveying, James Alexander also became a noted astronomer, and a member of Benjamin Franklin's American Philosophical Society. Much of his training in astronomy came directly from Hunter, who in 1718 led a project with Governor Keith of Pennsylvania, to plot and compare the declination of the stars and planets, from their respective latitudes. In 1753, working with Franklin's scientific circles, Alexander was the astronomer in charge of American preparations to record the transit of Mercury. He was also a key figure in Franklin's republican networks, and helped him organize support for the Albany Plan of Union, Franklin's nation-building scheme of 1754. His son William Alexander served in the French and Indian War, and became a general in the Continental Army early in the Revolution. In 1778, he helped to expose the Conway Cabal's plot against General George Washington.[68]

The list could go on. That Hunter had touched many lives for the better was evident in an address of thanks, passed by the New York assembly before he sailed:

> You have governed well and wisely, like a prudent magistrate, like an affectionate parent . . . We have seen many Governours, and may see more; and as none of those who had the honour to serve in your station were ever so justly fixed in the affections of the Government, so those to come will acquire no mean reputation, when it can be truly said of them, their conduct had been like yours.
>
> We thankfully accept the honor you do us in calling yourself our countryman; give us leave then, to desire you will not forget this is your country, and (if you can) make haste to return to it.[69]

Governor Keith made a special trip to New York for a final discussion of strategy. Then, on July 13, 1719, Hunter turned the governments of New York and New Jersey over to their respective council presidents, Peter Schuyler and Lewis Morris, and boarded H.M.S. *Pearle* for England.[70]

NOTES

1. *Jour. Coun. Va.*, III, 456; Byrd, *London Diary* for 1717, *passim*.

2. *Jour. Burgesses*, xxix.

3. *Ibid.*, 166–170.

4. Spotswood, *Letters*, II, 189–190.

5. *Ibid.*, 202–203.

6. *Ibid.*, 210–211.

7. *Ibid.*, 211.

8. *Ibid.*, 211–212.

9. *Ibid.*, 212.

10. *Ibid.*

11. *Jour. Coun. Va.*, III, 450.

12. *Ibid.*, 451.

13. *Jour. Burgesses*, 1712–1726, 174; *Jour. Coun. Va.*, III, 478.

14. Increase Mather, "Diary."

15. *Ibid.* For more on Penn's service to Mather, see chapter 3.

16. Swift, *Journal to Stella*, I, 45–46.

17. *Ibid.*, II, 464.

18. Tolles, *James Logan*, 114.

19. *Ibid.*, 117.

20. *Ibid.*

21. Quoted by Tolles, *op. cit.*, 118.

22. *Ibid.*, 105, 97.

23. *Ibid.*, 105; *Jour. Coun. Va.*, III, 456–457.

24. *Jour. Burgesses*, 189.

25. *Jour. Burgesses*, 174–175.

26. Quoted by Tolles, *James Logan*, 107.

27. *Ibid.*, 107–108.

28. *Jour. Burgesses*, 199, 213.

29. *Ibid.*, 207.

30. *Ibid.*, xxxviii, 212.

31. *Ibid.*, 213–214.

32. *Ibid.*, 216.

33. *Jour. Coun. Va.*, III, 479.

34. *Ibid.*, 464.

35. *Ibid.*, 479.

36. *Ibid.*, 480.

37. Quoted by Lustig, *Hunter*, 150.

38. *Ibid.*

39. *Ibid.*, 154.

40. *Ibid.*

41. Havighurst, *Spotswood*, 88.

42. This letter is not included in the published collection of Spotswood's official correspondence —perhaps to avoid treading on the toes of so many

of Virginia's "first families." The section here, from the original manuscript, is quoted by Havighurst, *Spotswood*, 89. The editorial interpolation, "efforts of the country," is Havighurst's, and probably refers to the support Spotswood was mobilizing at the county government level throughout Virginia.

43. Havighurst, *Spotswood*, 90.

44. Spotswood, *Letters*, II, 296–297.

45. *Ibid.*, 297–298.

46. Tolles, *Logan*, 107–108.

47. Spotswood to the Board of Trade, September 27, 1718, *Letters*, II, 302–303.

48. *Jour. Burgesses*, xxxviii.

49. *Ibid.*, 243.

50. *Ibid.*, 228–230.

51. *Ibid.*, 230–231.

52. *Ibid.*, 242.

53. *Ibid.*, xxxix; Havighurst, *Spotswood*, 78.

54. Quoted by Havighurst, *Spotswood*, 83.

55. *Jour. Coun. Va.*, III, 507.

56. Lustig, *Hunter*, 155.

57. *Jour. Coun. Va.*, III, 506–507.

58. *Ibid.*, 507.

59. *Ibid.*

60. *Ibid.*, 507–508.

61. *Ibid.*, 508.

62. Ibid., 508–509.

63. Quoted by Lustig, *Hunter*, 156.

64. Lustig, *Hunter*, 98.

65. *Ibid.*, 123–126.

66. Only two copies of *Androboros* are known to exist today. The plot summary and quotations above are drawn from Lustig, *Hunter*, 136–140.

67. Quoted by Lustig, *Hunter*, 140.

68. *Dictionary of American Biography; Columbia Encyclopaedia*; Ronald W. Clark, *Benjamin Franklin, A Biography* (New York, 1983), 123–127, 55, 105; Lustig, *Hunter*, 144, 147, 159.

69. Quoted by Lustig, *Hunter*, 157.

70. *Ibid.*, 159.

9

Winning the Treaty of Albany

Robert Hunter's mission to London came at a time of unusual flux in Britain's Hanoverian government. Besides the machinations around the South Sea Company, political warfare had erupted even in the royal household, over a feud between the King and his royal heir. Both Marlborough's and Walpole's Whig factions fought to control the outcome. An uncertain variable was Princess Caroline, wife of the future George II, who had been one of Leibniz's favorite pupils. Less than two months before Hunter left New York, word had also arrived that King George had declared war on Spain—further distracting London's attention from American affairs. In such a political climate, the Board of Trade was not inclined to take undue risks in matters of colonial policy.

Hunter kept his pledge "to promote the interest and welfare" of his adopted countrymen. He did not feel able, however, to return as their governor. He remained in great physical pain; he was a widower with five young children; and he had spent £21,000 of his own money on resettling the Palatine refugees—none of which had been repaid. Hunter began the task of selecting and organizing a potential successor to his post. There is every likelihood—though no published proof—that he communicated with his political ally Jonathan Swift, the friend whose company he had most delighted in, before his voyage to America nine long years ago.

The political outlook of the next governor of New York was of vital importance. Not only was the colony the strategic buffer against the French and Indian threat out of Canada. Its government was also indispensable for any treaty with the Iroquois Five Nations, to open the way for settlements beyond the mountains. Since all major factions in George I's government opposed such a development, gaining the appointment of a governor to continue Hunter's policies was not an easy matter. Hunter's tactic was to recruit someone already confirmed in office, and switch posts with him. His choice was William Burnet, comptroller of the customs service, whose functions included oversight of colonial trade. Hunter's experience as a colonial governor made him a legitimate candidate for Burnet's office. Burnet was also a fellow Scot and old personal friend, whose political acceptability to the crown was enhanced by the fact that he was the son of Anglican Bishop Gilbert Burnet, a longtime opponent of Jonathan Swift. Over the course of many discussions, Hunter convinced William Burnet to accept the exchange of positions, and to abide by Hunter's written statement of policy for New York. Burnet also agreed to retain the "Keeper's" loyal allies in office, including Lewis Morris, David ("Aesop") Jamison, and James Alexander.[1]

While Hunter worked to secure this arrangement, William Byrd was feverishly lobbying to save his political neck. Spotswood's defeat of Byrd's attempted legislative coup had already crushed Byrd's hopes of getting the Virginia governorship. Now he was about to lose his seat on the Council as well. Byrd appealed to the Duke of Argyll to write to the Earl of Orkney on his behalf. On October 28, 1719, he pled his case before the Committee of Lords at the Cockpit, who "agreed to recommend my case of the Council to His Majesty." A week later, he wrote to Argyll, retailing his shopworn slanders against Spotswood. He spent the month of November fluttering from parlor to parlor, seeking support among the Lords of Trade for his threatened seat, but politically getting nowhere. His diary records his growing anxiety—and a similar increase in attempts at fulfilling his sexual fantasies.   In early December, with no immediate prospect of resolving his status on the Council, he decided to return to Virginia.[2]

On February 4, 1720, Byrd landed privately at a friend's Tidewater estate—after shorting the ship's captain on the fare for his passage. Following an absence of five years, he had come home with one mission in mind: to get rid of Alexander Spotswood and his policies.   Soon he was meeting with Ludwell, Blair, Carter, and his other cronies; but there was no meeting with Spotswood. It was clear to the delighted governor why Byrd did not show his face at the Capitol. He had failed to secure confirmation as a member of the Council. Stripped of council status, Byrd was in an extremely weak position, which severely limited the influence of his faction as well. Now it was Byrd's turn to wait, hoping an order to reinstate him would arrive from London.[3]

Spotswood had already seized this new opportunity. On February 1, he had drafted the most ambitious proposal for western expansion yet submitted to the Board of Trade. Again he emphasized the need to break the French capability to "surround all the British plantations" in America. He reminded the board that Virginia's original charter grant included "most of the [Great) Lakes and great part of the head branches of [the] Mississippi." From a geographic-strategic standpoint, he outlined the measures needed to secure that vast interior. He enclosed an extraordinary map, the fruit of his relentless search for intelligence on the West:

> That your Lordships may have a clearer idea of the places I have now been describing, I herewith transmit a draught of the River Mississippi and the rivers communicating with it, and also of the seacoasts along the Bay of

Mexico and Gulf of Florida . . . . In it your
Lordships will see the many navigable rivers
that branch out from the Mississippi towards
the English plantations, and the situation of the
several Indian nations with whom both we and
the French trade.

To a high degree of accuracy, Spotswood's map traced the
Ohio ("Oubache"), Illinois, and Missouri rivers to the
points they flow into the Mississippi. He had also acquired
a more differentiated picture of the "great mountains"
beyond the Blue Ridge. He now identified the
"Appalachian Mountains" defining the western boundary of
the Shenandoah Valley, and beyond them "The Highest
Ridge," the Allegheny Front stretching down from
Pennsylvania. Long before the Age of Man, all of these
barriers had been higher than the Rocky Mountains are
today.

They were still formidable obstacles, but Spotswood
was confident they could be overcome. He proposed to the
Board of Trade that he undertake a private mission to
England, under pretense of ill health or personal business,
to present his entire strategy. Given Byrd's predicament,
which suggested that Hunter's return to London had opened
additional possibilities, Spotswood may have determined
that a decisive shift in colonial policy was attainable. He
reported that he had a plan for "acquiring possession of the
Lakes on the back of Virginia." Mindful of George I's war
against Spain, he also wished to discuss how taking
Spanish Florida could cut off the French from the Gulf
coast and the lower Mississippi. Yet none of his
recommendations received a response from London.[4]

Nearly three months later, it again appeared that a
stalemate had been reached on the issue of the West. On
April 24, an order from King George arrived, restoring

Byrd to the Virginia Council. It had been signed during a cabinet meeting on January 8. Byrd hurried into Williamsburg the following morning, picked up the order, and proceeded with Ludwell and Carter to the Capitol. For the first time in more than five years, he entered Spotswood's presence, to deliver his appointment from the King. Spotswood denounced him before the Council, as Byrd recorded that night in his diary, "and told me he would obey the King's order but if I had come without it he would not have admitted me."[5] Spotswood refused to administer Byrd's oath of office until the next day, and then announced he was "going out of Town on his Majesty's Service"— to organize his own countermoves. The following evening, April 27, Byrd and Ludwell met at "King" Carter's home, "where we discoursed about some 'treasonable' matters."[6]

By the afternoon of the next day, Byrd was bending ears in Williamsburg "about my quarrel with the Governor." In the evening, he met with five of his henchmen on the Council at Colonel Ludwell's, where they worked late into the evening on "the complaint to be made against the Governor," but did not finish it. When Spotswood summoned the Council the following morning, this "treasonable" gang confidently expected a final showdown. But Spotswood still had no word of Hunter's situation, and given Byrd's reappointment by the King, he needed time. Accordingly, he had a surprise in store for the "libellers of government."

As Byrd confided to his diary, the meeting began with

> abundance of hard words between the Governor and Council about Colonel Ludwell and Mr. Commissary [Blair] for about two hours till of a sudden the clouds cleared away and we began to be perfectly good friends and we agreed

upon terms of lasting reconciliation, to the great
surprise of ourselves and everybody else.

Spotswood had arranged a dinner party for the council
members at the newly completed governor's residence,
where he

> entertained us very hospitably and the guns
> were fired and there was illumination all the
> town over and everybody expressed great joy.
> The Governor kissed us all round and gave me
> a kiss more than other people. We had also a
> concert of music at the Governor's and drank
> the necessary healths till 11 o'clock and then
> we took leave.[7]

Like it or not, Spotswood had made Byrd the center of
public celebrations throughout the capital. Byrd liked it.
But the governor had not only displayed his disarming
charm.   During the Council meeting itself, his sudden
conviviality had won the signatures of Byrd's entire
faction, to a resolution

> that all past Controversys of what kind soever
> between the Governor and any of the Council
> be forever buried in Oblivion, and that there
> may be hereafter no other contention than who
> shall most promote the Kings Service and the
> publick benefit of the Colony.

With this stroke, the document Byrd and his allies had
toiled over most of the previous night was rendered
politically worthless.

Spotswood had also taken steps for the future. The
resolution further specified "that where any difference of
opinion shall happen between the Governor *and the Major*

part [emphasis added] of the Council," both sides were to draw up "fair and impartial" statements of the case for the Board of Trade. There would no longer be any legitimate back channel for Byrd's maneuvering:

> no separate Solicitations shall be made for either party, nor any thing represented on either side, but what shall be thus Stated and Signed here.

Finally, both the governor and the Council were to write to the Board of Trade, to notify their Lordships of the reconciliation, "and to Request that no notice be taken of any Representations heretofore made by either Party to the prejudice of the other."[8]

Spotswood had brilliantly neutralized his immediate enemies. By their own agreement, communicated to London, they had no complaints against their governor. Now they anxiously awaited each invitation to the governor's beautiful residence, to mingle with his friends in a house with marble floors, paneled walls, and ornate ceilings, and a main hall displaying hundreds of muskets and swords. Spotswood gave them an unprecedented social season, and prepared to renew his offensive in the fall.

He received word that summer that Robert Hunter had succeeded in his project with William Burnet. Burnet was officially appointed governor-general of New York and New Jersey on April 19, 1720. At the same time, the Board of Trade issued a formal endorsement of Spotswood's governorship.   Though they denied his appeal to restructure the membership of the Virginia Council, two of his nominees—Peter Beverley and Cole Diggs—were appointed to fill vacancies on the twelve-man body. According to the "reconciliation" agreement, Byrd's gang of six now lacked control of "the major part" of the

Council, and could not even force formal complaints against Spotswood's policies. They could still attempt to obstruct him, however, including in the House of Burgesses.

Agenda for Western Development

In his opening address to the new assembly on November 3, 1720, Spotswood referred to the "proofs that I have given of my disposition to peace and Union," and warned that he could not "but reckon them Enemies to the Country who shall endeavour to divide us again." He added that he was "sorry to observe Some men have been industrious still to keep up" the conflict. In deftly ironic language, he informed the burgesses that he had no agenda to put forth,

> but what you may be as forward to enact, as I to pass, and therefore I shall no more than barely hint what I think fit to propose, assuring you that if the needfulness thereof be not as obvious to you as to me, I will acquiesce with all the Indifference that is consistent with my Duty.

His proposal was straightforward: secure the colony for westward development, and make a treaty with the Iroquois Five Nations. He remarked on "the naked state" of Virginia's harbors and frontiers, and "the disarmed Condition of your Militia." He asked the burgesses to consider encouraging new settlements "to the high Ridge of Mountains," as the best way "to Secure this Colony from the Incursions of the Indians and the more dangerous Incroachments of the French." Finally, Spotswood laid before them his communications with the Lords of Trade on the proposed Indian treaty, including their general support for the plan.[9]

Byrd's followers were now confined largely to rearguard actions, given Spotswood's support in Virginia and political uncertainties in London. For a while, Byrd's committee chairmen in the House were able to stall any actions on Spotswood's suggestions, but could not defeat them. On the proposal for western settlements, the burgesses soon passed an address to King George, approved by the Council on December 13. They reviewed the French threat from the St. Lawrence to the mouth of the Mississippi, in the same terms Spotswood had argued to the Board of Trade. The assembly also reported that it had created two new counties, extending over the Blue Ridge, incorporating the upper reaches of the Rappahannock and the Roanoke rivers. They neglected to inform the King that they had named the first one, stretching beyond Swift Run Gap, *Spotsylvania*, and that its county seat was to be Germanna, Spotswood's base for his expedition beyond the Blue Ridge. (The second county, incorporating then Virginia's other known mountain pass to the south, was named Brunswick.)

What followed in the assembly's address was a report of some of the most extraordinary legislation in our colonial history. Spotswood's "hints" had been well received by Virginians who were tired of Byrd's Tidewater tantrums against development. The measures enacted laid the basis for Virginia's role in breaking through to settle Ohio, Kentucky, and Illinois—and for winning the American Revolution:

> To encourage People to go up and Seat these Two Countys—we have Exempted the Inhabitants thereof from Publick Taxes for the Space of Ten years. We have agreed to build them Churches and Courthouses, and to *furnish them with arms and ammunitions at the Publick Charge* [emphasis added].

For an assembly which had previously rejected Spotswood's efforts to lessen the burdens of time and expense on active members of the militia, this was quite a change indeed.

Beyond what they had already made law, the burgesses urged King George to yield all the quitrents for ten years from these counties on the "new frontier," and to use his current collections for "building a fort at each of the passes in the great Mountains." The address concluded with an unprecedented statement of support for Spotswood, who the assembly declared

> will be pleased to intercede with Your Majestie in our favour, [and] who has spar'd no fatigue or Expence to visit our Mountains in person and to inform himself of the Exceeding Importance of them, both for your Majesties Service and for the defense and Security of this Dominion.[10]

Byrd's followers understood the message, and moved the next day to undermine Spotswood's authority on the crucial element of his strategy—a treaty with the Iroquois. The "scurrilous" Corbin and the "conceited" Grymes, of whom Spotswood had warned Orkney in 1718, were also instructed to circumvent the reconciliation agreement, by getting the House to again make Byrd Virginia's official agent for negotiations in London. On December 14, Corbin presented the joint House-Council report on "preparing an address to the Governor relating to the Treaty with the Northern Indians." Despite Byrd's efforts, the report endorsed Spotswood's policies in all important respects. Grymes then introduced a resolution, with about one fifth of the burgesses absent,

> That it is necessary to appoint Some proper person to Solicit in *Great Britain* the Subject

matter of the address of the Council and Burgesses to his Majesty,. . . the affair relating to a Treaty with the five nations of Northern Indians at *Albany*, and all Such other matters as may hereafter be agreed on by this General Assembly.

No one was fooled by this test vote, but Byrd controlled the speaker, who resolved a 21-21 tie in favor of appointing "some proper person." It was no surprise, when the next motion passed, naming "*William Byrd* Esquire [to] be the person, and that he be desired to take upon him the Negotiation of the Said Affairs."[11]

The prospect of Byrd's representing Virginia in London, on the matters of western settlement and the Iroquois treaty, was outrageous to Spotswood. He also knew, of course, that Byrd would never confine himself to the issues specified by the assembly. On December 20, he sent to the House an amendment to the resolution, stating that as solicitor to London, Byrd must "enter into Bond to the Governor not to meddle in *Great Britain* with any other affair of this Government than what shall be contain'd in his said Instructions," which were to be signed by Spotswood. Now Byrd was furious, and the House rejected the amendment, with the reply that "we are entirely ignorant of any other affairs relating to this government intended to be by him meddled in." Spotswood held firm, explaining that he wished "to take away temptation from unquiet spirits who might be disposed to sow again the seeds of contention." Spotswood kept the House in session, though Christmas was just days away. Byrd must have worried that the House would concede to the amendment, for on December 23, following another unsuccessful confrontation with Spotswood, Byrd told him "not to keep the Assembly any longer on my account and begged he would put an end to it." Spotswood did so immediately.[12]

On his way out of town, Byrd stopped again at the Capitol, "where I told the Governor I had rather my tongue to be cut out than it should be tied up from doing my country service." At home again with his family on Christmas Eve, he said his prayers "but committed uncleanness with Annie," his maid. On Christmas night, he "read a sermon of Tillotson till 9 o'clock and then went to bed and committed uncleanness with Annie, for which God forgive me."[13]

Coordinating the Peace Effort

Spotswood had prorogued the House of Burgesses until the following November. For now, at least, Byrd was stymied, and would have to confine his "meddling" to Virginia. Spotswood rarely convened the Council either, during the next nine months, except to deal with the issue he was concentrating most of his energies upon—the treaty with the Iroquois Five Nations.

Thanks to Robert Hunter's work in London, the New York aspect of the problem was clearing up. As the new comptroller of customs, the former New York governor frequently testified before the Board of Trade, on the colony's situation with respect to French Quebec and the Indian trade. The board was perhaps more concerned with Hunter's estimate that the Albany traders were pocketing up to £12,000 a year duty-free, than by the fact that their goods were being used by the French to turn the Iroquois against the American colonies. William Burnet, the new governor of New York, was instructed to suppress this dangerous trade. Hunter's old friends in New York, led by Lewis Morris, saw to it that the assembly passed a bill prohibiting such 'free enterprise,' which Burnet signed into law shortly after his arrival.[14]

With Burnet installed in New York to carry out Hunter's instructions, Governors Spotswood and Keith went into action. In April 1721, Keith journeyed from Philadelphia to Williamsburg for a ten-day visit. Besides the opportunity to coordinate their plans, Spotswood made use of his reconciliation agreement with Byrd, inviting him to various official and social occasions during the Pennsylvania governor's stay. By smoothing his feathers, Spotswood may have hoped Byrd would endorse the planned Indian treaty. More likely, he made Keith's visit a public, ceremonial occasion, in order to impose further containment on Byrd's opposition. For Byrd to challenge Spotswood under their agreement, he had to do so with the formal backing of a majority of the Council. Spotswood convened the Council on the eve of Keith's departure. Though Byrd's diary reports that "the Governor could make no impression upon us, notwithstanding he endeavored it very much," Byrd had no countermove to play—especially against three colonial governors. The next day, Byrd served as part of Keith's farewell escort from Williamsburg, "as did abundance of gentlemen at the Governor's request." A week later, Spotswood adjourned the Council for the summer. Byrd's forces in Virginia had again been outflanked. It was not long before he decided to return to London, on matters of "business."[15]

The fruits of Spotswood's discussions with Keith soon appeared. On July 7 and 8, 1721, Keith met with deputies from the Five Nations in Pennsylvania, and secured their agreement to come to Virginia to negotiate a treaty with Spotswood. Spotswood convened the Virginia Council on August 10, to inform them of Keith's progress. He suggested that the Iroquois delegation might meet him at Germanna, "as being a shorter Journey" than to Williamsburg. Though Byrd had departed, his allies on the Council sought to restrict the governor's freedom of action as much as possible. They urged that the meeting be "at Williamsburg at the General Court," or that otherwise the negotiations be entrusted to one of their own—Councilor Nathaniel Harrison. Harrison would then give the Iroquois negotiators "a Passport to Travel to Germanna in their Return, that such Treaty as shall be made with them may receive the Governor's Approbation." These proposals were overripe with intentions to tamper with the peace. Justly apprehensive, Spotswood chose Williamsburg as the site.[16]

In London, Robert Hunter was trying to buttress Spotswood's plans for securing the Great Lakes. On August 29, Hunter appeared before the Board of Trade, to urge construction of a fort on Lake Ontario near Niagara, as "the only way to secure and Maintain our claim" against the French.[17] No action was then taken on Hunter's proposal. Nor was there yet a treaty with the Iroquois, which was indispensable to placing a fort west of the Seneca Nation. (In 1727, after Jonathan Swift had led a politically devastating, three-year assault on Prime Minister Walpole, New York Governor Burnet established Fort Oswego on Lake Ontario. It was later the strategic base for defeating the British invasion of the Great Lakes during the War of 1812.)

Spotswood did not convene the Council again until October 16. He then signed a proclamation further proroguing the House of Burgesses, from its scheduled November meeting until the following May. The deputies from the Iroquois Five Nations were arriving in Williamsburg, and Spotswood wished to concentrate on nothing else. The delegation was the same which had met that summer with Governor Keith, as well as the governor of Maryland, who had provided them with a sloop at Annapolis for the trip to Virginia. Spotswood immediately had new grounds for alarm. The five deputies were housed at the College of William and Mary—where four of them collapsed with symptoms of possible poisoning. Stricken with severe nausea and fever, two of them died before they could even meet with Spotswood. But on October 19, the survivors staggered into the council chamber at the Capitol and presented their token of friendship. They assured the governor, though the representatives of two of the Five Nations were dead, that they had "authority from the whole."[18]

The stage was finally set. Spotswood had also been in communication with Burnet, who had met with the Iroquois chiefs at Albany on September 7 and 8. Burnet had presented "on the behalf of Virginia" Spotswood's key article of peace, the security of the western frontier. In the evening, following the first meeting with the Iroquois deputies in Williamsburg, Spotswood received word from Burnet that the Five Nations were willing to accept his terms. A messenger arrived, bringing copies of the agreement, as well as belts of wampum the chiefs had presented in acknowledgement.

The next morning, Spotswood triumphantly laid them before the Council. The terms were read:

> That none of the said Indians should for the future Cross Potomack River, or pass to the Eastward of the Great Ridge of Mountains without the Licence of the Governor of New York; [nor would the Virginia tribes] hereafter cross the said River of Potomack nor pass to the Westward of the Great Mountains without the Licence of the Governor of Virginia.

Spotswood reminded the Council that these terms were "exactly Conformable to the Preliminaries" he had first proposed in 1717. Byrd's faction had stalled any

Colonial Settlement by 1725

Comparing this pattern of colonization with that of 1660 (see p. 15) reveals a development of major significance. The areas of settlement continued to concentrate along coastlines and major waterways, with one important exception. Alexander Spotswood's policy of opening the West, during his governorship of Virginia from 1710-1722, created a surge of population toward the Blue Ridge Mountains, running south of the Potomac River toward the pass he discovered in 1716. Most of these newly settled lands lay within Virginia's Spotsylvania County, which he established in 1720, and in the Northern Neck Proprietary of Lord Thomas Fairfax, the patron of George Washington.

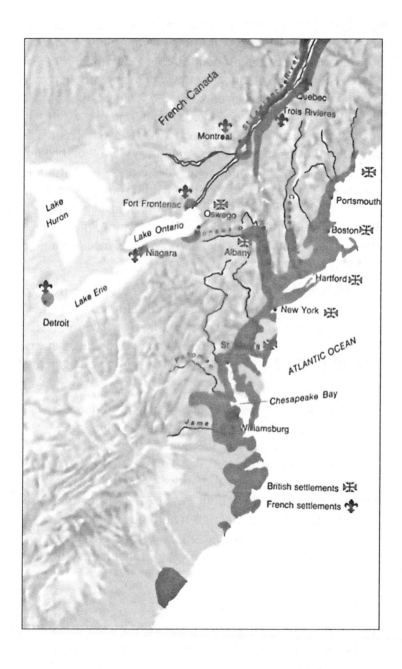

negotiating efforts for four years, by making acceptance of these preliminaries a precondition. Now, Spotswood told the Council, it was "incumbent on this Government to send Commissioners to Albany as soon as conveniently may be." Even Byrd's mouthpieces conceded to his proposal, but left his authority to proceed contingent upon "when the Governor of New York goes next to Albany to Treat with the said Indians." The Iroquois deputies were then brought into the chamber, along with the chiefs of Virginia's Nottoways and Saponies. Spotswood showed them the belts from the chiefs of the Five Nations, and told them of the agreements in Albany. The next morning, the Iroquois attended the Council meeting, and the plans for a settlement at Albany were endorsed.[19]

Suspicions that someone had tried to poison the Iroquois deputies in Virginia now hampered Governor Burnet's efforts to arrange a conference at Albany. Two more had died after leaving Virginia, though they had stayed nearly three months in Williamsburg. The surviving delegate had charged

> that the other four Deputys sent with him were all poisoned here by the Indians Tributary to Virginia; and that thereupon the said five Nations, expected that this Government should deliver up to them four boys as a satisfaction for the loss of their four Great Men; intimating that no other satisfaction would be accepted by them, and threatening in case of refusal to revenge themselves on the Inhabitants of Virginia. . . .[20]

Upon receiving news of these charges and threats, Spotswood convened the Virginia Council to deal with the matter on March 7, 1722. He reported the transactions between Governor Burnet's commissioners for Indian affairs and deputies for the Five Nations at Albany. He then reviewed the evidence against their "scandalous and groundless" charges, including the fact that the two delegates who died had arrived in Virginia "in a very bad state of health." Never in the three months the others remained, did they suggest they had been poisoned by Virginia Indians, with whom they maintained "all the outward signs of friendship imaginable." On the contrary, Spotswood suggested,

> if any foul practices were used toward the said Deputys in their journey home, it is most probable the same were committed by one of their own Number whose name is Sketowass, and is a Tuscarora Indian; who having in all his behaviour here, Acted the part of an Incendiary Rather than a Messenger of Peace, may be justly suspected guilty of destroying those of his Companions who would not join in his Designs.[21]

The Council endorsed a communiqué to Burnet, declaring that Spotswood was willing to refer further examination of the matter "to the intended Treaty at Albany." If the Iroquois rejected the proposal, and insisted on "revenging themselves," then Burnet was requested

> to send such timely intimation of their designs that this Country may be prepar'd to defend its Frontiers, and to give the said Indians such a reception as they deserve.[22]

Confronted with this response, the Five Nations thought it wiser to continue preparations for the peace.

The Death-Merchants of Venice

Spotswood's plans for the Iroquois treaty faced still greater dangers from London. So did the entire fate of the American colonies. The Venetian plague of economic ruin and war, from which Queen Anne had fought to free Britain, had returned in a more virulent form. Upon George I's taking the throne, the bludgeoning of Britain's nationalist institutions and political factions had resumed in earnest. But as a foreign king, George of Hanover had to proceed with some caution at first—especially against the landed gentry and aristocracy which had supported Robert Harley's challenge to the Bank of England's financial dictatorship. Harley's South Seas Act of 1711 had been aimed at wresting political control of Britain's debt from that Venetian-run institution. But in 1719, with George I on the throne of England and Philippe d'Orléans regent of France, schemes were set in motion to bring both countries under complete Venetian control.

In France, Venetian-Dutch agent John Law, with the regent's backing, pyramided stock companies controlling French colonial trade into a new Indies Company. This speculative swindle was then merged in 1720 with France's new royal bank—also created by Orléans—and given tax-farming powers over the nation's revenue. A speculative orgy soon drove stocks to unheard-of heights, before Law triggered a panic by forcing a devaluation of the currency. Orléans and selected insiders made a killing; thousands of other fortunes, great and small, died instantly.

In Britain, Law's admiring counterpart John Blunt, chief director of the South Sea Company, worked a similar fraud with devastating results. With no small thanks to George I, Britain's national debt by 1719 had risen to £50 million—as against the £10 million Harley's act proposed to retire in 1711. Now the South Sea Company moved to assume the entire debt, with a loan of £20 million from the Bank of England and the East India Company, and £30 million to be borrowed from the public at large, for stock in the company. By the summer of 1719, South Sea stock was also on a dizzying rise. Though no productive return on these investments was in sight, there were rumors of expanded trade in a typically Venetian commodity: slaves. Word went out from London's Exchange Alley, that Britain was about to make greater use of its monopoly on the slave trade in the Americas, and that the South Sea Company was negotiating for 'rights' in Africa. The British economy was being mortgaged to the slave trade.

John Blunt helped pump the bubble up further, by recycling monies from investors for further purchases of stock. The price of shares rose from £128 in January 1720, to £710 by the end of May. During the summer, the insurance company—that most distinctive Venetian institution, for managing the great oligarchical *fondi*—made its first appearance in Britain, with the establishment of the London Assurance Company and the Royal Exchange Assurance. By early August, South Sea shares hit £1,100. George I let it be known that he had bought and sold at a profit of £86,000, and made Blunt a baronet.

Robert Walpole played heavily, and guided both friends and enemies into the market. Stockjobbing companies of the wildest nature sprang up, and attracted investors for such ventures as "the Transmutation of Quicksilver," breeding silkworms in Chelsea Park, and "to carry on an undertaking of great advantage but nobody to know what it is."

With these added outlets for speculative mania, Exchange Alley became a giant roulette table, as players moved their bets from one number to another. Then director Blunt secured writs against the unchartered companies, collapsing their stocks and spreading the panic, as speculators rushed to cover their losses by selling South Sea stock. On August 18, the bubble burst; by the end of September, South Sea shares had plunged more than £900. An unprecedented wave of bankruptcies followed. The Duke of Chandos alone lost £500,000.[23]

Britain had been deliberately plunged into economic ruin, to the benefit of its Venetian 'directors,' and their Dutch and Swiss financial satellites. Their project to eliminate any vestiges of English sovereignty—begun with the invasion of William of Orange in 1688—had succeeded. The collapse of the South Sea Bubble restructured political and economic power within Britain to an unprecedented degree. The new age of the financier had arrived, and there was little that even the landed aristocracy could do about it. As one Tory lord wrote even before the blowout, the entire scheme

> was calculated for the enriching of a few and the impoverishment of a great many; and not only made for but countenanced and authorized the fraudulent and pernicious practice of stockjobbing, which diverted the genius of the people from trade and industry.[24]

Robert Walpole was most prominent among the winners. He sold out before the crash, and was then appointed by the King as Chancellor of the Exchequer, to 'resolve' the crisis. He then maneuvered to seize control of the cabinet during 1721. There is no better demonstration of how thoroughly the South Sea affair transformed British politics, than the fact that Walpole controlled the cabinet for the next twenty years, well into the reign of George II. During the reign of Queen Anne, while Swift held influence within her cabinet, Walpole had been sent to the Tower of London, for defrauding the British navy while serving as its treasurer.

Swift had recognized the new Venetian onslaught. From his base in Dublin, as Dean of St. Patrick's Cathedral, he had been quietly laying the basis for a republican movement. When the South Sea mania reached Ireland in 1720, he caused a political uproar with an anonymous pamphlet entitled *A Proposal for the Universal Use of Irish Manufacture*, outlining measures to protect and strengthen the Irish economy. The principles he argued were the same which later served Benjamin Franklin and Alexander Hamilton in freeing America from British rule. George I was just as hostile to such notions; Swift's printer was arrested and charged with sedition. Later that year, following the collapse of the Bubble, Swift issued what became one of his most reprinted poems, "Upon the South Sea Project." Set in quatrains, totaling 228 lines, Swift's poem dissected the plot by the company's directors:

> As fishes on each other prey
> The great ones swallowing up the small;
> So fares it in the Southern Sea;
> But, whale directors eat up all.
>
> When stock is high, they come between,
> Making by second hand their offers,
> Then cunningly retire unseen,
> With each a million in his coffers.
> . . .
>
> Each poor subscriber to the Sea,
> Sinks down at once, and there he lies;
> Directors fall as well as they,
> Their fall is but a trick to rise.
> . . .
>
> But these, you say, are factious lies
> From some malicious Tory's brain,

For, where directors get a prize,
The Swiss and Dutch whole millions drain.
. . .

Oh, may some Western tempest sweep
These locusts whom our fruits have fed,
That plague, directors, to the deep,
Driven from the South Sea to the Red.

May He, whom nature's laws obey,
Who lifts the poor, and sinks the proud,
Quiet the raging of the sea,
And still the madness of the crowd.

But never shall our isle have rest
Till those devouring swine run down,
(The devil's leaving the possessed,)
And headlong in the waters drown.[25]

The blowout of the Mississippi and South Sea Bubbles
sent shockwaves throughout the civilized world. Besides
the chain reaction of economic disasters, the political
consequences were the subject of deep concern among
republican circles internationally. This was emphatically
the case in America. Employment levels plummeted in
Boston and Philadelphia; a reduced volume of trade
afflicted all of the colonies. By the fall of 1721, Cotton
Mather had written books on both the British and French
crises. All talk of public affairs, however, was dominated
by the question, what next? What could be expected of
Walpole's new order in Britain?

In Virginia, it was not long before Governor Spotswood
concluded that he was running out of time. At the meeting
of the Virginia Council of April 16, 1722, one of Byrd's
members, Nathaniel Harrison, presented his commission as
"Auditor of his Majestys Revenues within this Colony." It

was signed by Robert Walpole's younger brother Horatio, who was now "Auditor General of His Majestys Plantations." Harrison was followed by John Grymes, the burgess who in 1720 had introduced the resolution to give Byrd authority in London, over any negotiations with the crown concerning a treaty with the Iroquois. Grymes presented his commission as "Receiver General of all his Majestys Revenues within this Colony." His bond of office was secured by Philip Ludwell, Byrd's right-hand man; and Archibald Blair, the brother of James Blair, who had joined Byrd in London to lobby for Spotswood's removal. Spotswood had so far managed to outmaneuver Byrd's efforts to oust him, whether in Williamsburg or London. But the political map had been redrawn, and the Walpole touch was obvious.[26]

Despite these clear signs that his governorship was nearing its end, Spotswood did not waver. There was a long lag-time in communications between Britain and Virginia, and Walpole's new government had a pressing domestic agenda to deal with. It was also apparent that Walpole had not yet forced the Earl of Orkney to name a new lieutenant to govern the colony. The latest ship from England had brought only these lesser commissions for Byrd's allies. On April 19, Spotswood had the Council endorse his full letter to Governor Burnet of New York, on the terms for proceeding with the treaty with the Five Nations. He also took steps to prepare for the future. He asked approval for grants of large tracts of land, in the new county of Spotsylvania extending across the Blue Ridge Mountains. Spotswood told the Council "that he had hitherto delayed Signing the said patents," while awaiting the King's response to the proposal to waive quitrents for ten years, to further encourage settlement of the West. Now Spotswood wanted to secure such crucial titles to western lands while he was still governor.[27]

The Treaty of Albany

On May 9, Spotswood convened the House of Burgesses, to inform them that the Five Nations had accepted his preliminary articles of agreement, and that he had promised to send commissioners to Albany "some time this Summer." He requested funds for the mission, "to undertake a Negotiation which may according as it is managed lay a lasting foundation for the Peace and Tranquility of our frontiers." The House unanimously approved the plans for the treaty on May 17, and on May 29 even appropriated £300 to repay Spotswood for his 1717 trip to New York. In Virginia, at least, Spotswood was still in command. On June 1, the House and Council presented the following address to the governor:

> From the Experience of near Twelve years of Your Honor's Administration, we are very sensible of your great Application and discerning Judgment in all the Concerns of Government, and as we have observed more particular skill and Dexterity in your Managing the Indian Affairs, We think it will greatly conduce to the Establishing an honorable and lasting Peace, if your Honor will be pleased to preside in the Negotiations at *Albany*, by which they will be under the influence of your more Immediate directions. And as we believe it will Redound so much to the Safety and Honor of this Country, We hope your Honor will gratify our unanimous desire.[28]

Spotswood delivered what was to be his final address to the Virginia assembly on June 7, 1722. He commended the session for having displayed "Such Concord, and application to Business, Such good temper and generous disposition." He then announced that he was proroguing the assembly, "that you may attend your own private Concerns, while I am going a long Journey in order to lay a Lasting foundation for Your Safety."[29]

The Iroquois chiefs had agreed to meet at Albany on August 20. Spotswood made ready the H.M.S. *Enterprise*, berthed at Hampton Roads, for his voyage to New York. The man-o'-war's cargo included gifts to present the Indians, a good supply of cordials, and 360 bottles of Madeira wine. At New York, he joined Governor Burnet and Governor Keith of Pennsylvania. Together they sailed up the Hudson River, arriving on the designated day at the stockaded frontier town of Albany. But the Iroquois were in no hurry to negotiate. It was nine days before the last of the Mohawk, Oneida, Cayuga, Onondaga, and Seneca delegates arrived. Once this extraordinary council had gathered, Spotswood delivered the opening address:

> Sachems and warriors of the Five Nations: You
> often say that your covenant chain with Virginia
> is grown rusty, and have urged of late years that
> some commissioners from that colony should
> be sent to this place to brighten the same.

He offered to forget the Iroquois' treaty violations in the past, if they would agree to remain north of the Potomac River, and west of the "Great Ridge" of Mountains. They were to remain at peace with the Virginia Indians, who also pledged not to cross those barriers in the opposite direction.

Eight days later, after repeated deliberations and ceremonial rituals, the Five Nations agreed. Their leaders presented Spotswood with belts of friendship, to shouts of approval from the assembled Indians. On September 10, Spotswood reviewed the terms before the entire conference, and added that any Iroquois who violated the agreed-upon territorial boundaries would be put to death or sold into slavery. He then laid down ten guns, for the ten Virginia tribes, to emphasize his point.   As his own pledge of agreement, he presented the guns to the Iroquois, adding five more in honor of the Five Nations. Two days later, the Iroquois declared they would respect the boundaries forever.[30]

With the Treaty of Albany, Spotswood secured a vital gateway to the West.   The crucial provision was the agreement concerning the Potomac River.   Only a few Americans at the time, even in Virginia, fully grasped its significance, for most of them knew nothing of the Potomac's western reaches, beyond the Blue Ridge and the Shenandoah,   stretching   toward   the   Ohio   Country. Thousands of square miles of new lands to the west, beyond the Blue Ridge, *but south of the Potomac*, were now open to settlement.   The genie of continental development was out of the bottle, and Spotswood had already laid the foundations for the first phase of colonization.   The wilderness of Spotsylvania County, reaching through Swift Run Gap, was being cleared for new farmlands. During the 1720s, the county grew more rapidly than any other section of Virginia, and became the base station for development of the Shenandoah Valley a decade later.

At Albany in 1722, Governor Alexander Spotswood could only dream of what America might become. But from the moment he assumed office in 1710, and sent forth his scouts to find a pass through the Blue Ridge, he had been guided by a vision of its vast potential. Upon bidding farewell   to   the   Iroquois   chiefs,   he   presented   their spokesman with a final gift.   He removed from his lapel the miniature golden horseshoe commemorating his expedition across the Blue Ridge in 1716.   Should any Iroquois wish to visit Virginia, he said, this would be their passport.[31] With the Treaty of Albany, Spotswood had given new meaning to the horseshoe's inscription—"thus we crossed the mountains."

From New York, Spotswood sailed with Governor Keith to Philadelphia. They intended to meet with the Pennsylvania Indians, to extend the agreement reached with the Iroquois. Like Spotswood, Keith had won the support of the Pennsylvania House. But the Council, representing the Penn proprietors, led by James Logan and the Quaker merchants of Philadelphia, were already plotting Keith's removal, in defense of the rights of "aristocracy."[32] The Council rejected the proposal to negotiate with the Indians.[33] Keith offered to join Spotswood to meet them anyway at Conestoga, but Spotswood declined to risk Keith's position. The Virginia governor had grounds for concern.

On September 27, nearly a month before Spotswood returned to Williamsburg, an Oxford English major had been sworn in as the new governor of Virginia. On orders from Robert Walpole, Hugh Drysdale had been nominated by the Earl of Orkney, and confirmed by King George, to replace Alexander Spotswood.[34] Spotswood appeared before the Council on October 31, to report the success of his mission to Albany. Drysdale thanked him for maintaining the "honor and dignity" of the colony. The greatest governor in Virginia history retired to Germanna, and built his home overlooking the river he had named the Rapidanna—the south branch of the Rappahannock. For nearly two decades, until his death in 1740, he worked to ensure that America's opening to the West would never be closed. Hugh Jones, chaplain to the Virginia assembly during much of Spotswood's term as governor, paid him the following tribute in 1724, in his introduction to *The Present State of Virginia*:

> this Country is altered wonderfully, and far more advanced and improved in all Respects of late Years, since the beginning of *Colonel Spotswood's* Lieutenancy, than in the whole Century before his Government.[35]

NOTES

1. Lustig, *Hunter*, 162–163, concerning the fact, but not the circumstances, of Hunter's choice.

2. Byrd, *London Diary*, 333, 336n., 337*ff.*

3. *Ibid.*, 368*ff.*

4. Havighurst, *Spotswood*, 90–91.

5. Byrd, *London Diary*, 398–399.

6. *Jour. Coun. Va.*, III, 524; Byrd, *London Diary*, 399.

7. Byrd, *London Diary*, 400.

8. *Jour. Coun. Va.*, III, 524–525.

9. *Jour. Burgesses*, 250*ff.*

10. *Ibid.*, 298–299.

11. *Ibid.*, 299–300.

12. *Ibid.*, 308–310, 313–314; Byrd, *London Diary*, 490.

13. Byrd, *London Diary*, 490–491.

14. Lustig, *Hunter*, 166.

15. Byrd, *London Diary*, 519–523 *passim*.

16. *Jour. Coun. Va.*, III, 549.

17. Quoted by Lustig, *Hunter*, 166.

18. *Jour. Coun. Va.*, III, 551–552; IV, 8–9.

19. *Ibid.*, III, 552–554.

20. *Ibid.*, IV, 8.

21. *Ibid.*, 8–9.

22. *Ibid.*, 9.

23. Isaac Kramnick, *Bolingbroke and His Circle, The Politics of Nostalgia in the Age of Walpole*

(Cambridge, Mass., 1968), 65–67.

24. Quoted by Kramnick, *Bolingbroke*, 66.

25. Swift, *Poems*, Rogers, ed., 207-214, and notes.

26. *Jour. Coun. Va.*, IV, 10–11.

27. *Ibid.*, 11.

28. *Jour. Burgesses* (1712–1726), 319, 343, 347.

29. *Ibid.*, 354.

30. Havighurst, *Spotswood*, 100–102.

31. *Ibid.*, 103.

32. Tolles, *James Logan*, 121–127.

33. Leonides Dodson, *Alexander Spotswood, Governor of Colonial Virginia, 1710–1722* (Philadelphia, 1932), 108.

34. *Ibid.*, 271, 273.

35. Jones, *State of Virginia*, ii.

10

Who Was Benjamin Franklin?

The life of Boston-born Benjamin Franklin is generally the leading example historians offer, in arguing that America's Founding Fathers owed nothing to the nation-building conspiracy begun before 1630 by John Winthrop's Massachusetts Bay Colony. According to this typical historical fraud, Franklin rejected his own Puritan past, and modeled himself after eighteenth-century British liberalism and French Enlightenment radicalism. Centuries of lying must again be swept aside. Benjamin Franklin was Cotton Mather's most gifted protégé. When he moved to Pennsylvania, Franklin also raised the political banner of Jonathan Swift. In 1737, Alexander Spotswood appointed him postmaster of Philadelphia. Franklin became the crucial link between the in-depth republican citizenry of New England, and the strategically placed, republican elite fostered by Spotswood in Virginia. That combination won the American Revolution; but until now, the real story has never been told.

Alexander Spotswood's 1722 treaty with the Iroquois secured the opening to the West. Yet his immediate removal by George I, from the governorship of Virginia, eliminated the unique advantage of executive authority to seize that opportunity. In any case, the battle for a continental republic would depend on a vast army of citizens, to colonize—and fight for—the land beyond the mountains. The stronghold for the future republic was still Massachusetts, where George Washington would raise the Continental Army in 1775. The battle was raging there even in 1722, the year that the young Benjamin Franklin first appeared on the front lines, at the age of sixteen.

In 1722, Cotton Mather was the leading target of the same 'Venetian' powers behind the ouster of Spotswood. Mather never held political office, but he was the acknowledged leader of America's republican forces. He had proven that repeatedly, especially since organizing the overthrow in 1689 of Sir Edmund Andros' attempted dictatorship over New England. Mather had also given the signal in America for the republican offensive begun in 1710, which brought Jonathan Swift's friend Robert Hunter to the governorship of New York, and Spotswood to Virginia.

Contrary to popular mythology, Benjamin Franklin did not begin life on his own as a teenage runaway, seeking new thrills in Philadelphia. Nor was he merely a composite of the fortunate dilettante, the inventive tinkerer, the shrewd opportunist, and the insincere moralist who parlayed his talents to become the consummate pragmatic politician. His debt to Cotton Mather, for example, is acknowledged in his own writings. The importance of that connection, however, is partly obscured by an element of caution imposed by Franklin himself, virtually throughout his life. The reasons for that will become clear in later sections of this history. It should suffice to note here that Franklin was the leading agent of the American conspiracy to found a continental republic from the 1730s onward. During an active career spanning more than sixty years, Franklin was often forced, by circumstances of political warfare, to keep significant details of his activities and associations out of public view.

The Puritan Prodigy

Benjamin Franklin was born January 17, 1706, to Josiah and Abiah Folger Franklin, his father's second wife. Benjamin was one of seventeen children, and the youngest of ten sons. Like so many citizens of Massachusetts, his father Josiah was a political refugee, faced with persecution by the crown when he joined the nonconformist opposition to Charles II near the end of his reign. Benjamin was named for Josiah's brother, who also sided with the nonconformists while "the rest of the family remained with the Episcopal church," Franklin reports in his *Autobiography*.[1]

In 1685, Josiah Franklin became a parishioner at the Old South Church, built next to founding Governor John Winthrop's house, a venerated landmark which still stood at the time of the Revolution, when British troops tore it down and burned it for firewood during their occupation of Boston. Josiah's early years in New England were marked by intense political turmoil, during the attempt by the newly imposed royal governor, Sir Edmund Andros, to eliminate the colonists' republican freedoms.

The elder Franklin soon became a close associate of the colonial opposition led by Increase and Cotton Mather, who in 1689 spearheaded the overthrow of the dictator in the Andros Rebellion. That same year, Josiah Franklin, then a widower, married fellow parishioner Abiah Folger. Franklin proudly notes in his *Autobiography* that she was "the daughter of Peter Folger, one of the first settlers in New England, of whom honourable mention is made by Cotton Mather in his ecclesiastical history of that country, entitled *Magnalia Christi Americana*, as a 'godly and learned Englishman,' if I remember the words rightly."[2]

With support from Judge Samuel Sewall—the most prominent member of the Old South Church, a close ally of the Mathers, and a political leader in his own right—Josiah Franklin became a congregational leader. For a newcomer of little means financially, he also attained unusual influence in civic affairs. Besides serving the town as a constable, tithingman, and clerk of the market, Josiah presided over the "Associated Families" organization for his district, within the political network established by Cotton Mather.

Samuel Sewall's *Diary* notes that the weekly meetings for the Old South neighborhood took place at "Mr. Josiah Franklin's." Sewall adds that Josiah, a violinist who enjoyed playing regularly, was often called upon to "set the tune" for the hymns and offer the closing prayer for the meetings. The Franklin household became a gathering place for Boston's republican leaders, providing Benjamin from his childhood onward with an extraordinary view of their concerns and aspirations. As Franklin recalled of his father in his *Autobiography*, "I remember well his being frequently visited by the leading men who consulted him for his opinion in affairs of the town or of the church he belonged to, and who showed a good deal of respect for his judgment and advice."[3]

An artisan of modest income with a large family to support, Josiah apprenticed all of Benjamin's older brothers to various trades, but Benjamin was something of a child prodigy. He was a precocious reader ("I do not remember when I could not read," he noted later), and the evidence points to his attracting the attention of the Mathers and Samuel Sewall even as a boy. Josiah was encouraged by "the opinions of all of his friends that I should certainly make a good scholar," and accordingly Franklin was enrolled at the age of eight in Boston's prestigious Latin School, to prepare for entrance into Harvard and education for the ministry.

At the Latin School, Franklin quickly distinguished himself among the sons of leading Puritans. Entering the same year with Mather Byles, Increase Mather's grandson and Cotton's favorite nephew, Franklin rose in less than a year from the middle to the head of his class, and was "remov'd into the next class above it." But by all published accounts, including Franklin's own, his father felt financially unable to sustain his son through college, withdrew him from the Latin School, and placed him for one more year in a school teaching only writing and arithmetic. At the age of ten, Franklin returned home to assist his father in his candle-making trade, marking the end of his formal education.[4]

But this was far from the end of Franklin's education by the Mathers. Deliveries of his father's candles took him frequently to their homes, and his "bookish inclination" must have made him marvel at Cotton Mather's library, by far the largest in North America. "I remember well," he wrote to Cotton's son Samuel in 1784, "both your father and grandfather, having heard them both in the pulpit, and seen them in their houses." Franklin's voracious reading continued during this period, and in his father's "little library" he read Cotton Mather's *Essays to Do Good*, the book he credited as the single most important in shaping his life's work.

Franklin reports briefly in his *Autobiography* that *Essays to Do Good* "perhaps gave me a turn of thinking that had an influence on some of the principal future events of my life." Looking back later on his career as statesman, scientist, and founding father of his country, Franklin wrote to Samuel Mather that the book had "an influence on my conduct through life; for I have always set a greater value on the character of a doer of good, than on any other kind of reputation; and if I have been, as you seem to think, a useful citizen, the public owes the advantage of it to that book."[5]

Franklin also used *Essays to Do Good* as the republican organizing manual Mather intended it to be. The book set forth specific "Points of Consideration" for the members of

Mather's "reforming societies," just as Franklin posed "Standing Queries" for the Junto he founded in Philadelphia in 1727.

A comparison of the two documents clearly establishes how directly Franklin followed Mather's plan.   For example, Mather's "Points" include the following political agenda:

> VII. Does there appear any instance of OPPRESSION or FRAUDULENCE, in the *dealings* of any sort of people, that may call for our essays, to get it rectified?
>
> VIII. Is there any matter to be humbly moved unto the LEGISLATIVE POWER to be enacted into a LAW for public benefit?

Franklin's "Queries" raise the same issues:

> 14. Have you lately observed any defect in the laws of your country, which it would be proper to move the legislature for an amendment?   Or do you know of any beneficial law that is wanting?
>
> 15. Have you lately observed any encroachment on the just liberties of the people?

Point number nine in both the Mather and Franklin documents raises an identical question: whether the members know of any case of illness or affliction and the remedies to be used.   Appropriately, it was on the issue of how to deal with a smallpox epidemic that Franklin waged his first political fight on Cotton Mather's behalf.[6]

The Hell-Fire Contagion

During Franklin's adolescence in Boston, a new wave of corruption arose, with the further influx of speculators and

profiteers attached to the rum-molasses-slaves triangle
trade, built up by oligarchical shipping interests in New
England. By 1714, the British Whigs, whom Jonathan
Swift fought against, had toppled the ministry he had
guided under Queen Anne. The peace negotiations pressed
forward by Swift had brought the long war in Europe to an
end, but with Queen Anne's death and the accession of
George I of Hanover to the British throne, peace signaled a
new round of speculative looting of the major powers'
already war-weakened economies.

Related, worsening economic conditions in New
England—then shaping Josiah Franklin's decision to
withdraw Benjamin from the Latin School—also prompted
Cotton Mather to again champion in 1714 the creation of a
bank to promote economic recovery, as he had following
the Andros Rebellion a quarter of a century earlier.
Appealing to an influential contact in England, Mather pled
the cause of New Englanders, groaning under worthless
bills of credit and a wave of land seizures for unpaid
mortgages.

But his plan for establishing a sound credit system in
New England fell largely upon deaf ears among the vermin
now loose in London. Less than five months after George
I's coronation, Mather noted for his English correspondent,
"the Government" had sided with a faction who "have
appeared violently against this projection" for a new
banking policy in New England.[7]

New England's woes were compounded the same year
by a devastating smallpox epidemic in Boston, a scorching
summer, and another wheat shortage exacerbated by the
Belcher grain monopoly. In London, the oligarchy felt
secure enough to advocate bestiality as the ideal of state
policy.

Bernard Mandeville, a supposed professor of medicine
from Holland, brought into England in the wake of William

of Orange's 'Glorious Revolution', published in 1714 his *Fable of the Bees, or Private Vices, Public Benefits.* Already a cult figure among England's proliferating, Satan-worshipping, secret societies, Mandeville now openly argued that the interests of the state were nothing more than the aggregate fulfillment of its individuals' hedonistic pleasures. The precursor of such radical libertarians as Adam Smith and Jeremy Bentham, Mandeville became a celebrated "social theorist," through his public campaign against any state interference in "private vices." He was also the key figure behind London's not-so-secret Hell-Fire Club, whose members acted out their bestial rites under the names of the Holy Spirit, the Apostles, and several millennia's worth of the oligarchy's demons and devils.

In 1721, at the age of fifteen, Benjamin Franklin joined the battle against these forces, in the middle of one of the most intensive campaigns to destroy the Mathers that their opponents had ever mounted. On the enemy side, he found his eldest half-brother James, to whose printing business he had been unwillingly apprenticed in 1718, for the onerous term of nine years. James Franklin had returned the previous year from London, where he acquired his press and type for printing—and familiarity with the degenerate admirers of Bernard Mandeville. By 1722, the Mathers were to accuse James Franklin of promoting "an Hell-Fire club."

James Franklin set up his printing business in Boston, and soon fell in with a circle of radical Anglicans attached to Boston's only Episcopal church, and allied with the radical Whigs of Elisha Cooke, Jr.'s political machine in common cause against the Mathers' republican leadership. At the center of the Anglican operation was one John Checkley, born in Boston in 1680, but subsequently trained in England at the Anglican stronghold of Oxford. After an oddly-accounted-for decade in Europe "collecting art,"

Checkley surfaced in Boston again in 1710, the year Cotton Mather launched his broadened republican organizing effort with his *Essays to Do Good.* Setting himself up as a bookseller, Checkley went on to become a major propagandist against the Mathers' congregational doctrines, and the leading lay advocate for the Church of England in Boston. (He eventually became the ordained rector of King's Church in Providence, Rhode Island, the nesting place for so many enemies of New England republicanism.)

Checkley's initial tactic against the Mathers was to portray them as Presbyterians opposed to congregational order, as he did in a 1721 pamphlet entitled *Choice Dialogues, between a godly Minister and an honest Countryman, concerning Election and Predestination.* Cotton Mather took note of it in his diary as one of the "cursed Pamphlets and Libels, wherewith some wicked Men, are endeavoring to Poison the Country."[8] Mather countered by having his brilliant nephew, the Roxbury minister Thomas Walter, publish a reply under the title *A Choice Dialogue between John Faustus, a Conjurer, and Jack Tory his Friend.*[9]

A key figure within Checkley's circle of intriguers, all habitués of the notorious Hall's Tavern in Boston, was the Scottish doctor William Douglass, who had studied at Paris, Leyden, and Edinburgh, and was an avowed hater of the Puritan clergy. Douglass was to assume the role of scientific expert in Checkley's campaign to destroy the Mathers, and made enough noise to become a public figure soon after his arrival in Boston in 1716.

The Mathers' republican forces were simultaneously being battered by the radical Whig agitation directed by Elisha Cooke, Jr.'s political machine. Still determined to give the British monarchy an excuse to eliminate the liberties retained in the royal charter negotiated by Increase

Mather, Cooke's faction played on the real suffering which his friends had brought upon New England. They sought to force a hopeless confrontation that would end in the sort of thoroughgoing feudalist control which John Locke had advocated for all of the American colonies. In 1719, campaigning for ruinous, inflationary currency schemes to hoodwink Bostonians seeking economic relief, Cooke's allies took the lion's share of seats in the House of Representatives. On November 5, Cotton Mather preached a sermon warning of the "Satanic Party's" intentions to abolish the liberties remaining under the charter.[10] Four years later, Cooke's henchmen partially succeeded, forcing the resignation of Mather's ally, Governor Samuel Shute, through repeated violations of the legislature's obligations to the executive as set forth in the charter.

As Mather wrote then, to an English ally and later financial patron of scientific education at Harvard, Cooke's faction had acquired "the knack of perverting and misleading a Majority of poor, and weak (tho' sometimes honest) Countrymen in our House of Representatives; and so they produced *Votes* which any Governor must count Intolerable." Mather recalled his sermon from 1719, and noted that "I have since been an object for the utmost Rage of the Satanic Party, and not only had their printed Libels continually darted at me, but had Attempts made upon my very Life."[11]

The Battle for Science

It was nothing less than an issue of life or death which became the battleground between Cotton Mather and the oligarchical forces opposing him. The same struggle brought Benjamin Franklin into active political life for the first time, though in a manner which historians typically have blatantly distorted or obscured.

Late in the spring of 1721, an epidemic of the dreaded smallpox, which had blasted New England's hopes at so many critical times in the past, erupted again in Boston. As a member of Britain's Royal Society, Cotton Mather had read some of its reports in 1719 on experimental attempts at vaccination undertaken in the Levant in the Middle East, and had independently investigated similar reports from the Caribbean. He was convinced that small doses, drawn from the infected tissue of a smallpox victim, could be administered to inoculate others against the disease. Mather launched a campaign through his civic organizations to persuade citizens to come forward and be vaccinated. As administering physician, Mather enlisted Dr. Zabdiel Boylston (whose brother would become the great-grandfather of President John Adams). While certainly there were doubts about the new remedy proposed, Mather's opponents responded in frenzied rage against the prospect of his becoming the scientist-savior of the city.

John Checkley and William Douglass had drawn James Franklin, the restless printer still in search of steady business, deeper into their circle. They now chose him as a leading instrument for their propaganda barrage against the Mathers. With their backing, James Franklin agreed to start a new paper in Boston, the weekly *New England Courant*, to compete with the Boston *Gazette* and Boston *News-Letter*.

The smallpox epidemic spread rapidly during the summer of 1721, lasting through to the following spring, and ultimately striking half the population of Boston. Cotton Mather announced the inoculation campaign in a letter to the Boston Gazette of July 27, 1721, also signed by Increase Mather and four leading ministers. Simultaneously, the *Courant* made its first appearance. For its third issue, John Checkley wrote that it was "the chief design of which Paper to oppose the *doubtful* and *dangerous* practice of inoculating the *Small-Pox*."[12]

Cotton Mather was accused of spreading the disease by inoculation. On August 15, he inoculated his own son Samuel, who lived in good health until 1785, at the ripe old age of seventy-nine. On November 1, he brought his nephew, Thomas Walter, from nearby Roxbury for inoculation, and was then accused of bringing "outsiders" into town to infect them. On November 4, the Boston town meeting, dominated by Elisha Cooke, Jr.'s "Satanic Party," voted to prohibit anyone from entering Boston to be vaccinated, and extended the ban to anyone already inoculated. On November 13, while Thomas Walter lay asleep in Cotton Mather's bedroom, overcoming the mild effects of his vaccination, a bomb was thrown through the window at 3 a.m. The iron grenade struck the window casement, which fortunately knocked off the fuse, preventing the explosion. Tied to the bomb by a string, "that it might outlive the breaking of the Shell," Mather noted, was a message: "COTTON MATHER. You Dog, Dam you: I'l inoculated you with this, with a Pox to you. [sic]"[13] Within the Franklin household, the repercussions of this attempt to assassinate Cotton Mather must have been severe.

Franklin's *Autobiography* is no help. The portion of it covering his life up to 1730 was written in 1771 as a letter to his son William, when Franklin was still in England as the official diplomatic representative of Massachusetts. William Franklin, educated as a lawyer at the Inns of Court in London while living with his father, became royal governor of New Jersey, and sided with the crown during the American Revolution. William fled to England, and Franklin's account of his own early years in Boston passed through many enemy hands. On issues of obvious political significance, it must be read with an eye to what is missing, and with extensive cross-checking of other sources for further clues.

The precise moment of Benjamin Franklin's recruitment by the Mathers is not so far documentable. He was only fifteen when his brother James began publishing the *Courant*, though by several accounts the Mathers took Benjamin aside to discuss his brother's actions with him. How much sway Josiah Franklin still held over the renegade James is also unclear, but the issue of the Courant immediately following the attempted bombing of Cotton Mather's house carried Mather's account of the incident verbatim, "to prevent wrong Representations that may be made of a late Occurrence much talked of."[14] Governor Shute, also a political target of the Cooke machine, offered a hefty £50 reward for identification of the terrorist.

But the genocidal campaign against inoculation continued. The ethical equivalent of Britain's Hell-Fire Club appeared in Boston, with John Checkley as president, as "The Society of Physicians Anti-Inoculator," meeting at Hall's Tavern, where its members took oaths to destroy Mather. To the Cooke-controlled Boston selectmen, William Douglass submitted a translation, purportedly of a French army doctor's claims, that persons inoculated in the Near East during the previous century, had died twenty and twenty-five years later of ulcers and tumors! With the aid of Cooke's henchmen, and a strident campaign of public lying in the pages of the New England Courant, Checkley and his friends were rapidly creating an anti-science mob in Massachusetts.

Like the anti-science, environmentalist cults of today, deployed to smash the remaining vestiges of the American System's commitment to technological progress, the "anti-inoculators" had no interest in the scientific validity of the vaccine Mather and Boylston developed. Although the epidemic was well under way when Dr. Boylston began administering smallpox vaccinations, of the 286 persons he inoculated, only six died—barely more than two percent. The death rate among the rest of Boston's smallpox victims was approximately 700 percent higher, with 844 fatalities out of 5,759 cases.   Smallpox epidemics in Britain during this period were similarly devastating, but no one tried to assassinate Dr. Boylston when he inoculated the royal princesses, on a mission to London to demonstrate the efficacy of the new vaccine.

There is no precise count of how many Bostonians died needlessly because they refused inoculation under the sway of Checkley's vicious campaign. But there is no doubt that it took a heavy toll on that will to do good necessary to a people's survival. To Increase and Cotton Mather, the two remaining giants of the Puritan republic, it appeared that the dominion of Satan was at hand. In January 1722, as James Franklin's *Courant* continued its efforts to prevent inoculations, one of its scribblers went so far as to write, "Most of the Ministers are for it, and that induces me to think it is from the D[evi]l; for he often makes Use of good Men as instruments to obtrude his Delusions on the World."[15] Such blasphemy, such open celebration of evil, did not go unanswered, and Benjamin Franklin was inevitably an intimate witness.   Despite years of incapacitating illness, Increase Mather, now over eighty-two years old, rose from his bed to charge James Franklin on a public street with fostering "an Hell-Fire Club."

Increase Mather was a living link to the republican commonwealth founded by John Winthrop as the Massachusetts Bay Colony in 1630. Born in 1639, Mather was educated at Harvard and then at Trinity College, Dublin, where the Mathers' family relations remained intellectually influential into the lifetime of Jonathan Swift. After serving in England, as an intelligence agent of the republican cause until the Stuart Restoration of 1660, Mather returned to Massachusetts and an extraordinary career as minister, scientist, philosopher, and statesman. He earned the mantle of leadership in New England, succeeding the great John Winthrop, Jr., after the latter's death in 1676.

This second Winthrop—who molded the Connecticut colony into a broadened republican flank for Massachusetts, whose library in the wilderness abounded with the works of Machiavelli, Erasmus, Thomas More, Johannes Kepler, Jean Bodin, and Blaise Pascal, and who corresponded with the young Leibniz in Germany—was one of those New England heroes "worthy to have their Lives written, as copies for future Ages to write after," as Cotton Mather put it.   In 1675, John Winthrop, Jr., exemplified his political and military leadership by stopping an invasion of Connecticut by royal forces before they could even come ashore.   King Charles II's attempt to subjugate Connecticut was led by Sir Edmund Andros, the man later overthrown and clapped in irons during the Massachusetts rebellion of 1689, engineered by Winthrop's key collaborator of the 1670s, Increase Mather.

Whatever freedom Massachusetts retained by 1722, much of it was due to wariness on London's part after the Andros Rebellion, and to the liberties preserved even under royal government by the new charter secured by Increase Mather.   Despite the decay which spread through Massachusetts by the time of the smallpox fight, it was no small matter for James Franklin to be publicly threatened with the wrath of God, by the elder statesman of the Puritan republic.

"I that have known what New England was from the Beginning, cannot but be troubled to see the Degeneracy of this Place," Mather declared in response to the *Courant*'s latest blasphemy. In advertisements run in both the Boston *News-Letter* and *Gazette*, Mather added,

> I cannot but pity poor [James] *Franklin*, who tho' but a *Young Man* it may be Speedily he must appear before the Judgment Seat of God, and what answer will he give for printing things so vile and abominable?

Mather's rage focused on the *Courant*'s insinuation "that *if the Ministers of God approve of a Thing, it is a Sign of the Devil*; which is a horrid thing to be related![16]

In the midst of this situation, imagine sixteen-year-old Benjamin Franklin, whose father witnessed the Andros Rebellion and became a respected citizen-leader in Cotton Mather's drive against the cultural decline which was threatening to extinguish New England's republican aspirations. Yet according to standard historical accounts, Benjamin Franklin had no role in the most dramatic political battle Massachusetts had seen during his life— except that of a juvenile prankster eager to have fun at the expense of those crotchety old Mathers. But nations are not created that way, and their founders invariably demonstrate something more than a flair for juvenile delinquency.

Worsening Prospects

The deteriorating situation confronting Cotton Mather and his fellow republicans certainly permitted no frontal assaults, and demanded the most skillful flanking maneuvers. Royal license for the bestial ethics of a Bernard Mandeville had provided sufficient footing to deploy an irrationalist mob in Massachusetts, far enough to lend cover to an open attempt on Mather's life. His supportive circle of republican allies and friends, led by key colonial governors, had also been broken. Robert Hunter, a friend in common to Swift and Mather, had left the governorship of New York in 1719. Governor Shute of Massachusetts was under pressure both from London and from Cooke's "Satanic Party." Governor Spotswood of Virginia was removed from office in 1722, while negotiating the treaty with the Iroquois that opened the way for westward expansion.

Internationally, the situation was also deteriorating rapidly. Remaining nation-building factions in both Britain and France had been flattened, along with numbers of America's republican allies, in the economic crash of 1720, when the Venetian-rigged speculative schemes known as the South Sea Bubble in Britain and John Law's Mississippi Bubble in France were blown out.

The simultaneous efforts to ruin both the British and French economies drew considerable attention from Cotton Mather, who knew better than most that evil was not localized in one country or under one label. At the time of the attempt on his life in November 1721, Mather was just completing works on both cases: *The Roaring of the South Sea* on the collapse of the British bubble, and a book in French, *Une Grande Voix du Ciel, a la France, sous la Verge de Dieu* [*A Great Voice from Heaven, to France, under the Scourge of God.*] Mather's diary notes that he sought to offer "Seasonable Reflections and profitable instructions" for the "Unhappy Nation" of Britain, and urged the French "to come out of Babylon." He had consulted with Governor Shute on "how to get my *Grande Voix du Ciel*, into France," anticipating that if he could secure distribution of the book inside the country, then reeling under the Orléans' Venetian-Jesuit rampage, "very astonishing may be the Consequences of it."[17]

At the same time, Mather was "Writing Letters for Europe," where a series of smallpox epidemics were "making terrible Destruction," to circulate "a further and more distinct Account of the *Small-Pox Inoculated*, the Method and Success of it among us, and the Opposition to it; By which Means, I hope, some hundreds of thousands of Lives, may in a little while come to be preserved."[18]

Cotton Mather's situation in Massachusetts, as underscored by the *New England Courant*'s hate campaign against his effort to stop the smallpox epidemic, was more immediately distressing. For all the well-meaning people he had inclined to do good, he as yet had no one willing to *lead* a fight at the level of command required. After the *Courant* flaunted its claim at the beginning of January 1722 that the Mathers' support for inoculation meant it must be the work of the devil, Cotton put the problem before "a meeting of the Ministers" on January 15.

Citing his hopes in writing *Essays to Do Good*, Mather told his colleagues,

> my Opportunities to do good, which have been to me the Apple of my Eye, have been strangely struck at. Odd Occurrences have happened, which have produced unaccountable Combinations in all Ranks of Men, to disable me for doing what I have most inclined unto. The most false Representations imaginable have been made of me; and of my Conduct. And tho' I could easily have confuted the Slanders and Clamours, I have rather borne them with Silence. . . .
>
> I am at length reduced unto this Condition, that my Opportunities to do good, (except among a few of my own little remnant of a Flock,) appear to me almost entirely extinguished, as to this Country [New

England].   I must employ my Faculties, in
projections to do good in more distant Places.
And I bless God, I have there a Prospect of
some Things, whereof I shall know more
hereafter. But at present, *I have done! I have
done! I have done* treating you with any more
of my Proposals. If they should be never so
good, yet if they be known to be mine, that is
enough to bespeak a Blast upon them. Do you
propose as many good Things as you please,
and I will second them, and assist them and fall
in with them, to the best of my Capacity.[19]

Besides Mather's forceful challenge to his associates,
for whom he had served as intellectual leader and political
commander-in-chief for more than thirty years, the
interesting feature of this address is his reference to his
remaining opportunities to do good "among a few of my
own little remnant of a Flock." Just two weeks earlier, in
his diary entry for January 1, Mather reported that he was
privately forming a new society for "some of my Flock"
who desired to "be more fully acquainted" with the
"Mysteries of the *Kingdom of God*, wherein His *Will* shall
be done on Earth as it is in Heaven." The group was to
meet once a fortnight at Mather's house. He hoped "that
the Society may afford me Opportunities to do for the
Flock, some further considerable Services."[20]

The 'Silence Dogood' Papers

The legend constructed of Benjamin Franklin's alleged
mischief against the Mathers during the smallpox fight,
centers around his anonymous submission of a series of
letters to the *New England Courant*, under the pseudonym
"Silence Dogood."   His authorship was not initially
detected even by his brother James, the editor of the

Courant. Since the *Courant*'s primary target was Cotton Mather, widely known as the author of *Essays to Do Good*, it was first assumed in some quarters—and later retailed as historical "fact"—that Silence Dogood was an opponent of the Mathers, perhaps even a menacing one.

The actual evidence exposes a long list of fools and liars. Benjamin Franklin's debut as a political polemicist was a flanking and encirclement operation against the enemies of Cotton Mather, and led directly to Franklin's being developed into the trusted agent of leading Massachusetts republicans for nearly seventy years. The design of the trap Franklin helped to set for Checkley's "Anti-Inoculator" cult was an able variation on Jonathan Swift's *Bickerstaff Papers*, which Cotton Mather had copied so extensively into his diary in 1708.

Both the Mathers' still-considerable stature and the civic reputation of the Franklin family, intermarried with relations of the Mathers, left James Franklin vulnerable to pressure. Such had been the case following the November 1721 attempt to assassinate Cotton, when the *Courant* not only printed his account of the bombing attack, but ran as the lead some decidedly Matherian verses on the smallpox epidemic. They were written at the time of the outbreak in May by one Matthew Adams, who in November gave them to James Franklin to publish, and ascribed the "sickly Gloom" of the "infectious Clouds" to "an angry God," irked by "a black and awful List of all our Crimes."

Among the handful of intellectual influences Benjamin Franklin cites respecting his youth in Boston, is this same Matthew Adams,

> an ingenious sensible man . . . who had a
> pretty collection of books and who frequented
> our printing house, took notice of me, invited
> me to see his library, and very kindly proposed
> to lend me such books as I chose to read.[21]

In February 1722, following Cotton Mather's report to the ministers that his attempts to do good in his own name could no longer succeed, Matthew Adams again managed to have a contribution published in the *Courant*. This time Adams lifted a paragraph verbatim, ascribing it only as something "I had somewhere read," from Jonathan Swift's *A Tale of a Tub*, published anonymously in 1694. It was Swift's first scathing attack on "modern" perversions of religion—and on Thomas Hobbes' *Leviathan*, the "spiritual" predecessor of Bernard Mandeville's celebration of sodomic horror, *The Fable of the Bees*.

Adams' quoting from *A Tale of a Tub* without naming the work suggests more about the delicate counter-operation Cotton Mather was preparing against the *Courant*. Swift himself never publicly acknowledged authorship of the book that nonetheless brought him so much public attention. Even Swift's *Gulliver's Travels* (1726), an allegorical attack on the insanity of the oligarchy in general, and the rotten Whig ministry of Sir Robert Walpole in particular, was published anonymously. Those "freedom-loving" Whig governments, which dominated the reign of King George I and his Hanoverian successors, repeatedly sought to convict Swift as author of anything offending them, ordered the arrest and trial of his printers, or suppressed publication entirely. During the week following Matthew Adams' piece in the *Courant*, Mather noted in his diary that he had written several things "towards Suppressing and Rebuking those wicked Pamphlets, that are continually published among us, to lessen and blacken the Ministers, and poison the people . . . . Tho my poor Hand is the Doer of them, they must pass thro other Hands, that I may not pass for the Author of them."[22]

Ironically, one of Benjamin Franklin's later agents in Ireland had to flee to the United States to escape arrest, for reprinting Swift's *A Modest Proposal* half a century after Swift's death. The agent was Mathew Carey, republican economist in his own right, and the father of Henry Carey, the leading developer of American System economics during the period of Henry Clay and Abraham Lincoln. Mathew Carey's crime against the government of George III was to make available again Swift's devastating indictment of British genocide against Ireland, in which he anonymously offered a scheme for breeding babies for human consumption, as a solution for Ireland's poverty and misery.

The Whig literary "Wits" Joseph Addison and Richard Steele were models emulated by the "right-to-die" propagandists at the *New England Courant*. Addison and Steele were also the leading figures churning out sophisticated Whig propaganda for *The Spectator* from 1711 to 1714, in opposition to Swift's behind-the-scenes reorganization of the policies and the cabinet of Queen Anne's government. The *Courant*'s staff cribbed regularly from the *Spectator*'s old issues—but never from Swift.

Benjamin Franklin began his undercover contributions to the *Courant* as "Silence Dogood" in April 1722. Surviving texts of his *Autobiography* omit any references to the controversy then raging, or the content of the pieces he wrote, or even his celebrated pseudonym. What is reported is that since he knew "that my brother would object to printing anything in his paper if he knew it to be mine, I contrived to disguise my hand; and writing an anonymous paper, I put it at night under the door of the printing house. It was found in the morning and communicated to his writing friends when they called in as usual."[23]

For his literary persona of "Silence Dogood," Franklin introduced the modest widow of a country minister, seeking to comprehend the strange new mores and fashions of

Boston, while offering advice and admonitions from one not yet corrupted. His fictional advocate began by noting that "now a days" readers will not accept an author without knowing "who or what the Author of it is," his circumstances and manner of living, and whether he be "a Scholar or a Leather Apron Man"— the last qualification referring to the ongoing war between the Mathers and those tradesmen, like James Franklin, under the sway of the "Anti-Inoculators" and Elisha Cooke.[24]

The literary device with which Franklin introduced "Silence Dogood" was precisely chosen to fool brother James and "his writing friends." The very first piece *The Spectator* published, written by Joseph Addison to launch that paper in 1711, began with the sentence, "I have observed, that a reader seldom peruses a book with pleasure, till he knows whether the writer of it be a black or a fair man, of a mild or choleric disposition, married or a bachelor, with other particulars of the like nature, that conduce very much to the right understanding of an author."[25] Franklin had just forged his entry into the *Courant*'s "Hell-Fire" club, and the ruse worked.

Franklin's *Autobiography* reports that when the *Courant*'s scribblers arrived the next day and discovered his "letter,"

> They read it, commented on it in my hearing, and I had the exquisite pleasure of finding it met with their approbation, and that in their different guesses at the author, none were named but men of some character among us for learning and ingenuity. I suppose now that I was rather lucky in my judges and that perhaps they were not really so very good as I then believed them to be.[26]

Certainly they were not as clever as he might have imagined them. The account in the *Autobiography* adds that he "wrote and sent in the same way several other pieces, which were equally approved, and I kept my secret until my small fund of sense for such performances were pretty well exhausted," when he revealed his authorship. In his dealings with his brother James, the disclosure occasioned one "of the differences we began to have about this time." In the same paragraph, Franklin's *Autobiography* adds that his disputes with James were often brought before our father, and . . . the judgment was generally in my favor." James frequently beat him nonetheless, and the report continues, "I fancy his harsh and tyrannical treatment of me might be a means of impressing me with that aversion to arbitrary power that has stuck to me through my whole life."[27]

Looking beyond this family feud to the Silence Dogood papers themselves, the case for Benjamin Franklin's—and his father's—adherence to the Mathers becomes conclusive. Franklin's next two pieces continued mimicking the *Spectator*'s merely 'literary' show of abstract moralizing, in the 'sophisticated' Whig manner. With each printing of the latest witticisms of the "mysterious woman," the wags of Hall's Tavern and the 'enlightened' would-be Anglicans dominating Harvard College clucked approvingly, in their respective fashions.

The Harvard problem was especially troublesome to Cotton Mather. Increase Mather had battled to maintain the college's republican traditions even during the Andros dictatorship, and Cotton knew all too well the depths of miseducation reached since his father's ouster as president and the takeover of Harvard after 1700 by the Cooke machine and its merchant backers. Matters worsened after 1715. Boycotting Harvard's commencement day in 1717, Cotton Mather prayed "that our College, which is on many

Accounts in a very neglected and unhappy Condition, and has been betray'd by vile practices, may be restored unto better circumstances."[28] By the early 1720s, he feared outright Anglican usurpation of the institution, which had been the early mainstay of republican leadership in Massachusetts. His concern was well founded. In 1722, even as Benjamin Franklin continued his "Silence Dogood" papers in the *Courant*, an Anglican coup surfaced at Yale, the Connecticut college at New Haven founded in 1706, which the Mathers had hoped might outflank the subversion of Harvard.

Franklin's fourth Dogood essay appeared April 16, 1722, after considerable public gossip and speculation had developed concerning the identity of the apparent new ally of the *Courant*'s crusade against the Mathers and their ministerial allies. Franklin's authorship remained unknown to the *Courant*, and he ventured now for the first time into specific controversies of the day. Modern historians actually cite this particular "Dogood" letter as evidence of Franklin's hostility toward the Mathers.[29] In it, the modest widow has a conversation with one "Clericus," during a stroll in the country on a warm, sunny afternoon. Resting a while under a tree, she dozes off and has a dream about a visit to the "Temple of Learning," where she discovers too many "Dunces and Blockheads" and too much catering to wealth. To the *Courant*'s "clever" followers, Mrs. Dogood was commencing an attack on Harvard College and those nasty Mathers (Clericus). The Cooke machine, just as it had whipped up "popular opinion" against Cotton Mather's lifesaving inoculations for smallpox, was then attacking Harvard—and education in general—as a wasteful extravagance for the rich. Under Mather's enemy John Leverett, brother-in-law of Elisha Cooke, Sr., the college had certainly become vulnerable to such charges.

Benjamin Franklin took note of Harvard's fate since it had fallen into enemy hands. During Silence Dogood's dream of her visit to the "Temple of Learning," she discovers a "magnificent Throne" in the great hall. On "the top of it sat LEARNING in an awful State; she was apparelled wholly in Black, and surrounded on almost every side with innumerable Volumes in all languages." Following this image of benighted "learning" swamped by incoherence, Franklin springs the trap:

> She seem'd very busily employ'd in writing something on half a Sheet of Paper, and upon Enquiry, I understood she was preparing a Paper, call'd, *The New-England Courant* [!].[30]

Thus he identifies Leverett's Aristotelian "modernist" regime at Harvard as the intellectual ally of the *Courant*'s war against science. Franklin further characterizes the decay of the college in a passage reminiscent of Swift's *Battle of the Books*:

> [On Learning's left hand] were seated several *Antique Figures* with their Faces vail'd. I was considerably puzzl'd to guess who they were, until one informed me, (who stood beside me,) that those Figures on her left Hand were *Latin, Greek, Hebrew,* &c. and that they were very much reserv'd, and seldom or never unvail'd their Faces here . . . . I then enquir'd of him, what could be the Reason why they continued vail'd, in this Place especially: He pointed to the Foot of the Throne, where I saw *Idleness,* attended with *Ignorance,* and these (he informed me) were they, who first vail'd them, and still kept them so.

For what remained of Harvard's role in educating the ministry, Dogood adds her impressions of the "Temple of Theology" as well, reporting that there

I saw nothing worth mentioning except the
ambitious and fraudulent Contrivances of
Plagius, who (notwithstanding he had been
severely reprehended for such practices before)
was diligently transcribing some eloquent
Paragraphs out of Tilotson's *Works*, &c. to
embellish his own.

When Dogood awakens from her dream, she relates it to
Clericus, with "all its Particulars, and he without much
Study, presently interpreted it, assuring me, *That it was a
lively Representation of HARVARD COLLEGE, Etcetera!*
[emphasis in original]"[31] Thus Franklin's supposed diatribe
against Mather is in fact a dialogue *between* the two men,
developing the same arguments that "Clericus" Cotton
Mather had put forth himself. In targeting "the fraudulent
Contrivances of Plagius" from the works of Anglican
archbishop Tillotson, Franklin again focused on the same
current of philosophical corruption at Harvard which
Mather had been attacking for years—as well as on the
liberal Anglican patrons of the "Anti-Inoculators"
themselves.

The staff of the *Courant*, whatever their misgivings
concerning the actual identity of Silence Dogood, was
stuck with a celebrated columnist who might be digging
their own graves. Jonathan Swift's "Isaac Bickerstaff," the
fictitious astrologer who convinced the public of the death
of his (quite living) rival John Partridge, would have
appreciated the twist of "friend" revealed as foe. As to the
origin and intention of Franklin's choice of pseudonym, the
Courant's staff may have overlooked a clue in the very title
of the latest work Cotton Mather had published in Boston:
Silentiarus, printed in the fall of 1721, at the height of the
smallpox epidemic. The book was printed on the occasion
of the death of his daughter from other causes, with the

subtitle, *A Brief Essay on the Holy Silence and Godly Patience, that Sad Things are to be Entertained withal.* Mather's "Hell-Fire" antagonists were undoubtedly too benighted to detect another irony, in Mather's January 15 "address to the ministers" on the subversion of his "opportunities to do good." Before the leaders of many of his civic organizations, which included in their ranks Benjamin Franklin's father Josiah, he had declared, "And tho' I could easily have confuted the Slanders and Clamours, I have rather borne them with Silence."

Having thrown the enemy camp into sufficient disarray to make it vulnerable, Mather's circle now moved to eliminate its main propaganda weapon. First Mather arranged for some further cover for Silence Dogood, whose political loyalties the Courant could not expose, without making itself the laughingstock of Boston for having so warmly embraced the modest widow. In the Boston *Gazette* of May 28, Mather's son, Samuel, replied to Dogood's "attack" on the temples of learning and theology, without disputing any of its substance. Under the pseudonym "John Harvard," Samuel Mather addressed not Dogood but the *Courant*'s own sources of inspiration: "Sir, Desire Courante to no more put upon Plagius for fear of hurting himself." Mather's John Harvard proceeded to demonstrate that most of the *Courant*'s 'literary' pieces were plagiarized from old issues of *The Spectator, The Guardian,* and *The Tatler*—all produced by Whig propagandists who had become enemies of Jonathan Swift.

As Silence Dogood, Franklin wrote fourteen letters in all, from April to October 1722. In the face of the Courant's "Hell-Fire" campaign, they were his own "essays to do good." He had warned in his third, still as the undiscovered author, "that I now take up a resolution, to do for the future all that *lies in my Way* for the Service of my Countrymen." Franklin added,

> I have from my Youth been indefatigably
> studious to gain and treasure up in my Mind all
> useful and desirable Knowledge, especially
> such as tends to improve the Mind, and enlarge
> the Understanding.

The anonymous Silence Dogood had been warmly received
by the Hall's Tavern plotters thus far. Franklin concluded
this letter, "I think I have now finish'd the Foundation, and
I intend in my next to begin to raise the Building:"[32]

His next, of course, was his blast against the *Courant*'s
patrons in the corrupted "Temple of Learning." Following
that letter, Silence Dogood put forth the necessity of greater
education for women, as indispensable to ending the folly
and vanity in relations between the sexes—and to
developing a republican citizenry. For this piece, and more
extensively for a later one on an insurance plan for widows,
Franklin quoted from Daniel Defoe's *An Essay on Projects*,
published in London in 1697 in support of the economic
development program offered by Robert Harley, in
opposition to the monetarist swindle imposed by Montagu
and Marlborough's Bank of England. Defoe was also a
correspondent of Cotton Mather, and is cited as such in
Mather's diary. Silence Dogood's treatment of Defoe
included an endorsement for the "reforming societies"
proposed in Mather's *Essays to Do Good*—which Franklin
himself was to organize in Philadelphia:

> I would leave this to the Consideration of all
> who are concern'd for their own or their
> Neighbor's temporal Happiness; and I am
> humbly of opinion, that the Country is ripe for
> many such *Friendly Societies*, whereby every
> Man might help another, without any
> Disservice to himself.[33]

Cotton Mather's political heir was coming into his own.

The evidence concerning Franklin's first counterintelligence mission has been presented here in detail, for two essential reasons. First, to establish that counterintelligence work was a central feature of his career from the outset—for without knowing that crucial fact, one cannot accurately chart the course of Franklin's subsequent activities. Second, to demonstrate that his political career was a continuation of New England's commitment, from its founding, to a sovereign republic—John Winthrop's "city upon a hill," a model of freedom for the world.

From the moment Charles II in 1684 voided the Winthrop charter upon which New England's liberty had been built, *the preparations for the American Revolution had begun.* In 1689—only six years after Benjamin Franklin's father Josiah brought his family to Massachusetts—Increase Mather from London, and Cotton Mather in Boston, directed the armed overthrow of royal governor Edmund Andros by Massachusetts militiamen, and proclaimed again a New England republic. The rebellion was a temporary blocking action against the expected new tyrannies of William of Orange, the Dutch prince who had just overthrown James II and seized the throne of England.

In New England, the dates of decisive events were well remembered. When Mather protégé Benjamin Franklin, under the pseudonym Richard Saunders, began publishing *Poor Richard's Almanack* in Philadelphia in 1733, he left a calling card perhaps unnoticed since his lifetime. On the almanac's final page, Franklin provided a "Catalogue of the principal Kings and Princes in *Europe*, with the Time of their Births and Ages." Below a bar line at the end of the list, Franklin printed the birth date of "*Poor Richard,* an American Prince, without Subjects." The birthday given is October 23, 1684, the precise date on which Charles II revoked the Massachusetts charter!

Franklin's coded call to rebuild a republic in America may have gone unnoticed by the royal administrators of the colonies. But in 1775, they would painfully observe the withering fire of Massachusetts militiamen on British troops retreating from Concord and Lexington, drawn into a well-laid trap, sprung by Paul Revere's ride on the night of April 18—the same date as the Andros Rebellion of 1689.

With his Silence Dogood letters, Franklin had entered active duty in the American republican intelligence service founded by John Winthrop. Yet even though Franklin had been imbued from childhood with a vision of a new world by men gathering around his father's hearth, there was an important difference. The Massachusetts republic they had known, existed in Franklin's lifetime largely in memory. Its population and institutions were now corrupted, and the quality of education was a pivotal case in point. At Increase Mather's Harvard of half a century earlier, the power of reason essential to a republican citizenry was inculcated through instruction including Plato, Kepler, and Milton. Under the Aristotelian takeover of Harvard, following the revocation of the Massachusetts charter, classical education was steadily discarded in favor of the dead, mechanistic notions of "enlightened modernists," such as Descartes, Newton, and Locke. Predictably, Harvard commencements soon became riotous orgies, instead of celebrations of intellectual accomplishment.

It was, therefore, no coincidence that Benjamin Franklin's first political broadside was aimed at the corrupters of Harvard's role as the fountain of learning for New England republicanism. Nor was it incidental that Franklin's later organizing objectives in Pennsylvania included the founding of a new college as a major priority. But *overcoming* this cultural degeneracy, under conditions of virtual enemy occupation, was obstructed most of all by the population's tolerance of such evil.

Franklin himself vented his rage against those who pretended to affirm their loyalty to *New* England while blithely complying with every atrocity dictated by the British oligarchy.   In his ninth Silence Dogood letter, Franklin evoked ugly memories of Joseph Dudley, the man Cotton Mather had branded "our Criminal Governor," who had ostensibly prepared for the Puritan ministry at Harvard, graduating in 1665. The infamous Dudley then worked to destroy the Massachusetts charter, became Sir Edmund Andros' royal lieutenant-governor, and was arrested for treason by Massachusetts during the Andros Rebellion in 1689. In 1702, the "pious" Dudley was appointed royal governor of New England, under sponsorship of the Duke of Marlborough, whereupon he proceeded to employ pirates to sink Massachusetts ships, and sell arms to the French in Canada for use against New England. Yet he was sustained as governor until his death in 1716, when his passing was lamented by criminals and fools alike, including some ministers who offered him eulogies. Silence Dogood observed,

> A publick Hypocrite every day deceives his betters, and makes them the Ignorant Trumpeters of his supposed Godliness: They take him for a Saint, and pass him for one, without considering that they are (as it were) the Instruments of publick Mischief out of Conscience, and ruin their Country for God's sake.   This Political Description of a Hypocrite, may (for ought I know) be taken for a new Doctrine by some of your Readers; but let them consider, that *a little Religion, and a little Honesty, goes a great way in Courts* .   .   .   .   But the most dangerous Hypocrite in a Common-Wealth, is one who *leaves the Gospel for the Sake of the Law.* A

man compounded of Law and Gospel, is able to cheat a whole Country with his Religion, and then destroy them under *Colour of Law*: And here the Clergy are in great danger of being deceiv'd, and the People of being deceiv'd by the Clergy, until the Monster arrives to such Power and Wealth, that he is out of the reach of both, and can oppress the People without their own blind Assistance . . . . [And] when he happens to *die for the Good of his Country*, without leaving behind him the Memory of *one good Action*, he shall be sure to have his Funeral Sermon stuffd with *Pious Expressions* which he dropt at such a Time, and at such a Place, and on such an Occasion . . . .[34]

Such a state of affairs, with the oligarchy on the verge of ruling without the population's "own blind Assistance," was the Massachusetts of Franklin's youth—and of Cotton Mather's last years. The official institutions established by their republican forebears had too long been in enemy hands. Cotton Mather had turned to unofficial, voluntarist associations for reawakening the population, as evidenced by his 1710 *Essays to Do Good.* But his intent was always to reclaim the institutions of power, and to remake them in the service of a republic. To carry out this complex responsibility, it was also necessary to operate successfully under the enemy's noses. Franklin had demonstrated the ability to do just that. Soon, Cotton Mather sent him forth on a much more daring mission, reaching all the way to "Hell-Fire" London.

Discovering Franklin's Secrets

Benjamin Franklin left Boston in late September 1723, ostensibly because his half-brother James had blacklisted him among Boston's printers, and because he had made himself "a little obnoxious to the governing party." Cotton Mather's enemies in the Cooke machine controlled the legislature.[35] The only surviving account of Franklin's decision is the portion of his autobiography written in 1771, as a letter to his son William, who defected to the British during the Revolution. Franklin's own reluctance, to commit sensitive intelligence matters to paper, was by no means diminished by the fact he was writing to his son. William Franklin had been targeted while in London with his father, during the 1760s, for recruitment into the networks of the Hell-Fire Club. Sir Francis Dashwood, His Majesty's postmaster general at the time, was then Benjamin Franklin's official superior. Franklin directed the postal service for the American colonies. Dashwood was the head of the Hell-Fire Club.[36]

Yet this first part of the autobiography, covering Franklin's life to approximately 1730, was also written as a kind of "essay to do good" for his son. Thus the pattern of his activities, as related, is to a definite purpose, even though their particular significance is masked by withholding important details. Only by reading that pattern, in the context of precise knowledge of the time, can one learn the secrets of the young Benjamin Franklin's role in the battle for the American republic. When he departed for Philadelphia in 1723, the seventeen-year-old Franklin was no runaway adventurer. He had already worked as an undercover agent for Cotton Mather, against the Boston branch of the Hell-Fire Club.

With Robert Walpole's coming to power, George I's government had by 1723 openly embraced Bernard Mandeville's doctrine that "private vices" and official corruption were the basis for "public benefits." The strategic urgency of building an American republic was now all the greater. Virginia's Governor Spotswood, with

Pennsylvania's Keith and New York's Hunter and Burnet, had opened the door with the 1722 Treaty of Albany with the Iroquois. That agreement had removed the main threat to settling Virginia's Shenandoah Valley, beyond the Blue Ridge, and confirmed its route to the West along the Potomac River, deep into the Allegheny Mountains. The potential also existed to extend Pennsylvania's settlements to the Alleghenies, and to funnel waves of pioneers into the Shenandoah Valley, stretching toward Kentucky and Tennessee. America's republican command, however, was now weakened. Walpole had forced Spotswood's removal from office in 1722, and New York's Governor Burnet was unequal to the leadership of his predecessor Robert Hunter, the republican colleague of Swift and of Mather. In Philadelphia, Governor Keith remained in office, but was under siege by the Quakers' "monied men." Yet Pennsylvania was the keystone for building colonies beyond the mountains. It was no accident that Benjamin Franklin, Cotton Mather's most gifted protégé, was deployed there.

Consider the chain of events which Franklin reports, masked as mere happenstances. His departure from Boston was arranged in secrecy, for passage on a ship bound for New York, under a cover story established by his closest intellectual companion, whom he had known since childhood. The two "had read the same books together," and while Franklin lived in Boston,

> most of my hours of leisure for conversation were spent with him; and he continued a sober and industrious lad [and] was much respected for his learning *by several of the clergy* and other gentlemen. . . . [emphasis added].[37]

*The Jesuits of French Canada were notorious for their
'spiritual' assistance to the Indians—instilling them with
synthetic belief structures, to direct them in savage attacks
against America's colonial settlements. The Jesuit menace was
the chief target of repeated American operations against
Canada from 1690 through the American Revolution.*

*Harvard College, once the stronghold of New England
republicanism, fell on dark times after Increase Mather was
ousted from its presidency in 1701 by Elisha Cooke's 'Satanic
Party.' In this 1726 painting, imitators of royal fashions
parade in the foreground, while ominous clouds loom above.*

Left: Birthplace of Benjamin Franklin in Boston. His childhood home was a regular meeting place for Cotton Mather's circle of republican organizers. Franklin cited Cotton Mather as the leading influence on his life. The continuity from Puritan republic to American independence has been deliberately obscured. (clipart.com)

Right: The house of Increase Mather, reduced to a boarding house and ground-floor grocery, before its demolition by real estate speculators in the late nineteenth century.

The Mathers' tomb in Boston's North End. The British used it as a cannon-mount to fire on Bunker Hill in 1775.

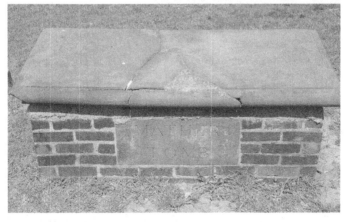

An outline of the home built in 1735 by Augustine Washington, Spotswood's fellow iron-maker in Virginia. (Courtesy of the Mount Vernon Ladies' Association) The house was later incorporated into the larger home built by George Washington—the famous Mt. Vernon (below). (Courtesy of H. Graham Lowry)

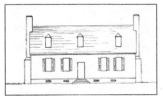

Right: Belvoir, the home of William Fairfax, overlooking the Potomac River just below Mt. Vernon. Damaged by fire in 1783, it was leveled to the ground by British warships in 1814. (Courtesy of a private collection)

Left: Spotswood's summer home overlooking the York River. Washington chose it as the site for the British army's signing of the articles of surrender at Yorktown in 1781.

Lord Thomas Fairfax (1693–1781), the republican proprietor of Virginia's Northern Neck—a land grant he transformed into America's route for developing as far as the Mississippi River. (Colonial Williamsburg Foundation)

Above: Lawrence Washington (c. 1717–1752). Like a second father to his younger brother George, he was the political heir-apparent to Alexander Spotswood. Working with Lord Fairfax, he founded the Ohio Company in 1747. (Courtesy of the Mount Vernon Ladies' Association)

Left: Portrait of the young George Washington (1732–1799). After Lawrence's untimely death, he became the leader of Virginia's republicans. (National Archives)

The surveying office at Lord Fairfax's home in the Shenandoah Valley. Beginning in 1748, George Washington spent nearly two years here, surveying the western reaches of the Fairfax grant.

The Fairfax Stone, at the head spring of the Potomac River, erected in 1746. The inscription 'Ffx 46' is still visible. Beyond the next ridge of the Allegheny Mountains, the Ohio Company extended America's claims to the West. (Courtesy of H. Graham Lowry)

Lord Fairfax was buried in Winchester, Va., which he fostered as America's westernmost town before the French and Indian War— and the strategic base for colonizing the Ohio country.

Massachusetts Governor William Shirley (1674-1771) designed a brilliant campaign in 1745 to capture Louisburg, French Canada's key stronghold. (Courtesy of H. Graham Lowry) At the Old State House (below left), built in 1711 during America's republican offensive, he presented the plan to the Massachusetts legislature— swearing them to secrecy to prevent British interference. His success drove the crown to a murderous frenzy. (I.N. Phelps Stokes Collection, Miriam and Ira D. Wallach Division of Art, Prints and Photographs, The New York Public Library, Astor, Lenox and Tilden Foundations)

Right: The Old State House today, surrounded by the money-changing temples of Boston's Anglophile financiers.

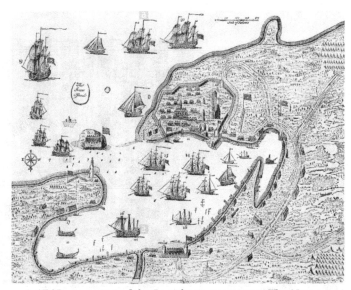

A 1745 engraving of the Louisburg campaign. The New England militia attacked overland (from upper right), seized the Grand Battery (lower center), and from Lighthouse Point (lower left) knocked out the Island Battery at the mouth of the harbor.

Robert Dinwiddie (1693–1770), governor of Virginia from 1751 to 1758. An ally of Spotswood's faction, he sponsored Washington's first mission to challenge French control of the Ohio country.

Portrait by Copley of Professor John Winthrop (1714–1779), the leading American scientist of his day, and a key figure in Franklin's intelligence network. (Courtesy of the Harvard University Portrait Collection, Gift of the executors of the Estate of John Winthrop, grandson, 1894)

A portrait of Franklin painted in 1748, when Franklin 'retired' to direct the battle for independence full-time. (Courtesy of the Harvard University Portrait Collection, Bequest of Dr. John Collins Warren, 1856)

Franklin's 1754 cartoon, 'Join, or Die,' was issued in support of the Albany Plan of Union. It was widely reprinted during the American Revolution.

JOIN, or DIE.

Upon arrival in New York, Franklin presented himself, as a young printer in search of work, to William Bradford, the publisher of Robert Hunter's satirical play, *Androboros.* Bradford forwarded him to his son Andrew, a printer in Philadelphia, telling Franklin, "If you go thither I believe he may employ you."[38]

By a series of boat trips and a fifty-mile hike through New Jersey to the Delaware River, Franklin proceeded to Philadelphia in a most inconspicuous fashion, where on arrival *he made certain he would be observed.* In work clothes dirtied by his long journey, he joined a procession of "many clean dressed people" entering "the great meetinghouse of the Quakers near the market." There he "sat down among them, and after looking round awhile and hearing nothing said, . . . I fell fast asleep and continued so till the meeting broke up, when someone was kind enough to rouse me." The next morning, dressed "as neat as I could," he went to the print shop of Andrew Bradford, where Franklin found "the old man his father whom I had seen at New York, and who traveling on horseback, *had got to Philadelphia before me* [emphasis added]."[39] Without directly making the point, Franklin here provides the evidence that William Bradford—a member of the circles of Swift, Hunter, and Mather—personally oversaw establishing Franklin's initial cover in Philadelphia.

Andrew Bradford offered Franklin the hospitality of his home, until a less obvious place of employment could be arranged. William Bradford then conducted Franklin to "another printer in town lately set up, one Keimer," who intended to challenge the younger Bradford for the business in Philadelphia. To the newcomer Keimer, the "old gentleman" Bradford pretended to be a local dignitary:

> "Neighbor," said Bradford, "I have brought to
> see you a young man of your business; perhaps

> you may want such a one.". . . And taking old
> Bradford, whom he had never seen before, to be
> one of the townspeople that had a good will for
> him, [Keimer] entered into a conversation on
> his present undertaking and prospects . . . .[40]

Even though Franklin told Keimer "who the old man was," he was soon hired. He began spending his evenings "among the young people of the town that were lovers of reading." He reported his new station to Boston, but only through the friend who had arranged his departure, "who was in my secret and kept it when I wrote to him."[41]

Soon after Franklin was established in Philadelphia, word of the arrangement was passed to Governor William Keith, by Franklin's brother-in-law Robert Homes, "master of a sloop that traded between Boston and Delaware." It was not long before Keith appeared "finely dressed" at Keimer's door, to request a meeting with Benjamin Franklin, the "promising" young man he had recently heard of, who "should be encouraged." The governor ignored Keimer,

> and with a condescension and politeness I had
> been quite unused to, made me many
> compliments, desired to be acquainted with me,
> blamed me kindly for not having made myself
> known to him when I first tame to the place,
> and would have me away with him to the tavern
> where he was going . . . to taste, as he said,
> some excellent Madeira. I was not a little
> surprised, and Keimer stared like a pig
> poisoned.[42]

At the tavern, Keith told Franklin that he wanted him to become the public printer for Pennsylvania—certainly an unusual offer for a supposed young vagabond from Boston.

Keith then suggested that Franklin's father—a longtime organizer for Cotton Mather—might provide him the money to set up his own print shop.[43]

> On my doubting whether my father would assist me in it, Sir William said he would set forth the advantages, and he did not doubt he should determine to comply. So it was concluded I should return to Boston by the first vessel with the Governor's letter of recommendation to my father. In the meantime the intention was to be kept secret, and I went on working with Keimer as usual.[44]

Letter in hand, Franklin sailed for Boston at the end of April 1724.

The *Autobiography* reports that Franklin's father refused to finance a new printing business for his son, "being in his opinion too young to be trusted with the management of an undertaking so important," but he was pleased that Benjamin had so impressed "a person of such note" as the governor of Pennsylvania.[45] But here the account makes a crucial omission, of enormous significance for deciphering the document as a whole. No mention is made of the fact that on this return to Boston, Franklin met privately with Cotton Mather!   Sixty years later, after Britain had conceded the sovereignty of the United States at the Treaty of Paris, Franklin wrote from France to Cotton's son, Samuel Mather, "The last time I saw your father was in the beginning of 1724, when I visited him after my first trip to Pennsylvania." The letter again paid tribute to Cotton Mather's determining influence on his life.[46]

Franklin returned to Philadelphia, making the first leg of the journey by sloop to New York. There he made contact with Robert Hunter's hand-picked successor:

The then Governor of New York, Burnet, son of Bishop Burnet, hearing from the captain that a young man, one of his passengers, had a great many books, desired him to bring me to see him . . . . The Governor received me with great civility, showed me his library, which was a very considerable one, and we had a good deal of conversation about books and authors. This was the second governor who had done me the honor to take notice of me, and for a poor boy like me was very pleasing.[47]

Next, Governor Keith arranged a mission to London for the "poor boy," ostensibly to purchase new type and printing equipment.   Keith told Franklin, "Then when there you may make acquaintances and establish correspondences in the book-selling and stationery way."[48]

In considerable detail the *Autobiography* reports Franklin's arrangements with Keith for the voyage. He was to sail in late October on the *Annis*, the annual ship from Philadelphia to England. Keith was to furnish him with recommendations to "a number of his friends," as well as a letter of credit for the printing purchases. During the months awaiting his passage, Franklin reports, Governor Keith "had me frequently to his house."[49] Much is made of Keith's repeated postponements in delivering the promised letters to Franklin, of his sailing from Philadelphia without them—expecting Keith to intercept the ship at Newcastle, and of arriving in England to discover Keith had supplied no letters at all. There Franklin made a great show of being "a poor ignorant boy," whose trusting nature had been betrayed by the Pennsylvania governor.[50]

From the higher level of evidence, it is clear that this episode with Keith was simply part of Franklin's cover story for a secret intelligence mission. Consider again the *pattern* of his accounts in the *Autobiography*, juxtaposed against the provable course of his activities. Franklin's career in political combat begins with his anonymous Silence Dogood papers, supposedly written to impress the Hell-Fire Club circle controlling his half-brother James, but in fact undertaken as an undercover operation in support of Cotton Mather. He flees Boston in secret, purportedly fearing reprisals from his brother's enemies, yet on his return is welcomed into Mather's home. Robert Hunter's friend, the New York printer William Bradford, arranges Franklin's first employment in Philadelphia, but sends him on an arduous overland and riverboat journey to get there, instead of letting Franklin accompany him on horseback. Perhaps no one took notice of Franklin's meeting with New York's Governor Burnet, but Keith's patronage could hardly be overlooked.

Governor Keith, after all, was the known ally of Robert Hunter and Alexander Spotswood. Franklin's own safety, as well as any prospects for a successful undercover mission in Britain, thus depended upon his having no apparent ties to Keith—nor to Cotton Mather. Franklin's *Autobiography*, written nearly half a century later, still preserves his cover, yet provides decipherable clues. He deliberately obscures his personal connection to Mather, while praising his *Essays to Do Good.* Keith's relationship is portrayed as duplicitous, but Franklin concludes that account by declaring that Keith was "otherwise an ingenious, sensible man, a pretty good writer, and a good governor for the people . . . . Several of our best laws were of his planning and passed during his administration."[51] The young Franklin, to the extent his actual connections could be hidden, was an ideal agent for a counterintelligence mission against Robert Walpole's Hell-Fire regime in London. The appearance of hostility to Keith was especially important, for the scrutiny of

Walpole's agents had already been attracted by another American arrival in 1724. Alexander Spotswood, the man who would later appoint Franklin postmaster of Philadelphia, had returned to London, ostensibly to reconfirm his land titles in Spotsylvania County, Virginia.[52]

Franklin arrived in London on Christmas Eve, 1724. Two things are certain. Whether Keith had furnished him with any letters or not, someone had paid his passage. Second, Franklin had not come to London simply to work in printing houses for more than a year-and-a-half.

Hell-Fire London

Coordinating a republican movement in the American colonies had always been hampered by the difficulty of obtaining adequate intelligence concerning machinations in London. Now the problem was even greater. Since the blowout of the South Sea Bubble, and the restructuring of power under the parliamentary regime of Robert Walpole and his "stockjobbers," Britain's political map had been drastically redrawn. London was fast becoming 'Venice-on-Thames,' and was threatening to supersede Sodom and Gomorrah. For a glimpse of how far London soon descended into the inferno, one need only study the engravings of Swift's ally, the artist William Hogarth.

Culturally, and thus politically, the nature of the beast had changed. Following George I's taking the throne in 1714, and the publication of Bernard Mandeville's *The Fable of the Bees* the same year, Satanic cults proliferated among Britain's elite. The most notorious were the various branches of the Hell-Fire Club, modeled after Mandeville's doctrine that evil, vice, and corruption were the ideal means of the state's controlling its servants, or the drones of the hive. Mandeville's bestial notions were later celebrated by such hedonistic "philosophers" as Voltaire, Helvetius,

Montesquieu, James Mill, and Jeremy Bentham. In 1720, the year of the Bubble and an unrestrained Venetian rampage against Britain, the Hell-Fire clubs played a major part in the intended shock treatment. The most prominent one was founded that year by the new Lord Wharton (later elevated to duke). The club's dining menu included "Hell Fire Punch," "Holy Ghost Pie," "Devil's Loins," and "Breast of Venus" (garnished with cherries for nipples).[53]

Even in London, such open Satan-worshipping was a bit ahead of its time, and in 1721 a King's Order-in-Council was issued banning the Hell-Fire clubs—at least in such public forms.[54] But the Satanic notion, that there is no distinction between good and evil, continued to rule government policy, and was promulgated quite directly by George I's chief minister, Robert Walpole.[55] Increase Mather was entirely accurate, when in 1722 he charged James Franklin with promoting a "Hell-Fire Club" in Boston, for publishing the claim that man cannot distinguish between the work of God and the work of the Devil.

When Benjamin Franklin arrived in London, a most vital intelligence task would have been to dissect this new form of the beast: the politically powerful networks of the Hell-Fire Club. In 1723, Bernard Mandeville had delivered another shock, by publishing an expanded version of *The Fable of the Bees*, and riding roughshod over his remaining opposition.[56] Yet Franklin's *Autobiography* generally recounts this visit to London simply as the experiences of a young printer trying to make the best of a bad situation. Again, the exceptions to this portrayal confirm the actual nature of his mission. As an eighteen-year-old just arrived from America, supposedly without references or recommendations, he nonetheless "immediately got into work at Palmer's, then a famous printing house in Bartholomew Close, and here I continued near a year."[57]

Soon, he constructed a variant on his Silence Dogood deception, by forging a literary passport into the very center of the Hell-Fire circles.

The composition was entitled "A Dissertation on Liberty and Necessity, Pleasure and Pain." Misled scholars and willful slanderers of Franklin have frequently cited this piece, as supposed evidence of his anti-Christian "deism" and philosophical affinity for British, Benthamite liberalism. Such claims, of course, assume the reader's willingness to walk blindly off the precipice of a major contradiction, by ignoring Franklin's lifelong career of fostering the divine spark of human creativity. His civic and educational ventures, his scientific discoveries and inventions, and his republican dedication to freeing America from the diseased minds governing Britain, are thus portrayed as mere opportunism, backed by an amateur's run of luck. What Franklin's enemies really hate, as exemplified in British historical and fictional writings to this day, is that he repeatedly outwitted and outmaneuvered them, right through to the founding of the United States.

Even in this portion of the *Autobiography*, Franklin repudiated this "Dissertation" as an "erratum" in his life. The account also provides more than enough evidence to indicate why he wrote it. His first mention of it is followed by a paragraph stressing that, during this same period, he made "as much use . . . as I could" of an "immense collection of second-hand books" he was able to borrow from a next-door bookseller. The "poor ignorant boy" had extensive resources at hand to produce his forgery. While working at Palmer's, he "printed a small number" of the "little metaphysical piece." In the *Autobiography*, Franklin makes no mention of its contents.[58]

An examination of the "Dissertation" itself provides the next level of the evidence that it was written as a piece of intelligence-deception.   It was addressed to his young friend   James   Ralph,   one   of   Franklin's   "chief acquaintances" in Philadelphia.   Ralph had sailed with him to England, roomed with him in London, and presented himself as a "freethinking" poet and job-hunter to the Venetian circles in such professions as theater, journalism, and law.   The *Autobiography* reports, "Ralph and I were inseparable   companions."[59]   The   connection   further established Franklin's cover.   The "Dissertation," printed early in 1725, begins with the following address to Ralph:

> SIR, I have here, according to your Request, given you my *present* Thoughts of the *general State of Things* in the Universe.   Such as they are, you have them, and are welcome to 'em; and if they yield you any Pleasure or Satisfaction,   I   shall   think   my   Trouble sufficiently compensated.   I know my Scheme will be liable to many Objections from a less discerning Reader than your self; but it is not design'd for those who can't understand it [emphasis in original].[60]

Note Franklin's emphasis that these *present*, objectionable thoughts are designed for people who already think this way.   He   adds   with   delicate   irony,   "You   will   easily perceive what I design for Demonstration. . . ."[61]

Further evidence that Franklin faked the "Dissertation" to impress a particular circle, is provided by his extensive use of barbaric spellings and contractions, such as *'em, can't, tho'*, and *us'd*.   Jonathan Swift had launched a major campaign in 1711 against such degradation of the language, which the "modernists" of the Kit-Kat Club and similar Venetian agencies were deliberately trying to impose. None of Franklin's other writings indulges in such liberal abuse, nor was he ignorant of the issue involved.   In his

Pennsylvania Gazette, Franklin published a piece in 1733, "On Literary Style," in which he noted the "Observation of Dr. Swift, that modern writers injure the Smoothness of our Tongue, by omitting Vowels wherever it is possible . . . ."[62]

From the arguments of the "Dissertation" itself, the intended victims of the piece become indisputably clear. Presenting a manic orgy of circular logic and sophistry, Franklin "proves" that good and evil, pleasure and pain, and life and death are all the same thing:

> If [God] is all-powerful, there can be nothing either existing or acting in the Universe *against* or *without* his Consent; and what He consents to must be good, because He is good; therefore, *Evil* doth not exist . . . .
>
> If there is no such Thing as Free-Will in Creatures, there can be neither Merit nor Demerit in Creatures . . . .
>
> Evil is hereby excluded, with all Merit and Demerit; and likewise all preference in the Esteem of God, of one Part of the Creation to another . . . .
>
> Pleasure is consequently equal to Pain . . . . Life is not preferable to Insensibility; for Pleasure and Pain destroy one another: That Being which has ten Degrees of Pain subtracted from ten of Pleasure, has nothing remaining, and is upon an equality with that Being which is insensible of both . . . .
>
> Since every Action is the Effect of Self-Uneasiness, the Distinction of Virtue and Vice is excluded . . . .

> No State of Life can be happier than the
> present, because Pleasure and Pain are
> inseparable . . . .[63]

To a sane mind, such logic is a virtual parody of Satanic ideas. But to promoters of evil, the entire exercise would be undeniably appealing. Franklin concludes the "Dissertation":

> I am sensible that the Doctrine here advanc'd, if it were to be publish'd, would meet with but an indifferent Reception . . . . "What! Bring ourselves down to an Equality with the Beasts of the Field! With the *meanest part of the Creation! 'Tis insufferable!*" But, (*to use a Piece of common* Sense) our *Geese* are but *Geese* tho' we may think 'em *Swans*; and Truth will be Truth tho' it sometimes prove mortifying and distasteful.[64]

The gaggle of historians who have cited this pamphlet, as proof of Franklin's embracing British philosophical radicalism, have demonstrated that there are a lot of silly geese out there. Concerning Franklin's purpose at the time, his *Autobiography* confirms that the quacks of the Hell-Fire Club eagerly consumed the crumbs he had thrown them:

> My pamphlet by some means falling into the hands of one Lyons, a surgeon, author of a book entitled *The Infallibility of Human Judgment*, it occasioned an acquaintance between us; he took great notice of me, called on me often to converse on those subjects, carried me to the Horns, a pale ale house in ——Lane, Cheapside, and introduced me to Dr. Mandeville, author of *The Fable of the Bees*

who had a club there, of which he was the soul, being a most facetious, entertaining companion.[65]

In his next sentence, Franklin also provides a clue that he was fully aware of who controlled the pathetic Isaac Newton, the Venetian version of Aristotle. He reports that the same Mr. Lyons who brought him to Bernard Mandeville tried to arrange "an opportunity sometime or other of seeing Sir Isaac Newton, of which I was extremely desirous; but this never happened." [66]

Franklin's description of the remainder of his London stay does not mention how he may have followed up his successful penetration of the Hell-Fire Club—accomplished in early 1725. But a conversation he had, at his home near Paris in 1783, identifies the man who helped him through this dangerous venture. He was none other than Dr. Zabdiel Boylston, Cotton Mather's right-hand man in the smallpox inoculation fight. A prime target of Boston's Hell-Fire networks, Boylston was in London during 1724–1725, when he inoculated Princess Caroline, who had been tutored by Leibniz as a young girl. Boylston's grandnephew recorded his introduction to Franklin years later, in the presence of other company:

> [He] arose from his chair and took me by the hand, saying, "I shall ever revere the name of Boylston; Sir, are you of the family of Dr. Zabdiel Boylston of Boston?" to which I replied that he was my great uncle; "then, Sir, I must tell you I owe everything I now am to him." He went on giving this account of himself, viz.: "When Dr. Boylston was in England, I was there reduced to the greatest distress, a youth without money, friends or counsel. I applied in my extreme distress to

him, who supplied me with twenty guineas; and *relying, on his judgment, I visited him as opportunities offered*, and by his fatherly counsels and encouragements I was saved from the abyss of destruction which awaited me, and my future fortune was based upon his parental advice and timely assistance" [emphasis added].[67]

Just as the *Autobiography* omits Franklin's meeting with Mather in 1724, it makes no mention of his relationship with Boylston in London. When Franklin met Boylston's young kinsman in 1783, he was beginning to prepare his *Autobiography* for publication. Not surprisingly, with other guests present, Franklin maintained the self-portrayal of "a poor boy in distress," in recounting the London mission of his youth.

Franklin's Lessons from Swift

There is another, more important name that Franklin does not mention. That is Jonathan Swift, and again the omission is revealing. When Franklin arrived in London at the end of 1724, all Britain and Ireland were consumed in a political war that Swift had initiated that year, by striking in force against a weak flank of Walpole's Hell-Fire regime. Although the cabinet had been reshuffled in 1721, to Walpole's immediate advantage, there were still a few wild cards in the deck. One was Lord John Carteret, a friend of Swift, who became secretary of state, and resisted Walpole's scheme of governing by maximum corruption. To get rid of Carteret, somewhat in the manner of Russia's exiling political troublemakers to Siberia, Walpole had Carteret appointed lord lieutenant of Ireland, in early 1724.[68] Before Carteret arrived in Dublin, Swift had sprung the trap—and surfaced the republican movement he had been building in Ireland.

Walpole's standards of graft were anything but small change. Walpole's first government service dated back to the period when Godolphin and Marlborough ran Queen Anne's cabinet, while enlarging their personal wealth to monumental proportions. Walpole had been dismissed as treasurer of the Navy and sent to the Tower in 1711, when it was discovered that £35 million in naval expenditures were unaccounted for.[69] In 1722, now as lord treasurer and chief minister to George I, Walpole had arranged a modest piece of corruption in issuing a patent to foist £108,000 in cheap copper coinage on the people of Ireland. The King's mistress pocketed £10,000 in the deal, and an ironmonger, William Wood, who bought the patent, saw an easy £30,000 on the bottom line for himself. The sums were trifling in the scale of Walpole's swindles, but *the issue* proved big enough to rock his ministry for the first time.

Following a protest by the Irish parliament, which had not been consulted on the new coinage, Swift went into action. Under the pseudonym M.B. Drapier, and using the persona of a small shopkeeper, Swift published a series of letters to mobilize Ireland against Wood's halfpence. They were addressed to the shopkeepers, tradesmen, farmers, and common people of Ireland, to the nobility and gentry, and finally "to the whole people of Ireland." From the printing of the first Drapier Letter, in April 1724, Swift made it clear that he was calling forth a mass republican movement:

> I do most earnestly exhort you as men, as Christians, as parents, and as lovers of your country, to read this paper with the utmost attention, or get it read to you by others; which that you may do at the less expense, I have ordered the printer to sell it at the lowest rate . .
> . . It is your folly that you have no common or general interest in your view, not even the wisest among you, neither do you know or

inquire, or care who are your friends, or who are your enemies.

About four years ago a little book was written, to advise all people to wear the manufactures of this our own dear country [Swift's *Proposal for the Universal Use of Irish Manufacture*]. It had no other design, said nothing against the king or parliament, or any person whatsoever; yet the poor printer was prosecuted two years with the utmost violence . . . . This would be good enough to discourage any man from endeavouring to do you good, when you will either neglect him, or fly in his face for his pains; and when he must expect only danger to himself, and to be fined and imprisoned, perhaps to his ruin.

However, I cannot but warn you once more of the manifest destruction before your eyes, if you do not behave yourselves as you ought.[70]

Swift counted on generating a special kind of political shock wave. For centuries, the Irish had succumbed to one oppression after another. Miserable poverty had been accepted as a normal way of life. Restrictions on their trade, industry, and agriculture were designed to keep it that way. Their parliament had no power; all their country's laws were made in England. Titles and estates in Ireland were awarded in London, though seldom to Irishmen, and the recipients' hostility to the natives was frequently increased by the "second-prize" status of their grants. For the people of Ireland, the worst of all this was their sense of being ruled by an unseen hand, with no enemy to strike at. Thanks to the stupidity of Robert Walpole, Swift was able to transform this sense of futility into anger, and focus it with accelerating speed against a known target.

Walpole never anticipated what hit him. A man with a gargantuan appetite for corruption, Walpole would not have had a second thought about endorsing Wood's patent for Irish halfpence. Yet it was precisely the "small change" aspect of this piece of graft, which led to Walpole's defeat. The poorest Irishman might be indifferent to still another case of exploitation on a grand scale. It was another matter, however, to reduce the value of the coins he had, so that he could not even afford "a quart of twopenny ale." Swift's plan of attack exploited Walpole's blunder to the fullest.

In his first Drapier Letter, Swift introduced as the perpetrator, "one Mr. Wood, a mean ordinary man," already cut down to size. He then described the swindle, that "Mr. Wood made his halfpence of such base metal, and so much smaller than the English ones," that they were worth only one-twelfth their face value. How, Swift asked, could "such an ordinary fellow as this Mr. Wood" be granted such looting rights, when "all the nobility and gentry here could not obtain the same favour?" The answer he pointed to was the issue of sovereignty:

> Now I will make that matter very plain. We are
> at a great distance from the king's court, and
> have nobody there to solicit for us, although a
> great number of lords and squires, whose
> estates are here, and are our countrymen, spend
> all their lives and fortunes there.

Wood was "an Englishman" with "great friends," and knew where to place his bribes to gain the attention of the king. Ireland was in no position to oppose the King's authority as such, but Swift was not afraid to challenge "the great lord or lords who advised him." Thus he warned Walpole:

> I am sure if his Majesty knew that such a
> patent, if it should take effect according to the

> desire of Mr. Wood, would utterly ruin this
> kingdom, which hath given such great proofs of
> its loyalty, he would immediately recall it, and
> perhaps show his displeasure to somebody or
> other: but a word to the wise is enough.[71]

For his readers, Swift reviewed the currency laws, which required acceptance of only gold and silver coins, despite the customary use of lesser metals for the smallest denominations. Nothing in English law required the Irish to take Wood's "vile halfpence . . . by which you must lose almost eleven pence in every shilling."[72]

In this first letter, Jonathan Swift, the Dean of Dublin's St. Patrick's Cathedral, raised a voice the Irish people had seldom heard. His strategy was later adopted by American patriots preparing the War of Independence: if you are governed by a kingdom which claims it honors liberty, claim that liberty for yourselves. The Drapier's first assault appeared to have little significance.   History proved otherwise.

> Therefore, my friends, stand to it one and all:
> refuse this filthy trash. It is no treason to rebel
> against Mr. Wood . . . . [The] laws have not
> left it in the king's power to force us to take any
> coin but what is lawful, of right standard, gold
> and silver. Therefore you have nothing to
> fear.[73]

In his subsequent letters, Swift's exhortations became calculatingly more militant:

> I will shoot Mr. Wood and his deputies through
> the head, like highwaymen or housebreakers, if
> they dare to force one farthing of their coin
> upon me in the payment of an hundred pounds.

> It is no loss of honour to submit to the lion, but who, with the figure of a man, can think with patience of being devoured alive by a rat.[74]

Soon he was directly raising the issue of Ireland's freedom:

> Were not the people of Ireland born as free as those of England? How have they forfeited their freedom? Is not their Parliament as fair a representative of the people as that of England? . . . Are they not subjects of the same king? Does not the same sun shine upon them? And have they not the same God for their protector? Am I a freeman in England, and do I become a slave in six hours by crossing the channel?[75]

Swift's *Drapier Letters* rallied all parties, all faiths, all Ireland against Wood and Walpole. "The Irish decorated and thronged the streets when the 'Drapier Dean' rode into Dublin. They proposed tearing down the statues of 'military murderers' to erect statues of Swift, the saviour of their country."[76] With an unprecedented breadth of popular support, Swift proceeded to close the trap. Walpole's propaganda machine in England had outdone itself, first by lying that the Irish welcomed the flood of Wood's debased coins, and then by charging they were "grown ripe for Rebellion, and ready to shake off the Dependency of Ireland upon the Crown of England."[77] Then the "Imposter [Wood] and his Crew" committed a fatal blunder, by underestimating both Swift's political power and his friendship with Carteret, the new lord lieutenant of Ireland. In October 1724, one of the British propaganda sheets for Wood declared "that the Lord Lieutenant is ordered to come over immediately, to settle his Half-pence."[78]

Swift's fourth and final Drapier Letter, "to the whole People of Ireland," appeared on October 13, the day

Carteret landed. Hawkers were crying it through the streets when he arrived in Dublin. Concerning Carteret's reported intention to impose Wood's halfpence, the Drapier answered,

> I intreat you, my dear Countrymen, not to be under the least Concern, upon these and the like Rumours; which are no more than the last Howls of a Dog dissected alive, as I hope he hath sufficiently been.   These Calumnies are the only Reserve that is left him.[79]

Claims concerning Walpole's intentions, however, were treated with ironic care:

> In another paper of [Wood's] contriving, it is roundly expressed, that Mr. Walpole will cram his Brass down our Throats. Sometimes it is given out, that we must either take these Halfpence or eat our Brogues. And, in another News-Letter, but of Yesterday, we read, that the same great Man hath sworn to make us swallow his Coin in Fire-Balls . . . . What vile Words are these to put into the Mouth of a great Counsellor, in high Trust with his Majesty, and looked upon as a Prime Minister? If Mr. Wood hath no better a Manner of representing his Patrons; when I come to be a Great Man, he shall never be suffered to attend my Levee.[80]

Whatever the reports of British intentions, the Drapier emphasized, they were

> no Concern of ours. For, in this point, we have nothing to do with English Ministers . . . . The Remedy is wholly in your own Hands; and therefore I have digressed a little, in order to

refresh and continue that Spirit so seasonably
raised amongst you, and to let you see, that by
the Laws of GOD, of NATURE, of NATIONS,
and of your own COUNTRY, you ARE, and
OUGHT to be a FREE PEOPLE, as your
Brethren in England.[81]

Two weeks later, Carteret issued a proclamation offering
a reward of £300 to anyone who would reveal the Drapier's
identity within six months, "so as he be apprehended and
convicted thereby." The edict was purely a matter of form,
for consumption at court in London. Swift immediately
revealed himself, and continued to be the regular dinner
guest of Lord and Lady Carteret at Dublin Castle. Even an
Oxford edition of Swift's writings, published in the 1930s,
reports, "The Lord Lieutenant discreetly did nothing. To
arrest Swift would have been to get himself promptly
lynched by the mob."[82] The entire affair of Wood's
halfpence ended in a stinging defeat for Walpole. Carteret
remained lord lieutenant until 1730, when he returned to
England to work for the opposition to Walpole. In a letter
written in 1737, Carteret reported, "When people ask me
how I governed Ireland, I say that I pleased Dr. Swift."[83]

Poor Richard's Almanack

Benjamin Franklin's later writings, on behalf of
America's independence, extensively demonstrate his debt
to Swift. As early as the first *Poor Richard's Almanack*,
which Franklin printed for the year 1733, he honored Swift
in a special way. Employing the pseudonym Richard
Saunders, instead of Isaac Bickerstaff, Franklin introduced
his almanac by predicting the death of his rival
"astrologer." Poor Richard, who did "nothing but gaze at
the Stars," had decided to enter the almanac business. He
had foreseen that the leading almanacker at the time was

soon to be removed, since inexorable Death, who was never known to respect Merit, has already prepared the mortal Dart, the fatal Sister has already extended her destroying Shears, and that ingenious Man must soon be taken from us. He dies, by my Calculation made at his Request, on Oct. 17, 1733, 3 ho. 29 m. P.M . . . .[84]

Like Swift's *Bickerstaff Papers*, Franklin's early editions of *Poor Richard's Almanack* provided follow-up accounts concerning his prediction.

The importance Cotton Mather attached to Swift's *Bickerstaff Papers* has already been noted. The young Franklin, recruited to political intelligence work by Mather, must have studied the Drapier's war against Walpole's Hell-Fire regime with intense interest, to say the least. Franklin's opportunity to profile the networks of the Hell-Fire Club followed Swift's rout of the halfpence scheme. Wood's patent was revoked by the crown in 1725 in an effort to end the matter, although he was granted a "pension" of £36,000.[85] Franklin, "the poor ignorant boy," had by his own account a position of privileged access to the propaganda battles raging in London while he was there. Some time after deceiving the Hell-Fire Club with his "Dissertation," Franklin left Palmer's "to work at Watts's near Lincoln's Inn Fields, a still greater printing house. Here I continued all the rest of my stay in London."[86]

Franklin did not sail for America until late July 1726. In March of that year, Jonathan Swift arrived in London, to coordinate an expanded campaign against Walpole. His undertaking such a mission, as the confessed author of the Drapier Letters, is further proof of the power of the movement he had built. On April 27, Swift even met privately with Walpole, to press his case for Ireland. Their meeting settled nothing, Swift reported, for Walpole had "conceived opinions . . . which I could not reconcile to the notions I had of liberty . . . ."[87] Swift's correspondence from this period in England is full of references to his meetings and exchanges of letters with leading figures of the Walpole opposition.

Franklin's *Autobiography* offers a possible clue to his own connections to Swift's circles at this time. Among Swift's contacts in 1726 was Sir William Wyndham, an old acquaintance from the Queen Anne period. It was at Wyndham's London house, in June 1711, that some members and close associates of Queen Anne's anti-Marlborough government, formed a sort of private advisory body of "men of wit or men of interest." Swift was a charter member of the group, known as the Society, or the Brothers Club. Wyndham became secretary at war in 1712 and chancellor of the exchequer the next year. He was arrested briefly in 1715, during the Whig Junto's purge on behalf of George I. At the time Franklin was in London, Wyndham was the co-leader of the Walpole opposition in the House of Commons.[88]

At the very end of Franklin's stay, while he was making final arrangements to depart for America, he reports, "I was, to my surprise, sent for by a great man I knew only by name, a Sir William Wyndham, and I waited upon him." Wyndham supposedly wanted Franklin to teach his sons how to swim— a little-known talent at the time.[89] It is more likely that Wyndham had some instruction to offer Franklin, but given the care he exercised in his *Autobiography*, he offers no further account of this extraordinary meeting.

Benjamin Franklin sailed from Gravesend on July 23, 1726. He returned to Philadelphia, where he immediately began building a republican machine of his own. It would soon begin to mesh with Spotswood's ongoing drive from Virginia, to open the continent. There were no governors in place, however, to push the project forward. Even Keith had been ousted during Franklin's absence. There was still, however, another crucial flank to exploit, which the enemy had so far failed to comprehend. This was Virginia's Northern Neck Proprietary, which under Lord Thomas Fairfax played an indispensable role in the success of the American Revolution.

NOTES

1. Jesse Lemisch, ed., *Benjamin Franklin, The Autobiography and Other Writings* (New York, 1961), 21.

2. *Ibid.*

3. *Ibid.*, 24.

4. *Ibid.*, 22–23.

5. Franklin to Samuel Mather, May 12, 1784, in A.H. Smyth, ed., *The Writings of Benjamin Franklin* (New York, 1907), IX, 209.

6. Franklin, "Standing Queries for the Junto," in *Writings*, Lemisch, ed., 199–200; Mather, *Bonifacius*, 136–137.

7. Mather to Sir Peter King, December 22, 1714.

8. Cotton Mather, *Diary*, March 2, 1721.

9. *Ibid.*, March 3, March 11, May 13, 1721.

10. "Mirabilia Dei," printed the same year.

11. Cotton Mather to Thomas Hollis, Nov. 5, 1723, in *Diary*, same date.

12. *New England Courant*, No. 3, Aug. 14–21, 1721.

13. Cotton Mather, *Diary*, Nov. 13, 1721.

14. *New England Courant*, Nov. 13–20, 1721.

15. *Ibid.*, Jan. 1–8, 1722.

16. Boston *News-Letter*, Jan. 22–29, 1722.

17. Cotton Mather, *Diary*, Sept. 14, Oct. 12, and Nov. 24, 1721.

18. *Ibid.*, Nov. 30 and Dec. 1, 1721.

19. *Ibid.*, Jan. 15, 1722.

20. *Ibid.*, Jan. 1, 1722.

21. Franklin, *Autobiography*, 27.

22. Cotton Mather, *Diary*, Feb. 25–26, 1722.

23. Franklin, *Autobiography*, 32–33.

24. New England *Courant*, April 9–16, 1722.

25. *The Spectator*, No. 1, March 1, 1711.

26. Franklin, *Autobiography*, 33.

27. *Ibid.*, 33.

28. Cotton Mather, *Diary*, July 3, 1717.

29. Bernard Fäy, *Franklin, The Apostle of Modern Times* (Boston, 1929); Arthur B. Tourtellot, *Benjamin Franklin; The Shaping of Genius, The Boston Years* (New York, 1977).

30. *New England Courant*, May 14–21, 1722.

31. *Ibid.*

32. *Ibid.*, April 30, 1722.

33. *Ibid.*, August 13, 1722.

34. *Ibid.*, July 23, 1722.

35. Franklin, *Autobiography*, 34–35.

36. Donald McCormick, *The Hell-Fire Club* (London, 1958), 42.

37. Franklin, *Autobiography*, 35, 46.

38. *Ibid.*, 35.

39. *Ibid.*, 37–40.

40. *Ibid.*, 40.

41. *Ibid.*, 40–41.

42. *Ibid.*, 41–42.

43. *Ibid.*, 42.

44. *Ibid.*, 43.

45. *Ibid.*, 44.

46. Franklin to Samuel Mather, May 12, 1784, in Smyth, ed., *Writings of Franklin*, IX, 209.

47. Franklin, *Autobiography*, 46.

48. *Ibid.*, 48.

49. *Ibid.*, 52–53.

50. *Ibid.*, 53–55.

51. *Ibid.*, 55.

52. Dodson, *Spotswood*, 287.

53. Bernard Mandeville, *The Fable of the Bees, or Private Vices, Public Benefits* (London, 1934; reprint of 1714 ed.); McCormick, *Hell-Fire Club*, 23; Kramnick, *Bolingbroke*, 201–204.

54. McCormick, *Hell-Fire Club*, 29.

55. Kramnick, *Bolingbroke*, 74.

56. Mandeville, *Fable*, editor's introduction, 4.

57. Franklin, *Autobiography*, 56.

58. *Ibid.*, 56.

59. *Ibid.*, 50, 55–56.

60. Franklin, "A Dissertation on Liberty and Necessity, Pleasure and Pain," in *Writings*, Lemisch, ed., 321.

61. *Ibid.*

62. *Pennsylvania Gazette*, August 3, 1733.

63. Franklin, "Dissertation," 322–327.

64. *Ibid.*, 327.

65. Franklin, *Autobiography*, 56–57.

66. *Ibid.*, 57.

67. Quoted in P.M. Zall, ed., *Ben Franklin Laughing* (Berkeley, 1980), 161.

68. Van Doren, ed., *Portable Swift*, intro., 28.

69. Swift, *Journal to Stella*, I, 252, 252n.

70. Swift, "The Drapier's First Letter," in *Writings*, Landa, ed., 423–424.

71. *Ibid.*, 424–425.

72. *Ibid.*, 430.

73. *Ibid.*, 430.

74. Quoted in *Portable Swift*, Van Doren, ed., 28.

75. *Ibid.*, 29.

76. William Alfred Eddy, ed., *Satires and Personal Writings by Jonathan Swift* (London, 1932), 296.

77. Swift, "A Letter to the Whole People of Ireland," *ibid.*, 311–312, 298.

78. *Ibid.*, 298.

79. *Ibid.*

80. *Ibid.*, 315.

81. *Ibid.*, 310.

82. *Ibid.*, 296. On the Carterets' hospitality, Van Doren, ed., *Portable Swift*, intro., 30.

83. Quoted in Swift, *Poems*, Rogers, ed., 911.

84. *Poor Richard*, 1733, facsimile of original edition (Philadelphia, 1977).

85. *Portable Swift*, intro., 31.

86. Franklin, *Autobiography*, 58.

87. Swift to the Earl of Peterborough, April 28. 1726, *Correspondence*, Williams, ed., III, 132.

88. Swift, *Journal*, I, 293–294, 293n.; Swift to Alexander Pope and John Gay, October 15, 1726, *Correspondence*, III, 172–173, 173n.

89. Franklin, *Autobiography*, 63.

11

The Fairfax Secret

The significance of Virginia's Northern Neck proprietary is one of the most misrepresented and misunderstood aspects of America's colonial history. During the proprietorship of Lord Thomas Fairfax (1693–1781), it became the front line for America's breakthrough beyond the vast mountain barrier of the Appalachians and Alleghenies. Its strategic importance to America was recognized as early as the 1670s—but except to a few, that was not revealed for more than half a century. Without the fact that Lord Fairfax was a patron of George Washington, few works on American history would mention either the proprietor or the proprietary. Even when they do, they fail to report—or fail to discover—the two most important facts. The first is that establishing the full extent of the Northern Neck grant, was crucial to America's becoming a republic. The second is that Lord Fairfax, a British peer who chose permanent residence in Virginia, used his power to promote that result. Therein lies the secret.

During America's colonial period, a proprietorship differed from a royal colony, in that it was not directly governed by the crown. The disposition of the property involved was instead placed in the hands of a proprietor, who, like a feudal lord, exercised local rights to the renting and selling of land. Such domains were otherwise subject to laws enacted in London, to the extent they could be enforced. Under George I, both the Maryland and Pennsylvania colonies were still governed by proprietorships, though both generally became pawns, for a time, of Robert Walpole's "Hell-Fire" ministry. Royal governors ruled New England, where John Winthrop's

Massachusetts Bay Colony had once thrived as America's first republic.

Virginia, although a royal colony, remained a special case. Its governors were appointed by the Scottish Earl of Orkney, by a grant from Queen Anne, from 1707 until the Earl's death thirty years later. Such a unique arrangement had enabled Alexander Spotswood to serve as governor of Virginia from 1710 until 1722, until Walpole forced Orkney to replace him. There was a still more unusual aspect of the Virginia colony. During the reign of Charles II, all of the land between the Potomac and Rappahannock Rivers, known as the Northern Neck, had been granted by the King to Lord Culpeper, as a proprietorship within the royal colony. Virginia's civil and criminal procedures remained in force. But until the founding of the United States, land use and development policies for the Northern Neck were under authority of the *proprietor*, not the crown. The distinction proved a decisive advantage in paving the way to America's independence.

The Original Grant

There was no momentous significance, from any vantage point, to be read into the grant which established the Northern Neck Proprietary in 1649. Charles II awarded the grant while in exile in Paris, with no kingdom to command. His father, King Charles I, had been executed for treason on January 30 of that year, by order of Parliament. Charles I had lost political control of England to the forces of the English Commonwealth. His military counterattack had been crushed by the New Model Army, led by Oliver Cromwell and Lord Thomas Fairfax—the ancestor of the later proprietor of the Northern Neck. Following an orgy of corruption in England, directed by Venetian-Dutch financiers during the Cromwell Protectorate, Charles II gained the throne in 1660, after having been tutored in France by the bestial Thomas Hobbes.

The new King reconfirmed the Northern Neck grant to his loyal Culpepers. It was a paper fiefdom, which had not even been settled. Colonization in Virginia was still concentrated along the Tidewater areas of the James and York Rivers, converging upon the mouth of the Chesapeake Bay. The Culpeper grant was defined as the neck of land to the north, between the Potomac and the Rappahannock, from the Chesapeake shore to the "heads of the Rivers."[1] Charles II had no intention of allowing any real development in America, as he soon demonstrated by his attacks on New England's sovereign status. As the figure who once again imposed a monarchy on England, over the ruins of the Commonwealth, he generally had to pay for his friends. On immediate account, the Culpeper grant cost him nothing, yet earned the political dividend of support for his regime. Abstractly considered, the grant was generous enough, even though construed at the time as an undeveloped peninsula, between the navigable stretches of the Potomac and Rappahannock Rivers. Their inland reaches had not even been explored.

By the early 1670s, it became clear to some that the Northern Neck grant was of far greater dimensions than anyone had imagined. In 1668, the German geologist John Lederer's explorations for Virginia Governor Berkeley established that the Rappahannock River stretched much farther into the interior. Lederer also reported that these lands were extremely fertile—far more so than the increasingly depleted and preempted Tidewater area. In 1673, the grant's northern boundary was also discovered to extend dramatically farther west, when Augustine Hermann reported to Maryland's proprietor Lord Baltimore, that one branch of the Potomac River originated in the "mighty high and great mountains" beyond the Blue Ridge.[2] The

Northern Neck Proprietary was therefore a passageway to the West. Such news certainly reached New England's leaders, since Lederer proceeded to spend several years working for John Winthrop, Jr., the governor of Connecticut and a correspondent of Leibniz.

Lederer also found a pass through the Blue Ridge, and crossed into the Shenandoah Valley. His discovery of such vast, new prospects was hardly welcome among the great landowners of Tidewater Virginia. Lederer tried to demonstrate the feasibility of western development by leading a company of "gentlemen" on a similar expedition. They turned back, and abandoned him even before they reached the mountains, then falsely reported him dead, and upon Lederer's return declared that he was lying in reporting a passage to the West. Soon, a blunter message was delivered by the enemies of America's hopes for westward expansion. In 1676, under sponsorship of William Byrd I, Bacon's Rebellion in Virginia fomented Indian warfare throughout the interior, and culminated in Bacon's "democratic" mob burning down the capital city of Jamestown. At the same time, unprecedented Indian warfare laid waste to much of New England, until the tribes under the Indian chief "King Philip" were defeated by the army of John Winthrop's New England Confederation. The barbaric Indian attacks during King Philip's War were coordinated by Sir Edmund Andros, then Charles II's royal governor of New York.[3]

The Virginia events were well-known to the 18th-century Lord Fairfax who became proprietor of the Northern Neck. His father's cousin, Colonel Thomas Fairfax, was named deputy governor to Sir William Berkeley in September 1676, during the height of Bacon's Rebellion. His grandfather, 2nd Lord Culpeper, was appointed governor of Virginia when Berkeley died, soon after the rebellion had been put down. Despite Bacon's defeat, his terrorist onslaught had taken its toll.   John Washington, the great-grandfather of America's first President, was among those who refused to join Bacon's self-proclaimed new government.   In retaliation, Bacon's rebels looted and vandalized his home.   More damaging was the greater restraint now placed on Virginia's settling any lands beyond the Tidewater, as a result of Bacon's having inflamed the colony's Indian friends and foes alike.   The bright prospect of opening new territories for colonization had been nearly extinguished, and was not rekindled until Alexander Spotswood took charge in 1710.

A Momentous Amendment

The potential expanse of the Northern Neck grant was not entirely forgotten.   The 2nd Lord Culpeper maneuvered to acquire the entire proprietary for himself.   In 1688, when his patent from Charles II was about to expire, he sought its renewal from James II, the successor whose throne was about to topple under the invasion of the Dutch Prince William of Orange.   On September 27, just three months before James II fled the country, he awarded the Northern Neck as a permanent, hereditary grant to Lord Culpeper.[4] The circumstances were not unlike those of Charles II's original patent.   Nor did the new grant differ in any apparent respect, except for its being made perpetual. Since James II had no foreseeable future as King, that alteration could hardly have troubled him.

Three little words, seemingly innocuous, had also been inserted to the text of the document.   The boundaries of the original grant were defined by the Rappahannock and Potomac to the "heads of the Rivers."   The new patent described it as their *"first heads or springs."*[5]   The slight change in wording would have seemed meaningless in London.   In Virginia, however, the amendment proved to be the basis for incorporating a vast new territory, stretching beyond the Blue Ridge Mountains, into the Northern Neck Proprietary—once Alexander Spotswood and his circle went to work on it.

There are some additional, intriguing circumstances surrounding the revised grant. During the period Lord Culpeper was seeking its renewal in 1688, Increase Mather, New England's political leader, was also in London. He arrived at the end of May, to negotiate the restoration of the Massachusetts Bay Charter, revoked by Charles II in 1684. Should that fail (as it did), he was prepared to draft a new charter securing as much self-government for the colony as he could. He was granted an audience with King James, almost immediately upon his arrival, and met with William Penn, the proprietor of the new Pennsylvania colony, later the same day. Penn had some influence at court, and promoted Mather's efforts behind the scenes, while meeting regularly with him to consider strategies and evaluate their progress.

Mather's political maneuvering in London proceeded from consideration of the American colonial situation as a whole. Even his dealings with the Quaker proprietor of Pennsylvania demonstrate that conclusively. Three consecutive entries in Mather's daily log of his activities are especially suggestive. On June 18, 1688, he met with Penn at Whitehall to review the situation at court with regard to New England, now ruled by royal governor Sir Edmund Andros. Penn discussed possible measures against Andros "which would settle his nose." The next day, Penn reported that "things should be done for N. E. [New England] to content, that Nicholson should be removed." Francis Nicholson, later the butt of Robert Hunter's satirical play *Androboros*, was at this time lieutenant to Governor Andros, assigned to administer the New York colony. In his next entry, for June 20, Mather cites another exchange at Whitehall, bearing on Virginia: "Discourse with my Lord Culpeper."[6]

Three months later, Culpeper was awarded proprietorship to Virginia's Northern Neck, with the crucial addition "to the first heads or springs" in the description of the grant. The security of his claim was soon in doubt, however, for in late December James II fled from the invasion of England by William of Orange, who then seized the throne. Increase Mather remained in London, awaiting a new round of bargaining with King William, while exploiting this violent disruption of political authority to strengthen his hand. In April 1689, his son, Cotton Mather, directed a bloodless coup in Boston against Governor Andros. In New York, Leisler's Rebellion overthrew Governor Nicholson. The future course of Virginia was soon altered by a remarkable sequence of events.

In 1690, Lord Culpeper died, leaving five-sixths of his Northern Neck grant to his daughter Catherine, his only child, and one-sixth to his widow Lady Margaret. Later that year, Thomas, 5th Lord Fairfax, the grandson of the commander of the Commonwealth's New Model Army, married Catherine Culpeper. King William sustained the Culpeper grant to the Northern Neck Proprietary in 1692, and confirmed the title to Catherine's share to her husband.[7] Lord Fairfax's service during the Glorious Revolution left the King little choice. He had been second in command of the Yorkshire cavalry, which secured the north of England for the invader, and was elected to the Parliamentary Convention which ratified William's claim to the throne. He was also a lieutenant in the Life Guards, the elite unit assigned to the personal protection of the King.[8] But King William and his Venetian-Dutch bankrollers had no interest in developing Virginia. That same year the King appointed Sir Edmund Andros governor of Virginia.

The Young Lord Fairfax

Thomas, 6th Lord Fairfax, was born October 22, 1693, at the family seat at Leeds Castle in England. Like much of the landed aristocracy, the Fairfax family's financial position steadily declined as the speculators and "monied men" behind the Bank of England seized control of the economy. The Fairfax farms in England were operating at a loss, and their Virginia proprietary was too undeveloped to generate any significant income. Thomas Fairfax did not grow up expecting to inherit great wealth. Upon his father's death, the major item left to him was a mass of debts.

He was only sixteen when his father died in January 1710, leaving his five-sixths share of the Northern Neck to his widow, who then willed it in trust to her son. The holder of the remaining one-sixth interest, Lord Culpeper's widow, also died that same year, leaving her share to her grandson, the new Lord Fairfax.[9] The young Fairfax had in effect become the sole proprietor of the Northern Neck at a momentous time, for in 1710 Jonathan Swift helped launch a broad offensive to break the Marlborough cabal's stranglehold on Britain, and Alexander Spotswood became governor of Virginia.

There are a number of indications that Thomas Fairfax was soon influenced by Swift and his circles. The same month his father died, Fairfax was enrolled at Oxford's Oriel College, where the provost was an old acquaintance of Lady Fairfax, and also a relative by marriage. Another relation, one of his closest friends, was already attending the same college. During the period Fairfax studied at Oxford, until July 1713, Swift was the most controversial writer of the day, whose political polemics rocked Britain on a regular basis. But Fairfax appears to have had greater involvement in these matters than most of his fellow students. His older friend wrote to him during a college break in 1712, when Fairfax was about to pay a visit, urging that he bring "if possible, Dr. Swift's *Tale of a Tub*."[10]

An English traveler to America, who visited Fairfax in Virginia during the French and Indian War, reports that at Oxford, Lord Fairfax was "highly esteemed . . . for his learning and accomplishments," and that "his judgment upon literary subjects was then, and at other times, frequently appealed to; and he was one of the writers of that incomparable work, *The Spectator*."[11] The *Spectator* was the weekly journal of London's literary "wits," and Swift was a frequent contributor.[12] Another intriguing note comes from a later Virginia historian, William Meade (1789–1862), who grew up on his father's farm adjoining Lord Fairfax's home in the Shenandoah Valley, Greenway Court. Meade reports that when Fairfax moved to London in 1715, he frequented the coffee houses and became "a member of the club of which Addison was the head."[13] Swift and Addison had formerly been close friends, until Addison continued as a Whig propagandist against Harley. In 1715, Addison became secretary of state for a brief term. Swift had returned to Ireland the previous year, following Queen Anne's death.

These few clues to Fairfax's early life provide no proof of his outlook during that period. They do establish, however, that Swift was no stranger to him politically—and that he was directly involved with the same circles. Fairfax was nominally a Whig—a label once worn both by Swift and Harley. His mother had supported the Whigs, which perhaps secured Lord Fairfax's appointment to a minor post on King George's palace staff in 1715, in the office of the Treasurer of the King's Household.[14] That a peer of the realm was assigned such an obscure position, is a strong indication that he was not favored by the Whig Junto lords.

More significant is the fact that Fairfax soon became known as an *anti-Walpole* Whig, aligned against the apostle of corruption who brought his "Hell-Fire" ministry to power in 1721. Walpole's political coup immediately resulted in the removal of Fairfax from his post in the King's household. As the Fairfax heir, descendant of several English military leaders, Lord Thomas then obtained a commission as Cornet in the Royal Regiment of Horse Guards, the "Oxford Blues." The commander was a leading Walpole opponent, Charles, Marquess of Winchester. Fairfax later honored him in naming Winchester, Virginia, the Shenandoah Valley base for George Washington's expeditions to the Ohio country.

The Virginia career of Lord Fairfax, as a proprietor of the Northern Neck, establishes beyond any doubt his support for America's republican cause. Subsequent portions of this history will demonstrate that, but it is useful in this section to look ahead to one particular piece of evidence. Following the death of Lord Fairfax at his Virginia home, not long after the British army laid down its guns at Yorktown in 1781, an inventory was taken of his library at Greenway Court. One entry stands out, by far the largest for any single author: "13 vols. Swift's *Works*."[15]

The Fight for Control of the Northern Neck

Lord Fairfax did not set foot in Virginia until 1735, and the full extent of his proprietary claim was not confirmed by the British crown until 1745. No bullets were fired, no armies engaged, yet the fight over the Northern Neck was a crucial, preliminary battle of the American Revolution. At command levels, both sides knew the potential stakes involved in the Fairfax grant, long before Fairfax came to Virginia. Once Alexander Spotswood became governor in 1710, the issue began to be one of practical significance.

Virginia's Northern Neck Proprietary

The Northern Neck grant, dating back to Charles II, was the only proprietary within Virginia. As such, its land policies and settlement rights were not dictated by the crown, but were under the authority of the proprietor. The distinction proved crucial to preserving a staging ground for westward development, especially after Robert Walpole's "Hell-Fire" ministry took command of Britain's Hanoverian monarchy in 1721. In 1722, Walpole forced the removal of Queen Anne's appointee, Alexander Spotswood, from the governorship of Virginia. The Northern Neck Proprietary then became the key to continuing Spotwood's efforts to break the coastal containment of the American colonies. The original grant described the neck of land between the Potomac and Rappahannock Rivers, from their "heads" to the Chesapeake Bay. In 1688, a slight change in the wording of the claim, to "the first heads or springs," extended the Northern Neck Proprietary beyond the Blue Ridge and deep into the Allegheny Mountains, incorporating the entire shaded area on the map. Spotswood himself helped ensure this expansion of Lord Fairfax's claim, by establishing the Rapidan as the main fork of the Rappahannock River. Note that the grant's southern boundary is flanked by both Spotswood's Germanna settlement and Swift Run Gap. The northern boundary, to the headspring of the Potomac, was surveyed in 1736 by political allies of Spotswood. The contested Fairfax claim was not finally confirmed until 1746, by King George II. Soon it became George Washington's passage to the Ohio country, and the staging ground for western colonization.

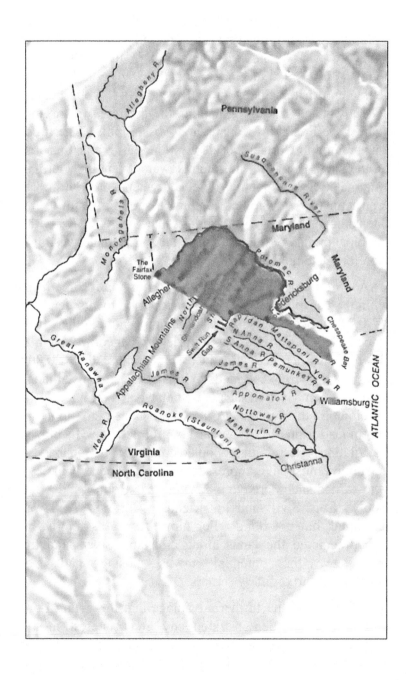

An expedition in 1706 had charted the Shenandoah, from its northern junction with the Potomac, down the valley to what is now Edinburg, more than fifty miles south. In 1709, Queen Anne authorized establishing a settlement on the Shenandoah River, as a "public benefit and advantage by strengthening the frontier of Virginia against the French of Canada and Mississippi." The order was granted to Christopher de Graffenreid, to resettle some of the victims of Marlborough's wars from the German Palatinate. The project was blocked when Lord Baltimore, proprietor of the Maryland colony, asserted a claim to the Shenandoah Valley, by arguing that its river was the principal branch of the Potomac, and that the land west of it therefore belonged to him.[16]

A more immediate threat to the Fairfax grant came from within. The previous Lord Fairfax, prior to his death in 1710, had been persuaded to appoint none other than Robert "King" Carter as the proprietary's agent in Virginia. By 1712, Carter had already assigned more than 20,000 acres of Northern Neck lands to himself. Using his alliance with William Byrd II against Spotswood's programs for developing the colony, Carter proceeded to loot an enormous fortune from the Fairfax proprietary. His brazen speculation, fraudulent bookkeeping, and unabashed corruption must have impressed even Sir Robert Walpole—who earned such derisive nicknames as "Robin" and "Bob Booty" from Swift and his friends. Carter's greed was unlimited, but not blind. For himself and his family, he also preempted the lands along navigable rivers and the best sites for potential towns—closing paths of development to ordinary settlers.

Carter had the further advantage that the young Lord Fairfax had not demonstrated any great interest in the Northern Neck Proprietary, even for personal gain. On that score, of course, Carter's falsified reports would have given him little encouragement. In 1722, the year Spotswood was removed by Robert Walpole from the governorship of Virginia, Carter again became agent for the Northern Neck, and took a ten-year lease on the proprietary as well. In 1723, he inserted a clause giving him full authority over issuing grants of land. True to form, Carter made sure that the bulk of applications for title were his own.

Spotwood's 1722 Treaty of Albany had removed the Indian threat to Virginia's western frontiers, including the uninhabited lands toward the Blue Ridge and beyond. "King" Carter lost no time in seizing these newly opened tracts for himself. In 1724 alone, he claimed 89,937 acres, adding extensively to his control of the interior. Many thousand more acres on the frontier were granted to Tidewater planters and speculators with no intention of developing the land. The net revenue that year to Lord Fairfax was £300.[17]

Even while Spotswood held the governorship, there was nothing he could do to prevent the feudalist looting of the Northern Neck Proprietary. That power lay in Lord Fairfax's hands, and he did not exercise it until 1734, when he named his cousin William as proprietary agent. By that time, without Spotswood's earlier accomplishments in fostering Virginia's republican potential, the Northern Neck's significance for America's future would already have been lost.

From the moment he took office in Williamsburg, it is clear that Spotswood understood the importance of designating the "first heads or springs" of the Potomac and Rappahannock rivers, as the boundaries of the Fairfax proprietary. Maryland had claimed in 1709 that the Shenandoah was the source of the Potomac, despite the findings of Hermann's 1673 expedition, commissioned by Lord Baltimore himself. Refuting the Maryland claim awaited full exploration of the western source of the Potomac, high in the Allegheny Mountains. But that remained impractical until Spotswood's 1722 treaty with the Iroquois Five Nations, by which they pledged to confine their sometimes violent excursions to territory north of the Potomac River. Extending settlements that far west depended on reversing "King" Carter's policies as agent for the Northern Neck. During the 1730s, Spotswood played a major role in resolving that issue as well; but during his governorship, he ensured the potential of the Fairfax proprietary where he could—on its southern flank, to the head spring of the Rappahannock River.

Spotswood's bold program for Virginia had been centered from the outset on opening the West. Prior to 1714, Jonathan Swift's role, in freeing Queen Anne from the grip of the Marlboroughs, enabled Spotswood to attack Virginia's feudalist aristocracy on all fronts. When the pressures of Marlborough's planned coup became intense, in early 1714, Spotswood moved to secure a crucial flank in the continuing battle. With help from Baron de Graffenreid, whom he had rescued from the Tuscaroras in 1711, he established his fortified settlement of German miners at Germanna, on the south bank of the Rapidan River. Explorations by Spotswood and his rangers had confirmed that the Rapidan, the south branch of the Rappahannock fork above what is now Fredericksburg, was in fact the principal source of the Rappahannock River. Originating in the Conway River beside the Blue Ridge Mountains, the Rapidan would extend the Northern Neck's lower boundary much further south and west, than the line formed by the Rappahannock's north fork. When finally confirmed, in 1745, the Rapidan boundary added 900 square miles to the Fairfax grant.[18]

During the long dispute over the land between the forks, neither officials of the crown, nor agents for the proprietor, could legitimately grant tracts in the area. Especially after Spotswood's removal from the governorship, that constraint had the beneficial effect of preventing "King" Carter from feudalizing the area south of the Rappahannock, during his second scandalous administration of the Fairfax proprietary, from 1722 to 1732. Spotswood, meanwhile, respected the Rapidan boundary line and built a powerful base for development below it. At Swift Run Gap, where Spotswood led his expedition over the Blue Ridge mountains in 1716, his rangers had found the nearest pass south of the Rapidan line. With his formation of Spotsylvania County in 1720, reaching through the gap to the Shenandoah Valley, he accelerated frontier settlement over a huge area west and south of Germanna.

The Spotsylvania Flank

Alexander Spotswood soon proved as dangerous to his enemies as a private citizen, as he had been as governor of Virginia. He turned Spotsylvania County into America's leading model for rapid development of the wilderness. Proceeding under his earlier reforms in land policy, and the tax incentives in his bill establishing the county in 1720, he demonstrated America's potential for growth to an unprecedented degree. In doing so, he gave inspiration to generations which followed him, and set the terms for the policies Lord Fairfax adopted in Virginia.

Following Spotswood's mission across the "Euphrates" in 1716, his supporters had helped him establish a 15,000 acre iron-mining tract at Germanna, which in 1723 became the county seat for Spotsylvania. To prevent the Carters, Byrds, and Ludwells from buying up the county as their wilderness preserve, Spotswood used his last months in office to protect this new frontier against the uncertain future. Between May 8 and July 27, 1722, he issued patents for new land holdings in Spotsylvania totaling nearly 179,000 acres. Included in these were nearly 60,000 acres Spotswood acquired for himself, in trust or through intermediaries. His policy for his own holdings was the same he had promoted for the colony—populate, cultivate, and move west. By 1725, fifty-seven large farms had been established on Spotswood's lands, by settlers with long-term leases. Throughout his holdings, his improvements on the land exceeded the requirements he had set as governor by seventy-five percent.[19]

Spotswood's personal enterprise continued to focus on iron manufacturing until his death in 1740. Faced with British restraints on colonial manufacturing of finished goods, he never matched the automated, water-powered complex of blast furnace, rolling mill, and slitting mill, that John Winthrop, Jr., had established during the 1640s in republican Massachusetts. But the air furnace Spotswood introduced provided cast iron for a variety of uses in Virginia and other American colonies.[20] Continuing this example, young George Washington later built some of the earliest iron forges and bloomeries west of the Blue Ridge, on lands of the Fairfax proprietary.

The growth of Spotsylvania was phenomenal. Virtually an uninhabited wilderness before Spotswood's policies took effect, the new county soon had more acres under patent than any other county in Virginia. Before its western division to form Orange County, Spotsylvania generated one-sixth of the quitrents for the entire colony.[21] By 1726, the county had also developed a militia of nearly 300 soldiers, plus a cavalry unit of seventy-five men.[22] The initial surge was stimulated by Governor Spotswood's ten-year exemption from quitrents for new settlers. William Byrd and his crew quickly realized, that removing Spotswood from office, had not extinguished his dream of developing the continent.

By the spring of 1723, Walpole's agents, including the puppet Governor Drysdale, challenged Spotswood's title to all of his new holdings in Spotsylvania. Orders were also issued to limit further land grants and quitrent exemptions in the county. With the backing of the Council, Virginia's deputy auditor Nathaniel Harrison (a Walpole appointee) declared that no one holding more than 1,000 acres could claim exemption. The Council prohibited legal surveys for any larger claims, past or future. Byrd's old crony John Grymes, Walpole's receiver general, next persuaded Drysdale to argue that all existing claims over 1,000 acres in Spotsylvania were invalid. In other parts of Virginia, Drysdale at this time was awarding grants of more than 10,000 acres, without much scruple over whether the holder even met requirements for improving the land. The Council adopted the Grymes proposal, which would have wiped out Spotswood's holdings in the new county, and many others as well. All of these measures, however, applied only to the new frontier counties established by Spotswood in 1720— Spotsylvania and Brunswick. Even the Council thought it best to refer such extraordinary notions to the British Board of Trade, before attempting to enforce them.[23]

Spotswood took his own case to London in 1724, the same year the young Benjamin Franklin arrived there on an undercover mission, designed by Cotton Mather and Pennsylvania's Governor William Keith, Spotswood's close ally. It was the year of Swift's *Drapier Letters*, when the Walpole ministry first rocked under the impact of Swift's new republican force in Ireland. Spotswood's own counterattack, on Walpole's machinations in Virginia, was of a Swiftian character:

> And to deprive a Man of his Possessions, after he has bore the Brunt of the Danger, & maintained them 'til the Terror of the Indians is

over; after he had Expended thereon more than double their prime Value; after he has cleared Roads & Bridges, Set up Mills, drove out Stocks of Cattle, transported Household Goods, removed Families of Women and Children [to Spotsylvania], with all the Necessaries of Life to support People in the wild Woods; & in short, after he has passed through the immense Troubles, Fatigues, Dangers, & Expenses, which are inseparable from new Settlements in America, whenever they are made at any distance from the Seated part of the Country: to Dispossess him then of his Lands, for a mere Chicane in Words, & to transfer his Improvements to Others, who never had the Courage or Industry, to gain an Acre of Land out of the Woods, where there was either Danger or Difficulty; would be such an Oppressive Act & cruel Proceeding, as would in no wise resemble Royal Justice.[24]

Such an appeal could not reach King George I directly; he did not even speak English. "Royal justice" was an uncertain prospect at best; but Swift had demonstrated that Robert Walpole, chief minister for the King, could be kicked effectively, when bent in the proper fashion.

Swift Strikes Again

During 1726 and 1727, Jonathan Swift undertook two missions to England, to build a political opposition designed to overthrow Robert Walpole's Hell-Fire regime. Although he failed in that objective as such, he sufficiently destabilized the Walpole government to take advantage of two key developments, thereby achieving some tactical victories which aided America's cause. The first was the death of King George I in 1727, which forced Walpole to defend his position under siege. The second was the bitter conflict between King George II and his heir, Frederick, Prince of Wales, which enabled the Walpole opposition to function in part under the banner of the House of Hanover. The resulting factional situation was complicated enough so that Walpole could never be sure he held all the keys to the kingdom, though he remained at the head of the cabinet until 1742.

Swift's "Drapier" campaign against Walpole had become the most celebrated feud of the time, and Swift did little to downplay it. In late 1725, he wrote to Alexander Pope, "I am no more angry with [Walpole] than I was with the kite that last week flew away with one of my chickens, and yet I was pleased when one of my servants shot him two days later."[25] But it was a broader offensive, centered in cultural warfare, that Swift prepared on his first mission to England, from March to August of 1726.

He met again with old acquaintances from the days of Queen Anne—the Earl of Peterborough, John Gay, John Arbuthnot, and Lord Bolingbroke. Bolingbroke had just returned from exile in France, and his country house at Dawley quickly became a gathering place for Swift's old associates from the Scriblerus Club, as well as younger politicians in Walpole's parliamentary opposition.[26] After several months in London, Swift moved to the country in May, spending most of the next two months at the home of Alexander Pope, "or rambling with him and Mr. Gay for a Fortnight together," during which he also visited the Earl of Bathurst, a leader of the Walpole opposition in the House of Lords.[27] In August, Swift concluded his tour by returning to London, to work with John Gay, and set out for Ireland again on the fifteenth of the month.[28] He left behind a large manuscript, for a London printer, which became the opening salvo of his new offensive.

That salvo was fired on October 28, 1726, with the publication of *Travels into Several Remote Nations of the World*, under the pseudonym Lemuel Gulliver. Since known as *Gulliver's Travels*, it was Swift's most far-reaching analysis of the degenerate axioms, destructive superstitions, and cultish ideologies then engulfing European civilization. With biting satire and profound irony, he fought the stupefied notions of readers great and small, generating that special laughter that comes with newly found insight, upon recognizing old foolishness in the mirror. The weapon was humor, forged by Socratic method. His targets appeared in a variety of contemporary modes—Cartesian physics, Newtonian mathematics, Lockean psychology, Venetian economics—exposed not by name, but by nature.

Gulliver's Travels was no mere political broadside. After all, Swift's enemies could generally identify an idea only by the label. Such nominalism, among both oppressors and victims, is attacked throughout the book. A useful sample can be found in Swift's description of the Grand Academy of Lagado's school of language. Three professors were at work on

> a scheme for entirely abolishing all words whatsoever; and this was urged as a great advantage in point of health as well as brevity. For it is plain, that every word we speak is in some degree a diminution of our lungs by corrosion, and consequently contributes to the shortening of our lives. An expedient was therefore offered, that since words are only names for *things*, it would be more convenient for all men to carry about them such *things* as were necessary to express the particular business they are to discourse on. And this invention would certainly have taken place, to

the great ease as well as health of the subject, if the women in conjunction with the vulgar and illiterate had not threatened to raise a rebellion, unless they might be allowed the liberty to speak with their tongues, after the manner of their forefathers; such constant irreconcilable enemies to science are the common people. However, many of the most learned and wise adhere to the new scheme of expressing themselves by *things*, which hath only this inconvenience attending it, that if a man's business be very great, and of various kinds, he must be obliged in proportion to carry a greater bundle of *things* upon his back, unless he can afford one or two strong servants to attend him. I have often beheld two of those sages almost sinking under the weight of their packs, like pedlars among us; who when they met in the streets would lay down their loads, open their sacks and hold conversation for an hour together; then put up their implements, help each other to resume their burthens, and take their leave.

But for short conversations a man may carry implements in his pockets and under his arms, enough to supply him, and in his house he cannot be at a loss; therefore the room where company meet who practise this art is full of all *things* ready at hand, requisite to furnish matter for this kind of artificial converse.[29]

Soon all of Britain was buzzing about the foibles and follies of yahoos, Lilliputians, and Houyhnhnms. Political and literary journals were filled with speculations over the possible identities of the peoples and personages in

Gulliver's Travels.   Swift's authorship was soon generally discovered, but Walpole's circles failed to realize how thoroughly his brush had tarred them, until they read about it in the opposition press. They soon perceived, however, that they were under coordinated attack. Six weeks after publication of Swift's work, a new opposition paper appeared—*The Craftsman*, headed by Bolingbroke, which applied the lessons of *Gulliver's Travels* to the state of affairs under Walpole.   Immediately following Swift's return to England in April 1727, Gay published his satirical *Fables*, a collection of verse attacking tyranny, sycophancy, and greed in both court and "administration."

At the same time, Swift added "a letter from Capt. Gulliver" to a new edition of his book, with the jibe that not one of the "abuses and corruptions" had been eliminated among the yahoos during the six months which had elapsed. He complained that his publisher had yet to report that

> party and faction were extinguished; judges learned and upright; pleaders honest and modest, with some tincture of common sense; and Smithfield blazing with pyramids of law-books; the young nobility's education entirely changed; the physicians banished; the female yahoos abounding in virtue, honour, truth, and good sense; courts and levees of great ministers thoroughly weeded and swept; wit, merit and learning rewarded; all disgracers of the press in prose and verse condemned to eat nothing but their own cotton, and quench their thirst with their own ink.[30]

Swift himself was soon under fire, and Walpole's agents began tracking his every move. On May 13 he wrote to his Irish friend Thomas Sheridan,

This goes by a private Hand, for my Writing is
too much known, and my Letters have been
stopt and open'd . . . . We are here in a
strange Situation; a firm, settled Resolution to
assault the present Administration, and break it
if possible. It is certain that *W- - - - [Walpole]*
is Peevish and Disconcerted. . . .

That same week, Swift had two private audiences "by her
own Commands" with Princess Caroline, Leibniz's former
but not very wise pupil.[31] She was shortly to become
Queen. King George I, during one of his many trips to
Hanover, died of an apoplectic fit on June 3, 1727; and
Caroline's husband succeeded to the throne, as George II.

For a few short weeks, expectations ran high that
George II would name a replacement for Robert Walpole.
But the master of corruption had a legion of thieves behind
him, who valued friends in high places. Queen Caroline
herself assented to Walpole's continuance as chief minister,
and George II reversed his earlier inclination to get rid of
him. Swift was disgusted by this display of how far
English politics had sunk into depravity. Echoing the
words of David in the Old Testament, he wrote a poem
emphasizing that "we should put no trust in princes."[32] In
America, and especially in Massachusetts, that same
warning was issued repeatedly concerning the House of
Hanover, until the American Revolution removed any need
for further discussion.[33]

Swift returned to Ireland in September, but he was not
through with Walpole. He had encouraged his close friend
John Gay, who had worked with the composer Handel in
London as far back as 1712, to prepare an opera in the form
of "a Newgate pastoral." The result was *The Beggar's*
Opera, which transposed the criminal doings of the
Walpole regime to their proper setting—the world of

cutthroats, prostitutes, blackmailers, and highwaymen, who moved in and out of London's Newgate Prison. Gay's production consisted of comic dialogue, interspersed with English and Scottish ballads, for which he wrote new lyrics to suit the occasion. Several were set to music previously composed by Handel; and one of Handel's students, Johann Christoph Pepusch, composed the overture and provided the bass counterpoint for the popular airs adapted by Gay. From its premiere on January 24, 1728, *The Beggar's Opera* began a record-setting run as the hottest ticket in town. From Dublin, Swift soon provided a most favorable review, in his newly established paper, *The Intelligencer*:

> In this happy Performance of Mr. GAY's, all the Characters are just, and none of them carried beyond Nature, or hardly beyond Practice. It discovers the whole System of that Common-Wealth, or that *Imperium in Imperio* of Iniquity, established among us, by which neither our Lives, nor our Properties are secure, either in the Highways, or in publick Assemblies, or even in our own Houses. It shows the miserable Lives and the constant Fate of those abandoned Wretches; for how little they sell their Lives and Souls; betrayed by their *Whores*, their *Comrades*, and the *Receivers* and *Purchasers* of these Thefts and Robberies . . . . [The] Author takes Occasion of comparing those *common Robbers of the Publick*, and their several Stratagems of betraying, undermining and hanging each other, to the several Arts of *Politicians* in Times of Corruption.[34]

With uproarious laughter, night after night, London audiences delighted in Gay's portrayal of Walpole's gang, done as a composite drawing of the chief minister himself. There was Macheath, given like Walpole to gentlemanly pretensions and sexual infidelities—the leader of a band of highwaymen. And Peachum, a receiver of stolen goods —"for 'tis but fitting that we should protect and encourage cheats, since we live by them." And his "brother" Lockit, who runs Newgate Prison as a free-enterprise zone, charging increased fees for more "comfortable" chains. One of the thieves is introduced as "Robin of Bagshot, alias Gorgon, alias Bluff Bob, alias Carbuncle, alias Bob Booty."

The Beggar's Opera created such a sensation that even King George II's chief minister, alias Robert Walpole, could not stay away. At one point in Act II, he must have wished he had. During a scene in Newgate Prison, Peachum complains that the government debt has reached a level which threatens his usual income for delivering fellow thieves to the hangman: "Can it be expected that we should hang our acquaintance for nothing, when our betters will hardly save theirs without being paid for it?" Peachum underscores his point, by noting that "like great statesmen, we encourage those who betray their friends." Lockit nervously asks him "to be more guarded" in his language, and sings

> When you censure the age,
> Be cautious and sage,
> Lest the courtiers offended should be;
> If you mention vice or bribe,
> 'Tis so pat to all the tribe,
> Each cries, "That was leveled at me."

The entire audience then turned to Walpole and broke out laughing.[35]

Walpole did not take ridicule graciously. When Gay announced later the same year that he had written a sequel to *The Beggar's Opera*, Walpole banned its production on the stage.   It was entitled *Polly*, and the plot included the deaths of both Peachum and Macheath.

A Renewed American Campaign

Jonathan Swift's 1724–1728 campaign against Robert Walpole put "Bob Booty" under sufficient strain to open some significant breaks.   Perhaps the most important beneficiary was Alexander Spotswood, who remained in London throughout this period.

Soon after his arrival from Virginia in 1724, Spotswood was married for the first time, to Anne Butler Brayne, goddaughter of the Duke of Ormond.[36]   A former lord lieutenant of Ireland, Ormond had been appointed in 1711 by Queen Anne, to replace the Duke of Marlborough as captain-general of the British army.   He was ordered to impose a cease-fire in Europe, to ensure the 1713 Peace of Utrecht.   For this "crime," he was dismissed by George I in 1714 and charged with treason.   He was very close to Swift, who admired him above all others in Queen Anne's government.   Ormond joined the Scottish rebellion of 1715, and afterward lived in exile in France until his death in 1745.   It is not presently known whether Swift, during his 1726 and 1727 missions to England, met with Spotswood —though their common associations and purposes would make that very likely.   One thing is virtually certain: Spotswood, a lover of theater who brought plays to Williamsburg, must have thoroughly enjoyed *The Beggar's Opera*.

Documentary evidence does establish, that Spotswood's repeated efforts to confirm his land holdings and exemptions, got nowhere until May 1727—at the height of Swift's campaign to oust Walpole.   The Board of Trade then ruled in Spotswood's favor, and advised the crown of its recommendation.   The board noted that Spotswood had personally recruited more than 300 immigrants to Virginia, and that his improvements on his lands entitled him to much larger holdings under Virginia law. Two months later, the matter was referred to a committee of the newly crowned King George II's Privy Council. Following Walpole's retention as prime minister, the council committee delayed further action until December 1728— the month that laughingstock Walpole banned John Gay's *Polly* from the stage. The committee then endorsed Spotswood's claims, with minor qualifications. George II finally signed an order to that effect in February 1729.[37]

Spotswood's operational base on the Virginia frontier was thus secured. During these protracted negotiations in London, Spotswood had also been seeking a new official position—one of crucial importance for coordinating colonial plans for western development. A little more than a year later, he got it: the appointment as "Postmaster General of His Majesty's province in North America," from which he could build and direct the only regular system of communication among the colonies. In effect, the position also made Spotswood the chief of America's intelligence service. Sworn in on August 4, 1730, he established new headquarters, which he called New Post, near the Rappahannock River below Fredericksburg, Virginia.[38] By 1732, he had invigorated a moribund postal system, extending it for the first time south of Philadelphia, as far as Williamsburg.[39]

The exact circumstances of Spotswood's appointment are not clear. A clue may lie in the undertakings of his Virginia allies at the time. As soon as word of the death of George I reached Williamsburg in 1727, the Virginia assembly passed a bill authorizing the creation of a new town in Spotsylvania, below the falls of the Rappahannock River. It was named Fredericksburg for Frederick Louis, the heir to the new King George II. Frederick was much at odds with his father's politics, and remained in Hanover for more than two years after his father's coronation. The King ordered him to stay out of Britain, although by protocol of the Act of Settlement, he should have been quickly confirmed as the Prince of Wales. Unannounced and uninvited, Frederick finally stormed into his father's court in London to claim his rights, late in 1729. Such a public conflict inside the royal family had readily drawn the attention of Walpole's opposition. For Virginia to honor the dissident Prince so quickly, however, was a word of caution which even Walpole could hear.

Fredericksburg was actually Virginia's first attempt at city planning. Its boundaries, streets, and lots were designed and surveyed before any development of the tract. The surveyor was George Hume, a protégé and distant relation of Spotswood, who later instructed the young George Washington in the art of surveying. At the age of seventeen, George Hume had taken part in the 1715 Scottish rebellion against George I. Spared execution because of his age, he was released from prison in 1721 and allowed to emigrate to Virginia. His uncle, Francis Hume, preceded him, having been deported to Virginia in 1716, apparently through the intervention of the Earl of Orkney. Francis Hume is said to have been one of the Knights of the Golden Horseshoe, who accompanied Spotswood across the Blue Ridge in the fall of 1716.[40]

The site chosen for Fredericksburg was a mile below the falls of the Rappahannock. It was designed as an inland river port, to supply the westward thrust of settlement in Spotsylvania County. The sense of purpose associated with the building of the new town had a definite and long-term effect. Fredericksburg became the leading point of socialization for much of Virginia's leadership in the American Revolution— including Commander-in-Chief George Washington.

In Philadelphia, another crucial undertaking was begun during Swift's campaign against Walpole. In the fall of 1727, Benjamin Franklin founded his own republican organizing committee, along the lines of Cotton Mather's earlier model in Boston.[41] He described it as a "club for mutual improvement," and ironically named it "the Junto." With less than a dozen young men from among his "ingenious acquaintance," Franklin generated a citizens' movement which soon made Philadelphia a model of cultural and scientific progress in America. The club reproduced republican leaders for nearly forty years, and from its beginning "was the best school of philosophy and politics that then existed in the province."[42]

Franklin soon lost the mentor of his youth. Cotton Mather died in February 1728, having lived to see this new endeavor by the finest student of his *Essays to Do Good.* As New England buried the last great leader of its Puritan republic, Franklin knew the torch had been passed to him.

The responsibility might have seemed overwhelming to Franklin, especially since he was still struggling to establish himself in Pennsylvania. He was a son of Massachusetts, which then had the most literate population in the world, and the only system of public education. Yet even in Philadelphia, "so few were the readers at that time" that Franklin could only find fifty people, "mostly young tradesmen," to subscribe to a circulating library. It was the first in America—organized in 1731 as a project of the Junto. The idea soon spread through the colonies, and Franklin later noted with satisfaction,

> our people, having no public amusements to divert their attention from study, became better acquainted with books, and in a few years were observed by strangers to be better instructed and more intelligent than people of the same rank generally are in other countries.[43]

Despite the Walpole regime's celebration of evil, Franklin pursued his task with dedicated cultural optimism. In 1731, he wrote a memorandum outlining his political course—a paper he still carried with him in 1784. His critique of the general conduct of politics echoed Swift, in language reminiscent of Mather. He noted that parties become their own interest, and within them "each man has his particular private interest in view." Consequently, Franklin observed, "few men in public affairs act from a mere view of the good of the country," and "fewer still . . . act with a view to the good of mankind." Franklin turned his thoughts to "*a great and extensive project*" to correct the problem:

> There seems to me at present to be great occasion for raising a united party for virtue, by forming the virtuous and good men of all nations into a regular body, to be governed by suitable good and wise rules, which good and wise men may probably be more unanimous in their obedience to than common people are to common laws. I at present think that whoever attempts this aright and is well qualified, cannot fail of pleasing God and of meeting with success.[44]

Franklin followed the advice he had received from Cotton Mather during their last meeting in 1724. He often pursued his efforts to do good behind the scenes, and through the work of others, instead of putting his projects forward only under his own name. Franklin's Philadelphia Junto "had from the beginning made it a rule to keep our institution a secret," and to limit its membership to twelve.[45] Once this leadership for "a party of virtue" was consolidated, Franklin directed each member "to form a subordinate club . . . without informing them of the connection with the Junto."

The fact of having to adopt such procedures, reflects the tyrannical nature of the policies Britain had already imposed on the colonies. The Junto's organizing for public improvements— libraries, fire departments, better education, paved streets, street cleaning, and police protection—were 'subversive' assertions of *citizenship*, by people who were supposed to be His Majesty's *subjects*. There was nothing more political than attempting to do good—as Mather had certainly discovered during the smallpox epidemic in Boston.

Franklin proposed creating a network of clubs under the Junto, to promote

> the improvement of so many more young citizens by the use of our institutions; our better acquaintance with the general sentiments of the population. . .; and the increase of our influence in public affairs and our power of doing good by spreading through the several clubs the sentiments of the Junto.[46]

When he launched *Poor Richard's Almanack* in 1733, his imitation of Swift's *Bickerstaff Papers* was a message which must have attracted some attention. Yet by then, any opposition had to confront the fact that it was dealing not merely with a man, but an emerging political force. In 1736, Franklin was elected clerk of the Pennsylvania General Assembly, a valuable position from which to determine new undertakings.

The following year, "Col. Spotswood, late Governor of Virginia, and then Postmaster-General," appointed Franklin postmaster of Philadelphia, which improved his position to "great advantage."[47] From Boston to Williamsburg, the potential for coordinating a republican movement was becoming a reality. What was still required was a concrete strategy, against British opposition, for colonizing the vast territories beyond the mountains.

Fairfax Joins the Fight

Virginia's land claims west of the Blue Ridge mountains remained the most practical approach to the Ohio country. Pennsylvania had barely begun to develop its interior, and William Penn's proprietary heirs had placed their short-term, mercenary interests before any consideration of the colony's future. The Virginia case was still complicated, however, by unresolved disputes over the Northern Neck claims of Lord Thomas Fairfax. The most crucial issue was determining the western source of the Potomac, upon which the entire Fairfax claim west of the Shenandoah River depended. Development of the Shenandoah Valley was the precondition for moving further west. The northern stretches of the valley afforded the most direct access to the rivers feeding into the Ohio, and constituted the only possible base of supply at the time.

In 1730, a Swiss group, headed by Jacob Stauber (or Stover) and Johann Ochs, petitioned the crown to establish a new colony on the western side of the valley—on lands claimed by the Fairfax proprietary. In September of the same year, "King" Carter illegally preempted more than 50,000 acres of prime tracts for development in the Shenandoah, under his self-augmented powers as agent for the Northern Neck. It would have been a reasonable suspicion, that attempts were under way to shut the door that Spotswood had opened to the West. The Swiss petitioners even proposed that the administration, legal system, and education in the new colony be conducted exclusively in German—and all under a Swiss governor to be confirmed by George II.[48]

Any skepticism regarding the Swiss proposal had nothing to do with the fact they did not speak English. As colonial governors, Spotswood, Robert Hunter, and William Keith had all recruited German-speaking immigrants. Stauber and Ochs, however, were requesting that a strategic approach to the West—incorporating lands owned either by Virginia or by Lord Fairfax—be placed under a new colonial jurisdiction. This new colony, moreover, would be financed and controlled by Swiss, who had already become notorious as willing agents of the financial powers of Venice. In Virginia, it was probably no secret that one of Ochs' promoters was also Spotswood's old enemy, William Byrd II.[49] The most conclusive grounds for alarm were that the proposal was given serious consideration in London. The monarchy had always opposed America's westward development—except during the second half of Queen Anne's reign.

The Swiss petition triggered a remarkable series of events, which brought Lord Fairfax into active contention for his proprietary rights for the first time. Most intriguingly, the affair involved both Spotswood and Keith, who had been reunited in London before the end of Spotswood's stay in England. By May 1731, Keith managed to become a sponsor of the Stauber-Ochs proposal. As an embittered ex-governor of the Penn proprietary, he must have appeared a useful advocate to the Swiss negotiators, who planned to violate some proprietary rights themselves. Step by step, however, he turned their petition into a proposal for a new English-speaking colony, to be governed by Alexander Spotswood!

First Keith recommended to the Board of Trade that all official business be conducted in English, and that "a free school be supported at the public Expence for teaching to read and write English." The "public school Master" and all those involved in "transacting Public Business [should] be named and appointed by the Governor." In August, Stauber and Ochs signed Keith's petition to the King for a colonial grant "to the Westward of the great Ridge of Mountains back of Virginia," to be placed under "an English Government." The new colony in America would "secure and defend all the British Colonies already planted there," and would "be called the Province of Georgia, or such other name as Your Majesty shall think fit . . . ." In a separate petition to the Board of Trade at the end of August, Stauber and Ochs presented a formal demand that their Swiss colonists be naturalized with the rights of Englishmen, yet under a government "administered in German," by a governor chosen from their own nominees.

Keith countered with his own petition to the board on August 30, urging that a "fit person with proper Authorities" be appointed to issue any land grants in the new colony, to "Foreigners as well as others." He made two more, significant recommendations:

> That as the person so appointed must be Invested with the Necessary Powers of Government and directing the first settlement of so Important a Colony, He ought to be a Man of Experience, in Military as well as Civil, affairs, possessed of a character in all Respects Equal to the Trust and likeways upon the spot to Execute it with Effect.   That Colonel Spotswood, whose present situation in Virginia is in a Manner contiguous to the proposed settlement, seems to be of all others the fittest person to be Employed by His Majesty in that Service.   But this Gentleman's Integrity and great abilities are so well known to your Lordships, That I am sensible His Character with the Board can Receive no Addition by any Applause of mine.

Having made this proposal to again put Spotswood in command of America's great western project, Keith withdrew from the negotiations.[50]

The Swiss petitioners attempted several further maneuvers, but soon found they had been outflanked on both sides of their position. The first setback was on the Spotswood issue. Keith's proposal was not frivolous, and Postmaster General Spotswood was again a significant public figure. Yet the Walpole regime, not to mention the Swiss, could hardly be expected to endorse such a plan. The second was on the Fairfax claim—a confrontation the Swiss provoked themselves, with a petition Ochs presented to the board two months later, on October 28, arguing that "Lord Fairfax's grant is to go no further than to Shanantoe [Shenandoah] River."[51] On December 9, the Board of Trade heard from Lord Thomas Fairfax, who formally challenged the Ochs petition, as the proprietor of Virginia's Northern Neck.[52]

The Swiss proposal soon died quietly. George II did act on one minor aspect of the affair. In 1732, he authorized the formation of a new American colony, not beyond the mountains, but on the southern Atlantic seaboard. He named it Georgia, and converted it into a penal colony for British convicts.

The defeat of the Stauber-Ochs scheme may well have involved some private collaboration between Fairfax and Spotswood, with Keith taking the public role. Spotswood certainly aided Fairfax in Virginia, during 1735–1737, in confirming the maximum extent of the Northern Neck Proprietary. Keith dedicated his 1738 map of Virginia, published in his history of the colony, "to the Right Honorable Thomas Lord Fairfax"—and provided a glowing account of Spotswood's governorship as well.[53] In any case, Lord Fairfax now began publicly to assert his proprietary interests, with particular attention to the dispute over his western claims.

"King" Carter's terms as agent and lessee of the Northern Neck expired in 1732. Fortunately, Carter himself expired shortly thereafter. To his derisive nickname, a popular ditty soon added an epitaph:

> Here lies Robin, but not Robin Hood,
>
> Here lies Robin that never was good,
>
> Here lies Robin that God has forsaken,
>
> Here lies Robin the Devil has taken.[54]

Largely through robbing the Fairfax proprietary, Carter had amassed roughly 300,000 acres of land in Virginia. At the time of his death, he held £10,000 in cash and 1,000 slaves —not counting the booty already distributed to other members of his family. Lord Fairfax prevented further looting by Carter's heirs, by suspending issue of any new grants in the Northern Neck. He also petitioned the King's Privy Council as a peer of the realm, requesting an official survey to "settle the marks and boundaries" of his proprietary claim.

After consulting the Board of Trade, the Privy Council issued an order on November 29, 1733, that the issue be settled by survey, to be jointly conducted by representatives of Lord Fairfax and the colony of Virginia.[55]

Fairfax now moved to ensure he would have a loyal agent in Virginia to represent the proprietary. There are intriguing circumstances surrounding this aspect of the story as well. William Fairfax (1691–1757), the proprietor's first cousin and close friend since childhood, had seen duty in the army, navy, and colonial service under Queen Anne. His career in public life ended temporarily in 1717, after George I had taken power in Britain. In 1725, William Fairfax was appointed Collector of His Majesty's Customs for the ports of Salem and Marblehead, Massachusetts. Following his wife's death in 1731, he married a twenty-three-year-old widow, Deborah Clark, whose former husband's family included a prominent Salem minister, well known to Cotton Mather. (Another member of the Clark family, who died in infancy in 1747, was christened Deborah Franklin Fairfax Clark.)[56] In 1734, Lord Fairfax persuaded his cousin William to become his agent for the Northern Neck. Bryan Fairfax, Lord Thomas's former guardian, was one of George II's Commissioners of the Customs at that time. He arranged to have William reassigned as Collector of Customs for the South Potomac district—the settled portion of the Northern Neck Proprietary.[57]

The strategic potential of the Fairfax grant was finally in friendly hands. "Robin" Walpole apparently preferred to gamble against a member of the House of Lords, rather than confront Spotswood's forces directly. Politically, Lord Fairfax was also a British domestic consideration. Within his county of Kent, he had used his influence against Walpole's party for years.[58] Whatever calculations Walpole may have made, he soon found that Spotswood still had the upper hand in Virginia. The Fairfaxes had also hidden their first move.

When William Fairfax arrived in the Northern Neck, his appointment as proprietary agent was still a secret. To official knowledge, he was simply the new customs collector for the South Potomac, reporting to Commissioner Bryan Fairfax in London. His undercover assignment was to gather political intelligence concerning the Fairfax grant, which posed the difficulty of making "proper inquiries without giving suspicion."[59] Beyond discovering the "exorbitant" extent of Carter's defrauding the proprietary, William Fairfax learned that "vast tracts of land . . . towards the first springs of Potomac" were being granted by agents of Pennsylvania. He urged "a scrutiny and search after the utmost limits" of the Fairfax claim.[60]

Lord Fairfax sailed for Virginia in March 1735, arriving in May to set foot in the Northern Neck for the first time. During that rainy spring and summer, he stayed with his cousin William's family at a rented house in Westmoreland County, near the broad stretches of the Potomac approaching Chesapeake Bay. The location was just above the Washington family's Northern Neck plantation, which was situated along the river near Pope's Creek. The Washingtons had lived there since 1662, when John Washington established one of Virginia's northernmost settlements at the time, more than fifty miles above the colonized area between the York and James rivers.

When Lord Fairfax visited in 1735, the head of the family was Augustine Washington (1694–1743), whose son George was then three years old. Augustine was already involved in a significant way with Alexander Spotswood's policy of westward development. In 1727, the same year as the founding of Fredericksburg, he began producing iron on his lands along Accokeek Run in Stafford County—within the Northern Neck grant, eight miles northeast of Fredericksburg. (At about the same time, another furnace went into operation at a newly established mining community at Fredericksville, in Spotsylvania County south of Fredericksburg.)[61]   During the next several generations, no family was closer to the Washington family than the Spotswoods. Yet even before their paths joined in the field of ironmaking, Alexander Spotswood had taken notice of the Washingtons. As governor, he had nominated another John Washington for sheriff of Stafford County in 1717—and did so again in 1718 (when he also nominated Thomas Jefferson, grandfather of the President, as sheriff for Henrico County).[62]

The Confrontation in Virginia

The arrival of Lord Fairfax signaled a renewal of political warfare in Virginia, over the issue of colonization beyond the Appalachian mountain barrier. Spotswood's return in 1730, as postmaster general for the American colonies, must have caused some alarm among his old enemies. But the lord proprietor's personal assertion of his western claims was a more tangible threat, to the Tidewater feudalists who believed they again had a stranglehold on Virginia's future. The danger was clear. If Virginians in the Northern Neck had the freedom to develop new settlements in the West, how could the rest of the colony be restrained?

William Byrd II was already worried. In September 1732, he had bestirred himself to journey on horseback to Spotswood's home at Germanna. He planned to try out the role of a genial old acquaintance, in order to profile Spotswood's current activities, especially concerning his iron industry. En route to Germanna, Byrd may have anticipated an unhappy ending to his plot. He stopped at Tuckahoe, the home of Thomas Randolph on the James River, about thirty-five miles northwest of Byrd's Westover estate. Heavy rains delayed him there another day. To pass the time, his host and another guest produced a copy of *The Beggar's Opera*, and they all read the parts aloud. Gay's brilliant satire was obviously a hit on the Virginia frontier, as it had been in London. Byrd noted in his journal of the trip, "This was not owing altogether to the wit or humor that sparkled in it, but to some political reflections that seemed to hit the [Walpole] ministry."[63]

By the time he reached Germanna, Byrd had recast himself as an admiring toady—so much so that he sustained the part in the record he made in his journal. He arrived in the afternoon at "Col. Spotswood's enchanted castle"—the large frame house on a brick foundation which he had built for his wife and children. "In the evening the noble Colonel came home from his mines"; and the next morning Byrd told him "that besides the pleasure of paying him a visit, I came to be instructed by so great a master in the mystery of making of iron, wherein he had led the way. . . ." Spotswood acknowledged that his iron works had inspired other colonies to expand and improve their own production. In the case of Pennsylvania, he noted,

> they have so few ships to carry their iron to Great Britain, that they must be content to make it only for their own use, and must be obliged to manufacture it when they have done. That he hoped he had done the country very great service by setting so good an example. That the four furnaces now at work in Virginia circulated a great sum of money for provisions and all other necessaries in the adjacent counties. That they took off a great number of hands from planting tobacco. . . .

Byrd learned that Spotswood had opened a new mine "thirteen miles below Germanna"—near the present town of Mine Run in Spotsylvania County. He was transporting the ore ("which was very rich") to a new furnace he had built at Massaponax, below Fredericksburg, about fifteen miles to the east. There Spotswood had perfected America's first air furnace, which would enable him "to furnish the whole country with all sorts of cast iron, as cheap and as good as ever came from England."[64] Adding to Byrd's discomfort, Spotswood conducted him on a tour of his various mines and furnaces, after which Byrd made his own inspection of Fredericksburg, the emerging supply base for the next phase of pushing West. Byrd had certainly seen enough to know, that were Lord Fairfax to follow Spotswood's course, the Tidewater oligarchy would be in serious trouble.

That anxiety among Byrd's circle rose considerably once Fairfax was in Virginia. The Northern Neck proprietor waited five months, before making his first appearance in the colonial capital at Williamsburg. The delay provided him with ample opportunity to do some profiling of his own. Since Spotswood's removal from the governorship in 1722, corruption in high office had again become the rule in Virginia. Members of the Council, in 1735, by royal appointment, included William Byrd, John Grymes, and John Carter (the principal heir of the late, unlamented "King" Carter). William Gooch, governor since 1727, had already disposed of approximately 300,000 acres within the Fairfax claim, through land grants issued without any authority.[65]

Accompanied by his cousin William, Lord Fairfax finally made his way to Williamsburg in October. Titled visitors were rare enough, but his plain clothing apparently caused as great a sensation. He stopped to pay his respects to Governor Gooch, who now occupied the magnificent official residence designed by Spotswood. Not long thereafter, pleasantries gave way to business, when Lord Fairfax delivered the Privy Council's order of November 29, 1733, to resolve the disputed boundaries of the Fairfax claim. Although the Privy Council had specified that any surveys be directed by commissioners representing both sides, Lord Fairfax offered to leave the matter in the hands of any three commissioners named by the governor, so long as they were members of the Virginia Council.[66] Such a move by Fairfax was probably designed to convey his confidence, that any survey would have to reflect where the rivers actually flowed, rather than where others might wish they did. His tactic also put responsibility for initiating any confrontation squarely upon the Council.

Whatever Fairfax's expectations were, the Council immediately showed its hand. Upon receiving the proprietor's offer on December 9, Gooch and the gang rushed through their appointments of the survey commissioners. Topping the list was none other than William Byrd, followed by his old crony John Grymes, Walpole's receiver general for Virginia.[67] To present at least the veneer of impartiality, they awarded the third position to John Robinson, an ally of Spotswood. As governor, Spotswood had first nominated Robinson to the Council in 1716, during his attempt to reverse Byrd's majority control. In 1720, Spotswood succeeded in appointing Robinson to the Council, to fill the vacancy resulting from the death of his oldest friend in Virginia, William Cocke.[68]

Winter had already set in, and there would be no surveys attempted before the spring. Fairfax returned to William's home near the Potomac. During the fall, their Washington family neighbors had moved further up the Potomac, to establish a new home near Little Hunting Creek. It later became famous as George Washington's Mount Vernon.[69] The move may have been undertaken in conjunction with Lord Fairfax's push for his western claims. Certainly it came at a time when Byrd's circle was nervous about any westward motion.

Governor Gooch even paid Fairfax a personal visit that winter, to argue that the Northern Neck grant should "be construed to extend no higher than the falls" of the Rappahannock and Potomac rivers![70] Under that interpretation, the western boundary of the Fairfax proprietary would run from just above Fredericksburg, to a point on the Potomac about ten miles above today's Washington, D. C. Gooch had no serious grounds for expecting Fairfax to accept such a proposal—which would have terminated the proprietary well before the Blue Ridge Mountains. But the governor had been sent to roll back the western borders as far as he could manage. His alternative contention was that the limits of the Fairfax grant were the *forks* of the boundary rivers, "especially [the forks) of the Potomac, the main branches whereof are called Shenandoah and Cohongarooton."

Strategically, this offer was not much better than the first. A line from the fork of the Rappahannock, just west of the falls above Fredericksburg, to the junction of the Potomac and Shenandoah, would entirely exclude the Shenandoah Valley, and all of the proprietary claims to the Piedmont east of the Blue Ridge—except at the northern end, opposite today's Harpers Ferry, West Virginia. Since 1688, by royal grant, the Northern Neck proprietor had claims to the "first heads or springs" of the Rappahannock and Potomac. Lord Fairfax observed that it was a "mystery" to him, how Gooch could argue the limits to be either their falls or forks.[71] The "Cohongarooton," moreover, was plainly the western reaches of the Potomac itself, flowing down from the Allegheny Mountains. Fairfax stated his case to the governor, and awaited the survey, to begin in the spring of 1736.

Warm days and spring blossoms generally grace Virginia before the end of March, yet no surveying parties had set out by late April. Gooch and Byrd were stalling in Williamsburg. On April 22, Lord Fairfax dispatched his cousin William with instructions "to move the Governor for orders that the commissioners begin the survey." The proprietor himself set out two days later "towards the mountains," to make his own inspection of the upper Shenandoah and the "Cohongarooton." He assured the early pioneers of the Shenandoah Valley that he "wanted to have the country settled." He would not contest any grants Gooch had issued in the crown's name, prior to October 1735, provided they had been "surveyed in an honest and equitable manner." Fairfax also informed them that he "would not have any poor man quit the place for want of land." Such an unheard-of policy quickly attracted attention, and Fairfax soon learned that a number of "gentlemen of fortune" were circulating petitions in the Valley against his claim.[72]

Before he could explore the western Potomac, Fairfax also learned that the colonial government had still done nothing to begin the survey. In the middle of May, he returned to William Fairfax's temporary home, where his cousin informed him that for "unanswerable reasons," the commissioners had decided to wait until September, as the "properest season." The Council also threw up roadblocks, delaying until August 11 its approval of instructions for the surveyors. Then Lord Fairfax was asked to sign a paper, binding him to accept the commissioners' findings on all matters concerning the grant, including the interpretation of its limits. Fairfax was not about to allow Byrd's crew to assume such powers. In a written reply to Gooch, Fairfax noted that "the main dispute is . . . what is meant and understood to be the first heads or springs of the two rivers Rappahannock and Potomac." The proprietor insisted that it "seems most equitable to have the case determined by His Majesty in Council, before whom the case may be fairly argued on both sides." Fairfax had no objection to a geographic survey of the rivers and their sources, but he declared he would not give any "other or fuller power to any commissioners."[73]

The issue was now fully joined. Byrd's forces were still committed to stopping westward development, even if that meant cheating a lord proprietor out of his royal grant. A sycophant like Byrd would only have undertaken such highhanded measures against a British lord, if he were assured of powerful support from the Walpole government. Such assurance clearly extended to Governor Gooch and the Council as a whole. They unanimously replied to

Fairfax's refusal to sign over complete jurisdiction, by declaring that since his proposal gave "no authority . . . to mark and settle the . . . boundaries," it "ought not to be accepted or executed by His Majesty's commissioners."[74] The forces behind William Byrd had plainly stated their position. They had no interest in any survey to determine the actual extent of the Fairfax grant. They simply wanted to prevent its reaching beyond the mountains.

There was a weakness in Byrd's position, however, which Fairfax had learned enough to exploit. The King's Order-in-Council, after all, had mandated that both sides— the colony and the proprietor—name the commissioners to resolve the disputes. To force a survey, Fairfax now named his own commissioners, headed by William Fairfax. On September 25, 1736, both sides met at Fredericksburg to hammer out terms for proceeding. Byrd still tried to claim authority to determine the Northern Neck boundaries, but finally conceded "to drive the nail that would go," when the Fairfax commissioners again refused.[75] It was agreed that the surveys of both the Rappahannock and Potomac rivers would begin on September 29. Both sides were empowered only to make a fact-finding report, and the Potomac surveyors were directed to trace its source beyond the junction with the Shenandoah, to its first head or spring.[76]

Against his opposition in Virginia, Lord Fairfax had attained an important victory. His primary objective at this stage was to obtain a legal survey of the sources of the boundary rivers, regardless of who the commissioners were. The most telling evidence would be the natural dictates of the rivers themselves; and those would be ascertained by licensed surveyors, not by commissioners. In Virginia, surveyors had to be certified for competence by the College of William and Mary. Many of them had been trained and licensed during the governorship of Alexander

Spotswood, the leading geometer and mathematician in the colony. Even the commissioners for the King had to select a number of surveyors who were associated with Spotswood.

For the Potomac survey, they named Robert Brooke, one of Spotswood's "Knights of the Golden Horseshoe." The Rapidan, the south branch of the Rappahannock, was strictly Spotswood territory. To determine whether the Rapidan could claim the headspring, the surveyors named by the colony were John Graham (or Graeme) and George Hume. Graham was Spotswood's cousin, an astronomer whom Spotswood had left in charge of his ironworks at Germanna during his absence in London. George Hume was the protégé of Spotswood who had been the surveyor for the founding of Fredericksburg in 1727.[77] On October 2, William Fairfax, Byrd, and the other commissioners spent the night at Spotswood's Germanna home, where the former governor regaled them with war stories from the days when he had fought in Europe.[78]

The Rappahannock survey went swiftly enough, but the team following the upper Potomac repeatedly haggled and broke down over various difficulties along the way. Lord Fairfax complained that the colony's commissioners were the cause of the delays. Not until the summer of 1737 did they meet in Williamsburg to approve a map based on the surveys.

Byrd's group still insisted on labeling the Potomac west of the Shenandoah River the "Cohongarooton," thus leaving three million acres in dispute. Fairfax concluded he would have to return to London to break the stalemate. He decided not to submit his own commissioners' report to the governor, and "very privately" embarked on a ship in the Rappahannock, bound for England. He took with him a map, prepared from the results of his own surveyors' work.

On matters of geography, it differed only slightly from the one produced by Byrd's group. What remained was the interpretation of the origins of the boundary rivers of the Fairfax grant—and that was a political question. The final decision remained in the hands of King George II.[79]

Lord Fairfax's departure put the development of the Shenandoah Valley on hold. Neither Fairfax nor the Virginia Council would issue grants while their authority remained in dispute, pending a ruling on the Potomac question. At the same time, however, a series of moves occurred in Virginia which helped to shape a much larger outcome.

One was the consolidation of an alliance between the Fairfax and Washington families, of major significance to the future course of American independence. Following Augustine Washington's move to his new Potomac home which became Mt. Vernon, William Fairfax acquired a tract immediately below it in 1736. On this neighboring estate, which he named "Belvoir," William built a beautiful brick mansion overlooking the Potomac River. The construction was completed in 1741. About 350 yards up river, closer to the Washington estate, William Fairfax built his customs office, which he named "the White House." In 1743, his daughter Anne married Lawrence Washington, Augustine's twenty-five-year-old son, who took charge of his younger brother George, when their father died that same year.[80]

Much later, the British navy paid its own perverse tribute to the importance of the Fairfax-Washington connection. During the War of 1812, the British expressed their frustrations over their failure to destroy the United States, by pillaging the nation's capital, designed under George Washington's supervision. En route to burning the White House in 1814, the British squadron sailing up the Potomac paused, within shooting range of Belvoir.

Training their guns on the mansion, British warships leveled it to the ground. At less expense, British soldiers had done the same to John Winthrop's house in Boston, during the American Revolution.[81]

There was another significant move in Virginia, after Lord Thomas Fairfax departed for London in 1737. It underscored the connection to Spotswood, without whom neither the Fairfaxes nor the Washingtons could have contributed to founding a new nation. In 1738, Augustine Washington acquired a tract of land along the north bank of the Rappahannock River. With the Fairfax claim yet unresolved, he moved his family again in 1739, to a new home across the river from Fredericksburg. The location was closer to his own iron-mining operations, and to Spotswood's as well. Spotswood's headquarters as America's postmaster general were just a few miles downstream, at New Post. Not far above Fredericksburg was Spotswood's home at Germanna. In these surroundings, George Washington grew to age fifteen, with a republic still to win.[82]

NOTES

1. Stuart E. Brown, *Virginia Baron, The Story of Thomas 6th Lord Fairfax* (Berryville, Va., 1965), 26.

2. Quoted by Brown, *Virginia Baron*, 33.

3. *Cf. supra*, chapters 2, 5, and 7.

4. Brown, *Virginia Baron*, 34.

5. *Ibid.*

6. Increase Mather, "Diary."

7. Charles Morrison, *An Outline of the Maryland Boundary Disputes and Related Events* (Parsons, W.Va., 1974), 24.

8. Brown, *Virginia Baron*, 35–36.

9. Morrison, *Boundary Disputes*, 26.

10. Brown, *Virginia Baron*, 16.

11. Andrew Burnaby, *Travels through the Middle Settlements in North America, in the Years 1759 and 1760* (New York, 1904), 197–198.

12. The *Spectator* ceased publication in December 1712, after Swift had broken with the paper, and taken over the Examiner, to support the Harley ministry against the Whig Junto and Marlborough.

13. William Meade, *Old Churches, Ministers, and Families of Virginia* (Philadelphia, 1857), 282–283.

14. Brown, *Virginia Baron*, 18.

15. *Ibid.*, 172.

16. *Ibid.*, 40–41.

17. *Ibid.*, 39, 56–57.

18. *Ibid.*, 38.

19. Dodson, *Spotswood*, 282, 298–299.

20. *Ibid.*, 296–297.

21. *Ibid.*, 293.

22. *Ibid.*, 290n .

23. *Ibid.*, 283, 285, 285n., 290n .

24. Quoted by Dodson, *Spotswood*, 290–291.

25. Swift to Pope, November 26, 1725, *Correspondence*, Williams, ed., III, 118.

26. Bertrand A. Goldgar, *Walpole and the Wits* (Lincoln, Nebraska, 1976), 40–41.

27. Swift to Thomas Tickell, July 7, 1726,

Correspondence, Williams, ed., III, 137, 136*n.*, 137*n.*

28. *Ibid.*, 149*n.*, 151*n.*

29. Swift, *Gulliver's Travels*, Landa, ed., 150–151.

30. *Ibid.*, 4.

31. Swift to Sheridan, May 13, 1727, *Correspondence*, Williams, ed., III, 206–207.

32. Swift, " A Pastoral Dialogue between Richmond Lodge and Marble Hill, Written June 1727, Just After the News of the King's Death," *Poems*, Rogers, ed., 322.

33. Notable are sermons preached in Boston, even on the death in 1751 of Frederick, Prince of Wales, considered "the people' s prince" and the only friend America ever had in Britain' s House of Hanover. Jonathan Mayhew, pastor of Boston' s West Church, took for his text, "It is better to trust in the LORD than to put confidence in Princes." Cf., Jonathan Mayhew, *A Sermon preached at Boston in New-England, May 26, 1751. Occasioned by the much-lamented DEATH of His Royal Highness Frederick, Prince of Wales* (Boston, 1751). Rare Book Room, Library of Congress.

34. *The Intelligencer* (No. 3), facsimile reprint (New York, 1967), 27–28.

35. Goldgar, *Walpole*, 69; John Gay, The Beggar's Opera, II:x, 7–26. For readers who would like to further enjoy the humor and music of Gay's "ballad opera," there is an inexpensive, paperback edition available. Though not a performance version, it includes the music for the ballads and a keyboard

arrangement of the basses supplied by Pepusch. Edited by Edgar V. Roberts, it is published by the University of Nebraska Press.

36. Campbell, *Spotswood Genealogy*.

37. Dodson, *Spotswood*, 291.

38. Order Book of Spotsylvania County, 1724–1730, 405.

39. Dodson, *Spotswood*, 301.

40. *Virginia Magazine of History and Biography*, Vol. XXXVIII, 337–345.

41. *Cf.* Chapter 10.

42. Franklin, *Autobiography*, 72–73.

43. *Ibid.*, 90.

44. *Ibid.*, 105–106.

45. *Ibid.*, 112.

46. *Ibid.*, 113.

47. *Ibid.*, 113–114.

48. *Virginia Magazine of History and Biography*, Vol. XXXVI, 66–67; Vol. XXIX, 184–185; Brown, *Virginia Baron*, 46.

49. Byrd, *London Diary*, intro., 41.

50. *Virginia Magazine of History and Biography*, Vol. XXIX, 188–190.

51. *Ibid.*, 188.

52. Brown, *Virginia Baron*, 43.

53. Sir William Keith, *The History of the British Plantations in America, Part I, Containing the History of Virginia* (London, 1738), map; and 172–

174.

54. Quoted by Brown, *op. cit.*, 57.

55. *Ibid.*, 45–47.

56. Edward H. Schultz, "Belvoir on the Potomac," typescript ms. [1932?], 2, Manuscript Division, Library of Congress; Salem, Mass., Record of Deaths.

57. Brown, *Virginia Baron*, 46.

58. *Ibid.*, 93.

59. William Fairfax to Bryan Fairfax, July 20, 1734, quoted by Brown, *op. cit.*, 47.

60. William Fairfax to Bryan Fairfax, July 30, 1734, *ibid.*

61. Margaret T. Peters, *A Guidebook to Virginia's Historical Markers* (Charlottesville, 1985), 26, 31.

62. *Jour. Coun. Va.*, III, 448, 470–471.

63. Byrd, "A Progress to the Mines," in *London Diary*, etc., 626–627.

64. *Ibid.*, 682–630.

65. Brown, *Virginia Baron*, 62.

66. *Ibid.*, 61–62.

67. *Ibid.*, 62.

68. Dodson, *Spotswood*, 148, 259.

69. United States George Washington Bicentennial Commission, *History of the George Washington Bicentennial Celebration* (Washington, D.C., 1932), I, 211–213.

70. Quoted by Brown, *Virginia Baron*, 63.

71. *Ibid.*

72. Quoted by Brown, *Virginia Baron*, 64, 77. The quotations concerning Fairfax's policy toward the Shenandoah Valley settlers are largely drawn from their own depositions, in a court case later promoted by the "gentlemen of fortune" against the Fairfax claim.

73. *Ibid.*, 80–81.

74. *Jour. Coun. Va.*, IV, 377–378.

75. Quoted by Brown, *Virginia Baron*, 83.

76. *Ibid.*

77. *Cf. supra*; Dodson, *Spotswood*, 298; Brown, *Virginia Baron*, 83.

78. Brown, *Virginia Baron*, 85.

79. *Ibid.*, 86–93.

80. Schultz ms.; Brown, *Virginia Baron*, 101–102.

81. The graves of William and Deborah Fairfax, and the excavated ruins of their home, lie today within the gates of Fort Belvoir, the U.S. Army base protecting Washington, D.C.

82. *Washington Bicent. Hist.*, I, 214; and *supra*.

12

The Road to the French and Indian War

By 1737, the ministry of Robert Walpole could boast of having kept Britain out of a major war for a decade and a half. To his opponents, however, the result of his policies seemed more like the peace of the grave. The crisis which had brought him to power—the collapse of the South Sea Bubble in 1720—had not been resolved. Without resorting to another stock market crash, the Venetian party managers of Britain's economy were steadily bleeding it to death. Needed infusions of investment in productive industry and agriculture were still cut off, to feed the demands of debt repayment, taxation, and speculation. The leading opposition newspaper charged in 1736 that such measures had

> more than doubled the price of the common necessaries of life within a few years past, and thereby distressed the poor labourer and manufacturer, disabled the farmer to pay his rent, and put even gentlemen of plentiful estates under the greatest difficulties to make a tolerable provision for their families.[1]

Walpole's personification of the bestial outlook of the Hell-Fire clubs also remained the object of some hostility. Even a British historian writing a century ago, while describing Walpole as "a great minister," acknowledged that

> politics and obscenity were his tastes . . . . the extreme coarseness into which he usually glided when speaking to and of women, drew down upon him much ridicule and some

contempt. His estimate of political integrity was very similar to his estimate of female virtue. He governed by means of an assembly which was saturated with corruption, and he fully acquiesced in its conditions and resisted every attempt to improve it. He appears to have cordially accepted the maxim that government must be carried on by corruption or by force, and he deliberately made the former the basis of his rule. He bribed George II . . . . He bribed the Queen . . . . He employed the vast patronage of the Crown uniformly and steadily with the single view of sustaining his political position, and there can be no doubt that a large proportion of the immense expenditure of secret service money during his administration was devoted to the direct purchase of Members of Parliament.[2]

Beyond his domestic difficulties, Walpole confronted an increasingly volatile international situation, as the general economic breakdown led to a falling-out among thieves, even in the Venetian-controlled capitals of Europe. Relations between the Bourbon monarchies of France and Spain were strained; the Hapsburg empire was at odds with both; and Britain's efforts to cut deals with all of them inevitably failed. Hapsburg power was at a low ebb; but France was still Europe's leading military power, and Spain had begun to challenge Britain's only significant asset: its overseas commercial looting, backed by its fragile margin of naval superiority. Whether by peace or by war, Britain was headed for ruin. The prevailing structures of faction or party were coming unglued, as was Walpole's elaborate edifice of corruption. To the oligarchical managers confronting this crisis, the most dangerous threat was any emergence of a real national interest. For America's republicans, the moment they had awaited was at hand.

Walpole's Undoing

Lord Fairfax returned to London in 1737 in the midst of this dramatic upheaval. It was the year that Frederick, Prince of Wales, heir to George II, brought his disputes with the King to the floor of the House of Commons, demanding from Parliament the allowance he had been denied by his father. The move was tantamount to splitting the administration between the current and future king, yet Walpole barely bought enough votes to defeat the opposition bill. Frederick's own court became the center of intrigue against Walpole, for principled opponents as well as corrupt manipulators—both seeking to determine the outcome. Walpole's authority was further weakened in November 1737, with the death of Queen Caroline, his most important supporter throughout the time he had been in power.[3]

As the crisis unfolded, Jonathan Swift again sought to rally his contacts in England, for a republican offensive against the Walpole regime. The first salvo came from his longtime friend Alexander Pope, who had maintained his career as a poet with an ample supply of political caution—and a resulting limit on his creativity. In May 1737, Pope published his *Epistle to Augustus*, a lengthy poem which ironically compared the reigns of the Roman emperor Augustus and King George Augustus II of Britain. The poem included lines praising Swift's revolutionary *Drapier's Letters*, for which Pope was almost prosecuted, according to Swift's friend from the days of Queen Anne, John Barber—now an alderman of London.[4] After a year of polemical attacks on Walpole by numerous writers, the government press complained that Swift's *Gulliver's Travels* had proved a treasure trove for the opposition.[5]

Swift's own role was hampered by a worsening affliction from a nerve disorder of the inner ear, producing dizziness and deafness. It was a degenerative condition which he had suffered off and on for more than forty years. During 1738–1739, it began causing him acute distress, but his voice was still heard.

In April 1739, the opposition paper *Common Sense* printed the poem he had written in late 1731, on "The Character of Sir Robert Walpole":

> With favour and fortune fastidiously blessed,
>
> He's loud in his laugh and coarse in his jest;
>
> Of favour and fortune unmerited vain,
>
> A sharper in trifles, a dupe in the main.
>
> Achieving of nothing, still promising wonders,
>
> By dint of experience improving in blunders;
>
> Oppressing true merit, exalting the base,
>
> And selling his country to purchase his peace.
>
> A jobber of stocks by retailing false news;
>
> A prater at court in the style of the stews;
>
> Of virtue and worth by profession a giber,
>
> Of juries and senates the bully and briber:
>
> Though I name not the wretch you know who I mean--
>
> 'Tis the cur-dog of Britain and spaniel of Spain.[6]

It was the epithet "spaniel of Spain" which struck Walpole's most vulnerable flank. Under the Venetian system of economic looting, the nations of Europe had little wealth beyond what they could steal—either from one another, or from one another's colonies. By the terms of the 1713 Peace of Utrecht, Britain was entitled to send only one 600-ton ship a year to trade with Spain's American colonies, but held an exclusive contract to supply them with slaves—the infamous Asiento. The revenues in both cases were assigned to the South Sea Company. Especially since Walpole's coming to power, British policy had been to violate Spain's commercial restriction as extensively as possible—but not so far as to jeopardize the Asiento. By 1731, Spain had begun exercising its right of search and seizure of British ships, suspected of smuggling goods beyond the agreed-upon limit. Walpole's protests against these occasionally violent proceedings were hollow indeed, for he dared not provoke Spain to cancel the agreement on the slave trade. In such unprincipled grounds of foreign policy, were planted the seeds of war.

Britain's long peace with France was also nearing an end. Its only real basis—a mutual desire to engage in the great enterprise of nation-building—had been shattered almost immediately, by the death of Queen Anne in 1714, and the simultaneous Jesuit-Orléans coup in France. France was also dying under its own version of Robert Walpole, the longtime chief minister Cardinal de Fleury. Though he had kept France generally at peace, the greatest industrial nation of Europe was only a shadow of its former self. Its enterprise was mortgaged to commercial looting abroad. Between 1715 and 1738, the number of French trading vessels increased from 300 to 1,800. During the same period, there was no increase whatsoever in the population of France.[7] With the minor exception of Louisiana, there were no *French* colonization projects to loot anywhere. In 1733, the Bourbon Kings of France and Spain signed the Family Compact, a secret treaty pledging France to aid Spain against the encroachments of British merchant shipping, in return for Spain's promise to revoke Britain's transatlantic trade privileges and grant more extensive ones to France.[8]

Assured of French support, Spain stepped up its retaliations against British commercial violations; and by 1738, London merchants were feeding a general clamor for declaring war in defense of England's 'honor.' Walpole was still negotiating accords to resolve the dispute in January 1739, and his urgings for moderation and concessions strengthened opposition charges that he was indeed the "spaniel of Spain." His position was politically untenable: There was little prospect of rallying sufficient support for "Peace and the Slave Trade!"—or whatever slogan he might have devised, for the actual interests he was defending. With regard to Spain, the issue of Britain's slave-trading interest, however, soon became moot. The *Asiento* contract expired on May 6, 1739, and Philip V of Spain refused to renew it. Britain declared war on October 19.[9]

For the next nine years, almost to the day, Europe was engulfed in continent-wide warfare, culminating in the War of Austrian Succession. The lineup of antagonists would again pit the British, the Dutch, and the Hapsburgs, against France and Spain. By the time of the Treaty of Aix-la-Chapelle, signed October 18, 1748, the military phase of America's drive for independence had begun, and its preparations for taking the Ohio and Mississippi River valleys were under way.

Spotswood's Last Campaign

From Virginia, Alexander Spotswood had followed the unfolding strategic crisis with great interest. He was still America's postmaster general when Britain declared war, and remained the highest-ranking military officer in the colonies. Throughout his career in America, he had looked forward to the day, when the web of political restraint by Britain, and military encirclement by France and Spain, could be broken—freeing the American colonies to develop the West. From the beginning of his Virginia governorship in 1710, he had fought to assert Virginia's claims against French inroads from the Great Lakes and the Mississippi River. As early as 1720, during a previous conflict between Britain and Spain, he had pressed London for a campaign to drive the Spanish from Florida, from which they threatened the Carolinas and controlled the choke-point for access to the lower Mississippi. He fully understood the corrupt bargain with Spain enforced by Robert Walpole, who had ousted him from his governorship in 1722.

During William Byrd's visit to Germanna in 1732, he recorded at least part of Spotswood's thinking on that subject:

> Then my friend [sic] unriddled to me the great mystery why we have endured all the late insolences of the Spaniards so tamely. The *Asiento* Contract and the liberty of sending a ship every year to the Spanish West Indies make it very necessary for the South Sea Company to have effects of great value in that part of the world. Now these, being always in the power of the Spaniards, make the directors of that company very fearful of a breach and consequently very generous in their offers to the [Walpole] ministry to prevent it . . . . All this moderation our peaceable ministry showed even at a time when the Spaniards were furiously attacking Gibraltar and taking all the English ships they could.

Despite a political outcry against Walpole even then, Spotswood sarcastically noted, "the courage of these worthy patriots soon cooled and the arguments used by the South Sea directors persuaded them once again into more pacific measures."[10]

Following Britain's declaration of war against Spain, Spotswood sought to ensure for the American colonies an active role in shaping the outcome. Certainly he well remembered the last mobilization of American militia during a European war, and how Marlborough's treasonous faction had sabotaged the expedition against Quebec in 1711. In 1739, it was still the case that Britain's enemies in war, might be her police force in peace, against America's westward hopes. Outside of New England, there was again not much in place from which to raise an American army, especially since the Walpole regime had never wanted to see one enter the field. Whatever agreements the combatting powers of Europe might arrange concerning America, the colonies would need to generate a military capability of their own, or remain a defenseless pawn.

With the *Asiento* revoked and all Britain clamoring for war, Spotswood made an offer which London could not refuse. He proposed to raise an American regiment for the British army. At the age of sixty-four, the veteran colonel was commissioned brigadier general, and was appointed quartermaster general and second in command to Lord Cathcart, for the British army contingent which was to attack Spanish strongholds in the Caribbean. He was also assigned to raise an American regiment, under his own command as colonel. Once his orders reached him in late March 1740, Spotswood set up recruiting operations in Williamsburg. Within two months, he had enlisted 400 officers and men from Virginia, including Captain Lawrence Washington, Augustine's son by his first wife, and George's revered half-brother.[11] As postmaster general, Spotswood had long played an important role with the various colonial governments. Now he rallied colonial executives for the common military effort ahead.

At the beginning of June, Spotswood set out for Annapolis, Maryland, where his American regiment was to embark for the Caribbean. He also planned to confer with the colonial governors on measures to build up American forces. Then, suddenly, at Annapolis, he was stricken by a fatal illness, the nature of which remains unknown and unreported to this day. His only two biographers, both of whom obscure his actual significance, bury him without a thought for the consequences. The more detailed account, based on British sources, concludes with this report:

> He struggled, it seems, against the death which would snatch from his grasp the opportunity [to fight again] awaited for so many years. His illness was concealed, and no one was allowed to see him. As so often where knowledge is not available, rumor rushed in to fill the vacuum. The day before his death [Governor] Gooch, who was entitled to know the truth if ever a man was, received word that Spotswood was too ill to be shown the letter which the governor had written to him, that his doctors declared he could not live more than a day or two, and that he was to sail for Virginia the following day! But on June 7, 1740, the end came to Spotswood, at the age of sixty-four.[12]

The Missing Corpse

Available accounts of Spotswood's death raise more questions than answers. Whatever doubt "rumor" created, over whether he died solely of natural causes, there is no question that his enemies sought to murder all memory of him. No funeral, nor memorial service, was reported, even though Spotswood was the leading newsmaker in America at the time. Upon learning of his death, Benjamin Franklin printed a brief, yet moving tribute in his *Pennsylvania Gazette* of June 12. But there is no record of any ceremonial observance, even in Virginia, where Spotswood had been the most prominent political figure of his time. Most astounding of all, according to the record of history, is that his corpse simply disappeared without a trace. To this day, no location has been confirmed as the grave of Alexander Spotswood, royal governor of Virginia, postmaster general of America, brigadier general of the British army, and commander of colonial forces. Had he died on some lonely mission in the wilderness, the fate of an unknown burial place might be understandable. But with a public spotlight on Annapolis, on the eve of an expedition known throughout the colonies, it would seem impossible.

It is more than possible, however, that Spotwood's enemies did their utmost at the time to prevent any public expressions of acknowledgement and support, for the leading champion of America's further development. During the reign of Queen Anne, he had seen the plots of Marlborough's gang to decimate the colonial militia, as cannon-fodder in battles meant to be lost. Had he lived, Spotswood certainly would have raised his voice against British policy, in the war which now unfolded. Though Walpole had conceded to war, he had no intention of securing any decisive victories. To Walpole's dismay, his outspoken opponent, Admiral Vernon, had already seized the Spanish stronghold at Porto Bello, on the Isthmus of Panama. Spotswood's American regiment was assigned to join an amphibious assault on Cartagena (Colombia), where Vernon's attack was repulsed with the unexpected assistance of British army general Wentworth. The British surrendered Porto Bello for lack of reinforcements, thanks to Walpole's holding back Britain's Mediterranean fleet on the pretext of defending Gibraltar.

Military strategy was a mere subsidiary, of a larger game run by the living dead—the Venetian-centered oligarchic cults. Among Walpole's literary opponents, Alexander

Pope now referred to him as "Magus the Wizard"; and even Henry Fielding stepped forward in 1741 to portray Walpole as Mammon, bribed by the Devil to obstruct reinforcements for the campaign in the Americas. By official policy, Britain had no moral objectives in the war. There was a desired result, however, in sacrificing Spotswood's effort to mobilize an American colonial army. After Cartagena, one defeat followed another, and Walpole ensured there would be neither reinforcements nor new supplies. Tropical fevers added a heavy toll, even on the lives of British sailors and soldiers. According to estimates of the time, ninety percent of the American regiment died.[13]

Among the survivors was Lawrence Washington, though weakened by illness which led to his death in 1752, at only thirty-four years of age. In 1743, Augustine Washington died, leaving his son the Potomac River estate, which Lawrence named Mt. Vernon, in honor of the admiral who had opposed Robert Walpole. For the remainder of his life, Lawrence Washington became like a father to his younger brother George, who lived to make Mt. Vernon one of the world's most famous homes. Both of them fought to realize Spotswood's dream for America.

Years later, following the British defeat at Yorktown, George Washington paid an especially fitting tribute to Spotswood. The Commander-in-Chief ordered that the meeting set between British and American representatives, to draw up the articles of surrender, be held at the home of Augustine Moore, a grandson of Alexander Spotswood. A beautiful house, which still stands today, it is located south of the battlefield, on a point overlooking the York River. By the best available evidence, it is also Spotswood's burial place. An old Virginia historian, whose father was Lord Fairfax's neighbor in the Shenandoah Valley, reports that Spotswood acquired the York property during his governorship, for use as a summer retreat, "where he built a new and larger house, and where he is buried." By another account from the early nineteenth century, the property's owner in 1834 discovered a pile of broken tombstones, "and on putting the fragments together found the name of Governor Spotswood."[14]

Washington was certainly in a position to know the facts. Spotswood's youngest son had accompanied him in battle during the French and Indian War, and was killed near Fort Duquesne (Pittsburgh) in 1756. Spotswood's grandson and namesake, Alexander, married Washington's niece Elizabeth in 1769, served during the Revolution as his personal chief of security in Virginia, and attained the rank of brigadier general in the Continental Army. Political circumstances may have constrained the recognition Washington could give to a former royal governor—but not any lack of knowledge.[15]

America Mobilizes in Earnest

As Britain became more deeply engaged in the war with Spain, the power of Robert Walpole—architect of 'peaceful' ruin collapsed. Even George II had demanded war. In his continuing role as Elector of Hanover, he also intended to use Britain against France, in support of a Hapsburg succession to the throne of the Holy Roman Empire. For squeezing from Britain the resources for a major war, Walpole was politically useless. He was swept from office in 1742. The new Whig war cabinet included Henry Pelham and the Duke of Newcastle, old acquaintances of Lord Thomas Fairfax.[16] Britain had been on a collision course with France since 1739, and that reality made the situation in the American colonies one of increasing strategic importance.

Even from a strictly commercial standpoint, British interests could not afford to be indifferent to the French threat to the colonies. As Spotswood had repeatedly warned, the French arc extending from the lower Mississippi through the Great Lakes, and across the northern frontiers of New York and New England, kept the colonies in constant danger of being overrun. Were France and Spain to control the seas as well, Britain might lose her American possessions. At the very least, she would lose the American trade. In 1740, the French military advantage in America was further increased, by the completion of its mighty fortress at Louisburg on Cape Breton Island, guarding the access to the St. Lawrence River—and thus to the Great Lakes. Faced with this worsening strategic and economic crisis, Britain might be forced to depart from her long reliance on French containment of the American colonies.

Even in 1740, while Spotswood was still mobilizing his American regiment, a leading British colonial official called attention to the economic stakes involved. His name was Robert Dinwiddie (1692–1770), appointed in 1738 as surveyor general of customs for the Southern District, including all British possessions from Pennsylvania to Bermuda. Dinwiddie later became governor of Virginia, and supported George Washington's expeditions during the French and Indian War. On April 29, 1740, Dinwiddie presented in London a report to the Board of Trade, emphasizing certain aspects of the American trade which were not generally noted in the balance sheets. New England alone had more than 1,000 ocean-going ships, and the Atlantic colonies as a whole had nearly 2,000 trading and fishing vessels. The number of British ships trading with those colonies was fewer than 600. Dinwiddie offered figures demonstrating that British dependence on America's "natural and improved annual produce" exceeded her earnings from exports to the colonies. Even including "that private Branch of Trade," in "Negroes" and goods sold to

Spanish and French colonies in the Americas, British exports still could not "over Rate our American Trade."[17]

Dinwiddie prefaced his report by assuring the board it was based on "the best informations I possibly could get. If it's thought worthy your Notice, it will fully answer my hopes.[18] He had made a special trip to Virginia in the summer of 1739, when his "hopes" may have been given a particular turn by Alexander Spotswood, whom he almost certainly consulted.   Dinwiddie had longstanding connections to Spotswood and his circle.

Born in Scotland in 1692, the son of a Glasgow merchant, Dinwiddie had an older brother John, who settled in Virginia during Spotswood's governorship.   John Dinwiddie established himself along the Rappahannock River, within the Fairfax Northern Neck Proprietary.   In 1716, he married Simpha Mason, daughter of the third George Mason, one of Spotswood's Knights of the Golden Horseshoe, who accompanied him that same year on the expedition across the Blue Ridge.   In 1721, Spotswood appointed John Dinwiddie sheriff for his district, the newly formed King George County.   Simpha Dinwiddie's sister married John Mercer, a Dublin-born classical scholar who owned one of the finest libraries in the colonies, and whose home was a center of intellectual life for northern Virginia. Mercer also knew Spotswood in Virginia, and may have had other connections as well, for Spotswood's stepfather was a Mercer of Ireland.   In 1726, John Mercer purchased a large selection of books from Spotswood's library at Germanna.   He was also the tutor of the fourth George Mason, who became a leading figure of the Ohio Company, beginning in 1749, along with Lawrence Washington.[19]

Robert Dinwiddie chose to make Virginia his headquarters when he took up his customs post, moving his family to the vicinity of Norfolk in the spring of 1741.

Though his brother John had died in 1726, his widow and children remained an active entree to the society of many of Virginia's leading families, including the Masons, Mercers, Washingtons, and Fairfaxes. Dinwiddie's own association with the Fairfax family dates from this period on a significant, official level. William Fairfax, the proprietary agent for the Northern Neck, still held the post of collector of customs for the South Potomac District, and in that capacity now worked under Dinwiddie. In July 1742, Dinwiddie secured a seat on the Virginia Council, despite opposition from Governor Gooch, thus winning a voice in the colony's affairs—as did William Fairfax at about the same time.[20]

As Robert Walpole's corrupt system of control broke down, further cracks appeared in Britain's containment of the American colonies. The strategic crisis had far outstripped his capacity for bribery, though it was he who coined the degenerate maxim, "all men have their price."[21] In 1741, Governor Belcher of Massachusetts—son of the old grain monopolist who had helped bankroll the "Satanic Party"—was removed from office. The new royal governor was William Shirley, appointed with the backing of his longtime patron, the Duke of Newcastle, friend of Lord Fairfax.[22] In Pennsylvania, Governor George Thomas, despite protests by the Quaker-controlled assembly, seized the occasion of the unfolding war to launch a vehement campaign for military preparedness.[23] In 1742, already anticipating hostilities with France, he also began negotiating a new treaty with the Iroquois, seeking their alliance against the Jesuit-controlled tribes of Canada.[24]

Within a year, British and French troops were engaged in full-scale combat in Europe, even though neither side had yet declared war on the other. In America, Pennsylvania's Quaker leaders kept insisting that peace was just around the corner, but events began to be dictated by reality. On August 15, 1743, an order was issued in London directing America's colonial governors to institute broad measures for defense. Word reached the colonies at the beginning of November. Governor Gooch met with the Virginia Council, and appointed Lawrence Washington adjutant general of the Virginia militia. In Philadelphia, Governor Thomas issued a proclamation calling for the creation of a militia, but the assembly rejected his enforcement legislation, and his request for arms and ammunition. The British crown had already issued another directive, on September 3, 1743, that the colonies be placed on a footing for offensive war, but it was not received in America until April of the following year.[25]

The Massachusetts colony, which still represented America's most important war-fighting capability, was immediately threatened. Beginning in May 1744, the French military governor at Louisburg launched a series of attacks against British-controlled Acadia (Nova Scotia today). The major target was the naval port and garrison at Annapolis Royal, the only military obstacle against French attacks on New England from Louisburg. Under Walpole's regime, the fort at Annapolis had fallen into such disrepair, that cows walked easily over its ramparts.[26] Nearly a hundred French regulars, and 300 to 400 Indians led by their Jesuit "missionary," laid siege to Annapolis in August. Governor Shirley sent reinforcements of Massachusetts militiamen and Indian rangers, and the French gave up the attack in late September.[27]

Efforts were also under way to extend the potential theater for the Virginia militia further west, by enlarging upon Spotswood's 1722 treaty with the Iroquois Five Nations. In June 1744, Governor Thomas of Pennsylvania, along with commissioners from Virginia and Maryland, met with the Iroquois, now the Six Nations, at Lancaster, Pennsylvania. The Six Nations agreed not to let the French or their Indians invade the lands claimed by the British colonies.[28] More importantly, they conceded for the first time to Virginia's colonial claims beyond the Allegheny Mountains, as far west as the Mississippi River. The Iroquois gave Virginia's commissioners a deed "recognizing the King's right to all the lands that are, or shall be, by His Majesty's appointment in the colony of Virginia."[29] If honored by the Iroquois, the agreement meant that only the French, or their Indian assets, could prevent Virginia's developing the strategically crucial Ohio country.

Among these coordinated efforts to end America's containment, Benjamin Franklin made a special contribution, on a higher level. In April 1744, he unveiled his newly founded American Philosophical Society, which reestablished the institution first created by Increase Mather in the 1680s. Intended to function as a scientific "committee of correspondence," it was Franklin's attempt to begin unifying the American colonies around a cultural commitment to reason—the indispensable requirement for a strong republic. He had begun the project the year before, with the publication of his "Proposal for Promoting Useful Knowledge among the British Plantations in America," urging that "one society be formed of *virtuosi* or ingenious men, residing in the several colonies, to be called *The American Philosophical Society*, who are to maintain a constant correspondence."[30] The proposed subjects of correspondence included botany, medicine, geology, and metallurgy; "new mechanical inventions for saving labour" in such applications as milling, transportation, and irrigation;

> all new arts, trades, and manufactures, that may be proposed or thought of; surveys, maps, and charts of particular parts of the seacoasts or inland countries; course and junction of rivers

and great roads, situation of lakes and mountains, nature of the soil and productions; new methods of improving the breed of useful animals; introducing other sorts from foreign countries; new improvements in planting, gardening, and clearing land; and all philosophical experiments that let light into the nature of things, tend to increase the power of man over matter, and multiply the conveniences or pleasures of life.[31]

Against Britain's cannibalizing colonial policies, Franklin offered a clear program for building a nation. The more widely he organized around it, the more readily Americans would decide, whether they had any future under British rule. Franklin recruited the core of the American Philosophical Society from his original organizing committee—the Junto and its network of "improvement" clubs. The first president of the Society was Thomas Hopkinson, whose son Francis became a signer of the Declaration of Independence, a member of the Continental Congress from New Jersey, and an organizer for the adoption of the Constitution. Beyond the founding group in Philadelphia, the Society's first recruits included "Mr. Alexander, of New York," and "Mr. Morris, Chief Justice of the Jerseys."[32] Both were protégés of Jonathan Swift's old friend, Robert Hunter, governor of New York from 1710 to 1719. Franklin made a special trip to New York to enlist them. James Alexander, trained in astronomy by Hunter, served on the councils of both New York and New Jersey, and backed Franklin's plan for unifying the colonies during the French and Indian War. His son became a general in the Continental Army under George Washington, during the American Revolution. Robert Hunter Morris was the son of Hunter's leading ally in New York, Lewis Morris, and became governor of Pennsylvania in 1754, supporting Franklin's efforts to mobilize for the French and Indian War. Governor Morris's son was also a signer of the Declaration of Independence, a member of the Continental Congress, and rose to the rank of brigadier general during the Revolution.[33]

The Breakthrough Achieved

The royal directive received in spring 1744, that the colonies make preparations even to initiate military operations, provided a major opportunity for advocates of America's westward development.   The Treaty of Lancaster signed that June also gave a tremendous boost to Virginia's plans for settling its lands west of the Shenandoah River, and far down the southwestern reaches of the Valley of Virginia. Though Lord Fairfax was still in London seeking final ratification of his claims, in 1744 the Northern Neck proprietor authorized the establishment of Frederick Town (later Winchester), at the northern end of the valley. Named for Frederick, Prince of Wales, it was the first town beyond the Blue Ridge, and became the base for further expeditions beyond the Appalachian and Allegheny mountain ranges.

The reality of a major war between Britain and France overturned the prevailing rules of the game. James Patton, ancestor of America's World War II General George Patton, had applied to the Virginia Council in 1743, for extensive land grants in the western stretches of the Valley, along the later route to Kentucky and Tennessee. Patton reported that Governor Gooch and the Council refused

> at that Time [to] Grant my Petition, not knowing how the Goverm't at Home would approve of their Granting Land [there] lest it might Occasion a Dispute betwixt them and the French who claimed a Right to the Land . . .

and as the distance was so great from any Part of the Atlantick Ocean, They could not conceive that any benefit could arise to his Majesties Revenues or to the Strength of this Colony, by an handfull of Poor People that might Venture to settle [there]. But if a War broke out betwixt England and France, they would then Grant my Petition.

Shortly after war was declared in 1744, Patton was notified to appear before the Council, and was informed that the grant was approved.[34]

The same circumstances finally forced a decision on the western claims of the Fairfax proprietary, which Robert Walpole had managed to block to the end of his ministry. Early in 1745, Lord Fairfax went before a committee of the King's Privy Council, offering to confirm all patents issued by Virginia within the disputed areas of his grant, and acknowledging the crown's claims in such cases to any uncollected quitrents. On April 11, the Privy Council issued an order in favor of Fairfax, setting the boundaries of the Northern Neck Proprietary as the "first springs" of the farthest branches of the Rapidan and Potomac Rivers, and the straight line between them.[35] Independent of the whims of royal policy, both in London and in Williamsburg, Lord Fairfax was now free to launch a crucial colonization effort, across the strategic western front approaching the Ohio River Valley.

New England was already poised to strike a stunning blow against French encirclement of America's frontiers. In the fall of 1744, Governor Shirley of Massachusetts began quietly forming plans for an attack on Louisburg. Returning Massachusetts prisoners, exchanged for French troops captured in the earlier fighting in Acadia, provided him with detailed information, based on their confinement inside the supposedly invulnerable fortress on the Gulf of St. Lawrence.[36]   If begun before reinforcements arrived from France the next spring, an overland attack from the rear might succeed.   Louisburg had been designed to control the sea lanes, and the batteries outside the fort were positioned to defend the narrow access to its harbor.   On performance, the French would never have expected the British to mount an all-out naval assault—and even less imagined that their colonists might attack on their own.

Popular sentiment for an expedition against Louisburg grew steadily in Massachusetts once its prisoners had returned.   The legislature heard a number of proposals to petition the British government to undertake such a campaign with colonial support, but no action was taken. Governor Shirley wrote to the Duke of Newcastle, warning that Acadia and New England's fisheries were in danger, and requesting that British warships be sent for their protection.   Still with no signal from London, Shirley initiated one of the most daring moves in American colonial history.   On January 9, 1745, he convened the Massachusetts General Court, the name its legislature had borne since the days of John Winthrop. He announced that he had a message of such importance, that he would deliver it only if the members swore themselves to secrecy. They consented, and then heard his astonishing proposal that Massachusetts immediately prepare an expedition against Louisburg, to reduce the greatest French fortress in the New World, *on the colony's own authority, and without the involvement of Britain!*

Here was a plan worthy of Winthrops and Mathers in its boldness, and calculated to rekindle the republican sense of identity which had previously distinguished the Massachusetts Bay Colony. Despite the oath taken by the legislators, the secret was soon out, even while they cautiously deliberated for several days.   Though Shirley had developed a good working relationship with the General Court, more than a streak of stubbornness remained, concerning any proposal granting extraordinary authority to a royal governor. In addition, the colony was virtually without funds, and had been for some time. In 1741, the British parliament had rejected the colony's proposals, both for issuing silver coinage and for printing currency backed by a land bank. On the advice of a special joint committee to consider Shirley's plan, the General Court voted to oppose it.[37]

The setback was only temporary. Shirley was no stranger to Massachusetts, having moved to Boston in 1731 to practice law and manage the local affairs of friends in London. Through a stint as advocate general of the British admiralty court for New England, he was also familiar with its merchant and shipping interests. They had their own reasons for removing the French fortress and naval port at Louisburg.[38] As governor, he had come to know even more about the political mood of its citizens. A general backlash had developed, especially in the older cities and towns established by the Puritans, against the corrupt excesses of the Walpole regime. Beginning in 1734, they had also witnessed the danger within, dramatized by a wave of religious irrationalism in the Connecticut River valley of western Massachusetts, led by Jonathan Edwards. Indoctrinated at Yale in John Locke's psychology of "sensations," Edwards was the grandson of Cotton Mather's bitter enemy, Solomon Stoddard, and the grandfather of some of America's worst traitors—including Aaron Burr, the murderer of Alexander Hamilton. A horde of British-sponsored fundamentalist preachers followed in Edwards' wake, offering mindless subjection to a "loving" instead of an "angry" God. Either way, the intended victim was the morality of Cotton Mather's *Essays to Do Good*, which insisted that human responsibility, even in government, was "the good of mankind." The young Sam Adams, a future leader of the Revolution, had struck the right chord for Massachusetts in 1740. Delivering the salutatorian's address at Harvard's commencement, he had called for a revival of "the Puritan Commonwealth of our fathers."[39]

Supporters of Governor Shirley's proposal soon circulated a petition, signed by some of the leading merchants in the colony, demanding that the General Court reconsider its vote. The legislature had been controlled since the late 1690s by a rigged game of poor versus rich, supervised to make the interests of Massachusetts the loser. Such old habits were hard to break, but the legislature accepted the petition and resumed a lengthy debate. The intelligence gathered by Shirley included reports that the garrison at Louisburg was undermanned, and that low morale and dissension among the troops had even led to mutinous incidents. But opponents of the plan called the information unreliable, and stressed that in any case Massachusetts lacked the naval power to mount a blockade against reinforcements from France. They further argued that the colonial militia, untested in battle, were no match for French regulars in any case. Supporters, however, had the most telling argument of all: Were Massachusetts to wait for Britain to undertake the attack, the opportunity to seize Louisburg would be lost. By a single vote, the General Court approved the expedition.[40] The long period of stagnation and containment was over.

Victory at Louisburg

On January 26, 1745, Governor Shirley issued a proclamation directing the people of Massachusetts to prepare for the conquest of Louisburg. On the difficult matter of financing, Shirley had an ace up his sleeve, which enabled him to circumvent British prohibitions on colonial currency issues. He had previously won permission to issue up to £50,000 in bills of credit, "to meet any pressing exigency of war."[41] After some wrangling, the legislature appropriated credits totaling £13,000, to be redeemed from tax revenues over a ten-year period, beginning in 1751.[42] The General Court also called 3,250 Massachusetts militiamen to service; appeals to the other colonies brought 500 more from Connecticut, and 250 from New Hampshire. Naval requirements were met almost entirely by Massachusetts, with three twenty-gun frigates, and six ships with eight to twelve guns, in a squadron totaling over 200 guns, supported by ninety transports. Artillery for the siege consisted of eight twenty-two-pound cannon, twelve nine-pounders, four mortar, and ten eighteen-pound guns from New York. Most of the Massachusetts artillery was stripped from Castle Island, the fort established by John Winthrop, commanding Boston harbor.[43]

Shirley had kept the risk of British interference to a minimum. From his years in Massachusetts, if nothing else, he certainly knew of the British navy's sabotage of the 1711 expedition against Quebec. He also knew that transatlantic communications, back and forth, took nearly four months generally, and often more during winter. On February 1, he wrote to the Duke of Newcastle, informing him of the resolution of the Massachusetts General Court to organize an expedition against Louisburg. On March 24, the Massachusetts fleet sailed from Nantasket Roads. Only after the troops had embarked, did Shirley report to Newcastle the fait accompli, that in April New England would besiege the fortress with 4,000 men.[44]

He had sought to arrange, however, some additional naval backup, against the possible arrival of French warships. To Commodore Peter Warren, at the time commanding a small British squadron of three warships at Antigua in the Caribbean, Shirley had sent a special message by ship, revealing the plans for the attack on Louisburg, and requesting his aid. Warren was known as a friend of the colonies, who had married an American and purchased land in New York's Mohawk River valley, the northern gateway to the West. Commodore Warren presented the appeal to his officers, who insisted that they could not take part in any attack made without the approval of the King. Reluctantly, Warren informed Governor Shirley of the decision, who kept the news from all but the senior commanders of the New England forces. The expedition sailed without promise of additional support. But a few days after Warren replied, the commodore received a long-delayed directive from the Duke of Newcastle, responding to the warning Shirley had sent the previous fall. Warren's squadron was ordered to Boston, to join with Shirley in measures "for the annoyance of the enemy, and his Majesty's service in North America." Warren took Newcastle's message as sufficient authority to join Shirley's attack, and set out for Massachusetts under full sail.[45]

The New England forces made their rendezvous in early April at Canseau, at the northeastern tip of Acadia, about fifty miles southwest of Louisburg. An unusually late spring delayed them there nearly a month, while they waited for the ice around Cape Breton Island to break up. On April 23, Warren's three ships caught up with the expedition, adding 140 guns to New England's fleet. By Governor Shirley's standing order, Warren took command of the most heavily armed Massachusetts cruisers as well, and joined their blockade of the approaches to Louisburg from the open ocean.[46] News that the ice had receded arrived in Canseau on April 27; three days later, the fleet stood off Flat Point on Gabarus Bay, several miles west of Louisburg, prepared to attack. The plan called for establishing a beachhead near Flat Point, where the full expeditionary force would then land and attack across the narrow neck. Louisburg lay on the opposite side, with most of its defenses oriented north and east, guarding its inner harbor. Within the fortress, the French had 560 professional soldiers, including several companies of Swiss mercenaries, and roughly 1,300 Canadian militia.[47]

In simple numbers, the New England militia held the advantage in ground forces by slightly more than two to one. For an attacking army, however, against the massive fortifications designed by Vauban, that numerical margin was insignificant or nonexistent. In sheer firepower, as well as position, the French superiority was dramatic. The fortress itself had well over eighty cannon in place, all of them much heavier than the biggest guns in New England's artillery. Outside its walls were two heavy batteries of thirty guns each: Grand Battery, northeast of the fort on the harbor's inner shore, and Island Battery, built on rocks standing in the mouth of the harbor. The fortress was surrounded on three sides by harbor and ocean; on the landward side, its bastions overlooked a vast marsh, sure to hinder any besieging army. Yet in Boston, Governor Shirley had designed a plan of attack he was confident would work—"a mad scheme," in the words of the anglophile Francis Parkman, the nineteenth-century New England historian who cynically produced the most detailed account of the Louisburg campaign.[48]

There were four key elements in Shirley's plan of attack, which was premised on throwing the defenders off balance, by striking overland against the rear fortifications of Louisburg. The first and most crucial objective was to overrun the detachment defending the Grand Battery, and then to turn its heavy guns against the French themselves. The main force of the army was to assault the narrow arm of the fortress, at its innermost reach along the harbor's west shore, while the New England batteries dragged their cannon over difficult terrain, to siege positions overlooking the western walls. Artillery fire was also to be trained on the Island Battery, to level the enemy's primary defense of the harbor entrance. The final ingredient of the strategy was to use the combined naval squadron under Warren, to prevent reinforcement of the garrison by sea.

In Shirley's mind, this last measure was more precautionary than indispensable. Given political and military realities in Europe, he had no reason to believe that France would dispatch any extraordinary force, to accompany the previously scheduled resupply of Louisburg that spring. Warren's three warships were welcome backup, but Shirley had been willing to proceed without them, counting on the New England squadron to fend off whatever might already be lumbering across the Atlantic from France. Once Louisburg were taken, word would reach London before Paris in any case. Both capitals might be stunned by the victory, but Shirley did not imagine any combination of military responses which might endanger an American-held Louisburg.

Nor did the French commander of the fortress imagine that any colonial attack might succeed. Through their Indians, the Jesuits had learned of New England's preparations, and of the expedition's landing at Canseau. The reports were initially discounted at Louisburg, but there was little its officials could do about the threat anyway. For more than a month before the attack, New England cruisers had roamed the waters near the harbor, in view of the garrison. The occupants of the fortress could only wait, and keep a sharp watch toward the sea.

On April 30, 1745, coordinated from the flagship Shirley, the New England expedition landed at Freshwater Cove, above Flat Point, well beyond the range of Louisburg's guns. A French detachment from the fort, of

120 men, raced to meet them, but were routed by the 100-man landing party, whose casualties totaled two men slightly wounded. Two thousand more were on the beach by evening, and the remaining half of the army landed without incident the following day. On May 2, Shirley's plan of attack was set into motion, further honed by weeks of drilling while the army had waited at Canseau. A Massachusetts division of 400 men, selected to accomplish the first objective, began its mission with a brilliant gesture. Upon reaching the hills above Louisburg, the militiamen paused to salute the fort and the town within it with three cheers. Then disappearing beyond the hills, they marched quickly to a point behind the Grand Battery, and proceeded to set fire to the magazines and supply warehouses on the northwest shore of the inner harbor.

The Grand Battery's detachment, numbering by French accounts 400 men, panicked in the face of these unexpected moves, and received permission to withdraw to the fort. The next morning, when the heavy smoke from the burning storehouses had cleared, Massachusetts soldiers discovered that the battery had been abandoned. Its munitions had only been partially disposed of, and its forty-two-pound cannon were intact, save for spikes in their match-holes. Four boatloads of French troops crossed the harbor from the fort to reclaim the battery, but were held off on the beach by a dozen or so Massachusetts men, until their own reinforcements arrived. A unit of engineers under Major Seth Pomeroy, a gunsmith from Northampton, proceeded to unspike the guns and train them on the fortress. The lighter Massachusetts artillery, commanded by the expert engineer Richard Gridley, had been equipped with forty-two-pound shot expressly for this purpose. The next morning, a French eyewitness reported, "The enemy saluted us with their own cannon, and made a terrific fire, smashing everything within range."

Louisburg still possessed plenty of firepower. A weeks-long siege ensued, during which the Massachusetts gunners often had to maintain a furious barrage simply to hold their initial positions, against artillery and rifle fire from the fifty acre fortress. The Island Battery remained intact. Munitions and supplies were running low on both sides, but a protracted stalemate could only favor the French. From mainland Quebec, the Jesuits had managed to bring hundreds of Indians, who harassed positions behind New England's lines, taking numbers of prisoners who were tortured and murdered. On May 19, the French warship *Vigilant* had appeared off Cape Breton Island, with sixty-four guns and 560 men, bringing munitions and supplies for Louisburg.

Intercepted by the *Shirley*, and chased into the midst of the blockading squadron, the French vessel soon surrendered. Commodore Warren reported prisoners' accounts to the effect that more French vessels were on the way, which later proved to be false. Such claims did not deter the New Englanders. Employing the munitions from the *Vigilant* for their own use, they stepped up their barrage against Louisburg. But a militia assault against the Island Battery was repulsed on the night of May 26, and the first wave of 120 men who landed were taken prisoner. The French claimed many more were killed or drowned. Within the fortress, the garrison cheered, still unaware of the fate of the *Vigilant*. Heavy fire from New England's batteries, however, continued to pour into Louisburg. Its rear bastions were damaged, the walls of its main gate were crumbling, and the houses of the town were all but obliterated. The long siege had taken its toll.

Under direction of Colonel Gridley, chief of the Massachusetts artillery, a battery was established at Lighthouse Point, at the eastern mouth of the harbor, directly in line with the Island Battery. The position was considered inaccessible, but was attained by hauling cannon up a steep cliff, and dragging them more than a mile to the point overlooking the target. Gridley's artillery then bombarded the Island Battery with such precision, that the French soldiers ran more than once into the sea for refuge. Many of their heavy guns were blown off their mountings and rendered useless. The same fate was descending upon the French batteries within the fortress. The surrender of Louisburg, supposedly invincible, was merely a matter of time.[49]

His Majesty Turns Thumbs Down

New England's capture of Louisburg sent shock waves across the capitals of Europe. The astonishing feat upset the prevailing rules of warfare, and especially the managed system of mutual mayhem known as "preserving the balance of power." Particularly in Britain and France, new calculations began to be made, on the possibility that America might assert its independence.

Though British policy was to give New England as little credit as possible for the accomplishment, the facts of the matter soon became widely known. A French witness of the siege wrote,

> It was an enterprise less of the English nation and its King than of the inhabitants of New England alone. This singular people have their own laws and administration, and their governor plays the sovereign. Admiral [Commodore] Warren had no authority over the troops sent by the Governor of Boston [Shirley], and he was only a spectator. . . . Nobody would have said that their sea and land forces were of the same nation and under the same prince. No nation but the English is

> capable of such eccentricities ,—which,
> nevertheless, are a part of the precious liberty
> of which they show themselves so jealous.[50]

There was jubilation throughout the colonies over the victory at Louisburg. Word reached Boston on July 3, 1745, at one o'clock in the morning; bells pealed and cannon roared, despite the hour. Before dawn, cheering throngs filled the streets. Celebrations continued throughout the day and into the night, when fireworks and bonfires added to the brightness of the occasion. New York and Philadelphia greeted the news with similar displays, and everywhere people eagerly anticipated removing the French threat at last. New York, New Jersey, and Pennsylvania authorized funds to reduce the financial burden of Massachusetts, and to maintain the colonial garrison at Louisburg. As far south as Virginia, plans for the conquest of Canada were rapidly being drawn up.[51] Such general enthusiasm among the colonies meant only one thing: on the issue of opening the West—and therefore, of *nation-building*—they might readily unite.

That message was not lost in London. The American question was pulling apart the synthetic consensus of George II's war ministry. Both British and French oligarchical interests were already at work, redrawing future settlements to preserve their joint containment of America. While those arrangements proceeded, official British policy was to project the illusion of supporting the colonies' hopes, until the opportunity to take Canada had passed. For the time being, Louisburg was to be held, at American expense, with nothing more from Britain than the promise that the garrison would be relieved by troops from Gibraltar.

Governor Shirley and William Pepperell, the commander he had chosen for New England's troops, were named colonels of the British army, to command regiments to be raised in America. They were to supply any relief of Louisburg until British troops arrived. The powers in London had decided to let Shirley twist in the wind. On April 4, 1745, even before the New England expedition had completed its rendezvous at Canseau, Shirley had written to Newcastle that if the mission succeeded, New England and the other colonies would eagerly undertake the conquest of Canada.[52] Beyond having made his intentions clear from the outset, Shirley now represented an even greater danger. Both the military and political outcomes of the campaign were exactly as he had projected.

In the summer of 1745, over 3,000 New England militiamen remained encamped at Louisburg. Their siege of the fortress had been so devastating, that any talk of a "garrison" must have seemed ludicrous. Living quarters within the walls had been largely reduced to ruin. The drinking wells were dangerously contaminated, and the island was completely dependent on external supplies. Only a major military and civil reconstruction effort could make Louisburg into a fortress once more. Two months passed, with no sign of any such intention from the government of King George II. Foul odors from London were soon detected in Boston, and rumors spread that Britain was plotting to return Louisburg to the French.[53]

Shirley reported little progress in recruiting to the new regiments, since a number of commissions had been claimed for the British army, "and men will not enlist here except under American officers."[54] In August, Shirley had to travel to Louisburg, and exert his personal authority to quell a mutinous mood in the militia. The death toll was rising. He managed to get Warren's British seamen to cooperate with New England's militiamen in building a mess hall, barracks, and latrines, as well as a hospital to treat those with dysentery and other illnesses. Week after week, he supervised the effort, while waiting nearly two months for the relief promised from Britain. Still none came, and in late October he returned to Boston.[55]

Whatever future role in life Shirley might have imagined, as a young Englishman seeking his way during the last years of Queen Anne, he had attained a position of historical responsibility. He was the royal governor of Massachusetts, yet he had become an official advocate of the policies which Hanoverian Britain feared most. He realized that, even before he mobilized the expedition against Louisburg; and he knew even more after it succeeded. He did not retreat. From Boston, he informed the British ministry that it were easier to recruit 10,000 Americans for an attack on Canada, than to find 1,000 willing to lie idle at Louisburg, or anywhere else. Defeating the French in Canada, he argued, was "the most effectual means of securing . . . the whole northern continent as far back as the French settlements on the [lower] Mississippi, which are about 2,000 miles distant." He offered the modest estimate, that without French containment, the population of the American colonies would rival that of France, within a century or so. He was confident that, should his Majesty command it, America would raise 20,000 men against Canada, to ensure such a prospect.[56]

While Shirley waited for a reply to his proposals, his men at Louisburg were forced to endure a much longer vigil. Nearly ten months after the French surrender, there was still no sign of the relief promised from Britain. Fevers, dysentery, and inadequate supplies left the American garrison in poor condition to face the winter. By the time the modest detachment of troops from Gibraltar arrived, in April 1746, nearly 900 New England militiamen had died waiting for them. The survivors finally sailed for home, bringing with them a deepening hatred of British rule.[57]

Another Winthrop Joins the War

Massachusetts had picked a fight which could not be won by simple resistance against injustice. Certainly the Louisburg campaign had reawakened its people's republican temperament, after so many decades of grinding despair. Yet resentment alone would not restore the liberty defined by the colony's founder, John Winthrop, who had demanded in 1645 that freedom be based on "the moral law, and the . . . constitutions amongst men themselves . . . to do that only which is good, just, and honest."[58] For these higher tasks, of the longer war resumed in 1745, there was another heir of the Puritan republic, whose contributions have never been properly acknowledged. He also bore the name of John Winthrop, and was America's foremost scientist of the eighteenth century—as well as the direct descendant of the founder of Massachusetts.

Most wrongly, he has been virtually excluded from our history books, though for significant reasons. His entire career, culminating in a prominent role in the Revolutionary government of Massachusetts, dramatizes the continuity in republican outlook from the days of the Puritan founders. According to historical frauds prevailing since the nineteenth century, that continuity is not supposed to exist. John Winthrop's importance to science has also been obscured, since his method and accomplishments belie similar claims, that our eighteenth-century culture was simply a poor imitation of "mother" England's. Beyond such motives to deny or suppress Winthrop's role, there is another factor to consider. Until preparations for the Revolution were sufficiently in place, he himself was careful to keep the full nature of his activities out of enemy view.

Like fellow-Bostonian Benjamin Franklin, John Winthrop (1714–1779) was a protégé of Cotton Mather.

Baptized by Mather at the North Church, he enjoyed not only the grandfatherly affection of an old family friend, but the intellectual resources of the most accomplished scholar and prolific writer in America. Like Franklin, the young John Winthrop was acknowledged as something of a child prodigy. Prepared at Boston Latin, he was admitted to Harvard College in 1728, when he was still thirteen. Cotton Mather died that same year; and Winthrop was soon testing the knowledge of his new professors, against that of his old mentor.

Winthrop's "commonplace book," begun in his freshman year, has been preserved. It offers several insights concerning his intellectual development. His reading notes on scientific questions frequently cite an alternative source for comparison: Cotton Mather's *The Christian Philosopher* (1721), which rejected the notion of a conflict between science and Christianity, in determining the laws of the universe. Kepler and Pascal were among Mather's examples.[59] His book had been published in London, where the very mention of Leibniz or his method had long been banned by the Venetian party. Winthrop's notes from his freshman year begin, however, with even more telling references. Against the Newtonian hucksters promoted at Harvard since the removal of Increase Mather, Winthrop turned to Jonathan Swift. Of William Whiston and Humphrey Ditton, whose works peddled Newton's incompetent plagiarism concerning planetary motion and the calculus, Swift had written a devastating ditty. It could only have been known to Swift's private circles, for the verses were never published, then or since. From Winthrop's notebook they are printed here for the first time:

A Poem on the Longitude by Dr. Swift

> The longitude mist on
> By wicked *Will. Whiston*

> And not better hit on,
> By good master *Ditton*.
> So Ditton and Whiston
> May both be bep - - st on,
> And Whiston and Ditton
> May both be besh - - t on.[60]

John Winthrop was no adolescent troublemaker, merely bent on ridiculing academic authority. He had a healthy disrespect for intellectual fraud, and had a tradition of scientific achievement behind him. His own patrimony included John Winthrop, Jr., the seventeenth-century governor of Connecticut and correspondent of the young Leibniz. Certainly he enjoyed the work of Jonathan Swift, Leibniz's leading ally in Britain, both of whom he first learned of through Cotton Mather. Winthrop graduated salutatorian of his class in 1732, and in 1738 was appointed to the only academic chair in science in America. This was Harvard's Hollis Professorship of Mathematics and of Natural and Experimental Philosophy, endowed by the London merchant Thomas Hollis, to whom Cotton Mather had dedicated his *Christian Philosopher*.

The endowment prescribed the topics for instruction, including

> Pneumaticks, Hydrostaticks, Mechanicks, Staticks, opticks etc. in the Elements of Geometry, together with the doctrine of Proportions, the Principles of Algebra, Conic Sections, plain and Spherical Trigonometry, with the general principles of Astronomy and Geography, viz. The doctrine of the Sphere. . .[61]

Such a Leibnizian curriculum, based upon classical scientific method, ran counter to the schemes of Harvard's controllers even then; but Hollis had set the terms, and John

Winthrop was the best hope of meeting them. Benjamin Franklin reported on the ceremonies for Winthrop's installation in his *Pennsylvania Gazette*.[62]

John Winthrop remained one of Franklin's most trusted friends throughout his life, which was ended by pneumonia in 1779. From evidence of the Revolutionary period, Winthrop was also at the very center of Franklin's republican networks in New England. There are clear suggestions that Winthrop began such a role by the 1740s, though both men took steps to conceal it. He was consulted by George Washington, during the French and Indian War, and again during the Revolution, when Washington appointed him to oversee the munitions for the Continental Army's siege of Boston. Winthrop's influence in developing the power of reason, among the several generations he taught, is beyond measure. His students included Sam Adams, John Hancock, and John Adams, who were in constant communication with him during the Revolution. When John Adams agonized over whether the Continental Congress should declare independence from Britain, Winthrop warned him in April 1776, that unless the decision were made "pretty soon," Massachusetts would "do it for themselves."[63]

In 1745, with its siege of Louisburg, Massachusetts had done just that. Benjamin Franklin visited Boston at the time, on "business" of the American Philosophical Society.[64] For that purpose, at least, he must have sought out John Winthrop, who was already engaged in research into electricity and electromagnetics. Franklin was back again the following year, and reports in his *Autobiography* that it was then, "at Boston," that he first witnessed experiments in electricity, "a subject quite new to me." In the same, typically cautious account, Franklin attributes the experience to an "imperfectly performed" demonstration by a touring Scottish scientist, "a Dr. Spence," who was not very expert."[65] Yet on May 10, 1746, John Winthrop presented at Harvard the first controlled experiments in America in electrical phenomena.[66] Franklin began his own work in electricity soon after returning to Philadelphia that year, and there is no question that these students of Cotton Mather collaborated in the newest field of science. For Winthrop's ongoing research, he commissioned Franklin to obtain an electric battery from London. Following an earthquake in New England in 1755, Winthrop publicly attacked malicious claims that it had resulted from growing use of Franklin's invention, the lightning rod—which applied the lessons of Winthrop's earlier experiments. (He also reported that earthquakes produced "undulatory" motions of "a wave of earth," generating "both an horizontal and perpendicular motion at the same time." Winthrop's 'shockwave' theory of earthquakes was not appreciated in Europe until 1759.)[67]

The Strategy for Independence Emerges

British betrayal of the Louisburg campaign was only beginning in 1745, yet the evidence was already sufficient for America's republicans to steer the colonies toward determining their own destiny. Massachusetts had already pointed the way. During 1746 and 1747, a definite strategy emerged, which laid the basis for the later success of the American Revolution. Regardless of whether Britain provided actual support, colonial leaders continued to mobilize the American population to end the French containment. The more the Americans mobilized, the more fearful the British became. Each time the British stepped back from defending their colonies' interests, the colonies stepped forward to assert their own. At the same time, Virginia's patriots prepared the western flank, to knock out both Britain and France, from control of the Ohio country.

In Massachusetts, Governor Shirley continued to press for a full-scale attack on French Quebec. Finally, at the end of May 1746, he received word from the British ministry. Though there was still no authorization for an expedition against Canada, the provincial governors were to request their assemblies to raise troops for that possibility. Since the return of the New England men from Louisburg, colonial support for Shirley's plan was, if anything, even greater—despite the needless loss of so many lives, while the garrison had been left stranded.

Massachusetts voted to raise 3,500 men; Connecticut, 1,000; New Hampshire, 500; and Rhode Island, 300. The Duke of Newcastle, now chief minister, had promised to send a squadron with eight battalions of British regulars, to join the New England troops at Louisburg, for an attack up the St. Lawrence against Quebec. Like the expedition of 1711, the plan called for a simultaneous assault by land on Montreal, from northern New York. For this second army, New York raised 1,600 men, New Jersey 500, and Maryland 300. Virginia managed one hundred more, despite the decided lack of enthusiasm on the part of Governor Gooch. Gooch's attitude did not bode well, since the ministry had designated him brigadier general, to command the American attack on Montreal.[68]

The Massachusetts regiments were mustered and ready by mid-July, less than six weeks after Shirley's proclamation calling them to service. Once more they were to wait in vain. The support promised from Britain was to have sailed at the beginning of May.[69] In the waning days of August, there was still no news of the British ships, then a month and a half overdue. On August 22, Shirley wrote to Newcastle, emphasizing that London's delay had already ruled out a successful campaign, which now could not be begun until October—too late to avoid the winter ice.[70] Shirley did not know, that a far more monstrous betrayal of the colonies, had already been arranged by His Majesty's government, through such jesuitical influences as the Duke of Bedford, Lord John Russell—a cabinet member from one of Britain's most infamous Venetian party families.

British and French oligarchical forces had long worked in parallel, though generally behind the scenes. Both governments were subject to such manipulations. While the colonies still awaited Britain's authorization and support for the attack on Canada, the promised battalions were deployed instead for a ghastly deception. The apparent plans to send a British force against Quebec were naturally picked up by French intelligence networks. Then the troops were loaded onto transports at Portsmouth— provoking a countermove by France. The French response was to assemble in June a fleet of more than thirty warships, with thirty-four transports carrying 3,150 veteran troops—intended to retake Louisburg and flatten any assault against Canada. Meanwhile, the British troops were unloaded from their ships, and the expedition for America was canceled. Lord Russell had objected that such a campaign might further a tendency toward "independence" by the colonies.[71] There were definite suspicions in America, that the British had never intended to support the conquest of Canada in the first place. Whether by arrangement or by deception, London's maneuvers ensured that the French fleet was free to attack Louisburg—and the entire New England coast.[72]

While Shirley was left in the dark, concerning the decision in London, the Jesuits of Quebec launched new Indian attacks against New England's frontiers. Shirley proposed that the colonial army, already raised to attack Montreal, be deployed to seize the French and Indian base in upper New York instead. It had been established at Crown Point, on Lake Ticonderoga, as a staging ground for their incursions against the northern colonies. Virginia's

Governor Gooch, brigadier general but Tidewater puppet, refused to lead the campaign.[73] Shirley enlisted the support of Governor Clinton of New York, however, and by late September, 1,500 Massachusetts troops were on their way to Albany, to rendezvous with New York militiamen, and drive the French from Crown Point.[74]

This independent assertion of colonial interests was also contrary to British policy, and was defeated in this case by a threat from France. While the Massachusetts contingent was still marching toward New York, word arrived that a French fleet had been sighted off Nova Scotia. Though long delayed by illness, unfavorable winds, and the lagging pace of the transport ships, the fleet had not been challenged by the British navy at any point. The Massachusetts regiments deployed to take Crown Point were recalled, and the militia fully mobilized. Within days, more than 8,000 men-at-arms crowded the narrow streets of Boston, Connecticut prepared to send 6,000 more, and the defenses of Boston harbor were strengthened on several fronts.[75]

Fortunately for New England, the French fleet was nearly destroyed in a fierce storm, and rendered incapable of assaulting even Louisburg. The returning remnants reached France in December 1746; yet it was six months later, before the Duke of Newcastle even wrote to Shirley, that there would be no British support for any undertaking against Canada. The ministry ordered that the American regiments, raised for the original expedition, be disbanded "as cheap [sic] as possible," and that *no more military actions* be undertaken by the colonies.[76]

Thus, the government of King George II had not only betrayed colonial efforts to remove the French threat from Canada. It also demanded that America confine itself for the future, to waiting for French attacks. By the time this 'right to die' directive reached the colonies, in August 1747, they had endured two years of escalating warfare, since the French surrender at Louisburg. Jesuit tribes had overrun settlements from Rochester, New Hampshire to Saratoga, New York and in 1746 had seized Fort Massachusetts, the key to that colony's western defense. Within lands claimed by Virginia beyond the Ohio River, the French also began strengthening their western line, building up Forts Miami, Ouiatenon, and Vincennes. By 1747, French and even Spanish ships began making hit-and-run attacks along the Atlantic seaboard. One French raiding party ventured that summer up the Delaware River, to within twenty miles of Philadelphia.[77]

For America's nation-building project of opening the West, the Louisburg campaign had generated tremendous momentum. British and French countermeasures now restricted the colonies, however, to pursuing the course which least depended on immediate military considerations. The most feasible route still lay through the western mountains of northern Virginia—the gateway established by Alexander Spotswood a generation before. The King's confirmation in 1745, of Lord Fairfax's entire Virginia claim, had vastly improved that prospect. Its importance became even greater, as the betrayal of the American war effort became clearer. In September 1746, surveying parties set out to establish the final boundary of the Northern Neck proprietary: the northwest line from the Blue Ridge headspring of the Rapidan River, to the Allegheny source of the Potomac—where the Fairfax Stone still stands today, north of Thomas, West Virginia. One of the surveyors was Peter Jefferson, the father of President Thomas Jefferson.[78]

Lord Thomas Fairfax was well informed of the treacherous turns of British colonial policy. He had spent eight years in England, before winning the settlement of his claim. He remained there for two years more, however, during the period from the Louisburg campaign to the order disbanding the American army. Following that miserable decision, he returned to Virginia in the summer of 1747. From the subsequent pattern of developments, it is clear that he brought with him some new tactics for the battle for the West. He proceeded directly to Belvoir, the Potomac estate of William Fairfax, which lay within full view of Mt. Vernon, the home of Lawrence Washington—now married to William's daughter Anne. Fifteen-year-old George Washington—largely in Lawrence's care since their father's death—was already a frequent guest at Belvoir.[79]

Lawrence Washington was no ordinary planter. Perhaps more than any other Virginian at the time, he was inspired by the example set by Alexander Spotswood. Lawrence maintained his father's ironmaking enterprise—as did John Spotswood, the eldest son of the founder of Virginia's iron industry.[80] He also looked to America's future in the West. In 1747, he purchased 700 acres in the Shenandoah Valley from Lord Fairfax, and 1,300 more the following year.[81] But during that first year of the proprietor's return, Lawrence Washington also took an extraordinary initiative to push forward the western frontier. With obvious collaboration from Fairfax, Washington circulated a petition seeking subscribers to a new venture, to be chartered as the Ohio Company.[82]

The western portions of the Fairfax grant were now open to settlement, and no longer subject to the dictates of royal government, whether from London or from Williamsburg. At their farthest boundaries, the proprietor's lands nearly reached the Ohio River system—the key to the huge territory between the Great Lakes and the Mississippi River. Immediately beyond the Fairfax claim, the Ohio Company proposed to establish the necessary trading posts, settlements, and forts, to begin developing this vast potential of the Virginia colony. Among Lawrence Washington's initial partners were his brother, William Augustine Washington; and George Fairfax, the son of the proprietor's cousin, William Fairfax.[83] The company soon included Spotswood's former protégé John Mercer and his son George; Mercer's pupil George Mason, whose father was one of Spotswood's Knights of the Golden Horseshoe; and Robert Dinwiddie, whose brother had married Mason's sister.[84] From the outset, the company's London agent was John Hanbury, a leading merchant in the Virginia trade, which was overseen by Dinwiddie as surveyor general of customs. Hanbury was recruited in 1748, while his friend Dinwiddie was in London.[85]

On October 20, 1747, the Ohio Company's petition was presented to Governor Gooch and the Virginia Council. The subscribers proposed to settle half a million acres below the headwaters of the Ohio, and east and south of the Allegheny and Monongahela Rivers. The plan was tabled. Early in 1748, Hanbury presented their case to the crown, arguing that the 1744 Treaty of Lancaster had confirmed Virginia's western claims, and that expansion "to the branches of the Ohio and the Lake Erie" would extend his Majesty's trade as far as the Mississippi. The Board of Trade was persuaded that

> the settlement of the country lying to the westward of the great mountains, as it was the centre of the British dominions, would be for his Majesty's interest, and the advantage and security of Virginia, and the neighboring colonies; as, by means thereof, a more extensive trade and commerce might be carried on with the Indians inhabiting those parts; and it would likewise be a proper step towards checking the incroachments of the French, by interrupting part of their communication, from

the ledgements upon the great Lakes to the river
Mississippi, and that of the Indians in their
interest.[86]

The political heirs of Alexander Spotswood were about to
turn his dream into reality.

Franklin's Call to Arms

The formation of the Ohio Company was a clear signal
that Americans were preparing to take matters into their
own hands, and open the West regardless of Britain's foul
deal with France to prevent that. A Swedish traveler in
America at the time, who visited with Benjamin Franklin,
reflected the growing sentiment:

> There is reason enough for doubting whether
> the king, if he had the power, would wish to
> drive the French from their possessions in
> Canada. . . . The English government has
> therefore reason to regard the French in North
> America as the chief power that urges their
> colonies to submission.[87]

Franklin certainly had no doubts that Britain was the
enemy of the American colonies. In a lengthy history of
Pennsylvania, which Franklin published anonymously in
London in 1759, he reviewed the British betrayal of the
Louisburg campaign, and their cynical pledge to mount an
expedition against Quebec:

> In the beginning of the year 1746, the
> ministers *affected* to entertain a project for the
> reduction of Canada . . . . [The] northern
> colonies were severally called upon to
> contribute their respective quotas towards it,
> which they cheerfully concurred in doing,

seduced by their interests and their inclinations
into a belief, that the whole line of our colonies
would not be thus agitated, nor their Indian
allies induced to take up the hatchet in
conjunction with them, *merely by way of feint
to facilitate a peace* [emphasis added].[88]

The political fallout from this British hoax included a
worsening of relations with the Iroquois Six Nations—
important allies who once again had serious grounds for
doubting the word of the English colonies, and of their
"great chief," King George II. The French Jesuits were
busily at work trying to lure the Iroquois into their own
orbit, and their Canadian tribes continued a broad assault
on the colonies' frontiers. The settlements proposed by the
Ohio Company along the Monongahela and Allegheny
forks underscored a pressing problem for Pennsylvania. It
was the only colony without a militia system, thanks to the
Quaker proprietors and merchants who dominated its
government. Western Pennsylvania was largely unsettled,
and even though the Indian trade on this frontier "was
productive of great advantages to the proprietaries," there
were no provisions to defend this corridor against French
and Indian incursions from Lake Erie.[89]

A month after the Ohio Company filed its petition in
Williamsburg, in the fall of 1747, Benjamin Franklin took
action in Philadelphia, to break the political deadlock over
the issue of Pennsylvania's defense. Following a series of
articles on the subject in his *Pennsylvania Gazette*, he
published on November 17 the pamphlet *Plain Truth*,
signed simply by "A Tradesman of Philadelphia." It was a
devastating attack on the smugness of the city's wealthy
merchants, who imagined that they were safe from attack of
any kind. Franklin made the most of the recent raids by
enemy ships up the Delaware, "in two different Cruises this

last summer in our Bay," and denounced the indifference of
the colony's leading figures, both Quaker and non-Quaker.
"It seems as if our greatest Men . . . of both Parties, had
*sworn the Ruin of the Country, and invited the French, our
most inveterate enemy, to destroy it.*"[90]

Whether merchant or tradesman, Philadelphian or
frontiersman, the inhabitants of the colony required a
common defense, Franklin argued. He more than
insinuated that the people would not tolerate being placed
in mortal jeopardy, to gratify the selfish whims of a wealthy
minority. Concerning the prospects for western settlement,
Franklin made a special point, which also addressed
Britain's betrayal of the Louisburg campaign:

> The French know the Power and Importance of
> the Six Nations, and spare no Artifice, Pains or
> Expence, to gain them to their Interest. By
> their Priests they have converted many to their
> Religion, and these have openly espoused their
> Cause. The rest appear irresolute which Part to
> take . . . [though] we had numerous Forces on
> their Borders, ready to second and support
> them. What may then be expected, now those
> Forces are, by Orders from the Crown, to be
> disbanded; when our boasted Expedition is laid
> aside, through want (as it may appear to them)
> either of Strength or Courage; when they see
> that the French, and their Indians, boldly, and
> with Impunity, ravage the Frontiers of New-
> York, and scalp the Inhabitants; and when those
> few Indians that engaged with us against the
> French, are left exposed to their Resentment:
> When they consider these Things, is there no
> Danger that, . . . they may be wholly gained
> over by our Enemies, and join in the War
> against us? If such should be the Case, which

God forbid, how soon may the Mischief spread
to our Frontier Counties? And what may we
expect to be the Consequence, but deserting of
Plantations, Ruin, Bloodshed and Confusion![91]

Franklin proposed a bold tactic to protect the colony—
and the eastern flank of the settlements planned by the Ohio
Company. To circumvent opposition by Thomas Penn and
his corrupt proprietary supporters, Franklin urged the
creation of an independent, voluntary militia, to be paid for
by private subscription. He promised "to propose in a few
days an association to be generally signed for that
purpose."[92] Plain Truth had argued, "The Way to secure
Peace is to be prepared for War."[93] A week after the
pamphlet's publication, Franklin rallied a packed house in
Philadelphia to prepare for just that—regardless of the
policies ruling there or in London. On that night of
November 24, 1,200 men—soon joined by 10,000 more
throughout the colony—put their signatures to Franklin's
"Form of Association."[94]

The document declared

that this Colony is in a naked, defenceless State,
without Fortifications or Militia of any
Sort . . . . That we are at a great distance from
the Mother Country, and cannot, on any
Emergency, receive Assistance from thence:
That through the Multiplicity of other Affairs of
greater Importance (as we presume) no
particular Care hath hitherto been taken by the
Government at Home of our Protection, an
humble Petition to the Crown for that purpose,
sign'd by a great number of Hands, having yet
had no visible Effect. That the Assemblies of
this Province, by reason of their religious
Principles, have not done, nor are likely to do

any Thing for our Defence, notwithstanding repeated Applications to them for that Purpose: That being thus unprotected by the Government under which we live, against our foreign Enemies that may come to invade us, As we think it absolutely necessary, WE DO hereby, for our mutual Defence and Security, . . . form ourselves into an ASSOCIATION, and, imploring the Blessing of Heaven on our Undertaking, do agree *solemnly* with each other in the Manner following. . . .[95]

The subscribers pledged to furnish themselves with arms and ammunition by January 1, 1748; form themselves into companies of fifty to one hundred men, and elect their own officers, who would then establish regiments by county and elect regimental commanders.   All companies were required to hold regular exercises in military training. The regiments of each county, at their annual review, would also elect by ballot four deputies to serve on the General Military Council, whose orders and regulations "shall have the Force of LAWS with us."   The deputies were to be those "of most Note for their Virtue, Prudence and Ability"; and the entire Association was "to act *only* on Principles of REASON, DUTY AND HONOUR." [96] Ten companies were raised in Philadelphia, and more than a hundred in the rest of the colony.[97] The officers of the Philadelphia regiment elected Franklin to be their commanding colonel, but he declined, for he had an even larger command to fulfill.[98]

In most dramatic fashion, Franklin had displayed the power of a republican movement, when the policies of government deny the most basic interests of the governed. "Poor Richard," his fictional almanacker, born on the day Charles II revoked the Massachusetts charter in 1684, had indeed become an "American Prince, without Subjects."[99] The Association, Franklin insisted, was a "Militia of FREEMEN," which therefore would not tolerate the British army's barbaric mode of discipline. The General Military Council was specifically prohibited from ordering any form of corporal punishment, or even a system of fines. (Franklin's only concession, was that the militia companies themselves might impose "little Fines," for such offenses as failing to report, and that the proceeds be applied "to the Purchasing of Drums, Colours, &c. or to be given in Prizes, or to refresh their weary Spirits after Exercise.") [100] Franklin even designed heraldic banners for the militia companies, complete with mottoes "of patriotic defiance."[101]

In the spring of 1748, nearly a thousand armed men of the Philadelphia regiment paraded through the city's streets. Artillery companies were also being trained, equipped with cannon sent from Massachusetts and New York.[102] The president and members of the Pennsylvania Council reviewed the troops. They had endorsed the Association, and the proprietary colony had no royal governor to oppose it. The proprietor Thomas Penn, however, viewed these developments with alarm. He described the Association as "a Military Common Wealth," and declared it was "acting a part little less than Treason." Of Franklin himself, Penn wrote,

> He is a dangerous Man and I should be very Glad he inhabited any other Country, as I believe him of a very uneasy Spirit. However as he is a Sort of Tribune of the People, he must be treated with regard.[103]

The Battle for Ohio Begins

There was growing alarm in London as well, over the string of assertive demonstrations that the colonies would fight for their own interests.   From the seizure of Louisburg, to Franklin's founding of an independent army, British colonial policy had suffered a series of major defeats.   British troops fared even worse in the war in Europe, where the French army swept them from the field. By 1748, Britain had no hopes of winning anything militarily in Europe, and yet its continuing state of war with France had provided Americans with ample justification for their own military efforts.   The British crown, with nothing to gain in Europe, and much to lose in America, was forced to turn to peace—and prepare for a longer war.   Even Thomas Penn reflected the political dilemma, in commenting on Franklin's argument for the Association: "tho very true in itself, that Obedience to Governors is no more due than Protection to the People, yet it is not fit to be always in the heads of the Wild unthinking Multitude."[104]

On April 30, 1748, the British and Dutch signed preliminary articles of peace with France, at Aix-la-Chapelle.   The French demanded the return of Britain's only significant conquest of the entire war—the fortress at Louisburg.   George II is reported to have thrown a rhetorical bone to his subjects in Massachusetts, by replying that it was not his to give, since it had been captured by the people of Boston.   Yet at the Treaty of Aix-la-Chapelle, signed by the warring powers on October 18, Britain exchanged Louisburg for the French-held port of Madras, India.

The agreement was tantamount to Britain's declaring war on her own colonies.   The interests of the British East India Company were thus given official priority over the survival of America.   New England's heroic enterprise had been sacrificed, for the greater loot of Britain's charter venture in the opium trade. Beyond the outrage in America, there were voices even in England against the settlement. The contemporary historian and novelist, Tobias Smollett, wrote that the "British ministers gave up the important island of Cape Breton in exchange for a petty factory in the East Indies."[105]

Word reached the colonies in July that Britain was fully restoring the military capabilities of French Canada. Since those were already being directed against America, further French incursions were fully expected—peace or no peace. One of the provisions of Aix-la-Chapelle was that definite boundaries be established, between the British and French possessions in North America. Britain's return of Louisburg was sufficient grounds to suspect that George II had little interest in defending the vast territory between the Mississippi Valley and Lake Erie—claimed by Virginia, and contested by France. For America's republicans, settling and physically gaining possession of the Ohio country, thus became a matter of greatest urgency.

In Virginia, the Fairfaxes and Washingtons were already stepping up the pace of their activity. On March 11, 1748, Lord Fairfax dispatched sixteen-year-old George Washington, to begin mapping potential settlements on the western frontier of his proprietary grant, accompanied by George Fairfax, a charter member of the Ohio Company. They were instructed to proceed beyond the Shenandoah, to the Potomac River's south branch, which flows through a beautiful Appalachian valley, joining the river about twenty miles east of present Cumberland, Maryland.[106] On October 20, the Ohio Company met at Lawrence Washington's Mt. Vernon home, and resolved to recruit German Protestant settlers, through a Philadelphia merchant, John Stedman, who had been organizing passage to America for German immigrants since the 1730s.[107]

The decision to encourage German settlement involved more than the need to rapidly populate the territory beyond the mountains. British repression of colonial ironmaking had also left America without a sufficient supply of skilled labor for that vital industry. As Alexander Spotswood had done in 1714, so Lord Fairfax and the leaders of the Ohio Company now turned to the Germans for a solution. German ironworkers soon began a string of bloomeries and forges in the Shenandoah Valley, thus developing the expanded sources of domestic iron which proved crucial even to the time of the American Revolution.[108] Skilled German ironmakers and metalworkers were already at work on another essential enterprise.   In 1748, at the frontier town of Lancaster, Pennsylvania, German gunsmiths began producing the first actual rifles in America.   They were spiral-grooved, as opposed to smoothbore, and were deadly accurate at more than 250 yards—roughly triple the effective range of muskets.[109] Known as the Pennsylvania rifle, it was the basis for the later design of the legendary Kentucky rifle.

The Ohio Company met again on June 20, 1749—still awaiting approval of its charter from London, where John Hanbury had been diligently selling the Board of Trade on the commercial advantages of expanding the Indian trade in the Ohio country. Trade with the Indians was of more tactical importance to the leaders of the Ohio Company, than any considerations of profit. The Ohio Indians were generally hostile to the French, but sustaining any allegiance to the Americans would require meeting their needs in trade. The government in Williamsburg had done nothing to secure friendly relations, even though these Indians resided in Virginia's western territories.   At its meeting, the company decided to force the issue.   The members resolved "that the Indians at the Ohio be invited to a Treaty, and an Interpreter be provided at the Expense of the Government." The company also requested "Major [Lawrence] Washington" to proceed to London, to procure "a Good Gun Smith" and arrange with Hanbury the necessary articles of Indian trade.[110]

During Lawrence Washington's mission to England, another intriguing development occurred. Robert Dinwiddie, who had been in London for some time, resigned his customs post, and soon after sought appointment to the Virginia governorship, when William Gooch announced later that year that he was leaving office, for reasons of health.[111] On recommendation of the Board of Trade, King George II had signed an order in March, granting the petition of the Ohio Company. On July 12, 1749, Governor Gooch announced the decision at a meeting of the Virginia Council, authorizing the company to establish settlements on its proposed tract both north and south of "the River Alligane, otherwise the Ohio."[112]

Governor Gooch had already demonstrated that he had little taste for fighting, especially when the crown had quite different plans in mind. Certainly the events of 1749 might have hastened his decision to retire. The French were attempting to shut off all access to the Ohio country. In June, the military government of Canada dispatched Captain Céloron de Bienville, with a small force of French regulars and provincials, and a band of Iroquois and Abnaki Indians. Equipped with lead plates asserting the dominion of Louis XV, they marked a line from Lake Erie down the Allegheny River, to the forks of the Ohio, and claimed all the land west to the Mississippi. The inscription on the plates declared that they represented "a token of renewal of possession heretofore taken of the aforesaid River Ohio," and cited the authority of the treaty of Aix-la-Chapelle. Céloron's force continued down the Ohio to Logstown, ordering the American traders there to withdraw. Then they made a sweep through the valley, and back up the

Miami River to Detroit, warning the various Ohio tribes to have nothing to do with "the English."[113]

Having received word of this new French and Indian menace, the Ohio Company again determined to force Britain's hand. At its meeting on September 25, "at the falls of Potomack in Fairfax County," the company directed its London agent, John Hanbury, to seek a change in its royal charter. The original requirement that the members establish a fort to protect the venture, "out of their private fortunes," was "impracticable." The issue was now "of a Public Nature, and a fort there will Guard the other Colonies as well as this." On January 29, 1750, the company decided to establish its "factory" at Wills Creek— a branch of the Potomac near Cumberland—on land to be obtained from Lord Fairfax.[114] The Ohio Company was now the spearhead for a variety of efforts, both public and private, to extend America beyond its ancient mountain barrier.

Imperial Looting versus Nation-Building

The thrust for development within the American colonies had not escaped the attention of King George II. His Majesty's government had no objections to granting a charter to members of a trading company, who might risk their lives to exchange British goods for Indian furs. But it was firmly opposed to any growth of America's domestic agriculture and manufacture, which might free the colonies from British economic subjugation. Britain's own industry, such as it was, was based on grinding up its own population—including women and children— at miserable wages, under monstrous working conditions. Even with such brutal "cost-cutting" measures, its manufacturing profits were heavily dependent on foisting its products on the colonies at high prices—thus exporting poverty to America. In turn, Americans were expected to survive as suppliers of raw materials, under a growing burden of debt. In the southern colonies, the policy took the form of outright slave labor, which provided additional profit to British slave-trading interests.

By 1750, Britain had more than begun to fear, that America intended to break this cycle of imperial looting. The "mother country" issued new decrees, revealing the ugly face of her policies. The issues of the American Revolution were already being drawn. That same year, by act of Parliament, the colonies were officially prohibited from developing their own iron industry. No more furnaces, plating forges, or slitting and rolling mills were to be built.[115] No more necessities of life, such as ironwares for household use, tools for farming and construction, or hardware for horses and wagons, were to be available except from Britain. A "zero-growth" policy had been proclaimed for America.

The Iron Act of 1750 was followed by the Currency Act of 1751, which was specifically aimed at New England. Its history of issuing credit and currency for useful enterprises, dating back to the Puritans' Pine Tree shilling, was officially relegated to memories of the past. Now the British crown decreed, that no "paper bills or bills of credit, of any kind or denomination whatsoever, shall be created or issued under any pretence whatsoever." Any attempts to sustain or reissue notes already in circulation, were "hereby declared to be null and void, and of no force or effect whatsoever." As a warning to colonial governors, "whether commissioned by his Majesty, or elected by the people," the order declared that should one of them "assent to any act of assembly" against the decree, he "shall be immediately dismissed from his government, and for ever after rendered incapable of any publick office or place of trust."[116]

Since his Majesty's response to the American capture of Louisburg in 1745, any hopes in the colonies, for their future under royal rule, had steadily declined. The peace of Aix-la-Chapelle buried much of what remained, and the subsequent imperial decrees added to the toll. There were some who looked to the supposed future king, Frederick, Prince of Wales, the rebellious son of George II. He had been useful to Walpole's opposition, and still retained his image as "the people's prince," who might become a "patriot king." Even after Walpole had been driven from office, there had been some serious attempts to educate Frederick to such an idea. The argument that America should defer responsibility for its own future, however, died with the Prince of Wales, on March 20, 1751. Officially, his death was due to complications, from being struck in the side by a tennis ball the previous year.[117]

On the very day that Frederick died, Robert Dinwiddie wrote from London to Lawrence Washington, that the "direction" of the Ohio Company now fell upon him, so long as his failing health would permit.[118] In America, there were expressions of mourning when word reached the colonies in late May; and in Boston, several eulogies to the Prince were even published. They provide useful insights concerning the significance that Frederick's death held for America. One stressed the positive concern "he expressed for us, especially for our heroick and successful Enterprize at *Cape-Breton*."[119] Another sermon, preached by John Winthrop's close friend, Jonathan Mayhew, paid tribute to Prince Frederick as a "great encourager of husbandry, manufactures and commerce (the true sources of national wealth and felicity). . . ."[120]

Mayhew was also the leading champion at the time of the writings of John Milton. He took the occasion of Frederick's death, to exhort the people of New England to act like republican *citizens*, according to the dictates of reason and truth—instead of leaving their fate in the hands of the British monarchy. For his text, he chose Increase Mather's old rallying cry from the fight for the Massachusetts charter: "It is better to trust in the LORD than to put confidence in Princes." Mayhew reminded his audience that the Roman emperor Nero, was at first esteemed as a prince of justice:

> But what was he afterwards? A royal monster, and imperial butcher! The same is true of many others likewise. So that subjects can never have an absolute security, that even the best of kings will not alter their measures; and oppress and devour, instead of defending, them. They are as liable to fall, and *turn away from their righteousness*, as other men. It is a great mistake to imagine that any state of earthly power and greatness, can make a man *independent*; exalt him above the reach of temptation, or remove him beyond a possibility of doing the most cruel, unjust, and shameful things.[121]

His sermon also invoked reflection upon Massachusetts' former republican defiance, and upon the folly of believing that good rulers were beyond the reach of the forces of evil. First, he asked, what of the worst princes,

> whose power has been employed for destruction?. . . And do you imagine that our own nation has been wholly free from them formerly . . . ? Are the very name of CHARLES and JAMES forgotten! . . . Nor have there been wanting examples of whole nations brought to ruin, by well-meaning, but impolitic, princes, under the influence of wicked counsels . . . . [As for princes who

offer protection to their people,] they themselves may die before us . . . . They wither away, and fall with years, as others do; unless, perhaps, they find a premature death. A dagger, or a cannonball, or poison, is as fatal to the prince as to the peasant. The lives of the great, are in continual jeopardy, either from secret treachery, or open violence.[122]

By the conclusion of Mayhew's address, his eulogy for Prince Frederick had become a poetic device, for instructing the conscience of his listeners—as though asking them to think like Franklin's "American Prince, without subjects." He emphasized that Frederick's "application to reading and study, especially in the last years of his life, was very great, and, perhaps, something singular in a *modern* Prince." He added that Frederick "well understood the consequence and importance" of the American colonies, and was "accordingly desirous of cherishing and encouraging them."[123]

In the tradition of the Puritan "Jeremiads," whereby the earlier ministers of Massachusetts had issued marching orders in religious metaphor, Mayhew pointed the way to a true American republic. The possibility of revolution was not overlooked:

A person that so well understood how to govern *himself,* amidst the snares and temptations of *a court,* where it is not (God knows) always *the fashion* to be wise and virtuous; could not easily have failed to govern *others* with justice and wisdom . . .—But he is gone—gone from an earthly Kingdom, liable to changes and revolutions; to possess another, which hath more stable *foundations; a kingdom that cannot be shaken.*[124]

The actual foundations of a new nation were being laid more rapidly than the British realized. In 1751, Benjamin Franklin drafted his *Observations Concerning the Increase of Mankind, Peopling of Countries, &c.* It was not published for four years, and then anonymously, but was circulated privately as a kind of primer, on how to destroy the imperial rationale for such measures as the Iron Act. Franklin carefully constructed his argument, in such a way as to create short circuits in the 'limits-to-growth' maxims which Britain applied at home, while using the same paths to demonstrate that quite the opposite measures should be prescribed for the colonies. The trick was masterful. To the defective minds of oligarchical policy makers, Franklin appeared to use their own axiomatic assumptions—making his proposals for the colonies more difficult to refute. He confounded more than a few enemies. Decades later, Adam Smith and Thomas Malthus were still uncertainly grappling with this treatise.

In Britain, the long reign of Venetian party economic policies was taking a murderous toll. Between 1738 and 1758, the recorded number of deaths exceeded the number of births by almost 200,000—486,171 to 296,831.[125] Franklin began his treatise with a nod to British generalizations on this 'empirical' phenomenon:

> In Cities, where all Trades, Occupations and Offices are full, many delay marrying, till they can see how to bear the Charges of a Family; . . . hence Cities do not by natural Generation supply themselves with Inhabitants; the Deaths are more than the Births.

> In Countries full settled, the Case must be nearly the same; all Lands being occupied and improved to the Heighth: those who cannot get Land, must Labour for others that have it; when

> Labourers are plenty, their Wages will be low;
> by low Wages a Family is supported with
> Difficulty; this Difficulty deters many from
> Marriage . . . .[126]

He proceeded, however, *on the premise of American
development*, to argue that the same axioms dictated
different policies for the colonies:

> Land being thus plenty in America, and so
> cheap as that a labouring Man, that understands
> Husbandry, can in a short Time save Money
> enough to purchase a Piece of new Land
> sufficient for a Plantation, whereon he may
> subsist a Family. . . .

> Hence Marriages in America are more
> general, and more generally early, than in
> Europe. . . . [Thus] our People must be at
> least doubled every 20 Years.[127]

By axioms of British policy, such unbridled growth in
population would mean economic ruin. Franklin parried
that conclusion, by noting that "so vast is the Territory of
North-America, that it will require many Ages to settle it
fully." Until then, he added, "Labour will never be cheap
here," for the worker "goes among those new Settlers, and
sets up for himself . . . . " Here the duel turned, as his
adversary considered the benefits of America's facing a
prolonged struggle with high costs of labor—while the
colonies pushed westward!

Franklin's next thrust was so swift and sharp, that a
slow-witted opponent would hardly notice the wound:

> The Danger therefore of these Colonies
> interfering with their Mother Country in Trades

that depend on Labour, Manufactures, &c. is too remote to require the Attention of Great-Britain.

But in Proportion to the Increase of the Colonies, a vast Demand is growing for British Manufactures, a glorious Market wholly in the Power of Britain, . . . even beyond her Power of Supplying [it]: Therefore Britain should not too much restrain Manufactures in her Colonies. A wise and good Mother will not do it. To distress, is to weaken, and weakening the Children, weakens the whole Family.[128]

Following these beguiling and disarming strains, Franklin prepared to drive his point home. Anticipating an ideological counter in the name of "supply and demand," he turned that imperial argument against itself. To reap the bounties of an expanding American market, Franklin argued, Britain would have to accept technological development, or risk being eclipsed by other nations:

Besides if the Manufactures of Britain (by Reason of the American Demands) should rise too high in Price, Foreigners who can sell cheaper will drive her Merchants out of Foreign Markets; Foreign Manufactures will thereby be encouraged and increased, and consequently foreign Nations, perhaps her Rivals in Power, grow more populous and powerful; while her own Colonies, kept too low, are unable to assist her, or add to her Strength.

He also struck at the advocates of slavery:

'Tis an ill-grounded Opinion that by the Labour of Slaves, America may possibly vie in

Cheapness of Manufactures with Britain. The Labour of Slaves can never be so cheap here as the Labour of working Men is in Britain.[129]

In the more than pedagogical duel Franklin projected, these ironical flourishes left his antagonist at a fatal disadvantage. He offered quarter on the following terms:

[The] Prince that acquires new Territory. . . ; the Legislator that makes effectual Laws for promoting of Trade, increasing Employment, improving Land by more or better Tillage; providing more Food by Fisheries; securing Property, &c. and the Man that invents new Trades, Arts or Manufactures, or new Improvements in Husbandry, may be properly called *Fathers* of their Nation, as they are the Cause of the Generation of Multitudes, by the Encouragement they afford to Marriage . . . . We have been here but little more than 100 Years, and yet the Force of our Privateers in the late War, united, was greater, both in Men and Guns, than that of the whole British Navy in Queen Elizabeth's Time. How important an Affair then to Britain, is the present Treaty for settling the Bounds between her Colonies and the French, and how careful should she be to secure Room enough, since on the Room depends so much the Increase of her People?[130]

Franklin's *Observations* clearly defined the position America's republicans had taken by 1751. Their only allegiance by *consent* was to the necessity of progress. They had no intention of suffering the fate His Majesty had already imposed on his subjects in Britain, and they were committed to defending their interests by force of arms, if need be. Most of all, they were determined to pursue the great project begun by the Puritan founders of Massachusetts. They would not, as John Winthrop had put it, "suffer a whole Continent, as fruitful and convenient for the use of man, to lie waste without any improvement."

The Approaching Conflict

The year 1751 marked a turning point in American colonial history. The surge of nation-building aspirations which had begun during the 1740s, was being transformed into specific plans of action, which the British monarchy clearly intended to prohibit. Britain's dilemma was that it had no reasonable grounds for doing so, as Franklin and others were quick to point out. American mobilizations beginning with the Louisburg campaign had also changed colonial self-perceptions, such that British attempts at political repression were more likely instead to promote the idea of independence. Even before the Treaty of Aix-la-Chapelle, it was also no secret to Americans, that Britain encouraged French and Indian attacks against any attempts to develop the frontier. Since Louisburg, however, it was not so evident in London, that the French threat would hold America in line.

New colonial initiatives, to secure the vast territory beyond the Appalachian Mountains, developed rapidly after 1751. They proceeded from a clear strategic assessment, and were designed to open the West, with or without Britain. Under authority of the Ohio Company, plans were pushed forward to colonize the new lands. Benjamin Franklin, George Washington, Lord Thomas Fairfax, and Robert Dinwiddie became leading coordinators of the drive, which was strengthened by Dinwiddie's assuming office as governor of Virginia, in November 1751. Measures were pursued to secure the friendship of the Indians of the Ohio country, and forts began to be constructed to defend the territory against the French. Scouting expeditions proceeded far down the Ohio River, and gathered intelligence on boating conditions all the way to its junction with the Mississippi.

Politically, the road ahead led to inevitable confrontation with either France or Britain, and perhaps both. But the Americans' strategy was brilliant, and contained a fateful trap for Britain, from which there was no imperial escape. Were France to yield to American claims to the Ohio country, then only Britain could stand in the way of a great nation-building enterprise. For Britain to choose such a course—an extremely difficult one at best—would simply intensify America's movement toward independence. On the other hand, if the French attacked the new settlements, the Americans would fight. Were Britain to defend its colonial claims, it would thus endorse the opening of the West, and would have to abandon its own policies of containment. Britain's only remaining option—refusing to fight in support of the colonies—would immediately destroy its political hold over them, and lead as surely to their independence.

The story of how this trap was set belongs to the second volume of this work. Once it was sprung, the political dynamic leading to the American Revolution was fully in motion. It was sprung on May 28, 1754, by Colonel George Washington of the Virginia militia, when his troops engaged a body of French soldiers at Jumonville Glen, east of the Allegheny River. That victorious skirmish marked the beginning of the French and Indian War. There were those in Britain who recognized the trap, and they spent the next twenty years trying to wriggle out of it—to no avail.

After the news reached London, Horace Walpole, the brother of old "Bob Booty," wrote, "The volley fired by a young Virginian in the backwoods of America set the world on fire." In America, Benjamin Franklin convened a colonial congress at Albany, to begin work on a plan of union. In support of the project, Franklin published America's first political cartoon. Widely reprinted at the time, it later became a symbol of the American Revolution. The cartoon portrayed a serpent, divided into segments representing the separate colonies, over the motto, "JOIN, or DIE."

NOTES

1. *The Craftsman*, No. 502, quoted by William E. H. Lecky, *A History of England in the Eighteenth Century* (4 vols., New York, 1883), I, 369.

2. Lecky, *History of England*, I, 395–396.

3. *Ibid.*, 413–414. Frederick did not live to become Britain's King, for he died in 1751, while George II was still on the throne. Frederick's son was coronated as George III in 1760.

4. Goldgar, *Walpole*, 160–161.

5. *Ibid.*, 167.

6. *Ibid.*, 179; Swift, *Poems*, Rogers, ed., 472.

7. Lecky, *History of England*, I, 415; Will and Ariel Durant, *The Age of Voltaire* (New York, 1965), 261, 264.

8. Lecky, *History of England*, I, 415.

9. Durant, *Age of Voltaire*, 102.

10. Byrd, "A Progress to the Mines," in Louis B. Wright, ed., *The Prose Works of William Byrd of Westover* (Cambridge, Mass., 1966), 364–365.

11. Dodson, *Spotswood*, 302–303; Bernhard Knollenberg, *George Washington, The Virginia*

Period (Durham, N.C., 1964), 6.

12. Dodson, *Spotswood*, 303.

13. Goldgar, *Walpole*, 199; Lecky, *History of England*, 419; Charles P. Keith, *Chronicles of Pennsylvania* (2 vols., Philadelphia, 1917), II, 809.

14. Mansfield, *Early Spotsylvania*, 35; Meade, *Old Churches*, etc., I, 227; Philip Slaughter, *History of St. Mark's Parish*, cited by Mansfield.

15. Campbell, *Spotswood Genealogy*; George Washington to Alexander Spotswood, April 30, 1777, in Washington Bicent. Comm., *History*, III, 394.

16. Brown, *Virginia Baron*, 97.

17. Robert Dinwiddie to the Board of Trade, April 29, 1740, in Jack P. Greene, ed., *Settlements to Society*, 1584–1763 (New York, 1966), 276–279.

18. *Ibid.*, 276.

19. John R. Alden, *Robert Dinwiddie, Servant of the Crown* (Charlottesville, Va., 1973), 3–4; Pamela C. Copeland and Richard K. MacMaster, *The Five George Masons, Patriots and Planters of Virginia and Maryland* (Charlottesville, Va., 1973), 48, 52, 68, 72, 76.

20. Alden, *Dinwiddie*, 10–11; Brown, *Virginia Baron*, 46, 121.

21. Lecky, *History of England*, I, 399.

22. John A. Schutz, *William Shirley, King's Governor of Massachusetts* (Chapel Hill, N.C., 1961), 4-5, 40.

23. Keith, *Chronicles of Pennsylvania*, II, 849*ff.*

24. *Ibid.*, 865–866.

25. *Ibid.*, 867–868; Knollenberg, *Washington*, 6.

26. Parkman, *Conflict*, II, 79–80.4–5, 40.

27. *Ibid.*, 80–82; Schutz, *Shirley*, 86.

28. Keith, *Chronicles of Pennsylvania*, II, 870.

29. Copeland and MacMaster, *The Five George Masons*, 123; Treaty of Lancaster, quoted by Lois Mulkearn, ed., *George Mercer Papers, Relating to the Ohio Company of Virginia* (Pittsburgh, 1954), 403.

30. Franklin, "A Proposal . . . ," in *Autobiography* etc., 206.

31. *Ibid.*, 207.

32. Franklin to Cadwallader Colden, April 5, 1744, in Carl Van Doren, ed., *Benjamin Franklin's Autobiographical Writings* (New York, 1945), 43.

33. *Cf. supra*, chapter 8.

34. Quoted by Mulkearn, ed., *Mercer Papers*, 405.

35. Brown, *Virginia Baron*, 97–98.

36. Schutz, *Shirley*, 88–89.

37. Parkman, *Conflict*, II, 85–86, 102; Schutz, *Shirley*, 40, 90.

38. Schutz, *Shirley*, 4–5.

39. *Cf. supra*, chapters 1, 3, and 5.

40. Parkman, *Conflict*, II, 87–88.

41. *Ibid.*, 89.

42. Herbert M. Sylvester, *Indian Wars of New England* (3 vols., Boston, 1910), III, 320–321.

43. *Ibid.*, 319–322, 322n.

44. Parkman, Conflict, II, 104, 104n.

45. *Ibid.*, 102–103.

46. *Ibid.*, 109, 111.

47. *Ibid.*, 105, 111, 113.

48. *Ibid.*, 78, 112–113.

49. The foregoing account of the Louisburg campaign, from planning to execution, has been cross-checked from a number of sources, including Sylvester's *Indian Wars of New England*, which incorporates many records of Massachusetts at the time. Nearly all particulars are corroborated by Parkman's 1892 account, which also provides the most extensive treatment of French reports of the siege. Yet by fallacy of composition, willful distortion of chronology, and an abiding hatred of the American Revolution, Parkman obscured the essential facts of the Louisburg campaign, in a way designed to make his readers almost regret the outcome. In this attempt to defraud Americans of their history, Parkman cites the assistance of Theodore Roosevelt, who danced with joy on the news of President McKinley's assassination in 1901, and launched a hideous assault on America's republican institutions. Conventional footnoting of Parkman's history of the Louisburg expedition, as drawn upon here, would resemble a jumbled mass of lottery numbers. The relevant information is scattered throughout Parkman, *Conflict*, II, 78–151.

50. Quoted by Parkman, *Conflict*, II, 155.

51. Sylvester, *Indian Wars of New England*, III, 337–338; Parkman, Conflict, II, 158–159.

52. Parkman, *Conflict*, II, 164.

53. Schutz, *Shirley*, 102.

54. Parkman, *Conflict*, II, 164.

55. Schutz, *Shirley*, 102–106.

56. *Ibid.*, 107–108; Parkman, *Conflict*, II, 168.

57. Edward P. Hamilton, *The French and Indian Wars* (New York, 1962), 122; Parkman, *Conflict*, II, 167, 167n.

58. *Cf.* Chapter 1.

59. Cotton Mather, *The Christian Philosopher* (London, 1721), Rare Book Room, New York Public Library.

60. John Winthrop, Commonplace Book, manuscript, Rare Book Collection, Houghton Library, Harvard University.

61. Quoted in I. Bernard Cohen, *Some Early Tools of American Science* (Cambridge, Mass., 1950), 33.

62. *Pennsylvania Gazette*, February 1, 1739.

63. John Adams John Winthrop Correspondence, Massachusetts Historical Society *Collections*, 5th Series, IV, 271–313.

64. Fäy, *Franklin*, 208.

65. Franklin, *Autobiography*, 164.

66. "The Summary of a Course of Experimental Philosophical Lectures, by Mr. J. Winthrop," 1746, original manuscript in the Harvard College Archives. Both from the handwriting and internal evidence, these lecture notes are clearly those of one of his students at the time. In addition to documenting his pioneering role in electricity, they confirm Winthrop's study of Leibniz, and his public commitment to demolishing Descartes.

67. Franklin, *Autobiography*, 164–165; Clifford K. Shipton, *New England Life in the Eighteenth Century* (Cambridge, Mass., 1963), 349*ff.*; John Winthrop, *A Lecture on Earthquakes* (Boston, 1755), Houghton Library, Harvard University.

68. Hutchinson, *History of Massachusetts Bay*, II, 381*n.*; Parkman, *Conflict*, II, 169–170; Schutz, *Shirley*, 112; Keith, *Chronicles of Pennsylvania*, II, 879.

69. Keith, *Chronicles of Pennsylvania*, II, 879.

70. Parkman, *Conflict*, II, 171.

71. Sylvester, *Indian Wars of New England*, III, 338.

72. Parkman *Conflict,* II, 171-172, 174-175.   Even Parkman acknowledges that there were those who thought "the proposed attack on Canada was only a pretext to deceive the enemy." He does not mention the obvious implication, that since the French were deliberately *warned*, and not deceived, the British "enemy" in question could only be the colonies themselves.

73. Schutz, *Shirley*, 113.

74. Parkman, *Conflict*, II, 172–173.

75. Shirley to Newcastle, September, 29, 1746, quoted by Parkman, *op. cit.*, 173–174.

76. *Ibid.*, 172, 176–182.

77. *Ibid.*, 229–265; Marshall Sprague, *So Vast, So Beautiful a Land; Louisiana and the Purchase* (Boston, 1974), 164; Clark, Franklin, 96; Sylvester, *Indian Wars of New England*, III, 342*ff.*

78. Brown, *Virginia Baron*, 104.

79. *Ibid.*, 101–103, 108.

80. Washington Bicent. Comm., *History*, I, 145; Campbell, *Spotswood Genealogy*.

81. Julia Davis, *The Shenandoah* (New York, 1945), 55.

82. Mulkearn, etc., *Mercer Papers*, xi.

83. *Ibid.*, 2.

84. *Ibid.*, xiii, 143. The relationships cited are documented in a previous section of this chapter.

85. *Ibid.*, 2–3; Aldie, *Dinwiddie*, 13–14.

86. *The Case of the Ohio Company, Extracted from Original Papers* [1769], 2–3, facsimile reprint in Mulkearn, ed., *Mercer Papers*.

87. Peter Kalm, written from New York in 1748, quoted in Winsor, ed., *Memorial History of Boston*, II, 120.

88. Benjamin Franklin, *An Historical Review of the Constitution and Government of Pennsylvania, From Its Origin*, in Jared Sparks, ed., *The Works of Benjamin Franklin* (10 vols., Boston, 1836), III, 212.

89. *Ibid.*, 214.

90. Benjamin Franklin, *Plain Truth*, in Leonard W. Labaree, ed., *The Papers of Benjamin Franklin* (New Haven, 1961), III, 195, 202.

91. *Ibid.*, 194–195.

92. Franklin, *Autobiography*, 121.

93. *Franklin Papers*, III, 203.

94. Franklin, *Autobiography*, 122.

95. Franklin, "Form of Association" [November 24, 1747], *Franklin Papers*, III, 205–206.

96. *Ibid.*, 206–207.

97. *Ibid.*, 185*n*.

98. Franklin, *Autobiography*, 122.

99. *Cf.* Chapter 10.

100. Franklin, "Form of Association," *Franklin Papers*, III, 211–212.

101. *Franklin Papers*, III, 184.

102. *Ibid.*, 311–312.

103. *Ibid.*, 186.

104. *Ibid.*, 186.

105. Sprague, *So Vast, So Beautiful a Land*, 161; Parkman, *Conflict*, II, 270.

106. Brown, *Virginia Baron*, 110.

107. *Mercer Papers*, 167, 464*n*.

108. Lewis, *Iron and Steel in America*, 21.

109. Joseph and Frances Gies, *The Ingenious Yankees* (New York, 1976), 19.

110. *Mercer Papers*, 169, 618, 631.

111. Alden, *Dinwiddie*, 13–14.

112. *Jour. Coun. Va.*, Wilmer Hall, ed. (Richmond, 1945), V (November 1, 1739–May 7, 1754), 295.

113. Sprague, *So Vast, So Beautiful a Land*, 165–166; Francis Parkman, *Montcalm and Wolfe* (2 vols., Boston, 1896), I, 43.

114. *Mercer Papers*, 171.

115. *Franklin Papers*, IV, 226.

116. The Currency Act of 1751, in Greene, ed., *Settlements to Society*, 297–298.

117.   *Cf.* Henry Curties, *A Forgotten Prince of Wales* (London, 1912).

118.   Knollenberg, *Washington*, 144n.

119.   Thomas Prince, *God destroyeth the Hope of Man* (Boston, 1751), 24.

120.   Jonathan Mayhew, *A Sermon preached at Boston in New-England, May 26, 1751* (Boston, 1751), 27. Copies of both sermons are in the Rare Book Room, Library of Congress.

121.   *Ibid.*, 12–13.

122.   Ibid., 13–21.

123.   *Ibid.*, 26–27.

124.   *Ibid.*, 31.

125.   Lecky, *History of England*, I, 621*n*.

126.   *Franklin Papers*, IV, 227–228.

127.   *Ibid.*, 228.

128.   *Ibid.*, 228–229.

129.   *Ibid.*, 229.

130.   *Ibid.*, 231–233.

Bibliography

Primary Sources

Manuscripts and Published Sources

Addison, Joseph. *The Letters of Joseph Addison.* Walter Graham, ed. Oxford, 1941.

Boylston, Zabdiel. *An Historical Account of the Small-Pox Inoculated in New England, upon All Sorts of Persons, Whites, Blacks, and of All Ages and Constitutions.* London, 1726.

Byrd, William II. *The Prose Works of William Byrd of Westover.* Louis B. Wright, ed. Cambridge, Mass., 1966.

_____. *The Secret Diary of William Byrd of Westover, 1709–1712.* Louis B. Wright and Marion Tinling, eds. Richmond, 1941.

_____. *William Byrd of Virginia, The London Diary and Other Writings.* Wright and Tinling, eds. New York, 1958.

Churchill, Sarah. *The Character of Princes.* London, 1715.

Colonial Laws of New York. 5 vols. Albany, 1894–1896.

Davis, Andrew M., ed. *Colonial Currency Reprints, 1682–1751.* 4 vols. Boston, 1910.

Defoe, Daniel. *A Tour through the Whole Island of Great Britain.* Reprint of 1724–1726 edition. New York, 1983.

Executive Journals of the Colonial Council of Virginia. Vols. III and IV. R. H. McIlwaine, ed. Richmond, 1928. Vol. V. Wilmer Hall, ed. Richmond, 1945.

Fontaine, John. *The Journal of John Fontaine.* Edward P. Alexander, ed. Williamsburg, Va., 1972.

Franklin, Benjamin. *Autobiographical Writings.* Carl van Doren, ed. New York, 1945.

_____. *The Autobiography and Other Writings.* Jesse Lemisch, ed. New York, 1961.

_____. *Experiments and Observations on Electricity, made at Philadelphia in America.* 2 vols. London, 1751–53.

_____. *The Papers of Benjamin Franklin.* Leonard W. Labaree, ed. New Haven, 1961.

_____. *Poor Richard, 1733.* Facsimile edition. Philadelphia, 1977.

_____. *The Works of Benjamin Franklin.* Jared Sparks, ed. 10 vols. Boston, 1836.

_____. *The Writings of Benjamin Franklin.* A. H. Smyth, ed. 10 vols. New York, 1907.

Gay, John. *The Beggar's Opera.* Reprint of 1728 edition. Edgar V. Roberts, ed. Lincoln, Neb., 1969.

Greene, Jack P., ed. *Settlements to Society, 1584–1763.* Vol. I of *A Documentary History of American Life.* New York, 1966.

Hall, Michael G., et al. , eds. *The Glorious Revolution in America, Documents on the Colonial Crisis of 1689.* New York, 1972.

Jones, Hugh. *The Present State of Virginia.* London, 1724.

Journals of the House of Burgesses of Virginia. 1702–1712. 17121726. 2 vols. R. H. McIlwaine, ed. Richmond, 1912.

Keith, William. *The History of the British Plantations in*

America. *Part I, Containing the History of Virginia.* London, 1738.

Lederer, John. *The Discoveries of John Lederer.* Facsim. Reprint of 1672 edition. Charlottesville, Va., 1958.

Mandeville, Bernard. *The Fable of the Bees, or Private Vices, Public Benefits.* Reprint of 1734 edition. London, 1934.

Mather, Cotton. *Bonifacius, An Essay upon the Good.* Reprint of 1710 edition. Cambridge, Mass., 1966.

_____. *The Christian Philosopher.* London, 1721.

_____. *The Diary of Cotton Mather.* Worthington Ford, ed. 2 vols. Massachusetts Historical Society *Collections.* 7th series. Vols. VII–VIII. Boston, 1912.

_____. *Life of Sir William Phips.* Mark van Doren, ed. New York, 1929.

_____. *Magnalia Christi Americana.* Boston, 1702.

_____. *Mirabilia Dei.* Boston, 1719.

_____. *Parentator.* Boston, 1724.

_____. *Selected Letters of Cotton Mather.* Kenneth Silverman, ed. Baton Rouge, La., 1971.

_____. *Some Considerations on Bills of Credit.* Boston, 1691.

_____. *Things for a Distress'd People to Think Upon.* Boston, 1696.

Mather, Increase. "Diary." Microfilm typescript. Manuscript Division, Library of Congress.

_____. "The Mystery of Christ Opened and Applyed." Boston, 1686.

Mather, Samuel. *The Life of the Very Reverend and learned Cotton Mather.* Boston, 1729.

Mayhew, Jonathan. *A Sermon preached at Boston in New-England, May 26, 1751. Occasioned by the much-lamented DEATH of His Royal Highness, Frederick, Prince of Wales.* Boston, 1751.

George Mercer Papers, Relating to the Ohio Company of Virginia. Lois Mulkearn, ed. Pittsburgh, 1954.

Order Book of Spotsylvania County {Virginia}, 1724–1730.

Prince, Thomas. *God destroyeth the Hope of Man.* Boston, 1751.

Salem, Mass. *Record of Deaths.*

Sewall, Samuel. *The Diary of Samuel Sewall.* Harvey Wish, ed. New York, 1967.

Shirley, William. *Correspondence of William Shirley, Governor of Massachusetts and Military Commander in America, 1731– 1760.* Charles Henry Lincoln, ed. New York, 1912.

Shurtleff, N. B., et al., eds. *Records of the Governor and Company of the Massachusetts Bay in New England.* 5 vols. Boston, 1853–1854.

Spotswood, Alexander. *The Official Letters of Alexander Spotswood.* 2 vols. Richmond, Va., 1882–1885.

Swift, Jonathan. *The Bickerstaff Papers*, in Louis A. Landa, ed., *Jonathan Swift, Travels and Other Writings.* Boston, 1960.

_____. *Complete Poems.* Pat Rogers, ed. New Haven, 1983.

_____. *The Correspondence of Jonathan Swift.* Harold Williams, ed. 5 vols. London, 1963–1965.

_____. *Gulliver's Travels and Other Writings.* Louis Landa, ed. Boston, 1960.

_____. *Journal to Stella.* Harold Williams, ed. 2 vols. London, 1948.

_____. *The Portable Swift.* Carl van Doren, ed. New York, 1948.

_____. *Satires and Personal Writings.* William Alfred Eddy, ed. London, 1932.

_____. *The Works of the Reverend Jonathan Swift,* D.D. Thomas Sheridan, ed. 24 vols. London, 1803.

    Especially:

    A Tale of a Tub. Vol. III.

    The Battle of the Books. Vol. III.

    The Conduct of the Allies. Vol. V.

    Memoirs Relating to the Change in the Queen's Ministry. Vol. VI.

    History of the Last Four Years of the Queen. Vol. VII.

Walker, Hovenden. *Journal of the Canada Expedition.* London, 1720.

Winthrop, Robert C. *The Life and Letters of John Winthrop.* 2 vols. Boston, 1869.

Winthrop, Prof. John. Commonplace Book. Ms. Houghton Library, Harvard University.

_____. "John Adams John Winthrop Correspondence." Massachusetts Historical Society *Collections.* 5[Th] series. Vol. IV, pp. 271–313.

_____. "The Summary of a Course of Experimental Philosophical Lectures." [Student notes,

1746.] Ms. Houghton Library, Harvard University.

_____. *A Lecture on Earthquakes.* Boston, 1755.

Newspapers

Boston News-Letter. Boston, 1715–1723.

The Examiner. London, 1710–1711.

The Intelligencer. Dublin, 172 . Facsim. Reprint. New York, 1967.

New England Courant. Boston, 1721–1722.

Pennsylvania Gazette. Philadelphia, 1735–1754.

The Spectator. London, 1711.

The Tatler. London, 1710.

Secondary Works

Books

Alden, John R. *Robert Dinwiddie, Servant of the Crown.* Charlottesville, Va., 1973.

Andrews, Matthew Page. *Virginia, The Old Dominion.* 2 vols. New York, 1937.

Black, Robert C. III. *The Younger John Winthrop.* New York, 1966.

Brown, Stuart E. *Virginia Baron, The Story of Thomas 6th Lord Fairfax.* Berryville, Va., 1965.

Burnaby, Andrew. *Travels through the Middle Settlements in North America, in the Years 1759 and 1760.* Reprint. New York, 1904.

Campbell, Charles. *Genealogy of the Spotswood Family in Scotland and Virginia.* Albany, N.Y., 1968.

Clark, Ronald W. *Benjamin Franklin, A Biography.* New York, 1983.

Cohen, I. Bernard. *Some Early Tools of American Science.* Cambridge, Mass., 1950.

Copeland, Pamela C., and Richard K. MacMaster. *The Five George Masons, Patriots and Planters of Virginia and Maryland.* Charlottesville, Va., 1973.

Craik, Henry. *The Life of Jonathan Swift, Dean of St. Patrick's, Dublin.* London, 1882.

Crawford, M. MacDermott. *Madame de Lafayette and her Family.* New York, 1907.

Curties, Henry. *A Forgotten Prince of Wales.* London, 1912.

Davis, Julia. *The Shenandoah.* New York, 1945.

Dodson, Leonides. *Alexander Spotswood, Governor of Colonial Virginia, 1710–1722.* Philadelphia, 1932.

Dunn, Richard S. *Puritans and Yankees, The Winthrop Dynasty of New England.* Princeton, 1962.

Durant, Will and Ariel. *The Age of Louis XIV.* Vol. VIII of *The Story of Civilization.* New York, 1963.

————————————. *The Age of Voltaire.* Vol. IX of *The Story of Civilization.* New York, 1965.

Fäy, Bernard. *Franklin, The Apostle of Modern Times.* Boston, 1929.

Forbes, Esther. *Paul Revere and the World He Lived In.* Boston, 1942.

Francke, Kuno. *Cotton Mather and August Hermann Francke.* New York, 1897.

Freeman, Douglas Southall. *George Washington.* 5 vols. New York, 1948–1952.

Fricke, Waltraut. *Leibniz und die englische Sukzession des Hauses Hannover.* Hildesheim, West Germany, 1957.

Gies, Joseph and Frances. *The Ingenious Yankees.* New York, 1976.

Goldgar, Bertrand A. *Walpole and the Wits.* Lincoln, Neb., 1976.

Gordon, Armistead C. *Men and Events, Chapters of Virginia History.* Staunton, Va., 1923.

Green, David. *Queen Anne.* New York, 1970.

Gregg, Edward. *Queen Anne.* London, 1980.

Guizot, F. *History of France.* . 8 vols. London, 1872.

Hamilton, Edward P. *The French and Indian Wars.* New York, 1962.

Hartley, E. N. *Iron Works on the Saugus.* Norman, Okla., 1957.

Havighurst, Walter. *Alexander Spotswood, Portrait of a Governor.* New York, 1967.

Hutchinson, Thomas. *The History of the Colony and Province of Massachusetts Bay.* 2 vols. Boston, 1759.

James, Patricia. *Population Malthus.* London, 1979.

Keith, Charles P. *Chronicles of Pennsylvania.* 2 vols. Philadelphia, 1917.

Knollenberg, Bernhard. *George Washington, The Virginia Period.* Durham, N.C., 1964.

Kramnick, Isaac. *Bolingbroke and His Circle, The Politics of Nostalgia in the Age of Walpole.* Cambridge, Mass., 1968.

Leach, Douglas. *Arms for Empire, A Military History of the British Colonies in North America, 1607–1763.* New York, 1973.

Lecky, William E. H. *A History of England in the Eighteenth Century.* 4 vols. New York, 1883.

Lewis, W. David. *Iron and Steel in America.* Meriden, Conn., 1976.

Lustig, Mary L. *Robert Hunter, New York's Augustan Statesman.* Syracuse, N.Y., 1983.

Martin, Henri. *The Age of Louis XIV.* 2 vols. Boston, 1865.

Mansfield, James Roger. *A History of Early Spotsylvania.* Orange, Va., 1977.

May, Earl Chapin. *Principio to Wheeling.* New York, 1945.

McCormick, Donald. *The Hell-Fire Club.* London, 1958.

Meade, William. *Old Churches, Ministers, and Families of Virginia.* Philadelphia, 1857.

Morrison, Charles. *An Outline of the Maryland Boundary Disputes and Related Events.* Parsons, W. Va., 1974.

Murdock, Kenneth. *Increase Mather, The Foremost American Puritan.* Cambridge, Mass., 1925.

Parkman, Francis. *A Half-Century of Conflict.* 2 vols. Boston, 1896.

——————————. *Montcalm and Wolfe.* 2 vols. Boston, 1896.

Peters, Margaret T. *A Guidebook to Virginia's Historical Markers.* Charlottesville, Va., 1985.

Realey, Charles Bechdolt. *The Early Opposition to Sir Robert Walpole, 1720–1727.* London, 1931.

Schutz, John A. *William Shirley, King's Governor of Massachusetts.* Chapel Hill, N.C., 1961.

Sedgwick, Alexander. *Jansenism in Seventeenth-Century France.* Charlottesville, Va., 1977.

Shipton, Clifford K. *New England Life in the Eighteenth Century.* Cambridge, Mass., 1963.

Silverman, Kenneth. *The Life and Times of Cotton Mather.* New York, 1984.

Somerville, Dorothy H. *The King of Hearts, Charles Talbot, Duke of Shrewsbury.* London, 1962.

Sprague, Marshall. *So Vast, So Beautiful a Land; Louisiana and the Purchase.* Boston, 1974.

Sylvester, Herbert M. *Indian Wars of New England.* 3 vols. Boston, 1910.

Thompson, George Malcolm. *The First Churchill: The Life of John 1st Duke of Marlborough.* London, 1979.

Tolles, Frederick B. *James Logan and the Culture of Provincial America.* Boston, 1957.

Toppan, Robert N. *Memoir of Edward Randolph.* Reprint. New York, 1967.

Tourtellot, Arthur B. *Benjamin Franklin, The Shaping of Genius, The Boston Years.* New York, 1977.

United States George Washington Bicentennial Commission. *History of the George Washington Bicentennial Commission.* 5 vols. Washington, D.C., 1932.

Virginia Magazine of History and Biography.

Warden, G. B. *Boston, 1689–1776.* Boston, 1976.

Washburn, Wilcombe E. *The Governor and the Rebel.* New York, 1957.

Winsor, Justin, ed. *The Memorial History of Boston.* 4 vols. Boston, 1880.

Zall, P. M., ed. *Ben Franklin Laughing.* Berkeley, 1980.

Articles and Unpublished Manuscripts

Arnest, Dana. "Handel, Swift, and the Cultural War for the New World." *New Solidarity*, February 28, 1985.

Schultz, Edward H. "Belvoir on the Potomac." Typescript ms. {1932?} Manuscript Division, Library of Congress.

Valenti, Philip. "The Political Economy of Leibniz's English Allies." Unpub. ms. 1978.

_____. "The Politics of the Newton-Leibniz Controversy." Unpub. ms. 1977.

Wolfe, Kathy. "Handel and the Cultural War for the New World." *New Solidarity*, March 6, 1985.

About the Author

Born in Washington, D.C., in 1943, H. Graham Lowry graduated *magna cum laude* from Harvard College in 1965, majoring in American history. Awarded a Woodrow Wilson Fellowship, he enrolled for graduate study at the University of Wisconsin (M.A., 1968). He taught undergraduate history at Wisconsin, and subsequently at Rutgers (Newark) and Boston University. In 1979-80, he directed Lyndon LaRouche's Presidential primary campaign in New Hampshire, and he served for many years as a member of the National Committee of the National Caucus of Labor Committees, a philosophical association founded by Lyndon LaRouche in the late 1960s. In later years, nothing was more enjoyable to him than teaching members of the LaRouche Youth Movement, and taking them to see the historic sites where America's patriots had advanced the cause of the Republic.

A number of Graham's forebears, as ordinary citizens, took part in some of the episodes of this book; but none of

553

his academic colleagues ever suggested that America had such an inspiring past.   With his wife, Pamela, and twin sons, Colin and Malcolm, he visited and photographed most of the locations mentioned in this book.   Graham died on July 28, 2003 from the effects of hemochromatosis, a genetic disease that was diagnosed too late to save his life.

Original Back Cover Text

To restore America's founding purpose . . .

How the Nation Was Won reveals the continuous fight waged by America's republican movement, beginning with John Winthrop's Massachusetts Bay Colony in 1630. From New England's first battles for freedom, American historian Graham Lowry traces how . . .

- The strategy for a continental republic was designed under the reign of Queen Anne (1702-1714), with the help of the brilliant Jonathan Swift.
- The Scottish soldier and geometer Alexander Spotswood, governor of Virginia from 1710 to 1722, created America's gateway to the West—and Virginia's leadership for the Revolution.
- The Massachusetts Puritan Cotton Mather brought Benjamin Franklin into political warfare, against the "Hell-Fire" regime of Britain's Hanoverian kings.
- The stage was set for the young George Washington to start the French and Indian War—to break the half-century plot by Britain and France to keep Americans from crossing the Appalachian Mountains.

These are some of the startling features of "America's untold story" which reports the visions and accomplishments of those who paved the way for the American Revolution, long before the Declaration of Independence. How they did it—and even who they were—has never been so fully brought to light before.

To restore America's founding purpose . . .

How the Nation Was Won reveals the continuous fight waged by America's republican movement, beginning with John Winthrop's Massachusetts Bay Colony in 1630. From New England's first battles for freedom, American historian Graham Lowry traces how . . .

● The strategy for a continental republic was designed under the reign of Queen Anne (1702-1714), with the help of the brilliant Jonathan Swift.

● The Scottish soldier and geometer Alexander Spotswood, governor of Virginia from 1710 to 1722, created America's gateway to the West—and Virginia's leadership for the Revolution.

● The Massachusetts Puritan Cotton Mather brought Benjamin Franklin into political warfare, against the "Hell-Fire" regime of Britain's Hanoverian kings.

The stage was set for the young George Washington to start the French and Indian War—to break the half-century plot by Britain and France to keep Americans from crossing the Appalachian Mountains.

These are some of the startling features of "America's untold story" which reports the visions and accomplishments of those who paved the way for the American Revolution, long before the Declaration of Independence. How they did it—and even who they were—has never been so fully brought to light before.

ISBN 0-943235-21-9

51995>

9 780943 235219

$19.95
ISBN 0-943235-21-9

Made in the USA
Monee, IL
09 January 2025

76460411R00321